The Landlord's Law Book

Volume 1: Rights and Responsibilities

3rd California Edition

by Attorneys David Brown & Ralph Warner

Edited by Marcia Stewart and Mary Randolph

Illustrated by Linda Allison

NOLO PRESS   BERKELEY, CALIFORNIA

please read this

Nolo Press is committed to keeping its books up-to-date. Each new printing, whether or not it is called a new edition, has been revised to reflect the latest law changes. This book was printed and updated on the date indicated below. Before you rely on information in it, you might wish to call Nolo Press (415) 549-1976 to check whether there has been a later printing or edition. It's your responsibility to check all material you have read here before relying on it.

THIRD EDITION	September 1991

BOOK DESIGN	Jackie Mancuso
PROOFREADING	Ely Newman
INDEX	Sayre Van Young
PRINTING	Delta Lithograph

Nolo books are available at special discounts for bulk purchases for sales promotions, premiums, and fund-raising. For details contact: Special Sales Director, Nolo Press, 950 Parker Street, Berkeley, California 94710.

89=642318
ISSN 1042-6582

thank you

This book could not have been published without the generous assistance of many people. A special thank you to Stephanie Harolde, who, in addition to keyboarding virtually the entire manuscript, made numerous helpful suggestions, nearly all of which were incorporated. Steve Elias, Carol Pladsen and Carol Marciel also made extremely helpful comments and suggestions. We would also like to acknowledge the generous help of Mike Mansel, a commercial insurance specialist in Walnut Creek; Joe Kelly, President of K&S Company, specialists in property management; D. J. Soviero, an attorney specializing in landlord/tenant law based in San Francisco; Jo Biel, a legal administrator with Eviction Assistance in San Francisco; Ira Serkes, a Berkeley Realtor with Security Pacific; and Bradley Booth, Assistant Chief Counsel, Department of Fair Employment and Housing. Thanks, too, to Darlene Hopper and Coral Swain for their assistance in typing the earlier and later manuscripts, respectively.

Special thanks to Marcia Stewart and Mary Randolph. Thanks also to Terri Hearsh, Barbara Hodovan, Toni Ihara, Amy Ihara, Robin Leonard, Jackie Mancuso, Ely Newman, John O'Donnell, Kate Thill, Sayre Van Young and, especially, Keija Kimura, who was responsible for the wonderful front cover design.

Finally, Dave Brown expresses his special thanks to his wife, Nancy Brown, and his mother, Jane Fajardo, for their support and encouragement in putting together this book.

RECYCLE YOUR OUT-OF-DATE BOOKS
AND GET 25% OFF YOUR NEXT PURCHASE

OUT-OF-DATE = DANGEROUS

Using an old edition can be dangerous if information in it is wrong. Unfortunately, laws and legal procedures change often. Generally speaking, any book more than two years old is of questionable value. Books more than four or five years old are a menace.

To help you keep up-to-date, we extend this offer:

If you cut out and deliver to us the title portion of the cover of any old Nolo book, we'll give you a 25% discount off the retail price of any new Nolo book. For example, if you have a copy of *Tenants' Rights*, 4th edition, and want to trade it for the latest *California Marriage and Divorce Law*, send us the *Tenants' Rights* cover and a check for the current price of *California Marriage and Divorce*, less a 25% discount.

Information on current prices and editions is listed in the back of this book and in the catalog in the *Nolo News* (see offer at the back of this book).

This offer is to individuals only.

LBRT 9/91

contents

INTRODUCTION

1

RENTING YOUR PROPERTY: HOW TO CHOOSE TENANTS AND AVOID LEGAL PITFALLS

2

UNDERSTANDING LEASES AND RENTAL AGREEMENTS

3

BASIC RENT RULES

4

RENT CONTROL

5

SECURITY DEPOSITS

6

PROPERTY MANAGERS

7

GETTING THE TENANT MOVED IN

8

LAWYERS, LEGAL RESEARCH, EVICTION SERVICES AND MEDIATION

9

DISCRIMINATION

10

CO-TENANTS, SUB-TENANTS AND GUESTS

11

THE LANDLORD'S DUTY TO REPAIR AND MAINTAIN THE PROPERTY

12

LANDLORD'S LIABILITY FOR DANGEROUS CONDITIONS

13

LANDLORDS' RIGHT OF ENTRY AND TENANTS' PRIVACY

14

RAISING RENTS AND CHANGING OTHER TERMS OF TENANCY

15

RETALIATORY RENT INCREASES AND EVICTIONS

16

THE THREE-DAY NOTICE TO PAY RENT OR QUIT

17

LANDLORD NO-NO'S: SELF-HELP EVICTIONS, UTILITY TERMINATIONS AND TAKING TENANTS' PROPERTY

18

TERMINATING TENANCIES

19

WHEN A TENANT LEAVES: MONTH-TO-MONTH TENANCIES, FIXED-TERM LEASES, ABANDONMENT AND DEATH OF TENANT

20

RETURNING SECURITY DEPOSITS

21

PROPERTY ABANDONED BY A TENANT

APPENDIX

Introduction

Here is a concise legal guide for people who own or manage residential rental property in California. It has two main goals: to explain California landlord-tenant law in as straightforward a manner as possible, and to help you use this legal knowledge to anticipate and, where possible, avoid legal problems.

This book, *The Landlord's Law Book, Volume 1: Rights and Responsibilities* is the first of a two-volume set. Here we concentrate on the legal rules associated with most aspects of renting and managing residential real property. For example, we include information on leases, rental agreements, managers, credit checks, security deposits, discrimination, invasion of privacy, the landlord's duty to maintain the premises, and much more. We provide practical, easy-to-use checklists and forms throughout this book. *The Landlord's Law Book, Volume 2: Evictions*, contains all the forms and instructions necessary to end a tenancy, including a step-by-step guide to doing your own evictions.

We make frequent references to the California Civil Code (CC) and the California Code of Civil Procedure (CCP), important statutes that set out landlords' rights and responsibilities. The standard abbreviations "CC" and "CCP" are used throughout the book. There are many times when you will surely want to refer to the complete statute. (See Recommended Reading, below.) Chapter 8 shows you how to find and use statutes and other legal resources if you want to do more research on a particular subject.

We believe that in the long run a landlord is best served by establishing a positive relationship with tenants. Why? First, because it's our personal view that adherence to the law and principles of fairness is a good way to live. Second, your tenants are your most important economic asset and should be treated as such. Think of it this way. From a long-term perspective, the business of renting residential properties is often less profitable than is cashing in on the appreciation of that property. Your tenants are crucial to this process, as it is their rent payments that allow you to carry the cost of the real property while you wait for it to go up in value. And just as other businesses place great importance on conserving natural resources, it makes sense for you to adopt legal and practical strategies designed to establish and maintain a good relationship with your tenants.

We've tried a roughly chronological treatment of subjects important to landlords—beginning with taking rental applications and ending with returning security deposits when a tenant moves out. But you shouldn't wait until a problem happens to educate yourself about the law.

With sensible planning, the majority of serious legal problems encountered by landlords can be either minimized or avoided. For example, in Chapter 11 we show you how to plan ahead to deal with those few tenants who will inevitably try to invent bogus reasons why they were legally entitled to withhold rent. Similarly, in Chapter 9 we discuss ways to be sure that you, your managers and other employees know and follow anti-discrimination laws and, at least as important, make it clear that you are doing so.

A special word is appropriate for those of you who live in areas covered by rent control ordinances. These laws not only establish how much you can charge for most residential living spaces, they also override state law in a number of other ways. For example, many rent control ordinances restrict a landlord's ability to terminate month-to-month tenancies and require "just cause for eviction." We handle rent control in two ways. First, as we explain your rights and responsibilities under state law in the bulk of this book, we indicate those areas in which rent control laws are likely to modify or change these rules. Second, we provide a detailed discussion of rent control in Chapter 4. This chapter is designed to be used along with a careful reading of your local rent control ordinance.

Finally, may we wish you nothing but good managers, good tenants and above all else, good luck.

Note. This book doesn't cover mobile home, condominium, hotel or commercial property rentals.

Guide to Icons Used in This Book

 = **Warning**

 = **Cross Reference**

 = **Rent Control**

Recommended Reading

Here are essential additions to every landlord's (tax-deductible) library.

Landlording, by Leigh Robinson (Express Press). A practical guide to the day-to-day aspects of being a landlord, with general information on rental practices, recordkeeping, maintenance and other topics.

California Civil Code (CC) and *California Code of Civil Procedure* (CCP). The basic state laws which regulate the landlording business.

These books can also be ordered from Nolo Press (see the order form at the back of this book) and are also available at most public libraries.

If you own rental property in a rent control city, it's crucial that you have a current copy of the local ordinance. You can get a copy from your city rent control board.

California Rental Housing Reference Book, published by the state's residential income property owners' association, California Apartment Association (CAA). Available from CAA, 1414 K St., Suite 610, Sacramento, CA 95814, 916-447-7881 or from a local apartment association. Summarizes landlord-tenant law in detail, with copies of rental agreements and other legal forms available for purchase from CAA.

Renting Your Property: How to Choose Tenants and Avoid Legal Pitfalls

All landlords typically follow the same process when renting property. We recognize that a landlord with 40 (or 400) units is in a far different situation than a person with an in-law cottage in the back yard or a duplex around the corner. Still, the basic process remains the same:

1. Decide the terms of your rental, including rent, deposits and the length of the tenancy.

2. Advertise your property.

3. Accept applications.

4. Screen potential tenants.

5. Choose someone to rent your property.

In this chapter, we examine the practical and legal aspects of each of these steps, with an eye to avoiding several potential legal problems. Because the topic of discrimination is so important we devote a whole chapter to it later in the book (Chapter 9), including advice on how to avoid discrimination in your tenant selection process.

A. Adopt a Rental Plan and Stick to It

Before you advertise your property for rent, you'll want to make some basic decisions which form your lease or rental agreement—how much rent to charge, when it is payable, whether to offer a fixed-term lease or a month-to-month tenancy and how much of a security deposit to require. You'll also need to decide the responsibilities of a manager (if any) in renting out your property.

 If you haven't made these important decisions, the details you need are in Chapters 2, 3, 5, and 6.

In renting residential property, be consistent when dealing with prospective tenants. The reason for this is simple: If you don't treat all tenants more or less equally—for example, if you arbitrarily set tougher standards for renting to a racial minority—

you can fairly easily be accused of discriminatory conduct.

Of course, there will be times when you will want to bargain a little with a prospective tenant—for example, you may let a tenant have a cat in exchange for paying a higher security deposit—but as a general rule, you're better off figuring out your rental plan in advance and sticking to it.

B. Advertising

In some areas, small landlords are lucky enough to fill all vacancies by word of mouth. If you fit this category, skip to the next section.

There is one crucial point you should remember about advertising: Where you advertise is more important than how you advertise. For example, if you rent primarily to college students, your best bet is the campus newspaper or housing office. Whether you simply put a sign in front of your apartment building or work with a rental service, be sure the way you advertise reaches a sufficient number of the sort of people you want as tenants.

Legally, you should have no trouble if you follow these simple rules:

Make sure the price in your ad is an honest one. If a tenant shows up promptly and agrees to all the terms set out in your ad, you may run afoul of the law if you arbitrarily raise the price. This doesn't mean you are always legally required to rent at your advertised price, however. If a tenant asks for more services or different lease terms, which you feel require more rent, it's fine to bargain and raise your price.

Don't engage in bait-and-switch tactics by advertising something you don't have. Some large landlords, management companies and rental services have advertised units that weren't really available in order to produce a large number of prospective tenants who could then be "switched" to higher priced or inferior units. This type of advertising is illegal and many property owners have been prosecuted for bait-and-switch practices.

Be sure your ad can't be construed as discriminatory. Ads should not mention age, sex, race, religion, or adults-only (no children). In addition, any discrimination against any group that is unrelated to a legitimate landlord concern is illegal—for example, if you don't rent to unmarried couples regardless of their income. It is an excellent idea to state in your ads that you provide "equal opportunity housing" or something similar, just as most businesses routinely include this statement in employment ads.

EXAMPLE

An ad for an apartment that says "Young, female student preferred" is illegal on at least two counts, and perhaps three, since sex and age discrimination are forbidden by both state and federal law. Under California law, even ads based on the prospective tenant's occupation could be illegal, since there is no legitimate business reason to prefer tenants with certain occupations over persons with other occupations.

If you have any legal and nondiscriminatory rules, such as no pets, it's a good idea to put them in your ad. However, the wording of your ad does not legally obligate you to rent on any particular terms. In other words, just because your ad doesn't specify "no pets," you are not obligated to rent to someone with two Dobermans.

C. Dealing With Prospective Tenants

It's good business, as well as sound legal protection strategy, to develop a system for screening prospective tenants. Whether you handle reference checking and other tasks yourself or hire a manager or property management company, your goal is the same—to select tenants who will pay their rent on time, keep their rental in good condition and not cause you any legal or practical hassles later.

1. The Rental Application

Each prospective tenant—anyone and everyone age 18 or older who wants to live in your rental property —should fill out a written application, including employment, income, credit and references. This is true whether you're renting to a married couple sharing an apartment or four unrelated roommates moving into a four-bedroom house.

A sample Rental Application is shown below. You will find a tear-out version at the back of this book.

If you intend to collect a credit-check fee, you'll probably collect this charge at the time you take an individual's rental application. Our Rental Application form includes the amount and purpose of the credit-check charge. If you do not charge credit-check fees, simply cross out this section at the bottom of the form.

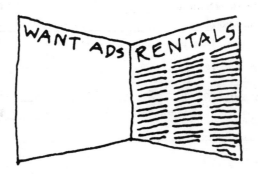

SAMPLE RENTAL APPLICATION

RENTAL APPLICATION
To Be Completed Separately By Every Adult Tenant

Property Address _____

BACKGROUND INFORMATION AND RENTAL HISTORY

Name _____

Home Phone _____ Work Phone _____

Driver's License No. _____ Social Security No. _____

Current Address _____

Years at Address _____ Reason for Leaving _____

Owner/Manager _____ Phone _____

Previous Address _____

Years at Address _____ Reason for Leaving _____

Owner/Manager _____ Phone _____

Number and Type of Pets _____

Please List Any Water-filled Furniture You Own _____

Name and Relationship of Every Adult Person to Live With You _____

_____

_____

_____

Name and Age of Every Minor Child to Live With You _____

_____

_____

_____

EMPLOYMENT HISTORY

Current Occupation _____

Name and Address of Employer _____ Phone _____

_____

Years with this Employer _____ Name of Supervisor _____ Phone _____

Name and Address of Previous Employer _____ Phone _____

_____

Years with this Employer _____ Name of Supervisor _____ Phone _____

Monthly Employment Income (before deductions) _____ $ _____

Sources and Average Monthly Amounts of Other Income _____

_____

_____ $ _____

Monthly Income of Other Adults to Live with You _____ $ _____

Total Monthly Household Income (sum of the three items above) $ ____

CREDIT HISTORY

Savings Acct. No. _____ Bank _____ Branch _____

Checking Acct. No. _____ Bank _____ Branch _____

Money Market or Similar Accounts (financial institution and account number)

_____

_____

Major Credit Card _____ Acct. No. _____

Other Credit Reference (e.g., car or student loan, department store credit card)

_____

_____

Acct. No.	Amount owed $	Average Monthly payment $
Acct. No.	Amount owed $	Average Monthly payment $
Acct. No.	Amount owed $	Average Monthly payment $
Acct. No.	Amount owed $	Average Monthly payment $

Have you ever filed for bankruptcy? _____ Have you ever been sued? _____ Have you ever been evicted? _____

Explain any "yes" to the above _____

_____

_____

MISCELLANEOUS

Vehicle Make _____ Model _____ Year _____ License Plate No. _____

Personal Reference _____

Address _____ Phone _____

Contact in Emergency _____ Relationship _____

Address _____

_____ Phone _____

I certify that all the information given above is true and correct, and I hereby authorize the Owner/Manager of the property listed above to verify any and all of the information and references provided to obtain all relevant credit information pertaining to me. I agree to pay the Owner/Manager a nonrefundable credit-checking fee of $ _____ to obtain a report on my credit from a credit reporting agency.

Date _____ Signed _____

NOTES (*Owner//Manager*)

2. Terms of the Rental

Be sure your prospective tenant knows all your general requirements and any special rules and regulations before you get too far in the process. This will help avoid situations where your tenant backs out at the last minute (he thought he could bring his three dogs and your lease prohibits pets) and help minimize future misunderstandings.

To put together a rental agreement or lease, see Chapter 2. Once you've signed up a tenant and want to clearly communicate your rules and regulations, see Chapter 7.

3. Landlord Disclosures

California landlords are legally obligated to make several disclosures to prospective tenants.

Shared utility arrangements. State law requires property owners to disclose to all prospective tenants, before they sign any rental agreement or lease, any arrangements where a tenant might wind up paying for someone else's gas or electricity use.[1] This would occur, for example, where a single gas or electric meter serves more than one unit, or where a tenant's gas or electric meter also measures gas or electricity that serves a common area—such as a washing machine in a laundry room or even a hallway light not under the tenant's control. Besides disclosing any shared utility arrangements, state law requires landlords to address this issue in lease or rental agreements. We discuss this aspect in more detail in Chapter 2. (See Clause 8 of our sample lease and rental agreement.)

Location near former military base. If your property is within a mile of a "former ordnance location"—an abandoned or closed military base in which ammunition or military explosives were used—you must notify all prospective tenants in writing.[2] Add something like the following statement to your rental application:

NOTICE

The property you're seeking to rent is within one mile of a former ordnance area as defined by California Civil Code Section 1940.7. Specifically, between 1942 and 1945, the United States Army used the nearby area bounded by 6th and 7th Streets and 1st and 3rd Avenues in the City of Stockton as a reserve training area. Unexploded rifle ammunition and other ordnance have been found there.

It is not necessary to warn prospective tenants of the existence of current ordnance locations, such as presently-existing army or navy bases.

Although there are no penalties stated in the law for failure to warn, and although the law applies only to former ordnance locations actually known by the owner, it's only a matter of time before someone sues their landlord for negligently failing to warn of a former military base the landlord "should have known about." Therefore, if you have the slightest idea your property is within a mile of a former military base or training area, check it out. You might start by asking the reference librarian at a nearby public library or by writing a letter to the local Congressional representative. If you have a particular location in mind, you can also check with the County Recorder, who will show you how to trace the ownership all the way back to the turn of the century for any indication the property was at one time owned or leased by the federal government.

Asbestos. Owners of apartment buildings that have 10 or more units and were constructed before 1979 must notify tenants and employees who work in the building if the building contains "asbestos-containing construction materials." The written notice must be given to each employee and tenant individually. Failure to notify can result in a fine of up to $1,000, imprisonment of up to one year, or both.[3]

---

[1]CC § 1940.9.

[2]CC § 1940.7.

[3]Health & Safety Code §§ 25915 through 25924.

4. Checking Background, References and Credit History of Potential Tenants

If an application looks good, there are several levels of screening prospective tenants, depending on how thorough you want to be. Obviously, you want tenants who pay their bills on time and consistently. At the very least, you should always make a few phone calls to check references from the previous landlord and to verify income and employment. You may want to go further—for example, to check whether eviction suits have ever been filed against a prospective tenant.

Here are various ways to screen applicants, beginning with the most basic steps:

Check with previous landlords or managers given as references. The key questions to ask include: Did the tenant pay rent on time? Was she considerate of neighbors—that is, no loud parties? Did she make any unreasonable demands or complaints? Why did she leave? Did she leave the place in good condition?

Make sure you speak to a legitimate landlord or manager, not a friend of the prospective tenant posing as one. Bad tenants often provide phony references. One suggestion is to call the number given for the previous landlord or manager and simply ask for the tenant by name, rather than begin by saying that you are checking references. If the prospective tenant

has really given you a friend's name, the friend will probably say something that gives away the scam.

If you still have questions, drive to the former address and check things out in person. Finally, if you have any doubts, ask the previous landlord or manager to pull out the tenant's rental application so you can verify certain facts, such as the tenant's Social Security number. If the so-called landlord can't do this, you are perhaps being conned.

Verify a potential tenants' income and employment. You want to make sure that all tenants have the income to pay the rent each month. Call the prospective tenant's employer to verify income and length of employment. Some employers require written authorization from the employee; this is included at the bottom of our Rental Application form. If you feel that verifying an individual's income by telephone, or accepting a note from her boss, is not reliable enough, you may require applicants to provide copies of recent paycheck stubs with their application. It's also reasonable to require documentation of other sources of income (such as disability or other benefits checks). Where a large portion of an applicant's income is from child support or alimony payments, you might want to ask for a copy of the court decree for the support payments. However, don't go overboard by asking for copies of tax returns or bank statements, except possibly from self-employed persons.

Obtain a credit report from a private credit Reporting agency. Many landlords find it essential to check a tenant's credit history with one or more credit reporting agencies. These agencies collect and sell credit and other information about tenants—for example, if they pay their rent on time or if they've ever been evicted. If asked to, these companies also will gather and sell "investigative reports" about a person's character, general reputation, personal characteristics or mode of living.

If you own many rental properties and need credit reports frequently, you should consider joining one of the three largest credit reporting agencies—CBI/Equifax, Trans Union or TRW—which may charge $40-50 in annual fees plus $5-10 per report. You can find their numbers and those of other companies that do tenant screening in the yellow pages of the phone book under "Credit Reporting Agencies." Or if you only rent a few units each year, see if your local apartment association (there are about two dozen in California) offers credit reporting services. With some credit reporting agencies, you can obtain a verbal credit report the same day it's requested, and a written one within a day or two.

It is legal to charge prospective tenants a fee (say $20) for the cost of the credit report itself and your time and trouble. Our sample application alerts prospective tenants of this fee. Be warned, though: It is not legal to charge a credit check fee if you do not use it for the stated purpose and pocket it instead. Also, excessive fees will only anger prospective tenants.

If you do not rent, or charge higher rent, to someone because of negative information in a credit report, you must so notify the tenant and give the person the name and address of the agency that reported the negative information. You must also tell the person that he has a right to obtain a copy of his file from the agency that reported the negative information, as long as he requests the file within 60 days.[4]

Check with the tenant's bank to verify account information. If an individual's credit history raises questions of his financial stability, you may want to take this additional step. If so, you'll probably need an authorization form such as the one included at the bottom of the Rental Application. Also, banks differ as to the type of information they will provide over the phone. Generally, banks will at most only provide information as to average account balances and bad checks, if any.

Be wary of an applicant who has no checking or savings account. It could be because the individual bounced so many checks her bank dropped her.

If your prospective tenant has lived in the area, you may want to review local court records to see if she has been named as a defendant in any collection or eviction suits. Checking court records may seem like overkill in many situations, but now and then it's an invaluable tool if you suspect a prospective tenant may be a potential troublemaker. Since court records are kept for several years, this kind of information can supplement references from recent landlords. You can get this information from your local municipal or justice court; for the nearest location, check your phone book under county listings.

You'll need to go in person and ask the civil clerk to show you the defendant's index, usually kept in microfiche form. If a prospective tenant's name is listed, jot down the case number so you can check the actual case file for details on the lawsuit and its resolution. You can often determine if a prospective tenant asserted a reasonable defense and if any judgment against her was paid off.

As an alternative to checking local court records yourself, see if any "tenant-reporting services" operate in your area. Just as regular credit-reporting agencies keep tabs on retail purchasers' creditworthiness, businesses such as UD Registry of Van Nuys keep tabs on eviction suits (called unlawful detainer, hence the "UD") filed against tenants. Your local apartment association may recommend other local services of this type. (Although it's illegal for companies to report eviction cases in which the tenant has won in court,[5] tenants usually don't win eviction suits; in most cases, the tenant fails to respond to the suit and is evicted, or negotiates a settlement.) Tenant-reporting services cost from $20 to $50, depending on the agency involved. As with credit-reporting agencies, if you don't rent to an applicant because of information from a tenant-reporting service, you must notify the applicant of the nature of the report and give her the name and address of the company.

---

[4]CC § 1785.20.

[5]CC § 1786.18(a)(4).

Get completed rental applications. Landlords are often faced with anxious, sometimes desperate people who need a place to live immediately. Some people tell terrific hard-luck stories as to why normal credit and reference-checking rules should be ignored in their case and why they should be allowed to move right in. Don't believe any of it. People who have planned so poorly that they will literally have to sleep in the street if they don't rent your place that day are likely to come up with similar emergencies when it comes time to pay the rent. Always make sure that prospective tenants complete the entire Rental Application including Social Security number, current employment and emergency contacts. You may need this information later to track down a tenant who skips town leaving unpaid rent or abandoned property (see Chapters 19 and 21). Never, never let anyone stay in your property on a temporary basis. Even if you haven't signed a rental agreement or accepted rent, you give the legally protected status of a tenant by giving a person a key or allowing him or her to move in as much as a toothbrush. Then, if the person won't leave voluntarily, you will have to file a lawsuit to evict him or her.

5. Choosing an Applicant

Once you have several applications, make your selection. Assuming you choose the candidate with the best qualifications to be a tenant (job, credit history, references), you have no legal problem. But what if you have a number of more or less equally qualified applicants? Can you safely choose one who happens to be an older white man over a young black woman? If two people rate equally, you can choose either one without legal risk in any particular situation, but not if you consistently avoid equally qualified minority applicants. See Chapter 9 for a detailed discussion on how to avoid discrimination when choosing an applicant.

6. Recordkeeping

A crucial use of any tenant-screening system is to document how and why you chose a particular tenant. Assuming you did choose a highly qualified tenant, you want your records to back you up to protect yourself against any charges of illegal discrimination. So maintain organized files of applications, credit reports and other materials and notes on prospective tenants for at least one year after you rent a particular unit. And, if your decision not to rent to an applicant is based on oral information provided by a former landlord or employer, make a brief note of your conversation and include it in your file. You can put your notes in the space provided at the bottom of our Rental Application form.

EXAMPLE
March 15, 199__ at 11:35 A.M.—Called Kate Steiner's former landlord, Larry Lewis, for property at 345 Mercer St., Apt.#4, San Francisco. Phone: 555-1313. Adams said that when Steiner was his tenant, she was occasionally one to two weeks late with her rent and kept a cat in her apartment, contrary to the rental agreement.

A final piece of recordkeeping advice: Make sure you update your records after a tenant moves in. You always want to know the tenant's phone number and where he works and banks. (You can get this latter information from the monthly rent check.) If a tenant leaves owing you money above the security deposit amount, a court may order that money be deducted from his wages or bank account to cover the amount owed you.

D. Holding Deposits

Accepting a holding deposit is legal, but we don't advise it. This type of deposit is usually offered by a tenant who wants to hold a rental unit pending the result of a credit check, or until she can come up with enough money for the rent and a formal deposit.

Why not take a holding deposit? Simply because they do you little or no good from a business point of view, and all too often result in misunderstandings or even legal fights.

EXAMPLE

Landlord Jim Chow takes a deposit of several hundred dollars from Michael Blake. What exactly is Jim promising Michael in return? To rent him the apartment? To rent Michael the apartment only if his credit checks out to Jim's satisfaction? To rent to Michael only if he comes up with the rest of the money before Jim rents to someone who comes up with the first month's rent and deposit? If Jim and Michael disagree about the answers to any of these questions, it can lead to needless anger and bitterness. This can sometimes even spill over into a small claims court lawsuit alleging breach of contract.

Another prime reason to avoid these deposits is that the law is very unclear as to what portion of a holding deposit a landlord can keep if a would-be tenant changes his mind about renting the property or doesn't come up with the remaining rent and deposit money. The basic rule is that a landlord can keep an amount that bears a "reasonable" relation to the landlord's costs, for example, for more advertising and for pro-rated rent during the time the property was held vacant. A landlord who keeps a larger amount is said to be imposing an unlawful "penalty."

If contrary to our advice you decide to take a holding deposit, it is essential that both you and your prospective tenant have a clear understanding. The only way to accomplish this is to write your agreement down, preferably on the holding-deposit receipt, including the amount of the deposit, the dates the landlord will hold the rental property vacant, the costs and term of the rental agreement or lease, and conditions for returning the deposit.

Here's a sample Receipt and Holding-Deposit Agreement which you can adapt to your situation— for example, if you have a one-year lease rather than a month-to-month agreement. A blank tear-out form is in the Appendix. If your agreement to rent property to a particular individual is not contingent upon your receiving a credit report and satisfactory references, simply delete this sentence from the last paragraph of the form.

SAMPLE RECEIPT AND HOLDING-DEPOSIT AGREEMENT

Receipt and Holding-Deposit Agreement

This will acknowledge receipt of the sum of $ ___200.00___ by ___Jim Chow___ _____ , "Owner," from ___Michael Clark___ _____ , "Applicant," as a holding deposit to hold vacant the rental property at ___123 State Street, City of Los Angeles, California___ until ___February 5___ , 19 ____ at ___5 P.M.___ . The property will be rented to Applicant on a ___month-to-month___ basis at a rent of $ __400__ per month, if Applicant signs Owner's written ___rental agreement___ and pays Owner the first month's rent and a $ __1,200__ security deposit on or before that date, in which event the holding deposit will be applied to the first month's rent.

This Agreement is contingent upon Owner receiving a satisfactory report of Applicant's references and credit history. Owner and Applicant agree that if Applicant fails to sign the Agreement and pay the remaining rent and security deposit, Owner may retain of this holding deposit a sum equal to the pro-rated daily rent of $ __20__ per day plus a $ __50__ charge to compensate Owner for the inconvenience.

Date: ___February 2, 199___

Michael Blake
_____
Applicant

Date: ___February 2, 199___

Jim Chow
_____
Owner

Understanding Leases and Rental Agreements

It is essential that every landlord understand California law as it applies to rental agreements and leases. Let's begin with the basics. There are three legal ways to create residential tenancies:

- written lease
- written month-to-month rental agreement
- oral rental agreement.

We'll look at each of these types of agreements in detail and provide sample lease and rental agreement forms with a description of each specific clause. We'll also point out illegal lease and rental agreement provisions.

A. Oral Agreements

Oral agreements are perfectly legal as long as they cover a year or less.[1] Typically, you agree to let the tenant move in, and she agrees to pay a set amount of rent, once or twice a month, or even weekly. If you want to raise the rent (subject to any rent control restrictions that apply) or terminate the tenancy, then the amount of notice you must give the tenant must correspond to the frequency of rent payment—unless you have specifically agreed to allow the tenant to stay for a longer period at an established rent.[2] Thus, if a tenant pays weekly, then she's entitled to a week's notice; she gets 30 days' notice if she pays monthly.

While oral agreements are easy and informal, it is rarely wise to use one. It's better business practice to clarify your agreement in writing, particularly if you want to impose conditions on the tenancy, such as no pets or no subletting. The main problem with oral agreements is obvious. As time passes and circumstances change, people's memories (including

yours) have a funny habit of becoming unreliable. Then, if something goes wrong, both sides are all too likely to end up in court, arguing over who said what to whom, when and in what context. This book is based on the assumption that you will always use either a written rental agreement or a lease.

B. Written Agreements: Which Is Better, a Lease or a Rental Agreement?

There are two kinds of written landlord/tenant agreements: leases and rental agreements. The crucial difference between the two documents is that written leases fix the term of the tenancy—most often for six months or a year, but sometimes longer. Written rental agreements usually run for a shorter period of time—typically 30 days (month-to-month) and are automatically renewed each month unless the tenant or landlord gives the other the proper amount of notice and terminates the agreement.

There is less legal difference between the two than there used to be because of legal developments in the last 20 years. What legal differences remain probably, on balance, favor the use of rental agreements. But don't jump to any conclusions. Read what

---

[1] Oral leases, while legal, are even more dangerous than oral rental agreements because they require that one important term—the length of the lease—be accurately remembered by both parties over a considerable time.

[2] CC §§ 827, 1944 and 1946.

follows, think about your own situation and then decide.

When you rent property under a month-to-month rental agreement, you can change the terms of the tenancy, including the amount of rent, or even end the tenancy, on 30 days' written notice in all cities without rent control ordinances.[3] (Chapter 14 describes how to raise rent and change other terms of tenancy.) With month-to-month agreements, a tenant who wants to leave needs to give you only 30 days' notice. With a fixed-term lease, you can't raise the rent or change other terms until the lease runs out (unless the lease says you can), nor can you evict before the lease term expires unless the tenant fails to pay the rent or violates another significant term of the lease. (The eviction process and rules are described in Chapter 18.)

It used to be that the major advantage of leasing for fixed terms such as a year or more was that a landlord obtained a fair degree of security. The tenant was on the hook to pay for a greater length of time than provided by month-to-month agreements. A tenant who broke the lease and left before it expired was still legally responsible for the rent for the entire lease term. And, if the tenant could be located, the landlord could sue and obtain a court judgment for the balance of the rent.

This is no longer true in most circumstances. Nowadays, landlords who sue the departing (lease-breaking) tenant for the rent due for the rest of the lease term are required to "mitigate" (or minimize) the damage they suffer as a result of the broken lease. That means the landlord must try to rent the unit to another suitable tenant at the same or a greater rent. If the landlord re-rents the unit, (or if a judge believes it could have been re-rented with a reasonable amount of effort), the landlord is presumed to have

suffered little or no damage, and the lease-breaking tenant is off the hook.

This all adds up to a simple truth: A lease no longer provides much income security to a landlord. Indeed, a lease is now something of a one-way street running in the tenant's direction. This is because, in most circumstances, the mitigation-of-damages rule allows a tenant to break a lease with little or no financial risk. And, even if the tenant does end up owing the landlord some money for the time the unit was empty, collecting the money can be more trouble than it is worth. (We discuss tenants' moving out and breaking leases in detail in Chapter 19.) Not surprisingly, many landlords prefer to rent from month to month, particularly in urban areas where new tenants can often be found in a few days.

There can still be, however, practical advantages to leasing for a fixed period, despite these legal rules. Many people do make a serious personal commitment when they enter into a long-term lease (partly because they think they'll be liable for quite a few month's rent if they up and leave). In other words, if you get the right tenant willing to sign a lease, you may reduce your turnover rate, even though the tenant could probably get out of the lease if he wished.

Finally, you'll probably prefer to use leases in areas where there is a high vacancy rate or it is difficult to find tenants. Remember, if you can't find another suitable tenant to move in, the former tenant whose lease hasn't expired is still liable for the rent. So, if you are renting near a college which is only in session for eight months a year, or in a vacation area which is deserted for months, you are far better off with a year's lease. Remember, though, that a seasonal tenant is almost sure to try to get someone to take over the tenancy, and you may very well not like the person they produce.

---

[3]Under just-cause eviction provisions of rent control ordinances in cities such as Los Angeles and San Francisco, you must have a good reason—one of those listed in the ordinance—to evict a tenant. We discuss rent control in detail in Chapter 4.

Variations on the Standard One-Year Lease

1. Long-Term Leases. *Most leases run for one year. This makes sense, as it allows you to raise the rent at reasonably frequent intervals if market conditions allow. Leasing an apartment or house for a longer period—two, three or even five years—can be appropriate, for example, if you're renting out your own house because you're taking a two-year sabbatical or if the tenant plans to make major repairs or remodel your property.*

One danger with a long-term lease is that inflation can eat away at the real value of the rent amount. A good way to hedge against this danger in all leases of more than a year is to provide for annual rent increases which are tied to the Consumer Price Index (CPI) increases during the previous year.

Here is a sample clause:

"Owner and Tenant agree that the rent shall increase on the ___ day of the _____ month of each year by the same percentage as the Consumer Price Index has increased during the previous twelve months."

The index most commonly used is the All-Urban-Consumers Consumer Price Index for the nearby large metropolitan area. The U.S. Department of Commerce publishes figures for the Los Angeles/ Long Beach/Anaheim/Santa Monica/Santa Ana area and the San Francisco/Oakland/San Jose area each May. In Los Angeles, the figure is published each May 30th by the Community Development Department. Other cities' rent-control boards keep records of the applicable figure, even where the rent increase allowed each year isn't directly tied to the CPI. (See Chapter 4 on rent control.)

For this sort of rent increase, no formal notice is required. Simply send the tenant a letter reminding him of the lease term calling for the increase and demonstrating how you calculated the amount.

2. Options to Renew a Lease. *Commercial leases often contain an option, perhaps at a higher rent, when the original lease period runs out. An option to renew is essentially a standing offer by the landlord to the tenant, which the tenant can accept or not in the manner and time frame set forth in the option. The option to renew concept is not commonly used in residential rentals, but a tenant occasionally requests one.*

We usually advise against using option clauses, for several reasons. First, an option to renew a lease leaves it entirely up to the tenant as to whether to continue the tenancy. Without such an option, both the tenant and the landlord must agree on a renewal. After all, by the time the lease is about to expire, you might not want to continue the tenancy. Unless you receive a very high guaranteed rent for the initial term, or a lump-sum payment in consideration for including the option clause, you have very little to gain and a lot to lose by giving an option to renew.

Second, options often allow the tenancy to continue, assuming the tenant exercises the option, on the same terms as before.[4] Since you may be able to obtain a higher rent after the initial term of six or twelve months, it's obviously not in your best interest to include an option that allows the tenant to remain at the same rent.

Finally, drafting option clauses can be very tricky. Even the slightest mistake may do you a great deal of harm or at the very least, render the option clause of no effect and add uncertainty to the entire situation. If you want to include a renewal or other option in a lease, contact an attorney.

---

[4]Option clauses must clearly set forth the terms of the renewed tenancy, including the new term, the rent (which can be different from the rent for the first term if the option clause clearly says so) and so forth. Most clauses do this by simply referring to the same terms of tenancy under the initial lease terms. An option clause which leaves any significant term, such as rent or length of term, to further negotiation, or words to that effect, is of no effect and is not legally binding.

3. Options to Purchase. *An "option to purchase"*
or "lease option" is a contract where an owner leases
her house (usually from one to five years) to a tenant
for a specific monthly rent (which may increase during
the contract term) and gives the tenant the right to buy
the house for a price established in advance. Depending
on the contract, the tenant can exercise the option to
purchase at any time during the lease period, or at a
date specified, or for a price offered by another person
who makes a purchase offer, subject to the tenant's
"right of first refusal," to match the offered price.

If your property should be easy to sell, why share
your chance at future appreciation with a tenant?
This, in addition to the fact that drafting option clauses
is pretty difficult, should give you pause.

Here are some situations when you might consider
a tenant's request for a lease-option:

- *If you have a negative cash flow and think the*
  short-run return (initial option fee, higher-than-
  normal rent, tax advantages) is worth it
- *If you plan to sell your property soon and think*
  that it might be difficult to sell
- *If you think your tenant will take better care of*
  your house, and perhaps even improve it.

Needless to say, never sign an option, whether in-
cluded in a lease or not, without consulting a lawyer.
If you're thinking of selling, and a tenant or
prospective tenant asks for an option to purchase, you
might simply reply that you'll consider selling at the
expiration of the lease.

C. Common Legal Provisions in Lease and Rental Agreement Forms

This section discusses each clause in the Lease and
Rental Agreement forms provided in this book.

Except for the important difference in how long
they run (see Clause 3 in our sample forms), leases
and written rental agreements are so similar that they
are sometimes hard to tell apart. Both cover the basic
terms of the tenancy (such as amount of rent and
date due). Except where indicated below, the clauses
are identical for the lease and rental agreements
included here.

In the Appendix, we provide you with two
clearly labelled tear-out forms: a Month-to-Month
Residential Rental Agreement and a Fixed-Term
Residential Lease. You should copy and use the one
more appropriate to your rental needs. We include
exerpts of a sample filled-in Rental Agreement in
throughout this chapter.

Spanish language note. If your lease or written
month-to-month rental agreement is negotiated primarily in Spanish, you must give the tenant notice in
Spanish of her right to request a Spanish translation
of the lease or rental agreement.[5] We recommend
that you routinely make Spanish-language
translations available to tenants who speak Spanish
as their first language.

**Choose your lease or rental agreement
carefully!** There are dozens of different
printed forms in use in California, and
provisions designed to accomplish the same result are
worded differently. Unfortunately, some of these
agreements are written so obtusely that it is hard to
understand what they mean. Ambiguous terms, fine
print and legalese will only lead to confusion and
misunderstanding with your tenants. Contrary to
what many form writers seem to believe, it is not
illegal to use plain English on lease and rental
agreement forms. We have done our best to provide
clearly written agreements. If you use a different
form, be sure to avoid leases or rental agreements
with illegal or unenforceable clauses (see Section E
below). You may need to use a special government
lease if you rent subsidized housing (see Chapter
9.B.1).

---

[5]CC § 1632.

CLAUSE 1. IDENTIFICATION OF OWNER AND TENANT

This Agreement is made and entered into on
_____19_____, between
_____, hereinafter "Tenants,"
and _____, hereinafter "Owner."

Every lease or rental agreement must identify the Owner and the tenant—usually called the "parties" to the agreement.

You should always list the names of all adults who will live in the premises, even if they are husband and wife. If you are renting to a family with minor children, you may want to simply list them as such (for example, "Sally Phillips and Steve Phillips and their minor children"). If you are worried about the possibility of overcrowding if the family has more children, you should state the number of minor children ("Sally Phillips and Steve Phillips and their two children, Adam and Amy"). But avoid using language that might be considered discriminatory. (We discuss this in Chapter 9.)

CLAUSE 2. IDENTIFICATION OF THE PREMISES

Subject to the terms and conditions below, Owner rents to Tenants, and Tenants rent from Owner, for residential purposes only, the premises at _____
_____, California.

This provision normally involves no more than filling in the blanks with the address of the unit or house you are renting.

Identifying exactly what the tenant is renting can be more difficult, however, in shared housing situations. Suppose, for example, you are renting a small cottage in your backyard that comes with kitchen privileges in your house, or you are renting a portion, but not all, of the house where you live. The best way to handle these sorts of situations is to add a sheet to the lease or rental agreement identifying exactly what property you are renting.

Simply fill in the address of the property and then add the words "as more fully described in Attachment 1 to this Agreement." Then, take a piece of paper, label it "Attachment 1" and define the particulars of what you are renting.

Finally, staple the attachment to the lease or rental agreement. When you and the tenant complete the paperwork, it's a good idea to ask the tenant to initial the attachment, as well as sign the agreement.

The words "for residential purposes only" are to prevent the tenant from using the property for conducting a business—for example, a day-care center that might affect your insurance or violate zoning laws. Before letting the tenant conduct any sort of business on the property, you should see a lawyer for advice on zoning laws and your potential liability.

Note on garages and out-buildings. If any part of a particular property is not being rented, such as a garage or shed you wish to use yourself or rent to someone else, make this clear by specifically excluding it from your description of the premises. For example, you might lease your "single-family house at 1212 Parker St., Visalia, California, except for the two-car garage located behind the house."

CLAUSE 3. DEFINING THE TERM OF THE TENANCY

a. Lease Provision

The lease form contains the following provision, setting a definite date for the expiration of the lease.

The term of the rental shall begin on _____ 19__, and shall continue for a period of _____ months, expiring on _____ , 19____.

NOTE: Should Tenants vacate before expiration of the term, Tenants shall be liable for the balance of the rent for the remainder of the term, less any rent Owner collects or could have collected from a replacement tenant by reasonably attempting to re-rent. Tenants who vacate before expiration of the term are also responsible for Owner's costs of advertising for a replacement tenant.

This provision in our Fixed-Term Residential Lease form obligates both the owner and the tenants for a specific term. It also includes a warning that explains the tenants' liability for breaking the lease. For reasons explained in Section E, it is not wise to include a specific monetary penalty (such as two months' rent) for tenant's breach of the lease. (See Chapter 19 for more details on tenant's liability for breaking a lease.)

b. Rental Agreement Provision

The rental agreement form contains the following provision for a month-to-month tenancy.

The rental shall begin on _____ , 19__ , and shall continue on a month-to-month basis. This tenancy is terminable by Owner or Tenants and is modifiable by Owner, by the giving of 30 days' written notice to the other (subject to any local rent control ordinance that may apply).

As the above provision implies, a owner's right to terminate or change the terms of a tenancy, even one from month-to-month, is limited by local rent control ordinances. Such ordinances not only limit rent and other terms of tenancies, but also require the owner to have a good reason to terminate a tenancy. We discuss rent control in detail in Chapter 4.

Reducing the notice period. A few rental agreement forms allow the landlord to modify or terminate the agreement by giving less than 30 days' written notice to the tenant. The law allows a rental agreement to contain a clause reducing the 30-day period to as little as seven days.[6] Though this may seem advantageous to landlords, it's not usually a good idea. This is because it is unclear under the law whether such a clause also allows the tenant to terminate his tenancy on short notice too, even if the provision is worded to only allow the landlord to do so.

Another legal uncertainty is whether a landlord can use this sort of short-notice clause to terminate a tenancy in less than 30 days if she has already accepted rent to cover a period beyond the end of the short-notice period. In other words, if you accept rent on January 1 for the whole month, your seven-day notice may not be valid unless served on or after the 24th, to take effect on the first day not covered by any rent you've accepted. Because of these uncertainties, and because a 30-day notice provision is the one traditionally used, we do not include a provision reducing the 30-day notice period.

Extending the notice period. You may, however, want to adopt a clause in a rental agreement giving a tenant a longer notice period—say 60 or 90 days. This may very well be appropriate where a tenant has occupied your premises for a long time, and some landlords report that they have fewer evictions when they give tenants a generous amount of time in which to find another place. You can modify the provision in the written rental agreement at the back of this book.

---

[6] CC § 1946.

CLAUSE 4. AMOUNT AND SCHEDULE FOR THE PAYMENT OF RENT

On signing this Agreement, Tenants shall pay to Owner the sum of $ _____ as rent, payable in advance, for the period of _____ , 19___ through _____ , 19 ___ . Thereafter, Tenants shall pay to Owner a monthly rent of $ _____ , payable in advance on the first day of each month, except when the first falls on a weekend or legal holiday, in which case rent is due on the next business day. Rent shall be paid to _____ at _____ , _____ , California.

In this provision, specify the amount of the monthly rent and where and to whom the rent is paid.

We discuss how to set a legal rent and where and how rent is due in Chapter 3. Please read this discussion and consider whether you wish to modify this clause which requires tenants to pay rent on the first of the month, with rent to be pro-rated between a move-in date (assuming it's other than the first) and the end of that month.

CLAUSE 5. LATE FEES

If Tenants fail to pay the rent in full within five days after it is due, Tenants shall pay Owner a late charge of $, plus $___ for each additional day that the rent continues to be unpaid. The total late charge for any one month shall not exceed $___. By this provision, Owner does not waive the right to insist on payment of the rent in full on the day it is due.

CLAUSE 6. RETURNED CHECK CHARGES

In the event any check offered by Tenants to Owner in payment of rent or any other amount due under this Agreement is returned for lack of sufficient funds, Tenants shall pay to Owner a returned check charge in the amount of $_____ .

It's legal to charge the tenant an extra fee if the rent is late or if his rent check bounces (assuming you agree to accept checks), if such fees are reasonable. If a bounced check fee or late charge is plainly excessive, chances are that a judge in an eviction lawsuit will rule that it is void. (This could cause you to lose the entire eviction suit if you included the amounts of the charge in a Three-Day Notice To pay Rent or Quit, as described in Chapter 16.)

A typical late charge provision on a low- or moderate-rent place is $10 after the fifth day the rent is due, plus $5 for each additional day, up to a maximum of $50. If you rent an expensive home or luxury apartment where the monthly rental amount is large, a bigger late fee will be legally enforceable as described in Chapter 3.

As for fees when the tenant's rent check bounces, you should charge no more than the amount your bank charges you for a returned check, (such as $5-10 per returned item) plus a few dollars for your trouble.

Month-to-Month Residential Rental Agreement

CLAUSE 1.   IDENTIFICATION OF OWNER AND TENANT

This Agreement is made and entered into on _____ August 18 _____ , 19 ___, between _____ Sally Phillips and Steve Phillips and their minor children _____, hereinafter "Tenants," and __ Olivia Matthews _____, hereinafter "Owner."

CLAUSE 2.   IDENTIFICATION OF THE PREMISES

Subject to the terms and conditions below, Owner rents to Tenants, and Tenants rent from Owner, for residential purposes only, the premises at ___ 123 Flower Lane, Unit 5, ___ _____ San Diego _____, California.

CLAUSE 3.   DEFINING THE TERM OF THE TENANCY

The rental shall begin on __September 1_____, 19 ____, and shall continue on a month-to-month basis. This tenancy is terminable by Owner or Tenants and is modifiable by Owner, by the giving of 30 days' written notice to the other (subject to any local rent control ordinance that may apply).

CLAUSE 4.   AMOUNT AND SCHEDULE FOR THE PAYMENT OF RENT

On signing this Agreement, Tenants shall pay to Owner the sum of $ __900__ as rent, payable in advance, for the period of __September 1_____, 19 _____ through ___September 30_____, 19 _____ . Thereafter, Tenants shall pay to Owner a monthly rent of $ __900_____, payable in advance on the first day of each month, except when the first falls on a weekend or legal holiday, in which case rent is due on the next business day. Rent shall be paid to _Olivia Matthews_____ at __456 Park St., San Diego_____, California.

CLAUSE 5.   LATE FEES

If Tenants fail to pay the rent in full within five days after it is due, Tenants shall pay Owner a late charge of $ __10_____ , plus $ 5_____ for each additional day that the rent continues to be unpaid. The total late charge for any one month shall not exceed $ __50_____ . By this provision, Owner does not waive the right to insist on payment of the rent in full on the day it is due.

CLAUSE 6.   RETURNED CHECK CHARGES

In the event any check offered by Tenants to Owner in payment of rent or any other amount due under this Agreement is returned for lack of sufficient funds, Tenants shall pay to Owner a returned check charge in the amount of $ __10_____ .

CLAUSE 7.   AMOUNT AND PAYMENT OF DEPOSITS

On signing this Agreement, Tenants shall pay to Owner the sum of $ _____ 1,800 _____ as and for security as that term is defined by Section 1950.5 of the California Civil Code, namely any payment, fee, deposit or charge to be used to compensate Owner for (a) Tenants' default in the payment of rent, (b) repair of damages to the premises, exclusive of ordinary wear and tear or (c) cleaning of the premises on termination of tenancy. Tenants, or any of them, may not, without Owner's prior written consent, apply this security deposit to rent or to any other sum due under this Agreement.

Within two weeks after Tenants have vacated the premises, Owner shall furnish Tenants with an itemized written statement of the basis for, and the amount of, any of the security deposit retained by the Owner. Owner may withhold only that portion of Tenants' security deposit necessary (a) to remedy any default by Tenants in the payment of rent, (b) to repair damages to the premises exclusive of ordinary wear and tear or (c) to clean the premises if necessary.

CLAUSE 8.   UTILITIES

Tenants shall be responsible for payment of all utility charges, except for the following, which shall be paid by Owner: _____ garbage pickup _____

_____.

CLAUSE 9.   LIMITS ON USE AND OCCUPANCY

The premises are to be used only as a private residence for Tenants listed in Clause 1 of this Agreement, a total of _____ 2 _____ adult occupants, and for no other purpose without Owner's prior written consent. Guests may stay up to ten days in any six-month period if Tenants notify Owner or Owner's representative by the third day of visiting. Occupancy by guests for more than ten days is prohibited without Owner's written consent and shall be considered a breach of Clause 10 of this Agreement.

CLAUSE 10.   PROHIBITION OF ASSIGNMENT AND SUBLETTING

Tenants shall not sublet any part of the premises or assign this Agreement without the prior written consent of Owner.

CLAUSE 11.   CONDITION OF THE PREMISES

Tenants acknowledge that they have examined the premises, including appliances, fixtures, carpets, drapes and paint, and have found them to be in good, safe and clean condition and repair, except as otherwise noted on the "Landlord/Tenant Checklist" which Tenants have completed and given Owner, a copy of which Tenants acknowledge receipt of, and which is hereby deemed to be incorporated into this Agreement by this reference.

Tenants agree to (a) keep the premises in good order and repair and, upon termination of tenancy, to return the premises to Owner in a condition identical to that which existed when Tenants took occupancy, except for ordinary wear and tear, (b) immediately notify Owner of any defects or dangerous conditions in and about the premises of which they become aware and (c) reimburse Owner, on demand by Owner or his or her agent, for the cost of any repairs to the premises damaged by Tenants or their guests or invitees.

CLAUSE 7. AMOUNT AND PAYMENT OF DEPOSITS

On signing this Agreement, Tenants shall pay to Owner the sum of $ _____ as and for security as that term is defined by Section 1950.5 of the California Civil Code, namely any payment, fee, deposit or charge to be used to compensate Owner for (a) Tenants' default in the payment of rent, (b) repair of damages to the premises, exclusive of ordinary wear and tear or (c) cleaning of the premises on termination of tenancy. Tenants, or any of them, may not, without Owner's prior written consent, apply this security deposit to rent or to any other sum due under this Agreement.

Within two weeks after Tenants have vacated the premises, Owner shall furnish Tenants with an itemized written statement of the basis for, and the amount of, any of the security deposit retained by the Owner. Owner may withhold only that portion of Tenants' security deposit necessary (a) to remedy any default by Tenants in the payment of rent, (b) to repair damages to the premises exclusive of ordinary wear and tear or (c) to clean the premises if necessary.

The use and return of security deposits is a frequent source of disputes between landlords and tenants. For example, a tenant may assume that the deposit, if it is equal to one month's rent, is the same as "last month's rent" and try to apply it this way a month before moving out. To avoid confusion, make sure that your lease or rental agreement is clear on the subject, and make the point again in a move-in letter. (See Chapter 7.)

The amount of security deposit is limited by state law. To determine the maximum amount of security deposit you can charge, read Chapter 5 before completing this section.

CLAUSE 8. UTILITIES

Tenants shall be responsible for payment of all utility charges, except for the following, which shall be paid by Owner: _____ .

This provision avoids misunderstandings. Normally, landlords pay for garbage (and sometimes water, if there is a yard) to make sure that the premises don't turn into a dump. Tenants usually pay for other services such as gas and electricity.

As mentioned in Chapter 1, state law requires landlords to notify all prospective tenants, before they sign any rental agreement or lease, if their gas or electric meter serves any areas outside their dwelling.[7] This law specifically applies where:

- there are not separate gas and electric meters for each unit; and

- a tenant's meter serves any areas outside his unit (even a light bulb not under the tenant's control in a common area).

If both these conditions apply, the landlord is required to do one of the following:

- pay for the utilities for the tenant's meter himself, by placing that utility in his (the landlord's) own name; or

- enter into a separate written agreement with the tenant, under which the tenant specifically agrees to pay utilities on his own meter, knowing he's paying for others' utilities too; or

- correct the situation by separately metering the area outside the tenant's unit.

We prefer the first and third methods above. Regardless of how few dollars a month a tenant may be paying for another tenant's or the landlord's common-area utilities, a tenant faced with this sort of uncertainty will usually demand a concession on rent; this will probably cost you more in the long run than if you either added a new meter or simply paid for the utilities yourself.

---

[7]CC § 1940.9.

In a situation where you share housing with the tenant, or where there is only one meter for several units, you may want to define who is responsible for what portion of the utilities in more detail. If you do, replace clause 8 of our form with these words:

Tenants shall pay for utility charges as follows:

CLAUSE 9. LIMITS ON USE AND OCCUPANCY

The premises are to be used only as a private residence for Tenants listed in Clause 1 of this Agreement, a total of __ adult occupants, and for no other purpose without Owner's prior written consent. Guests may stay up to ten days in any six-month period if Tenants notify Owner or Owner's representative by the third day of visiting. Occupancy by guests for more than ten days is prohibited without Owner's written consent and shall be considered a breach of Clause 10 of this Agreement.

CLAUSE 10. PROHIBITION OF ASSIGNMENT AND SUBLETTING

Tenants shall not sublet any part of the premises or assign this Agreement without the prior written consent of Owner.

Clause 9 spells out the total number of adult occupants, and lets the tenant know she may not move anyone else in as a permanent resident. Clause 10 enforces this with an anti-subletting clause, breach of which is grounds for eviction.

Clause 9 won't stop a tenant from bringing in a spouse or child later; in fact, if you tried to do so, you could be charged with illegal discrimination as discussed in Chapter 9. You may not want to enforce Clause 9's restriction on guests strictly, but it will be very handy to have if a tenant tries to move in a friend or relative for a month or two, calling her a guest. Restrictions on guests may not be based on the age or sex of the occupant or guest, as discussed in Chapter 10.

This clause is designed to prevent your tenant from leaving in the middle of the month or of a lease term and finding a replacement—maybe someone you wouldn't choose to rent to—without your consent (an "assignment"). It also prevents a tenant from subleasing during a vacation or renting out a room to someone unless you specifically agree.

If you include Clause 10 in a lease, you have the option not to accept a sublet or assignment if you don't like or trust the person your tenant proposes to take over the lease. If, however, the tenant wishes to leave early and provides you with another suitable tenant, you can't both hold the tenant financially liable for breaking the lease and unreasonably refuse to rent to another tenant who is in every way suitable. (We discuss this in detail in Chapter 19.)

The issue of who is and who is not a tenant, and legal liability for paying the rent and meeting all the conditions of the lease or rental agreement, can be very confusing and cause all kinds of problems. See Chapter 10 for a discussion of this topic.

CLAUSE 11. CONDITION OF THE PREMISES

Tenants acknowledge that they have examined the premises, including appliances, fixtures, carpets, drapes and paint, and have found them to be in good, safe and clean condition and repair, except as otherwise noted on the "Owner/Tenant Checklist" which Tenants have completed and given Owner, a copy of which Tenants acknowledge receipt of, and which is hereby deemed to be incorporated into this Agreement by this reference.

Tenants agree to (a) keep the premises in good order and repair and, upon termination of tenancy, to return the premises to Owner in a condition identical to that which existed when Tenants took occupancy, except for ordinary wear and tear, (b) immediately notify Owner of any defects or dangerous conditions in and about the premises of which they become aware and (c) reimburse Owner, on demand by Owner or his or her agent, for the cost of any repairs to the premises damaged by Tenants or their guests or invitees.

Clause 11 makes it clear that if a tenant damages the premises (for example, breaks a window or scratches hardwood floors), it's his responsibility to pay for fixing the problem.

Chapter 7 describes the use and value of the Landlord-Tenant Checklist and other means to minimize disputes about who's responsible for damage or repairs. A tear-out copy of the checklist is in the Appendix. If you decide not to use the checklist, simply cross-out the reference to it in Clause 11.

We can't emphasize enough the importance of establishing a system for tenants to regularly report on the condition of the premises and defective or dangerous conditions. This is covered in detail in Chapter 11.

CLAUSE 12. POSSESSION OF PREMISES

The failure of Tenants to take possession of the premises shall not relieve them of their obligation to pay rent. In the event Owner is unable to deliver possession of the premises to Tenants for any reason not within Owner's control, including but not limited to failure of prior occupants to vacate as agreed or required by law, or partial or complete destruction of the premises, Owner shall not be liable to Tenants, except for the return of all sums previously paid by Tenants to Owner, in the event Tenants choose to terminate this Agreement because of Owner's inability to deliver possession.

This clause protects you if you're unable, for reasons beyond your control, to turn over possession after having signed a lease or rental agreement.

CLAUSE 13. PETS

No animal or other pet shall be kept on the premises without Owner's prior written consent, except: properly trained dogs needed by blind, deaf or physically disabled persons and:

☐ **other _____, under the following conditions: _____**

_____ .

This clause is designed to prevent tenants from keeping pets without your written permission. This is not to say that you will want to apply a flat "no-pets" rule. It does provide you with a legal mechanism designed to keep your premises from being knee-deep in Irish wolfhounds. Without this sort of provision, particularly in a fixed-term lease that can't be terminated on 30 days' notice, there's little to prevent your tenant from keeping dangerous or non-house-broken pets on your property, except for city ordinances prohibiting tigers and the like.

It is illegal to forbid a blind person to keep a trained guide dog, a deaf person to keep a trained signal dog, or a physically handicapped person to keep a trained service dog on the premises.[8]

Print "None" next to the word "other" if you want to forbid pets. If you allow pets, check the box "other" and identify the type and number of pets—for example, "one cat." If you do allow a pet, you may want to spell out your pet rules. You may also want to charge a higher security deposit.

---

[8]CC § 54.1.

Should You Require a Separate Security Deposit for Pets?

Some landlords allow pets but require the tenant to pay a separate deposit to cover any damages caused by the pet. This is not legal if the deposit charged for the pet, when added to the amount charged for the security deposit exceeds the maximum amount that can be charged for a deposit. (See Chapter 5.) Generally, we do not think separate deposits are good ideas because they limit how you can use that part of the security deposit. If you want to protect your property from damage done by a pet, you are probably better off charging a slightly higher rent or security deposit to start with, assuming you are not restricted by rent control.

 Enforce no-pets clauses. When faced with tenants who violate no-pets clauses, landlords often ignore the situation for a long time, then try to enforce it later if friction develops over some other matter. This could backfire. In general, a landlord who knows a tenant has breached the lease or rental agreement (for example, by keeping a pet), and does nothing about it for a long time, waives the right to object. You can preserve your right to object by giving the tenant an informal written notice, then following through with a Three-Day Notice to Perform Covenant or Quit, or a 30-day termination notice if the tenancy is month-to-month —subject to any rent control law requirements. See Chapter 4 for details on rent control and Chapter 18 for a discussion of three-day and 30-day notices.

CLAUSE 14. OWNER'S ACCESS FOR INSPECTION AND EMERGENCY

Owner or Owner's agents may enter the premises in the event of an emergency, or to make repairs or improvements, supply agreed services, or exhibit the premises to prospective purchasers or tenants. Except in case of emergency, Owner shall give Tenants reasonable notice of intent to enter and shall enter only during regular business hours of Monday through Friday from 9:00 A.M. to 6:00 P.M. and Saturday from 9:00 A.M. to noon. In order to facilitate Owner's right of access, Tenants, or any of them, shall not, without Owner's prior written consent, alter or re-key any locks to the premises or install any burglar alarm system. At all times Owner or Owner's agent shall be provided with a key or keys capable of unlocking all such locks and gaining entry. Tenants further agree to provide instructions on how to disarm any burglar alarm system should Owner so request.

This clause makes it clear to the tenant that you as a owner have a legal right of access to the property to make repairs or show the premises for sale or rental, provided you give the tenant reasonable notice. As we'll see in Chapter 13, the law limits the landlord's right to enter property in the tenant's absence or without her permission. Although these limits apply regardless of what an agreement or lease says, it's best to put the limits in writing to avoid problems later on.

Clause 14 also addresses a few things not covered by law. It forbids the tenant from re-keying the locks or installing a burglar alarm system (which would frustrate your right of access) and provides that you or your manager are entitled to duplicate keys and instructions on how to disarm the alarm system. Also, the law allows entry by the landlord in non-emergency situations during "ordinary business hours" without defining those hours. Clause 14 defines these hours to include part of Saturday.

CLAUSE 15. PROHIBITIONS AGAINST VIOLATING LAWS AND CAUSING DISTURBANCES

Tenants shall be entitled to quiet enjoyment of the premises. Tenants shall not use the premises in such a way as to violate any law or ordinance, including laws prohibiting the use, possession or sale of illegal drugs, commit waste or nuisance, or annoy, disturb, inconvenience or interfere with the quiet enjoyment of any other tenant or nearby resident.

This type of clauses is found in most form leases and rental agreements. If the tenant causes a nuisance, seriously damages the property or violates the law, (for example, deals drugs, a subject covered in Chapter 12), you may be able to evict him even without such a provision in the agreement, but it will be easier to evict if you can point to an explicit lease provision. If you want specific rules—for example, no loud music played after midnight—add them to Clause 15 or Clause 19 (Tenant Rules and Regulations).

CLAUSE 16. REPAIRS AND ALTERATIONS

Except as provided by law or as authorized by the prior written consent of Owner, Tenants shall not make any repairs or alterations to the premises.

Especially with fixed-term leases for a year or more, the law is unclear on the extent to which a tenant may, in the absence of a provision in the agreement, remodel or make substantial alterations to the building. Clause 16 makes it clear that alterations and repairs without the landlord's consent aren't allowed. If you wish, you can make this clause more specific to prohibit the use of nails or tacks in the walls (very bad for lath-and-plaster walls, but okay on sheet-rock walls), adhesive hangers (which tear the outer layer off sheet-rock walls when removed), or whatever, or spell your rules out in a move-in letter. (See Chapter 7.)

The "except as provided by law" language is a reference to the "repair-and-deduct" remedy the tenant may use to repair health- or safety-threatening defects. (See Chapter 11.) The tenant always has the right to use this statutory procedure, no matter what a lease says. If you grant permission to install a bookshelf, security system, kitchen cupboards screwed to studs or anything that is firmly attached to your property, make sure the tenant understands that the fixture is to remain in place when she leaves. (Fixtures are completely defined in Civil Code Section 1019. They belong to the landlord except where "the removal can be affected without injury to the premises unless the thing has by the manner in which it is affixed become an integral part of the premises.") You might attach a statement to the lease or rental agreement, which both you and the tenant sign. A sample agreement is shown below.

You might also insist that you or a worker install the shelves or other fixture, to assure that the work meets your standards of quality.

SAMPLE AGREEMENT FOR INSTALLATION OF FIXTURE

```
     Olivia Matthew, the Owner of the premises at 123 Flower Lane, San
Diego, California, hereby grants to Steve Phillips, Tenant at Unit 5 at
this address, permission to install a set of bookshelves by use of four-
inch screws attached to the long wall of the rear bedroom of the
premises. Steve acknowledges and understands that the bookshelves, once
installed, are to be considered part of the premises, and are not to be
removed when his tenancy ends.


Date:    February 2, 199         Olivia Matthew
                                 Owner

Date:    February 2, 199         Steve Phillips
                                 Tenant
```

CLAUSE 17. DAMAGE TO PREMISES, FINANCIAL RESPONSIBILITY AND RENTER'S INSURANCE

In the event the premises are damaged by fire or other casualty covered by insurance, Owner shall have the option either to: (a) repair such damage and restore the premises, this Agreement continuing in full force and effect, or (b) give notice to Tenants at any time within thirty (30) days after such damage terminating this Agreement as of a date to be specified in such notice. In the event of the giving of such notice, this Agreement shall expire and all rights of Tenants pursuant to this Agreement shall terminate. Owner shall not be required to make any repair or replacement of any property brought onto the premises by Tenants.

Tenants agree to accept financial responsibility for any damage to the premises from fire or casualty caused by Tenants' negligence. Tenants shall carry a standard renter's insurance policy from a recognized insurance firm, or, as an alternative, warrant that they will be financially responsible for losses not covered by Owner's fire and extended coverage insurance policy. Repair of damage or plumbing stoppages caused by Tenants' negligence or misuse will be paid for by Tenants.

This clause speaks to what happens if the premises are seriously damaged by fire or other calamity. Basically, it seeks to limit your risk to thirty days' rental value, even if the damage was your responsibility, and to eliminate your risk entirely if the damage was caused by the tenant. This provision forces the tenant to assume responsibility for damage to her own belongings and for certain types of damage to your building caused by the tenant's acts.

Clause 17 gives tenants the option of obtaining renter's insurance or being held personally liable for damages they or their guests cause. One change you may wish to make in this clause involves requiring renter's insurance. If you absolutely wish to require insurance, substitute the following paragraph for the second paragraph of Clause 17:

Tenants, within 10 days of the signing of this Agreement, shall obtain insurance which will reimburse Owner for the cost of fire or water damage and vandalism to the premises and indemnify Owner against liability to third parties for any negligence on the part of Tenants or their guests or invitees, and cover damage to the tenants' personal possessions to a maximum of $_____. Tenants shall provide Owner with proof that this has been done.

Your move-in letter (see Chapter 7) is the place to highlight your policy on renter's insurance.

CLAUSE 18. WATERBEDS

No waterbed or other item of water-filled furniture shall be kept on the premises without Owner's written consent.

Whether or not you can refuse to rent to a tenant with a waterbed depends on when the property was built.

If your property's "certificate of occupancy" (final approval of initial construction by local building department) was issued before January 1, 1973, you may legally refuse to rent to a tenant who has a waterbed. This isn't to say that you should ban waterbeds if your property was built before 1973. Wooden floors built to current standards, or even the standards 20 or 30 years ago, can withstand pressures of at least 60 pounds per square foot, and a typical queen-sized waterbed exerts about 50 pounds per square foot. (Poured concrete floors, of course, pose no problem.)

If your property was built after 1973, you may have no choice. State law prohibits owners of such property from refusing to rent to (or renew leases with) tenants who have waterbeds, or refusing to allow tenants to use waterbeds, if:

- The tenant obtains a replacement-value $100,000 waterbed insurance policy.
- The pressure the waterbed puts on the floor does not exceed the floor's pounds-per-foot weight

limitation (as stated above, this should be no problem for dwellings constructed after 1973).

- The waterbed is held together by a pedestal or frame.
- The tenant installs, maintains and moves the waterbed in accordance with the manufacturer's or retailer's standards, or state standards, whichever are more stringent.
- The tenant gives the landlord at least 24 hours written notice of his intention to install, move or remove the waterbed, and allows the landlord to be present when this occurs.
- The waterbed conforms to construction standards imposed by the State Bureau of Home Furnishings and displays a label to that effect.
- The waterbed was constructed after January 1, 1973.[9]

If your property was built before 1973 and you wish to ban waterbeds, a simple clause to this effect will suffice.

For property built in 1973 or later, if you want all the protections of the law, add the following to your lease or rental agreement:

No waterbed or other item of water-filled furniture shall be kept on the premises unless tenant complies with all the requirements of Civil Code Section 1940.5. The provisions of that law with regard to insurance, pounds-per-square-foot weight, installation, moving and removal of bedding, notice to Owner, structural limitations, waterbed construction standards and inspection by Owner shall apply to this Agreement as though incorporated herein.

If you expect the tenant to comply with the provisions of the law, you will need to give him a copy or spell the rules out in your Tenant Rules and Regulations.

Note on security deposits and waterbeds. You can charge higher security deposits for tenants with waterbeds. (See Chapter 5.)

---

[9]CC § 1940.5.

CLAUSE 12. POSSESSION OF PREMISES

The failure of Tenants to take possession of the premises shall not relieve them of their obligation to pay rent. In the event Owner is unable to deliver possession of the premises to Tenants for any reason not within Owner's control, including but not limited to failure of prior occupants to vacate as agreed or required by law, or partial or complete destruction of the premises, Owner shall not be liable to Tenants, except for the return of all sums previously paid by Tenants to Owner, in the event Tenants choose to terminate this Agreement because of Owner's inability to deliver possession.

CLAUSE 13. PETS

No animal or other pet shall be kept on the premises without Owner's prior written consent, except properly trained dogs needed by blind, deaf or physically disabled persons and:
n other ___None_____,
under the following conditions: _____.

CLAUSE 14. OWNER'S ACCESS FOR INSPECTION AND EMERGENCY

Owner or Owner's agents may enter the premises in the event of an emergency, or to make repairs or improvements, supply agreed services, or exhibit the premises to prospective purchasers or tenants. Except in case of emergency, Owner shall give Tenants reasonable notice of intent to enter and shall enter only during regular business hours of Monday through Friday from 9:00 a.m. to 6:00 P.M., and Saturday from 9:00 A.M. to noon. In order to facilitate Owner's right of access, Tenants, or any of them, shall not, without Owner's prior written consent, alter or re-key any locks to the premises or install any burglar alarm system. At all times Owner or Owner's agent shall be provided with a key or keys capable of unlocking all such locks and gaining entry. Tenants further agree to provide instructions on how to disarm any burglar alarm system should Owner so request.

CLAUSE 15. PROHIBITIONS AGAINST VIOLATING LAWS AND CAUSING DISTURBANCES

Tenants shall be entitled to quiet enjoyment of the premises. Tenants shall not use the premises in such a way as to violate any law or ordinance, including laws prohibiting the use, possession or sale of illegal drugs, commit waste or nuisance, or annoy, disturb, inconvenience, or interfere with the quiet enjoyment of any other tenant or nearby resident.

CLAUSE 16. REPAIRS AND ALTERATIONS

Except as provided by law or as authorized by the prior written consent of Owner, Tenants shall not make any repairs or alterations to the premises.

CLAUSE 17. DAMAGE TO PREMISES, FINANCIAL RESPONSIBILITY AND RENTER'S INSURANCE

In the event the premises are damaged by fire or other casualty covered by insurance, Owner shall have the option either to: (a) repair such damage and restore the premises, this Agreement continuing in full force and effect, or (b) give notice to Tenants at any time within thirty (30) days after such damage terminating this Agreement as of a date to be specified in such notice. In the event of the giving of such notice, this Agreement shall expire and all rights of Tenants pursuant to this Agreement shall terminate. Owner shall not be required to make any repair or replacement of any property brought onto the premises by Tenants.

Tenants agree to accept financial responsibility for any damage to the premises from fire or casualty caused by Tenants' negligence. Tenants shall carry a standard renter's insurance policy from a recognized insurance firm or, as an alternative, warrant that they will be financially responsible for losses not covered by Owner's fire and extended coverage insurance policy. Repair of damage or plumbing stoppages caused by Tenants' negligence or misuse will be paid for by Tenants.

CLAUSE 18.   WATERBEDS

No waterbed or other item of water-filled furniture shall be kept on the premises without Owner's written consent.

CLAUSE 19.   TENANT RULES AND REGULATIONS

Tenants acknowledge receipt of, and have read a copy of, the Tenant Rules and Regulations, which are hereby incorporated into this Agreement by this reference. Owner may terminate this Agreement, as provided by law, if any of these Tenant Rules and Regulations are violated.

CLAUSE 20.   PAYMENT OF ATTORNEY FEES IN A LAWSUIT

In any action or legal proceeding to enforce any part of this Agreement, the prevailing party shall recover reasonable attorney fees and court costs.

CLAUSE 21.   MANAGER'S AUTHORITY TO SERVE AND RECEIVE LEGAL PAPERS

In addition to the Owner, any person signing this Agreement on Owner's behalf is authorized to manage the premises, and is authorized to act for and on behalf of Owner for the purposes of service of process and for the purpose of receiving all notices and demands, at the address indicated below Owner's signature below.

CLAUSE 22.   ENTIRE AGREEMENT

This document constitutes the entire Agreement between the parties, and no promises or representations, other than those contained here and those implied in law, have been made by Owner or Tenants.

CLAUSE 23.   ADDITIONAL PROVISIONS

Cross through with large X if none.

_____ See attached Addition to Rental Agreement regarding painting _____

_____

_____

This Agreement has been signed on the day and year first written herein.

Owner/Manager: _Olivia Matthews_____

Address: ___456 Park Street_____

_____San Diego, California_____

Tenant: ___Sally Phillips_____

Tenant : ___Steve Phillips_____

CLAUSE 19. TENANT RULES AND REGULATIONS

Tenants acknowledge receipt of, and have read a copy of, the Tenant Rules and Regulations, which are hereby incorporated into this Agreement by this reference. Owner may terminate this Agreement, as provided by law, if any of these Tenant Rules and Regulations are violated.

Many landlords don't worry about detailed rules and regulations, especially when they rent single-family homes or duplexes. However, in large buildings, rules are usually important to control the use of such things as elevators, pools, parking garages, lock-out charges and security systems. They are also commonly employed to lay down rules about such things as excessive noise, pets, use of grounds and maintenance of balconies (for example, no drying clothes on the balcony). If you do plan to use tenant rules and want the power to enforce them if a tenant doesn't want to cooperate, include a clause such as this in your lease or rental agreement, especially if you use a lease. Doing this gives you the authority to evict a tenant who persists in seriously violating your code of Tenant Rules and Regulations.

If you don't have a set of Tenant Rules and Regulations, cross out and initial Clause 19.

CLAUSE 20. PAYMENT OF ATTORNEY FEES IN A LAWSUIT

In any action or legal proceeding to enforce any part of this Agreement, the prevailing party shall recover reasonable attorney fees and court costs.

Many landlords assume that if they sue a tenant and win, the court will order the losing tenant to pay the landlord's attorney fees. This is usually wrong. As a general rule, a court will order the loser to pay the winner's attorney fees only if a written agreement specifically provides for it. This is why it can be important to have an "attorney fees" clause in your lease. That way, if you hire a lawyer to bring an eviction suit and win, the judge will order your tenant to pay your attorney fees.

An attorney fees clause in a lease or rental agreement works both ways. That is, if your tenant prevails in a lawsuit, and the lease or written rental agreement contains such a clause, you must pay her "reasonable attorney fees," in an amount determined by the judge.[10] This is true even if the clause is worded so that it requires payment of attorney fees only by the tenant if you win and not vice-versa. Many landlords don't use this provision because of this reason and because of their experience that, if they win a suit, these fees are very hard to collect.

If you intend to do your own legal work in any potential eviction or other lawsuit, even if the tenant hires a lawyer, you will probably conclude that it is wiser not to include Clause 20 in your agreements. You don't want to be in a situation where you'd have to pay the tenant's attorney fees if she won, but she wouldn't have to pay yours if you won because you didn't hire a lawyer.

CLAUSE 21. MANAGER'S AUTHORITY TO SERVE AND RECEIVE LEGAL PAPERS

In addition to the Owner, any person signing this Agreement on Owner's behalf is authorized to manage the premises, and is authorized to act for and on behalf of Owner for the purposes of service of process and for the purpose of receiving all notices and demands, at the address indicated below Owner's signature below.

If you plan to give a manager authority to serve and receive legal papers, include this clause. We discuss your legal rights vis-a-vis managers in Chapter 6.

CLAUSE 22. ENTIRE AGREEMENT

This document constitutes the entire Agreement between the parties, and no promises or representations, other than those contained here and those implied in law, have been made by Owner or Tenants.

---

[10]CC § 1717.

The meaning of this provision is obvious. It protects you from liability for anything a tenant claims you promised orally. It also works the other way: If a tenant with a written rental agreement or lease makes oral promises—such as paying extra rent if another person moves in—and doesn't do so, you're covered because the promises weren't written down. To repeat, get everything you want included in your rental agreement in writing before you sign. Any agreements made later should be done in writing in the form of an amendment.

CLAUSE 23. ADDITIONAL PROVISIONS

If you want to include additional clauses in your lease or rental agreement, put them here. If there are no additional provisions, simply put a large "X" through this section. If you need to make more extensive changes to the lease or rental agreement, see Section D below.

D. How To Modify and Sign the Form Agreements

Our lease and rental agreement forms have been designed to protect your broad legal interests, but they may not fit your exact situation. For example, if your building has a garage, you may want to incorporate rules in the lease or rental agreement regarding specific parking requirements.

1. Before the Agreement Is Signed

The easiest way to change a pre-printed form agreement is to cross out unwanted portions and write in desired changes on the standard forms. With major alterations, you may retype one of our forms and add your own provisions. If you make fundamental changes, however, you may wish to have your work reviewed by an experienced landlords' lawyer. (See Chapter 8.)

If the changes are lengthy, use a separate sheet of paper. Type the same heading as used on the original document, identify the parties, and make it clear that you are adding provisions to the lease or rental agreement.

For example, if you agree that the unit will be repainted before the tenant moves in, with you supplying the paint and painting supplies and the tenant contributing labor, you could add a clause to the rental agreement like the one shown below.

SAMPLE ADDITION TO RENTAL AGREEMENT

> The rental agreement for the premises at 123 Flower Lane, Unit 5, San Diego, California, entered into between Olivia Matthew, Owner, and Steve Phillips, Tenant, is hereby supplemented as follows:
>
> Owner will supply up to $150 worth of paint and painting supplies. Tenant will paint the living room, hall and two bedrooms, using off-white latex paint on the walls, and water-based enamel on all wood surfaces (doors and trim). Paint and supplies shall be picked up by Tenant from ABC Hardware and billed to Owner.
>
> Date: ___August 18, 199___   *Olivia Matthew*_____
> Olivia Matthew, Owner
>
> Date: ___August 18, 199___   *Steve Phillips*_____
> Steve Phillips, Tenant

2. Signing the Lease or Rental Agreement

At the end of the lease or rental agreement, there's space to include the signature and street address at which the owner and anyone authorized to manage the premises may be personally served with legal papers. There's also space for the tenants' signatures.

Be sure your tenant reviews the lease or rental agreement before signing and is clear about all your terms and rules and regulations. Chapter 7 discusses how to get your new tenancy off to the right start.

If you've altered a standard form, be sure that you and all tenants initial the changes when you sign the document.

Give the tenant a copy of the signed lease or rental agreement.

3. After the Agreement Is Signed

All amendments to your lease or rental agreement must be in writing to be legally binding.

If you want to change one or more clause in a month-to-month rental agreement, there is no legal requirement that you get the tenant's consent (although it's always a good idea to do so). You can simply send the tenant a 30-day notice of the change, unless a local rent control ordinance requires more notice or prohibits the change you want to make. However, if you use a lease, you can not unilaterally change the terms of the tenancy. We discuss the mechanics of changing terms of a rental agreement by use of a 30-day notice in Chapter 14.

If you wish to make mutually agreed-upon changes to a written rental agreement or lease after it is signed, there are two good ways to accomplish it. The first is to agree to substitute a whole new agreement for the old one. The second is to add the new provision as an amendment to the original agreement. An amendment need not have any special form, so long as it clearly refers to the agreement it's changing and is signed by the same people who signed the original agreement.

SAMPLE AMENDMENT TO LEASE

The written lease for rental of the premises at 123 Flower Lane, Unit 5, San Diego, California, entered into by Olivia Matthew ("Owner") and Steve and Sally Phillips ("Tenants") on August 18, 19__ is hereby amended as follows:

Beginning on June 1, 19__ , Tenants shall rent a one-car garage, adjacent to the main premises, from Owner for the sum of $75 per month. Accordingly, the rent of $900 per month set out in Clause 1 of lease agreement shall be increased to $975, effective June 1, 19__ .

Date: ___May 20, 199_____   _____Olivia Matthew_____
                                      Olivia Matthew, Owner

Date: ___May 20, 199_____   _____Steve Phillips_____
                                      Steve Phillips, Tenant

Co-signers

Some landlords require co-signers on rental agreements and leases, especially when renting to students who depend on parents or other persons for much of their income. The co-signer signs a separate agreement or the rental agreement or lease, under which she agrees to pay any rent or damage-repair costs the tenant fails to pay.

In practice, a co-signer's promise to guarantee the tenant's rent obligation often has little value, because the threat of eviction is the primary factor that motivates a tenant otherwise reluctant to pay the rent. However, you cannot sue a co-signer along with the tenant in an eviction suit. The co-signer must be sued separately in either a regular civil lawsuit or in small claims court. As far as going after the co-signer on the tenant's rent obligation is concerned, your best weapon—the possibility of an eviction lawsuit—is unavailable.

Another legal obstacle to enforcement of a co-signer's promise is that the promise is not enforceable if the lease or rental agreement has been changed without the co-signer's written approval. See Wexler v. McLucas, 48 Cal. App. 3d Supp. 9 (1975). Even the simple renewal of a lease involving the signing of a new document by the landlord and the tenant (but not by the co-signer) will eliminate the co-signer's liability—so may a rent increase or other change in the terms of tenancy. Taking this one step further, a court might refuse to hold a co-signer liable for any period beyond that of the original lease term, where the tenancy has since become a month-to-month agreement. Since lease expirations, renewals and rent increases usually occur over the life of a residential tenancy, a landlord who foregoes the nuisance of getting the co-signer's signature every time an element of the tenancy changes may wind up with a worthless promise.

The benefits of having a lease or rental agreement co-signed by someone who won't be living on the property are almost entirely psychological. A tenant who thinks you can look to the co-signer—usually a relative or close friend of the tenant—may be less likely to default on the rent. Similarly, a co-signer asked to pay the tenant's debts may persuade the tenant to pay.

E. Illegal Lease and Rental Agreement Provisions

Because some landlords have drafted leases and rental agreements that contained provisions that attempted to take away various tenant protections of California law, the Civil Code now expressly forbids the use of many types of illegal provisions.[11]

Unfortunately, a few landlords still intentionally include illegal provisions to try to intimidate tenants. Doing this is counterproductive, because a lease or rental agreement containing too many illegal clauses may be disregarded in its entirety should you ever end up in court. In addition, several district attorneys have sued landlords who routinely and flagrantly use leases with illegal clauses. As a result, several landlords were fined.

1. Waiver of Rent Control Laws

California has no statewide rent control law. However, all cities that do have rent control ordinances specifically forbid lease or rental agreement provisions by which a tenant gives up (or waives) any rights granted by the rent control ordinance. Thus, any rental agreement provision excusing the landlord from complying with rent ceilings or just-cause-for-eviction requirements would be of no legal effect.

 See Chapter 4 for a detailed discussion of rent control.

---

11 CC § 1953.

2. Waiver of Repair-and-Deduct Rights

Landlords must maintain and repair their rental property in accordance with certain minimum standards.[12] If a landlord refuses to do so, a tenant may arrange for certain repairs and deduct the cost from the next month's rent.[13] Further, a tenant cannot give up or modify those rights in a lease or rental agreement.[14]

There is one exception to this rule, however. If the tenant specifically agrees to repair and maintain all or part of the property in exchange for lower rent, the repair-and-deduct rule can be waived. Although in principle this would seem to be a broad exception, it is not broad in practice. Judges look to see if the tenant's promise to keep the premises in repair was really in exchange for lower rent and was not just a way for the landlord to avoid her legal responsibilities. Chances are the tenant's waiver will be upheld if, in the written lease, a tenant handy with tools agrees to repair or maintain the property in exchange for rent that's considerably lower than fair market rent, but not otherwise.

Here is an example of a valid clause which could be included in your lease or rental agreement:

Tenants agree to be responsible for all routine repairs and maintenance to the premises covered by this Agreement in exchange for a monthly rent of $900. This amount is approximately $200 less than the fair market rent for the premises, which is agreed to be $1,100.

All said and done, we advise against this sort of arrangement. For one thing, even if you include this provision, it doesn't relieve you of your obligation to the city or county to comply with local housing codes. You retain this obligation even if the tenant breaches a rental agreement or lease provision requiring her to maintain the premises in compliance with city and county regulations. In other words, the city and county has no interest in what you and the tenant agree to, but will hold you responsible if there is a code violation problem.

A better approach is this: If you want your tenant to fix up the property, fine, but pay him or her by the hour or the job for work agreed on in advance. It's better to pay the tenant separately and collect the regular market rent. That way, if you're unhappy with the tenant's work, you can simply fire her and still be entitled to the full rent. If, on the other hand, you agree to reduce the rent in exchange for work, you may be be stuck for a long time with reduced rent in exchange for the tenant's poor-quality work. (Chapter 11 discusses landlords' liability and tenants' repair and deduct rights in detail.)

3. Right of Inspection

A landlord can't just walk in any time to inspect or repair the property or to show it to prospective renters or buyers. Except in an emergency, the law requires a landlord to give a tenant reasonable notice. Nevertheless, some leases and rental agreements have provisions that purport to allow a landlord to enter with little or no notice. This type of provision

---

[12]CC § 1941.

[13]CC § 1942.

[14]CC § 1942.1.

is of no effect.[15] (Chapter 13 covers landlords' right of entry and tenants' privacy.)

4. Provision That the Owner Is Not Responsible for Tenant Injuries or Injuries to a Tenant's Guests

Often called an "exculpatory clause," this provision says that if the landlord fails to maintain the property and the tenant or her guests suffer injury or property damage as a result, the landlord can't be held responsible for paying for the loss. This provision is void and of absolutely no use to a landlord, should a tenant or a guest suffer personal injury or property damage and sue the landlord. (For more on landlords' liability, see Chapter 12.)

5. Provision Giving Owner Right of Entry

Some leases and rental agreements contain a clause that appears to allow the landlord to come in and throw the tenant out, or at least change the locks and remove her property, if she doesn't pay the rent. This clause is void.[16] If you do resort to illegal means to evict a tenant, this type of clause won't protect you in a tenant's lawsuit for unlawful eviction. No matter what the lease says, you have to sue and get a court order to remove an unwilling tenant legally. (See Chapters 17 and 18 and Volume II of this book for details on evictions.)

6. Waiver of Right to Legal Notice, Trial, Jury or Appeal

A lease or rental agreement clause under which a tenant gives up any procedural right in a lawsuit you might bring is also void.[17] This includes the tenant's right to proper service of a Three-Day Notice To Pay Rent or Quit (three-day notice periods *cannot* be reduced by agreement) or other termination notice and the rights to present a defense in a lawsuit, trial by jury, appeal, and so on.[18]

7. Waiver of Right to Deposit Refund

A landlord must, within two weeks after the tenant vacates the property, mail the tenant a refund of his deposit or, if the deposit is not completely refunded, a written itemization as to how it was applied to back rent, costs of cleaning, repairs, and the like. See Chapter 20 for details on returning security deposits. Any provision waiving or modifying the tenant's rights in this respect is void and of no effect.[19]

8. Other Illegal Provisions

Just because a particular type of lease clause isn't listed above doesn't mean it's legally enforceable. Courts can and do exercise the power to refuse to enforce what they consider to be illegal or outrageous clauses in leases and rental agreements. Some examples: provisions for excessive late charges (discussed in Chapter 3), and short-cuts the landlord can use to recover possession if he believes the property to be abandoned (covered in Chapter 21). Also, the legality of certain provisions may depend on such factors as the date your property was built (see, for example, Clause 18 of our rental agreement regarding waterbeds).

---

[15]CC § 1953.

[16]CC § 1953.

[17]A jury-trial waiver in a commercial (nonresidential) lease was upheld in *Trizec Properties, Inc. v. Superior Court,* 779 Cal. App. 3d 1616 (1991), but the case seems to apply only in the commercial leasing context.

[18]CC § 1953.

[19]CC § 1953.

Basic Rent Rules

To state the obvious, one of your foremost concerns as a landlord is receiving your rent—on time and without hassle. It follows that you need a good grasp of the legal rules governing rent.

 In this chapter, we review California's basic rent laws. However, several topics we discuss in other chapters can affect your rights under these laws, including:

Condition of the premises. If a landlord fails to fulfill his obligation to keep up the premises, the tenant's duty to pay rent is affected correspondingly. Under state law, a tenant may claim that the landlord's failure to repair and maintain the property justifies withholding rent. The validity of such claims, and the amount of rent, if any, that can legally be withheld, may ultimately be determined by a judge in an eviction lawsuit. We discuss this process in detail in Chapter 11.

Local rent control laws. Los Angeles, San Jose, San Francisco, Oakland and ten other cities have rent control ordinances that dictate how much rent you can charge (and many other aspects of your business). We discuss rent control in Chapter 4.

How and when you notify tenants of rent increases. Chapter 14 describes the legal process for raising rents.

How you enforce rent payments. You can give tenants who don't pay their rent on time a Three-Day Notice To Pay Rent or Quit. We show you how in Chapter 16.

A. How Much Can You Charge?

There is no state or federal law governing how much rent landlords can charge. In other words, you can legally charge as much rent as you want (and a tenant will pay) unless your premises are subject to a local rent control ordinance. Many wise landlords,

however, charge slightly less than the going rate as part of a policy designed to find and keep excellent tenants. You may wish to check newspaper want-ads for comparable rents in your area, or contact local real estate and property management companies.

 Cities With Rent Control Ordinances

Berkeley

Beverly Hills

Campbell (mediation only)

Cotati

East Palo Alto

Hayward

Los Angeles

Los Gatos

Oakland

Palm Springs

San Francisco

San Jose

Santa Monica

Thousand Oaks

West Hollywood

As with any business arrangement, it usually pays in the long run to have your tenants feel they are getting a good deal. In exchange, you hope the tenants will be responsive to your sensibilities as a landlord. This doesn't always work, of course, but it's our experience that tenants who feel their rent is fair are less likely to complain over trifling matters. Certainly, it's obvious that a tenant who thinks you are trying to squeeze every last nickel out of her is unlikely to think twice before calling you about a clogged toilet at 11 P.M.

B. When Rent Is Due

Most lease and rental agreements, including the ones in this book, call for rent to be paid monthly, in advance, on the first day of the month. The first of the month is customary and convenient because many people get their paychecks on the last workday of the month, just in time to pay rent on the first of the following month. Also, entry into a new month itself reminds people to pay monthly bills that are due on the first. (Hopefully, your tenant will learn to associate flipping the calendar page with paying the rent on time.)

It is perfectly legal to require rent to be paid on a different day of the month, and may make sense if the tenant is paid at odd times. Some landlords make the rent payable each month on the date the tenant first moved in. We think it's easier to pro-rate rent for a short first month and then require that it be paid on the first of the next month (see Chapter 7.C). But if you only have a few tenants, and don't mind having different tenants paying you on different days of the month, it makes no legal difference.

You are not legally required to have your tenant pay rent on a monthly basis. If you wish, you and the tenant can agree that the rent be paid twice a month, each week, or on whatever schedule suits you. The most common variation on the monthly payment arrangement is having rent paid twice a month. This is a particularly good idea if you have tenants who receive government benefits or who have relatively low-paying jobs and get paid twice a month. Such tenants may have difficulty saving the needed portion of their mid-month check until the first of the month.

If your rental agreement (whether written or oral) is for an unspecified term (as opposed to a lease for a specific period), you should be aware that the length of time between rent payments affects other important rights. Specifically, the notice period you must give your tenant in order to terminate the tenancy (and the notice he must give you), is normally the same number of days as the period between rent payments—typically 30 days.[1] This is true unless your rental agreement specifically establishes a different notice period, or a local rent control ordinance changes the rules on termination (a topic covered in Chapter 4). This general rule also applies to the notice period you must give your tenants to raise the rent, subject, of course, to any rent-increase limitations of local rent control ordinances.

EXAMPLE 1

On March 10, landlord Marion Carty signs a month-to-month rental agreement with Carol Tomson. Carol rents an apartment for $550, payable on the tenth day of each month. Because the interval between rent payments is a month, Marion must give Carol at least 30 days' written notice if she wants to raise the rent, change any other term of the rental agreement or terminate the tenancy. If Carol wants to leave, she too must give 30 days' notice to Marion.

EXAMPLE 2

Ken Tanaka rents out rooms on a weekly basis with the rent payable every Friday. Because the interval between rent payments is one week, Ken must give his tenants one full week's notice if he wishes to raise the rent or have them move out. So for a rent increase or termination of tenancy to take effect the following Friday, Ken must give his tenants written notice to that effect no later than the Friday before.

Once you have established the rental amount and the day of payment, you should insist that rent be paid in advance to cover the following month or other period. For example, rent should be due on the first day of the month for that month, and it should be paid on or before that day. It may seem obvious to require tenants to pay rent in advance. You would probably never consider allowing a tenant who moved in on the first day of the month to wait to pay rent until the 31st. We belabor this point because California law, following an ancient rule traceable to

[1]CC § 827.

feudal times, states that in the absence of an agreement to the contrary, rent is due at the end of the rental term.[2] In other words, unless the agreement states that rent is due in advance, you may have trouble getting the tenant to pay at the beginning of the rental period.

1. Weekends and Holidays

Even if a rental agreement says the rent is due on a certain day of the month, there are some exceptions. One instance is when the date rent is due falls on a weekend day or other legal holiday. When rent would actually be due on a Saturday, Sunday or holiday, it is legally due on the next business day.[3]

---

[2]CC § 1947.

[3]Although Civil Code § 7 defines holidays to include Sundays and special legal holidays, Section 12a of the Code of Civil Procedure (which governs three-day notices to pay rent or quit) defines holiday to include Saturdays also. Legal duties—including payment of rent—which fall on such a holiday need not be performed until the next business day. CC § 11, CCP § 12a.

EXAMPLE

If your lease or rental agreement says a tenant's rent is due on the first day of each month, and April 1 falls on Saturday, rent isn't due until Monday, April 3. If April 3 is a legal holiday, rent isn't legally due until Tuesday, April 4.

Figuring the exact due date isn't really all that important unless you have to file an eviction lawsuit based on the tenant's nonpayment of the rent, where counting days correctly can be crucial. Chapter 16 covers starting the eviction process with a Three-Day Notice To Pay Rent or Quit; evictions are covered in detail in *Landlord's Law Book, Volume 2: Evictions*

2. Grace Periods

Now let's clear up a giant myth. Lots of tenants are absolutely convinced that if they pay by the 5th (or sometimes the 7th or even the 10th) of the month, they have legally paid their rent on time and should suffer no penalty because they are within a legal grace period. This is not true. Quite simply, there is no law that gives tenants a five-day or any other grace period when it comes to paying the rent. As we'll discuss more thoroughly in Chapter 16, a landlord can legally proceed with the first step necessary to evict a tenant—serving a Three-Day Notice To Pay Rent or Quit—the day after the rent is legally due but unpaid.

In practice, most tenants get a grace period because landlords usually don't get upset about late rent until it's more than a few days late, and many rental agreements and leases do not begin assessing the tenant late charges until at least five days after the due date. But you are definitely within your legal rights to insist that the rent be paid on the day it is due, allowing for Saturdays, Sundays and legal holidays. In our opinion, if you wait more than five days to collect your rent, you are running your business unwisely, unless your particular circumstances warrant a longer period.

C. Where and How Rent Is Due

You may want to specify in your lease or rental agreement where, or even how, the tenant should pay her rent. (See Clause 4 in Chapter 2.C.) Some form rental agreements require the rent to be paid personally at the landlord's place of business. This makes the tenant responsible for getting the rent to the owner or manager at a certain time or place, and avoids issues such as whether or not a rent check was lost or delayed in the mail.

You may also wish to specify whether rent should be paid by cash, check or money order. Some landlords, concerned with security and the need to write receipts, accept checks only. Others are more concerned about bounced checks and will accept only cash, certified checks or money orders.

Once in a while, when relations between a landlord and a tenant are beginning to break down for other reasons, there will be misunderstandings about where and how the rent must be paid. Sometimes a landlord who's been burned by bounced checks from a particular tenant will suddenly decree that she'll accept nothing less than cash or a certified check or money order, and that rent may be paid only during certain hours at the manager's office.

Be careful. It may be illegal to suddenly change your terms for payment of rent—unless you are simply enforcing an existing term. For example, if your agreement states that you only accept cash or a money order, you are on solid ground when you tell a check-bouncing tenant that you'll no longer accept her checks, and that your previous practice of doing so was merely an accommodation not required of you under the rental agreement.

If, however, your lease or rental agreement doesn't say where and how rent is to be paid, the law states that past practice generally controls how rent is paid until you properly notify the tenant of a change. It's not a good practice to accept rent by mail, except as an accommodation where the lease or rental agreement requires rent to be paid personally to the owner or manager. In the absence of a provision requiring tenants to pay rent in person, a landlord's practice of accepting rent by mail may enable the tenant to continue paying by mail, and to claim "the check's in the mail" in response to a Three-Day Notice To Pay Rent or Quit. If you want to change this practice and require tenants to pay rent at your office, you must formally change a month-to-month rental agreement with a written 30-day notice. (We show you how in Chapter 14.) If you rent under a lease, you will have to wait until the lease runs out and change your terms for payment of rent in the new lease.

Now suppose you wish to make a change with regard to whether the rent must be paid by cash or check. The past-practice rule stated above doesn't apply in this case. The law presumes that a lease that doesn't specify how rent is to be paid requires the rent to be paid in cash.[4] So, if you don't want to continue accepting a tenant's checks, simply notify her of this fact, in writing. This kind of notice is effective immediately.

You should not accept post-dated checks under any circumstances. A post-dated check is legally a note promising to pay on a certain date. If you accept a post-dated check, you have accepted a note, rather than cash, for the rent, and a tenant facing eviction could argue that you accepted the "note" in lieu of cash.

D. Late Charges

A fairly common and sensible practice is to charge a late fee. Late charges provide an incentive for tenants to pay rent on time and make sense when used with discretion.

Most California cities and unincorporated areas do not regulate what you can charge for late fees.

---

[4]*Strom v. Union Oil Co.*, 88 Cal. App. 2d 78, 84, 198 P.2d 357 (1948).

Some large cities with rent control ordinances do regulate the amount of late fees. Check any rent control ordinances applicable to your properties.

Unfortunately, a few landlords try to charge excessive late fees and, by so doing, get themselves into legal hot water and incur tenant hostility. Some courts have ruled that contracts which provide for unreasonably high late charges are not enforceable.[5] Also, if a late charge is plainly excessive, chances are that a judge in an eviction lawsuit will rule that it is void.

While there are no statutory guidelines as to how much you can reasonably charge as a late fee, you should be on safe ground if you adhere to these principles:

- If you use a flat fee, it should not exceed four to six percent of the rent ($30 to $45 on a $750-per-month rental). A late charge much higher than this (say, a 10% charge of $75 for being one day late with rent on a $750-per-month apartment) would probably not be upheld in court.

- If you adopt a late charge which increases with each additional day of lateness, it should be moderate and have an upper limit. A late charge that increases without limit each day could be considered interest charged at a usurious rate. (Ten dollars a day on a $1,000 per month rent is 3650% annual interest.)

A more acceptable late charge would be $10 for the first day rent is late, plus $5 for each additional day, with a maximum late charge of $50. (See Clause 5 of our filled-in sample rental agreement in Chapter 2.) If you rent an expensive home or luxury apartment where the monthly rent is larger, a bigger late fee would probably be legally enforceable.

- The late charge should not begin until after a reasonable grace period of three to five days. Imposing a stiff late charge if the rent is only one or two days late may not be upheld in court.

Some landlords try to disguise excessive late charges as a "discount" for early payment of rent. One landlord we know concluded he couldn't get away with charging a $50 late charge on a late $425 rent payment, so instead, he designed a rental agreement calling for a rent of $475 with a $50 discount if the rent was not more than three days late. Ingenious as this ploy sounds, it is unlikely to stand up in court, unless the discount for timely payment is very modest. Giving a relatively large discount is in effect the same as charging an excessive late fee, and a judge is likely to see it as such and throw it out.

Anyway, we think all this fooling around with late charges is wasted energy. If you want more rent for your unit, raise the rent (unless you live in a rent control area). If you are concerned about tenants paying on time—and who isn't—put your energy into choosing responsible tenants. Be consistent about enforcing rent due dates, following through with a Three-Day Notice To Pay Rent or Quit—the first legal step in a possible eviction—no later than six or seven days after the rent is due.

If you have a tenant with a month-to-month tenancy who drives you nuts with late rent payments, and a reasonable late charge doesn't resolve the situation, terminate the tenancy with a 30-day notice, as described in Chapter 18.

 Local rent-control ordinances may regulate how this is done. If that isn't possible—either because the tenant has a lease or because rent control laws are too restrictive—serve the tenant with a Three-Day Notice To Pay Rent or Quit the day after the rent is due, and follow through with an eviction if the rent isn't paid in full within the three-day period.

---

[5]See *Fox v. Federated Department Stores,*94 Cal. App. 3d 867, 156 Cal. Rptr. 893 (1979), where the court held invalid a late charge clause in a promissory note because the charge exceeded reasonable administrative costs.

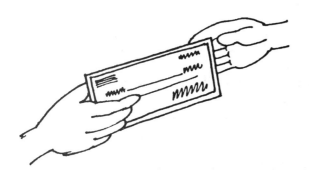

E. Returned Check Charges

In Chapter 2, we suggest a rental-agreement provision requiring the tenant to pay bad-check charges equal to what the bank charges you, plus a few dollars for your trouble. (See Clause 6 in Chapter 2.C.) State law provides that anyone who fails to pay a bounced check is liable for a penalty equal to three times the amount of the check up to $500, plus the amount of the check.[6] However, this penalty can be collected only by waiting 30 days after sending the person who wrote the check a demand letter, then filing a regular civil lawsuit in court. This law is of little use to landlords for two reasons:

- First, a landlord faced with a check-bouncing tenant should never wait 30 days, but should give the tenant a Three-Day Notice To Pay Rent or Quit right away, then sue for eviction if the tenant doesn't make the check good within three days.

- Second, even if a landlord served both a Three-Day Notice To Pay Rent or Quit on the tenant, plus a 30-day bad-check demand letter, he would have to file two separate lawsuits: a fast-moving unlawful detainer lawsuit for eviction, and a regular civil lawsuit for the bounced check penalty. Two lawsuits are necessary because the law doesn't allow landlords to ask for any money other than rent in eviction lawsuits.

---

[6]CC § 1719.

It's better to serve the tenant a three-day notice demanding the rent (but not a late charge or bad-check charge) as soon as you find out a tenant's check bounces. Then follow through with an eviction lawsuit—well before 30 days has passed—and forget about penalties you may ultimately be unable to collect anyway.

 Don't redeposit rent checks that bounce. It is a poor idea to let your bank redeposit rent checks that bounce, something they will normally do unless you request that bad checks be returned to you immediately instead. Why would you want to do this? For two excellent reasons. The first is that it alerts you to the fact that the rent is unpaid much sooner than if the check is resubmitted and returned for nonpayment a second time. You can use this time to contact the tenant to ask that the check be made good immediately. If it is not, you can promptly serve a three-day termination notice. (See Chapter 18.)

The second reason that you want to get the check back quickly is that, if it is resubmitted, and again there are insufficient funds to cover it, the normal bank procedure is to punch holes in it. If this is done, the check can never again be presented for payment. If it's returned to you before it is punched, however, you can hold on to it. Even after you succeed in evicting the tenant for nonpayment, or after she has just voluntarily left, you can periodically call the tenant's bank over the next few months to see if enough funds have been deposited to cover it. In a surprising number of instances, a tenant will eventually put more money in the account, often giving you the chance of collecting your money by cashing the check.

 Eviction warning! Do not demand late charges or bad checkcharges when you give a tenant a Three-Day Notice To Pay Rent or Quit. We discuss the proper procedures for giving a written three-day notice preceding an eviction lawsuit in Chapter 16.

F. Partial Rent Payments

On occasion, a tenant suffering a temporary financial setback will offer something less than the full month's rent, with a promise to catch up in partial payments as the month proceeds, or full payment at the first of the next month. Although generally it isn't good business practice to allow this, you may wish to make an exception where the tenant's financial problems truly appear to be temporary and you have a high regard for the person. But we recommend that you verify a tenant's hard-luck story by asking questions and then checking the story out by calling the hospital, employer or anyone else the tenant says can back her up.

1. Routinely Accepting Partial Payment

There is generally no legal problem if you accept partial rent payments. If you accept less than a full month's rent from a tenant, you certainly do not give up the right to the balance. Indeed, you can normally accept a partial payment one day and demand full payment the next. (Even the words "paid in full" on a tenant's check can be ignored; you will not lose your right to more money owed you by cashing the tenant's check if you cross out the offending language before you cash the check.[7])

If you regularly accept rent in installment payments (despite a written agreement that rent is due in one payment in advance), you may have legally changed the terms of your rental agreement.

---

[7]CC § 1526.

You routinely allow your tenant Larry, whose $800 rent is due on the first of the month, to pay $400 on the first and the other $400 on the 15th. Nine months later, you get tired of this arrangement. After receiving $400 on the first day of the month, you give Larry a three-day notice on the second of the month to pay the rest of the rent or quit. This may not work. You may be stuck with getting $400 on the first and $400 on the 15th for the balance of the term of the lease, or in the case of a written or oral rental agreement, until you give him a written notice of change in the terms of tenancy. (See Chapter 14.) Why? Because a judge in an eviction lawsuit may rule that, by giving Larry this break every month for almost a year, coupled with his reliance on your practice, you in effect changed the terms of the lease or rental agreement. Viewed this way, your three-day notice to pay the full rent or leave would be premature because the second $400 isn't due until the 15th.

If the tenancy is one from month-to-month, you can reinstate the original payment terms by "changing" the terms back to what the rental agreement says they are, with a 30-day written notice. A simple form is shown below, and a blank tear-out copy is in the Appendix. You don't have to worry about this problem if you accept partial payments only a few times on an irregular basis. And accepting partial payments more often than this really isn't good landlording anyway, unless you truly are willing to change the terms of the lease or rental agreement. If you are, do it in writing.

2. Accepting Partial Payment After a Three-Day Notice

It's a trickier situation if you accept partial rent payments after giving the tenant a three-day notice to pay the rent in full or quit. The basic legal rule is this: If your tenant responds to a three-day notice with less than the amount stated in the notice, you can either refuse to accept it or accept the lesser amount and serve a new three-day notice demanding the balance. You probably cannot accept the partial payment and base an eviction lawsuit on the original three-day notice. This is simply because the law requires that in any eviction lawsuit you file, the rent that's past due as of the date of filing must be the same as the rent demanded in the three-day notice.

For example, if you served a notice demanding the rent of $600, and the tenant paid $500, you would be filing a defective eviction suit based on a $600 three-day notice when only $100 was due. Also, any acceptance of rent by the landlord after serving the tenant a three-day notice is considered a waiver of the breach complained of in the notice, so that a new notice, demanding only the balance, would have to be given. This is more fully explained in Volume 2 of this book, which provides step-by-step advice on how to do your own evictions.

SAMPLE NOTICE OF REINSTATEMENT OF TERMS OF TENANCY

Notice of Reinstatement of Terms of Tenancy

To: __Sam Jones_____,
          (name)

Tenant(s) in possession of the premises at
      123 Fourth Street
_____,
                  (street address)

City of __Los Angeles_____, County of __Los Angeles_____, California.

When you rented the premises described above, your rent was due and payable on the first day of each month. While the undersigned has attempted to work with you in the past, your late rental payments can no longer be tolerated.

Therefore, please be advised that effective 30 days from the date of service on you of this notice, your monthly rent will be due and payable in advance on the first day of the month, for that month.

Date: __August 12, 199_____   *Roy Jefferson*_____
                                              Owner/Manager

---

3. Written Agreements To Accept Late Rent

If you do give a tenant a little more time to pay, monitor the situation carefully. You don't want to provide extension after extension, until the tenant is three months in arrears with no chance to bring her account current. One way to prevent this is to put a payment schedule in writing. This binds you—you can't get mad at the tenant and demand the rent or initiate an eviction lawsuit sooner. But more importantly, it also gives both you and the tenant a benchmark against which to measure her efforts to catch up on the rent. If you give the tenant two weeks to catch up and she doesn't, the written agreement precludes any argument that you had really said "two to three weeks." Here's a sample agreement; a blank, tear-out copy is in the Appendix.

SAMPLE AGREEMENT FOR PARTIAL RENT PAYMENTS

Agreement for Partial Rent Payments

_____John Lewis_____, Owner, and

_Betty Wong_____, Tenant, agree as follows:

1. That _Betty Wong_____ has paid
one-half of her $500 rent for Apartment #2 at 111 Billy St., Fair
Oaks, CA_____ on _March 1,_____, 19 ___,
which was due _March 1_____, 19 _____.

2. That _John Lewis_____ agrees to accept all the remainder of the rent
on or before _____March 15_____, 19 ____ and to hold off on any legal
proceeding to evict _Betty Wong_____ until that date.

Date: _March 2, 199_____   _John Lewis_____
                                       Owner

Date: _March 2, 199_____   _Betty Wong_____
                                       Tenant

If the tenant does not pay the rest of the rent when promised, you can, and should, follow through with a Three-Day Notice To Pay Rent or Quit (covered in Chapter 16), and if need be, initiate an eviction lawsuit if payment is still not forthcoming.

4. Oral Agreements To Accept Late Rent

Don't rely on an oral agreement with a tenant who promises to catch up on back rent. To be legally binding, an oral agreement must include a promise by the tenant to give you something over and above a promise to pay rent already due. For example, the tenant could agree to pay a late fee.

EXAMPLE 1

Nancy approaches her landlord Robin with a sad story about needing to send money to her ailing mother. Nancy asks if she can pay half the rent on the first of the month (the day it is due) and the remaining half two weeks late. Robin agrees, but nothing is written and Nancy does not promise to provide any extra payment or other advantage in exchange for Robin's forbearance. The next day, Robin finds out Nancy has lost her job and been arrested for possession of cocaine. He asks her to pay the full rent immediately. This is legal. Nancy's original promise was not legally binding because Robin made no promise in exchange for it.

EXAMPLE 2

Now let's change this example slightly and assume that in exchange for the right to pay half of the rent late, Nancy promised to sweep the parking lot twice a week and turn on the pool filter every morning. Now, Nancy and Robin have entered into a valid contract and Robin has a legal obligation to stick to his end of the bargain as long as Nancy honors her agreement.

Rent Control

California has no statewide rent control law. Cities may establish rent control on a local basis, either through the initiative process or by the act of a city council.[1] A county's board of supervisors also can enact rent control in unincorporated areas of the county (places where there are no cities).

Some form of rent regulation now exists in 15 California cities, including Los Angeles, San Francisco, Oakland and San Jose. (See list below.)

 Cities With Rent Control Ordinances

Berkeley

Beverly Hills

Campbell (mediation only)

Cotati

East Palo Alto

Hayward

Los Angeles

Los Gatos

Oakland

Palm Springs

San Francisco

San Jose

Santa Monica

Thousand Oaks

West Hollywood

Rent control ordinances generally control more than how much rent a landlord may charge. For example:

- Many cities' ordinances also govern how—and under what circumstances—a landlord may terminate a tenancy, even one from month-to-month, by requiring the landlord to have just cause to evict.

- Several cities, most notably Los Angeles, require landlords to register their properties with a local rent control agency.

- Finally, several cities regulate the amount of security deposits and impose notice requirements for rent increases and termination of tenancies that are different from the state law requirements we discuss in Chapters 5, 14, 16 and 18.

No two rent control ordinances are identical, even as to how rents may be increased. For example, some cities have elected or appointed boards which have the power to adjust rents; others automatically allow a certain percentage rent increase each year as part of their ordinances. We review basic rent control provisions in this chapter and how they compare among cities. We summarize each city's ordinance in a Rent Control Chart in the Appendix.

Cities change their rent control laws frequently, and court decisions also affect them. In short, you should read the material here to get a broad idea of rent control. If the property you rent is in a city that has rent control, it is imperative that you also contact your city or county to get an up-to-date copy of the ordinance and any regulations interpreting it.

---

[1] The California Supreme Court upheld the right of cities and counties to enact rent control ordinances in the cases of *Fisher v. City of Berkeley*, 37 Cal. 3d 644 (1984) and *Birkenfeld v. City of Berkeley*, 17 Cal. 3d 129 (1976). The U.S. Supreme Court upheld the *Fisher* decision in *Fisher v. City of Berkeley*, 475 U.S. 260, 106 S. Ct. 1045 (1986).

Where to Get Answers to Questions on Rent Control

The following organizations can help you with questions you might have about rent control ordinances in your area:

- *Your city rent control board can supply you with a current copy of the local ordinance, and sometimes also with a brochure explaining the ordinance. (Unfortunately, many cities' staffs are hostile to landlords' questions and don't provide much help over the phone on specific questions.) Check the Rent Control Chart in the Appendix or contact your mayor or city manager's office for the address of your local rent control board.*
- *Your local apartment owners association can also give you general information on rent control ordinances in the area they serve. For the name of your local association, contact the California Apartment Association, 1414 K St., Suite 610, Sacramento, CA 95814, 916-447-7881.*
- *Local attorneys can be an additional resource. Check the Yellow Pages for attorneys who specialize in "landlord/tenant" law, and whose offices are in or near the city about whose ordinances you have questions.*

A. Property Exempt From Rent Control

No city's rent control ordinance covers all rental housing within the city. New buildings as well as owner-occupied buildings with four (or sometimes three or two) units or less are often exempt from rent control ordinances. Some cities also exempt single-family dwellings and luxury units that rent for more than a certain amount.

Unfortunately, an ordinance can sometimes be ambiguous, leaving the landlord and tenant to wonder whether or not the property is covered. If the local rent board can't give you a straight answer—or you're reluctant to contact them—you may need to consult an attorney who's familiar with your community's rent control ordinance.

B. Local Rent Control Administration

Most rent control ordinances are administered by a rent control board whose members are appointed (elected in Santa Monica and Berkeley) by the mayor or city council (board of supervisors in San Francisco). In some cities, these boards determine the amount of an allowable across-the-board rent increase each year, applicable to all properties covered by the ordinance. They also conduct individual hearings where landlords seek an additional increase over and above that amount. As a general rule, appointed boards are more even-handed than elected ones. The name, address and phone number of each board is given in the Rent Control Chart in the Appendix.

C. Registration of Rental Properties

The cities of Berkeley, Cotati, East Palo Alto, Los Angeles, Palm Springs, Santa Monica, Thousand Oaks and West Hollywood all require the owners of rent-controlled property to register the property with the agency that administers the rent control ordinance. This allows the rent board to keep track of the city's rental units, as well as to obtain operating funds from the registration fees.

These cities forbid landlords who fail to register their properties from raising rent. In fact, cities may require a landlord to refund past rent increases if the increases were made during a period in which the landlord failed to register property. The courts have ruled that it is unconstitutional for rent control ordinances requiring registration to allow tenants to withhold rents just because the property isn't registered.[2]

Some cities, including Berkeley and Santa Monica, impose fines on landlords who fail to register property. However, both of these types of penalties are now limited by a state law[3] in cases where the landlord's failure to register was not in bad faith and was quickly corrected (that is, the landlord registered the property) in response to a notice from the city. To make things easier for landlords who make honest mistakes, state law now requires cities to allow landlords to phase in, over future years, any rent increases that would have been allowed had the property been registered, if the following conditions are met:

• The landlord's original failure to register the property was unintentional and not in bad faith.

• The landlord has since registered the property as required by the city and paid all back registration feess.

• The landlord has paid back to the tenant any rents collected in excess of the lawful rate during the time the property wasn't properly registered.

---

[2]*Floystrup v. Berkeley Rent Stabilization Board*, 219 Cal. App. 3d 1309 (1990).

[3]CC § 1947.7.

EXAMPLE

Three years ago, Carla bought a tri-plex in a rent control city. She planned to live in one of the units three months out of the year, and rent it out the other nine months. Carla had been advised by her family lawyer that her property was "owner occupied," and thus not subject to registration or rent controls, even though she only lived there three months out of the year. Each time Carla rented her property to a new tenant for nine months, she increased the rent by ten percent. She also increased the rent for the other units each year. A tenant complained to the rent board, which determined the property should have been registered. Since it hadn't been registered, Carla's three years of rent increases were illegal, and the proper rent was what she charged three years before. If Carla registers the property and refunds the excess rent she collected to all her tenants, she can phase in the increases the city would have allowed during her three years, had the property been registered. The city can't fine Carla for failure to register her property because she had acted in good faith on the poor advice of a lawyer.

This law is fairly complicated, as are the typical local ordinances and regulations in cities that require registration of units. Should you run afoul of your city's rent control board and be faced with having to refund back rent increases for a substantial period, or pay other substantial penalties, you should probably see a lawyer familiar with the local rent control ordinance and regulations.

D. Rent Formula and Individual Adjustments

Each city has a slightly different mechanism for allowing rent increases. All cities allow periodic (usually yearly) across-the-board increases. The amount of the increase may be set by the rent control board, or the ordinance may allow periodic increases of either a fixed percentage or a percentage tied to a local or national consumer price index.

1. Mild Rent Control

Rent control is considered mild in the Bay Area cities of San Jose, Oakland, Hayward and Los Gatos. To begin with, none of these cities' ordinances require landlords to register units with the board.

Although the rent control ordinances of these areas set forth a certain formula (usually fairly generous, in the 5-8% range) by which rents can be increased each year, it is possible for landlords to raise the rent above this figure and still stay within the law. Each of these cities' ordinances require a tenant whose rent is increased above the formula level to petition the board within a certain period (usually 30 days) and protest the increase. If no tenants protest the increase within the time allowed, the increased rent is legally effective, even though it is higher than the formula increase. If a tenant protests the increase, then the board schedules a hearing to decide if the entire increase should be allowed.

Rent Mediation

Some cities, most notably the Bay Area city of Campbell, have adopted voluntary rent guidelines or landlord/tenant mediation services. Voluntary guidelines, of course, do not have the force of law. However, it's often an excellent idea for you to comply with voluntary rent guidelines or to handle a dispute by mediation. The alternative may be hiring a lawyer to sue a tenant who refuses to pay a rent increase and going to court to obtain a money judgment you may never collect.

Keep in mind that several cities have rent control at least in part because some landlords completely ignored voluntary guidelines and mediation services, causing tenants to show up at polls and support rent control in record numbers.

We discuss mediation in more detail in Chapter 8.

---

2. Moderate Rent Control

The rent control laws of Los Angeles, San Francisco, Beverly Hills, Palm Springs and Thousand Oaks can all be described as moderate. They all require landlords who wish to increase the rent by more than a fixed formula amount to petition the board for a higher increase. The request must be based on certain cost factors listed in the ordinance, such as increased taxes or capital improvements.

3. Strict Rent Control

California's most extreme rent control laws are found in Berkeley, Cotati, East Palo Alto, Santa Monica and West Hollywood. Often, single-family rentals are not exempt from these cities' laws, unless a rental property has four or fewer units and the landlord lives on the property.

Landlords must register their units with the board, which decides on the amount of the across-the-board rent increase allowed each year. The increases tend to be very low. A landlord who increases rent by a greater percentage than that established by the board faces civil penalties unless the board has allowed an additional increase following the landlord's application.

In cities with strict rent control:

- Landlords bear the entire burden of justifying the need for a higher than routinely allowable rent increase.

- There is no vacancy decontrol (except for West Hollywood), which means that if a tenant moves out, the maximum rent for a property remains fixed.

- A landlord must show a good reason (just cause) to evict a tenant.

(Vacancy decontrol and just cause evictions are described in detail below.)

Of the strict rent control cities, Berkeley and Santa Monica also allow tenants to petition for lower rents based on landlord's failure to maintain or repair rental units.

4. Hearings and Rent Adjustments

Almost all cities with rent control have a hearing procedure to handle certain types of complaints and requests for rent adjustments. The hearing procedures are described in detail in Section I, below.

5. Rent Agreed To by the Tenant

In cities with moderate and strict rent control, which require the landlord to petition the board before increasing the rent over a certain amount, a landlord can't circumvent the ordinance by having the tenant agree to an illegal rent. Even if a tenant agrees in writing to pay a higher rent and pays it, he can sue to get the illegal rent back.[4] This cannot happen, however, in cities with mild rent control which require the tenant to object to a rent increase or have it go into effect.

E. Security Deposits

Several local rent control ordinances require landlords to keep security deposits (including "last month's rent") in interest-bearing accounts and to pay interest on them. See "Other Features" in the Rent Control Chart for details on various cities' deposit laws.

F. Certification of Correct Rent Levels by Board

Cities that require registration must certify in writing, on request of the landlord or tenant, the correct rent level for the property under state law.[5] When the landlord or tenant requests such a certificate from the board, the board must send copies to both the landlord and tenant. Each of them then has 15 days to file an appeal with the board, challenging the rent level, by filing a written notice on a form available from the board. The board must then decide the appeal within 60 days. If the certificate rent level is not appealed by the landlord or tenant within 15 days, it cannot be challenged later, except by the tenant if the landlord was guilty of intentional misrepresentation or fraud, with regard to information she supplied to the city in the request for the certificate.

G. Vacancy Decontrol

Most cities allow landlords free rein to raise the rent when a unit is vacated. This feature, called "vacancy decontrol," is built into their ordinances. In practice it means that rent control applies to a particular rental unit only as long as a particular tenant (or tenants) live there. If that tenant voluntarily leaves, or in some cities is evicted for just cause (defined below), this property, in most cities, is subject to rent

---

[4]*Nettles v. Van de Lande*, 207 Cal. App. 3d Supp. 6 (1988).

[5]CC § 1947.8.

control again after the new (and presumably higher) rent is established. However, in the cities of Hayward and Thousand Oaks, the property is no longer subject to rent control following a voluntary vacancy.

Cities with Vacancy Decontrol

Beverly Hills

Hayward

Los Angeles

Los Gatos

Oakland

San Francisco
(this may change—see Rent Control Chart in Appendix)

San Jose

Thousand Oaks

West Hollywood

Note on cities without vacancy decontrol. Berkeley, Cotati, East Palo Alto, Palm Springs and Santa Monica do not have vacancy decontrol and keep units under rent control even when a tenant moves out. The new tenant must be charged the same rent as the old one, unless it is time for a city-wide increase.

When more than one tenant shares an apartment or house, the rule in some cities with vacancy decontrol is that the rent can't be raised more than the annual increase allowed by the ordinance until all of the original tenants whose names were on the lease or rental agreement leave. At this point the landlord can raise the rent as much as he wants under the vacancy-decontrol provision. But this rule is subject to a number of different interpretations, depending both on the city and the precise situation, so check locally with the rent board.

 Tenants who try to get around vacancy decontrol. Some tenants try to keep the rent low by unofficially subletting part or all of the premises to a new tenant, who may in turn sublet to someone else, and so forth. You can't raise the rent, and you can't evict the tenant unless your lease or rental agreement (as ours does) forbids subleasing or assignment without your permission. As long as subletting is a breach of the lease or rental agreement, you can legally evict tenants who sublet their property.[6] If you evict the tenant who violated the lease or rental agreement, you can then legally raise the rent. But if the legal tenant corrects the problem by having the illegal subtenant move out, you won't be able to raise the rent (except as allowed under the ordinance) until the tenant leaves.

H. Tenant Protections: Just Cause Evictions

If a city has a vacancy decontrol provision (in other words, the rent can be raised when a tenant moves), the ordinance will have little impact unless a tenant can only be evicted for a legitimate reason. Why? Because if rents could be raised when a tenant left, landlords could get around rent control simply by evicting tenants who haven't done anything wrong.

To protect tenants, most rent control ordinances contain a just cause eviction provision, which requires landlords to give (and prove in court if necessary) a valid reason for terminating a month-to-month tenancy.

---

[6] A landlord's consent to a sublease cannot be unreasonably withheld. However, if the tenant's subleasing of the property is designed to circumvent the rent control ordinance's provision for higher rent when occupancy changes, the landlord's refusal to consent to the sublease isn't unreasonable. (For details on subtenants and subleasing, see Chapter 10.)

Cities That Require Just Cause for Eviction

Berkeley

Beverly Hills

Cotati

East Palo Alto

Hayward

Los Angeles

San Francisco

Santa Monica

Thousand Oaks

West Hollywood

Note. San Jose, Oakland and Los Gatos, three of the mild rent control cities, do not have just cause eviction. The ordinances, however, penalize a landlord who tries to evict a tenant in retaliation for asserting his or her rights. The tenant has the burden of proving that the landlord's motive was retaliatory. See Chapter 15 for details on retaliatory evictions.

Rent control ordinances that require just cause for eviction list acceptable reasons for eviction. The common reasons are discussed below.

See Chapter 18.C for more details and procedures on evicting tenants in rent control cities requiring just cause for eviction.

1. Tenant Violates Lease or Rental Agreement

If a tenant violates the lease or rental agreement, the landlord has just cause for eviction. The landlord must first serve the tenant with a three-day notice. (The particular type of notice depends on the violation—see Chapters 16 and 18.) City ordinances list violations which are just cause for eviction. Typical reasons are:

- Tenant has not paid rent after being served with a Three-Day Notice To Pay Rent or Quit. This is

the most common way tenants violate their lease or rental agreement.

- Tenant continues to violate a lease or rental agreement provision, such as keeping a dog on the property in violation of a no-pets clause, after being served with a three-day notice to correct the violation or leave.

- Tenant has caused substantial damage to the premises and has been served with an unconditional three-day notice specifying the damage done and telling her to vacate. Some cities require the landlord to give the tenant the option of repairing the damage.

- Tenant is seriously disturbing other tenants or neighbors, and has been given a three-day notice specifically stating when and how this occurred. Some cities require that the notice give the tenant the option of stopping the offending conduct.

- Tenant has committed an illegal activity on the premises and has been given a three-day notice setting forth the specifics. Minor illegal activity, such as smoking marijuana, is not sufficient cause, although dealing drugs is. In fact, landlords who fail to evict drug dealers can face serious liability (see Chapter 12).

Other activities which constitute cause for eviction include engaging in an illegal business (such as prostitution), or even an otherwise legal business that's in violation of local zoning laws, or overcrowding the unit in violation of local health codes.

Some just cause eviction provisions are more stringent than others. In Berkeley and Santa Monica, a tenant who violates a lease or rental agreement— for example, moves in too many people, damages the premises, makes too much noise—must first be notified of the problem in a written notice (often called a cease-and-desist notice) and given a reasonable time to correct it (even though state law does not always require this). What is "reasonable" depends on the circumstances. A tenant who makes too much noise should be able to stop doing so in a day at most, whereas a tenant who damages the premises by breaking a window might reasonably be given a week to fix the window. Only after this is done can you evict the tenant for the lease or rental agreement violation, starting with a three-day notice.

2. Landlord or Immediate Family Member Wants To Move Into Rent-Controlled Property

All rent control cities that require just cause to evict allow a landlord to terminate a month-to-month or other periodic tenancy if the landlord wants to reside in the unit, or wants to provide it to a member of his immediate family. These cities generally require that no similar unit be available for the landlord or family member in the same or in another building the landlord owns, and that the landlord give the tenant a 30-day termination notice setting this out as the basis for eviction.

"Family member" is defined differently in different cities. In Berkeley and Santa Monica, family members include only parents and children. In cities with somewhat less restrictive laws, such as San Francisco and Los Angeles, family members also include brothers, sisters, grandparents and grandchildren. When property is owned by several people, either as co-tenants or through a joint venture, small corporation or partnership, cities have different ways of defining who qualifies for the status of a landlord for purposes of claiming priority over an existing tenant if they, or a family member, wish to live in the property.

There has been some abuse of this provision by landlords who evict a tenant claiming they or a family member want to rent the premises, but then, after the tenant has moved out, simply move in a non-family member—at a higher rent. In response, cities have amended their ordinances, and the legislature has passed a law, to impose serious civil penalties (fines) on landlords who do this. State law requires that in rent-controlled cities that mandate registration, landlords who evict tenants on the basis of wanting to move a relative (or the landlord) into the

property must have the relative actually live there for six continuous months.[7] If this doesn't happen, the tenant can sue the landlord in court for actual and punitive damages. Typically, such suits are brought in superior court, with the tenant demanding well over the $25,000 minimum jurisdictional amount.

If a court determines that the landlord or relative never intended to stay in the unit, the tenant can move back in. The court can also award the tenant three times the increase in rent she paid while living somewhere else and three times the cost of moving back in. If the tenant decides not to move back into the old unit, the court can award her three times the amount of one month's rent of the old unit and three times the costs she incurred moving out of it. The tenant can also recover attorney fees and costs.[8] In a recent case, the court awarded a San Francisco tenant $200,000 for a wrongful eviction based on a phony-relative ploy.[9]

3. Other Reasons for Just Cause Evictions

In cities that require landlords to show just cause for eviction, landlords can also terminate a month-to-month or other periodic tenancy for any of the following reasons. The landlord must, however, give the tenant a 30-day termination notice which specifically sets out the basis for the eviction.

- The tenant refuses to enter into a new lease containing the same terms as a previous expired one.

---

[7] CC § 1947.10.

[8] CC § 1947.10. See also *Zimmerman v. Stotter*, 160 Cal. App. 3d 1067, 207 Cal. Rptr. 108 (1984). In this case, the landlord had earlier won an eviction lawsuit, on the basis that he didn't use the phony relative ploy. Despite the landlord's win, the tenant was allowed to bring suit for damages, claiming that the landlord did use the phony-relative ploy, although it didn't become obvious until after the tenant was evicted and the property re-rented. The tenant won the case.

[9] *Beeman v. Burling*, 216 Cal. App. 3d 1586, 265 Cal.Rptr. 719 (1990).

- The tenant refuses, following a written request, to allow the landlord to enter the premises when he has a right to do so. For example, the tenant refuses to allow the landlord access to fix a hazardous condition on the property, a reason for which the landlord has a legal right to enter. (See Chapter 13.)

- The landlord seeks to substantially remodel the property, after having obtained the necessary building permits. However, the current tenant must be allowed the right of first refusal to move back in after the remodeling is completed—at the original rent plus any extra "passthrough" increases allowed by the particular rent control ordinance. This provision is designed to allow the landlord to recoup part of the cost of capital improvements.

- The landlord, after having complied with any local condominium-conversion ordinance and having applied for and received the necessary permits, seeks to convert an apartment complex to a condominium complex.

I. Rent Control Board Hearings

Disputes over rent usually get hammered out in a hearing before the local rent board. The hearing may be initiated by a tenant who protests a rent increase over the formula amount in a mild rent control city,

or by a landlord in a city that requires her to first obtain permission before exceeding the formula increase.

In either case, the landlord must demonstrate the need for a rent increase higher than that normally allowed. This most often means establishing that business expenses (such as taxes, maintenance and upkeep costs, or applicable utility charges), as well as the amortized cost of any capital improvements, make it difficult to obtain a fair return on one's investment given the current rent.

1. Initiating the Hearing

A hearing is normally initiated by the filing of a petition or application with the rent board. In describing this process, let's assume that a landlord is filing a petition in a strict or moderate rent control city that requires him to obtain permission before raising rents above the formula increase allowed. This process is approximately reversed in mild rent control cities that require the tenant to protest such an increase.

In some cities, including Los Angeles and San Francisco, there are two types of petitions a landlord seeking an above-formula rent increase can file. If an increase is sought because of recent capital improvements, the landlord files a "petition for certification" of such improvements. If a rent increase is sought on other grounds, a "petition for arbitration" is filed. The rent board can tell you which document you need to file.

The application form will ask for your name and mailing address, the address of the property or properties for which you're seeking the increase, including the numbers of any apartments involved, the affected tenants' names and mailing addresses, the dollar amounts of the proposed increases and the reason for the requested increase, such as higher repair, maintenance, or utility charges or pass-through of recent capital improvements. Make sure that your justification for an increase is specifically allowed by your local ordinance.

Usually, you must pay a nominal filing fee, often based on the number of units or properties for which an increase is being sought. After your application is filed and your fees paid, you and the tenant (who in some cities may file a written reply to your request) are notified by mail of the date and place of the hearing, usually within a few weeks. In Los Angeles, San Francisco and some other cities, city employees may inspect your property before the hearing. You are, of course, well-advised to cooperate as fully as possible with such inspections.

2. Preparing for the Hearing

As a general rule, you will greatly increase your chances of winning your rent increase if you appear at the hearing fully prepared and thoroughly familiar with the issues, and make your presentation in an organized way.

Here's how to prepare:

a. Obtain a copy of the ordinance and any applicable regulations for the area in which your property is located. Then determine which factors the hearing officer must weigh in considering whether to grant your request. For example, in San Francisco the hearing board will consider the cost of capital improvements, energy conservation measures, utilities, taxes and janitorial, security and maintenance services. Your job is to show that the increase you are requesting is allowed by the rent control ordinance. Sometimes an outline on a 3" x 5" index card will help you focus.

b. Gather all records, including tax statements, employee pay statements, bills for repairs, maintenance and any other costs (remodeling, repairs or other capital improvements) having to do with the property.

c. Be prepared to testify how each item of documentation relates to your monthly operating costs. Also be prepared to produce witnesses who are familiar with any items you think might be contested.

For example, if you know tenants are likely to argue that you didn't make major improvements to the building when in fact you did, arrange for the contractor who did the work to appear at the hearing.

If for some reason your witness cannot appear in person, you may still present a sworn written statement or declaration from that person. The declaration should be as specific as possible, including a description of the work done, dates, costs and any other relevant information. At the end of the declaration, the contractor or other person should write "I declare under penalty of perjury under the laws of the State of California that the foregoing is true and correct," putting the date and her signature afterward. A sample Declaration follows.

d. Before your hearing, go and watch someone else's hearing. (If your city's hearings are not open to the public, you can almost always arrange to attend as an observer if you call ahead.) Seeing another hearing may make the difference between winning and losing at yours. This is because both your confidence and your capabilities will grow as you understand what interests the hearing officers who conduct the hearing. By watching a hearing, you will learn that while they are relatively informal, all follow some procedural rules. It is a great help to know what common practices are so you can swim with the current, not against it.

e. If you feel it's necessary, consult an attorney or someone else thoroughly familiar with rent board hearings to discuss strategy. You are permitted to have an attorney represent you at a rent adjustment hearing, but this is probably not a good idea. You might prefer to be represented by your apartment manager or management company. If you do a careful job in preparing your case, you will probably do as well alone as with a lawyer or other representative. And remember, hearing officers (and rent boards) are local citizens who may well react negatively to a landlord who pleads poverty at the same time he is obviously able to pay a lawyer to argue his case.

SAMPLE DECLARATION

Declaration of Terry Jarman, Contractor

I, Terry Jarman, Licensed Contractor, declare:

I am a general construction contractor, licensed by the California State Contractor's Licensing Board. My contractor's license number is A-1234567.

Between January 1 and February 1, 19__, I contracted with Maria Navarro, the owner of the apartment complex at 1234 Fell Street, San Francisco, to replace plumbing, heating and electrical systems installed in the 1930s and to repair a roof that had developed numerous leaks over six of the apartment units. The total cost was $25,600, which Ms. Navarro paid me in full.

Pursuant to the contract, I engaged the necessary plumbing heating, electrical and roofing subcontractors to perform the necessary work, which was completed on February 1, 19__.

I declare under penalty of perjury under the laws of the State of California that the foregoing is true and correct.

Dated: __April 1, 199__   _Terry Jarman_____
                                     Terry Jarman, Licensed Contractor

---

3. The Actual Hearing

Once you've prepared for the hearing, it's time to make your case. Here's how to be most effective.

a. Before the Hearing Begins

Arrive at the hearing room at least a few minutes before it is set to begin. Check in with the clerk or other official. Ask to see the file that contains the papers pertaining to your application. Review this material to see if there are any comments by office workers, rent board investigators or your tenants. Read the tenants' comments very closely and prepare to answer questions from the hearing officer on any of the points they raise.

As you sit in the hearing room, you will probably see a long table, with the hearing officer seated at the head. In a few cities, the hearing is held before several members of the rent board, and they may sit more formally on a dais or raised platform used by the city council or planning commission. In any event, you, any tenants who appear, your representative and any witnesses will be asked to sit at a table or come to the front of the room.

A clerk or other employee may make summary notes of testimony given at the hearing. In some cities hearings are taped. If under the procedure followed in your city no record is kept, you have the right to have the proceedings transcribed or tape recorded at your own expense.

b. The Hearing Officer's Role

Rent board hearings are usually heard by a "hearing officer" who is a city employee or volunteer mediator or arbitrator. In a few cities, hearings are conducted by the rent board itself, with the chairperson presiding over the hearing. The hearing officer or rent board chairperson will introduce himself or herself and any other people in the room. If you have witnesses, tell the hearing officer. The hearing officer, or sometimes an employee of the rent board, will usually summarize your application, taking the information from your file. At some point, you will be sworn to tell the truth; it is perjury to lie at the hearing. When these preliminaries are complete, you or your tenant, depending on who initiated the proceeding, will have an opportunity to speak. A rent adjustment hearing is not like court. There are no formal rules of evidence. Hearing officers will usually allow you to bring in any information that may be important, though it might not be admissible in a court of law . Relax and just be yourself.

c. Making Your Case

Present your points clearly, in a non-argumentative way. You'll normally have plenty of time to make your case, so don't rush. At the same time, don't get carried away in unnecessary details. The hearing officer may well ask you questions to help you explain your position. Make sure you present all documentary evidence and witnesses necessary to back up your case.

Later, the hearing officer will allow the tenant or his representative to present his case and to ask you questions. Answer the questions quietly. It is almost always counterproductive to get into an argument. Even if you feel the tenant is lying or misleading, don't interrupt. You will be given time later to rebut the testimony. Direct all your argument to the hearing officer, not to the tenant or his representative.

When your witnesses are given the opportunity to testify, the normal procedure is simply to let them have their say. You may ask questions if the witness forgets something important, but remember, this is not a court and you don't want to come on like a lawyer. Very likely, the hearing officer will also ask your witnesses questions. The tenant has the right to ask the witnesses questions as well. Similarly, you have the right to ask questions of the tenant and her witnesses.

In rare instances, you may get a hearing officer or rent board chairperson who dominates the hearing or seems to be hostile to you or to landlords in general. If so, you will want to stand up for your rights without needlessly confronting the hearing officer. Obviously, this can be tricky, but if you know your legal rights and put them forth in a polite but direct way, you should do fine. If you feel that the hearing officer is simply not listening to you, politely insist on your right to complete your statement and question your witnesses.

Just before the hearing ends, the hearing officer should ask if you have any final comments to make. Don't repeat what you have already said, but make sure all your points have been covered and heard.

At the end of the hearing, the hearing officer will usually tell you when you can expect the decision. A written decision will usually be mailed to you within a few days or weeks of the hearing. Some cities, however, do not issue written decisions; the hearing officer just announces the decision at the end of the hearing.

Be assured that it is illegal for hearing officers and rent boards to unfairly penalize landlords who made innocent mistakes filing or serving legal notices.[10] A landlord's good-faith ("substantial compliance") in attempting to obey an ordinance prevents a rent board from imposing penalties.

---

[10]CC § 1947.7.

4. Appealing the Decision

In most cities, in which applications for increases are heard by a hearing officer, you have the right to appeal to the full rent board if you are turned down. Your tenants have this same right if you prevail. A form for making an appeal will be available from the rent board.

If you make an appeal, you must file it within a certain time. You may or may not have the opportunity to appear in person before the rent board.

The rent board will probably take as truth the facts as found by the hearing officer and limit its role to deciding whether the hearing officer applied the law to these facts correctly.[11] On the other hand, the rent boards of some cities (including Los Angeles) will allow the entire hearing to be held all over again. (This is sometimes called a "de novo" hearing.) In addition, the board will not usually consider any facts you raise in your statement which you could have brought up at the hearing but didn't. If you've discovered a new piece of information since the time of the first hearing, however, the board may consider the new information.

If your tenants are appealing and you are satisfied with the earlier decision, you will want to emphasize the thoroughness and integrity of the earlier procedure and be ready to present detailed information only if it seems necessary.

The entire rent board will generally have more discretion to make a decision than does a single hearing officer. If your case is unique, the entire board may consider the implications of establishing a new legal rule or interpretation.

If you again lose before the entire board, or if your city only permits one hearing in the first place, you may be able to take your case to court if you are convinced the rent board or hearing board failed to follow the law or their own procedures. However, if yours is a situation where the hearing officer or board has broad discretion to decide issues such as the one you presented, you are unlikely to get the decision overturned in court. Speak to an attorney about this as soon as possible, as there is a time limit (usually 30 days) on how long you can take to file an appeal in court.

J. Legal Sanctions for Violating Rent Control

When rent control laws were first adopted in the 1970's, many landlords came up with imaginative ways to circumvent them. In cities with vacancy decontrol, landlords began terminating month-to-month tenancies so that they could raise rents. As noted above, this caused localities to enact just-cause-for-eviction protections. Similarly, where ordinances allowed landlords to evict tenants in order to make major repairs to the property or move in themselves or move in relatives, some landlords used these reasons to evict, but didn't follow through. That is, after evicting their tenants, they made few, if any, repairs, or failed to move themselves or a relative in for any length of time.

EXAMPLE

After purchasing a duplex, a Los Angeles landlord immediately served a 30-day notice on the tenant, on the grounds that she (the landlord) wanted to move her mother into the unit. The landlord evicted the tenant, but did not move her mother into the vacant unit. Instead, the landlord put the duplex back on the market for a much higher price. The duplex had a higher market value because the Los Angeles rent control ordinance had vacancy decontrol (discussed in Section G, above), which would allow any new buyer to charge higher rents. The tenant who had been evicted sued the landlord for many thousands of dollars and ultimately received a substantial settlement.

---

[11]There is an exception to this general rule in some cities. If you arranged for a typed transcript of the original hearing at your expense or have paid to have the tape recording of the hearing made by the hearing officer typed, the rent board may review it.

Other landlords deliberately reduced services or adopted obnoxious behavior to encourage their tenants to leave "voluntarily." This, in turn, was followed by more amendments to close such loopholes, with landlords devising more refined ways to avoid the new rules, and so forth.

Many landlords did get rid of low-paying tenants and raise rents. However, newer rent control ordinances, as well as recent changes in state law, have closed many of the original loopholes and now assess heavy financial penalties against landlords who try to circumvent a rent control or just-cause-eviction ordinance, such as evicting tenants on false grounds of moving in relatives. In addition:

- The law allows a tenant to sue a landlord for having made her life miserable, under the legal theory of "intentional infliction of emotional distress." The landlord's repeated refusals to repair (see Chapter 11), privacy violations (see Chapter 13) or threats can be the basis for such a lawsuit.[12]

- All rent control ordinances (except Palm Springs') forbid lease or rental agreement clauses where the tenant supposedly gives up or waives her rights under the law. Thus, lease clauses which say "tenant knowingly gives up all his rights under any applicable rent stabilization ordinance" are of no legal effect. (See Section D.5 of this chapter.)

- State law provides that in rent controlled cities that require registration, a landlord who charges illegally high rent can be sued by the tenant in court for up to three times the rent collected in excess of the certified level, plus attorney fees and costs.[13]

Finally, tenants and rent boards have become more sophisticated in spotting and countering landlord maneuvers.

The best way to avoid the possibility of legal hassles is to forget about trying to circumvent the intent behind a rent control law, if indeed you ever thought about it.

Be extra careful to avoid a "retaliatory eviction." The few cities that don't require just cause for evicting a tenant (see Section H, above) do forbid evictions intended to retaliate against a tenant who exercised her rights under the rent control law—by objecting to an illegal rent increase, for example. State law forbids this too. The tenant has to prove in court that the landlord's reason for eviction was retaliation. (See Chapter 15 and the *Landlord's Law Book, Volume 2: Evictions,* which covers evictions in detail, including all the causes allowed for eviction in rent control cities.)

Save your energies for working toward a repeal or amendment of any rent control law you think is unfair. If you live in a strict rent control city, you may want to consider selling your properties and buying others in areas that make it easier for you to operate. This may not be as difficult to do as you might imagine, given the number of groups of unrelated adults who are purchasing housing together as tenants-in-common.

---

[12]*Newby v. Alto Rivera Apartments,* 60 Cal. App. 3d 288, 131 Cal. Rptr. 547 (1976).

[13]CC § 1947.11

Security Deposits

Most landlords quite sensibly ask for a security deposit before entrusting hundreds of thousands of dollars worth of real estate to a tenant. But it's easy to get into legal trouble over deposits, because they are strictly regulated by state law, and sometimes also by city ordinance. State law dictates how large a deposit you can require, how you can use it, when you must return it and more. Some cities also require landlords to pay interest on deposits and a few require landlords to put deposits in a separate account. What's more, you cannot modify these terms—regardless of what you put in a lease or rental agreement. It goes almost without saying that it is absolutely essential that you know the laws on security deposits and that you follow them carefully.

Exception for short-term rentals. The rules on deposits discussed in this chapter do not apply to short-term rentals where the occupancy is for 30 days or less. Someone who frequently rents out a vacation house, for example, for short periods need not worry about the laws discussed in this chapter.

Related Topics

- Lease and rental agreement provisions on security deposits: Chapter 2

- Highlighting security deposit rules in a move-in letter to the tenant: Chapter 7

- Importance of insurance as a back-up to security deposits: Chapter 12

- Using 30-day notices to raise the security deposit: Chapter 14

- Procedures on returning tenants' deposits and how to deduct for cleaning, damages and unpaid rent: Chapter 20

A. Legal Definition of Security Deposit

The first thing to understand is that many terms, such as "cleaning deposit," "cleaning fee" and "security deposit," which used to be defined in a multitude of ways in leases and rental agreements, now all have the same meaning as far as the law is concerned.

Any "payment, fee, deposit, or charge," including last month's rent (but not first month's rent), paid by a tenant at the time she moves in is, legally, a security deposit.[1] That means it is subject to all the laws that control the amount and uses of security deposits. In other words, no matter what you call a deposit you collect from a tenant, the law calls it a security deposit. You can't limit your tenant's right to have all up-front payments treated as a security deposit. One court ordered a landlord to refund a nonrefundable "new tenant" fee because it was an obvious substitute for an illegal nonrefundable deposit, and served no legitimate purpose.[2]

Note on last month's rent. You can mistakenly limit your own rights under California's deposit law by calling part or all of a deposit last month's rent. See Section D, below.

B. Refundability of Deposits

Simply stated, it is not legal to collect nonrefundable fees or deposits; it's also illegal to charge a hidden nonrefundable deposit by charging considerably more rent for the first month than for later months.[3] For example, you can't require tenants to pay a cleaning fee or something other than a refundable deposit or

---

[1]CC § 1950.5.

[2]*People v. Parkmerced Co.*, 198 Cal. App. 3d 683, 244 Cal. Rptr. 22 (1988).

[3]*Granberry v. Islay Investments*, 161 Cal. App. 3d 382, 207 Cal. Rptr. 652 (1984). Also see *People v. Parkmerced Co.*, 198 Cal. App. 3d 683, 244 Cal. Rptr. 22 (1988).

last month's rent. It is simply not legal to charge a fixed fee for cleaning drapes or carpets. All such fees are legally considered security deposits, and must be refundable.

There are two exceptions to the law that all deposits and fees must be refundable. You don't need to refund:

• Credit check fees you charge prospective tenants for getting a report of their credit history;

• Holding deposits which tenants pay to hold or bind a deal before a lease or rental agreement is signed.

These two types of fees are described in Chapter 1.

State law controls how and when landlords must return security deposits.[4] You can withhold all or part of the deposit if the tenant skips out owing rent or leaving his apartment filthy or damaged. The deposit may be used by the landlord "in only those amounts as may be reasonably necessary" to do the following four things only:

1. To remedy defaults in payment of rent;

2. To repair damage to the premises caused by the tenant (except for "ordinary wear and tear");

3. To clean the premises, if necessary, when the tenant leaves;

4. If the rental agreement allows it, to pay for the tenant's failure to restore or replace personal property.

When a tenant moves out, you have 14 days to either return the tenant's entire deposit or provide an itemized statement of deposit deductions and refund the deposit balance, if any. Chapter 20 provides detailed procedures for handling security deposits when the tenant leaves, including inspecting the premises, making proper deductions, notifying the tenant and dealing with small claims lawsuits.

C. Dollar Limits on Deposits

State law limits the amount you can collect as a deposit.[5]

Unfurnished property. The deposit (including last month's rent) can't exceed two months' rent.

Furnished property. The deposit (including last month's rent) can't exceed three months' rent.

Property is considered "furnished" if it contains at least essential furniture, such as a bed in each bedroom, a couch or chairs for the living area, an eating table with chairs and a refrigerator and stove.

There are two situations where other deposit limits apply:

Rent control. Many cities with rent control ordinances (and at least two without rent controls—Santa Cruz and Watsonville) place further restrictions on deposit amounts and increases. (See Section D of this chapter.) Before attempting to set or raise a deposit in a rent-controlled city, be sure to obtain a copy of the rent control ordinance.

Waterbeds. If the tenant has a waterbed, the maximum allowed deposit increases by half a month's rent. So, if a tenant has a waterbed, you can charge a total deposit of up to 2.5 times the monthly rent for unfurnished property and 3.5 times the monthly rent for furnished property.[6]

EXAMPLE 1

Mario charges $500 per month rent for a two-bedroom apartment. Since Mario's apartment is unfurnished, the most he can charge is two months' rent, or $1,000 total deposit. It makes no difference whether or not the deposit is divided into last month's rent, cleaning fee and so forth. In other words, if Mario charges a $200 cleaning deposit, a $300 security deposit, and $500 last month's rent (total $1,000), he is just within the law. Remember, the rent Mario collects for the first month doesn't count for this purpose.

---

[4]CC § 1950.5

[5]CC § 1950.5 (c).

[6]CC § 1940.5(h).

EXAMPLE 2

Lenora rents out a three-bedroom furnished house for $1,000 a month. Since total deposits on furnished property can legally be three times the monthly rent, Lenora can charge up to $3,000 for last month's rent and deposits. This is in addition to the first month's rent of $1,000 that Lenora can (and should) insist on before turning the property over to a tenant. Realistically, Lenora might not find any takers if she insists on receiving $3,000 in deposits plus the first month's rent, for a total of $4,000. In the case of furnished property, the market often keeps the practical limit on deposits lower than the maximum allowed by law.

D. How To Increase Deposit Amounts

Since the amount of a deposit is tied to the rent, an increase in rent affects the amount of the deposit. You can normally change the amount of rent for a month-to-month tenancy, as well as other terms of the agreement, by giving the tenant a written 30-Day Notice of Change of Terms of Tenancy (see Chapter 14). If you increase the rent with a 30-day notice, you can also legally increase the amount of the deposit.

EXAMPLE

A landlord who rents an unfurnished house or apartment to a tenant for $750 a month can charge total deposits (including anything called last month's rent) of two times that amount, or $1,500. If the deposit is for this amount, and the landlord raises the rent to $1,000, the maximum deposit the landlord is allowed to charge goes up to $2,000. The required deposit does not go up automatically. To raise the deposit amount, the landlord must use a 30-day notice.

If you have a fixed-term lease, you may not raise the security deposit during the term of the lease, unless the lease allows it.

The ordinances of cities with rent control typically define controlled rent so broadly as to include all security deposits and last month's rent paid by the tenant. This means that if the city restricts your freedom to raise rents, it probably restricts your right to raise deposits as well. Also, since most cities that have special security deposit laws have them as part of a rent control ordinance, any property that is subject to that city's rent control laws is also subject to the city's deposit law. In such cities, the ordinance may therefore restrict the amount and manner in which you can raise a tenant's security deposit.

E. Last Month's Rent

Don't use the term "last month's rent" unless you want to be stuck with its literal meaning. If you accept an up-front payment from a tenant, and call it last month's rent, you are legally bound to use it for that purpose only. There's no advantage to using this term, as the total deposit you can collect (two or three times the monthly rent, depending on whether the property is furnished or not), does not increase.

Here are two examples:

- You give your tenant a year's lease, from January 1 to December 31, and require an up-front payment of last month's rent. In this case, the tenant has paid the rent for December in advance.

- If you rent to your tenant from month-to-month, the tenant's last month's rent will take care of the rent for the last month, after you or the tenant give the other a 30-day notice.

In either case, you can't use last month's rent as a security deposit for damage or cleaning charges.

If, instead, you require a security deposit and do not mention last month's rent, the tenant will have to pay the last month's rent when it comes due and then wait until after moving out to get the security deposit back. If the tenant damages the premises or fails to pay rent, you can hold on to the appropriate amount of the entire deposit.

EXAMPLE 1

Fernando's last tenant left his $600 per month apartment a mess when he moved out. Fernando wanted to charge his next tenant a nonrefundable cleaning fee, but couldn't because this is illegal. Instead, Fernando decided to collect a total of $1,200, calling $600 a security deposit and $600 last month's rent. His next tenant, Liz, applied this last month's rent when she gave her 30-day notice to Fernando. This left Fernando with the $600 security deposit. Unfortunately, when Liz moved out, she left $700 worth of damages sticking Fernando with a $100 loss.

EXAMPLE 2

Learning something from this unhappy experience, Fernando charged his next tenant a simple $1,200 security deposit, not limiting any part of it to last month's rent. This time, when the tenant moved out, after paying his last month's rent as legally required, the whole $1,200 was available to cover the cost of any repairs or cleaning.

Avoiding the term "last month's rent" also keeps things simpler if the rent, but not the deposit, is raised before the tenant's last month of occupancy. The problem arises when rent for the tenant's last month becomes due. Has the tenant already paid in full, or does he owe more because the monthly rent is now higher? Legally, there is no clear answer. In practice, it's a hassle you can easily avoid by not labeling any part of the security deposit last month's rent.

EXAMPLE

Artie has been renting to Rose for three years. When Rose moved in, the rent was $400 a month, and Artie collected this amount as last month's rent. Over the years he's raised the rent to $500 without collecting any more also for last month's rent. During the last month of her tenancy, Rose applies the $400 last month's rent to the current $500 rent. Artie thinks that Rose should have to pay the $100 difference. Rose, however, thinks that, by having previously accepted the $400 as last month's rent, Artie had implicitly agreed to accept the $400 as full payment for that month. They end up in court fighting over something that could have been avoided.

F. Interest, Accounts and Recordkeeping on Deposits

No state law requires landlords to pay interest on security deposits. In most localities, you don't have to pay tenants interest on deposits, or put them in a separate bank account—unless you require this in your lease or rental agreement.[7] In other words, you can simply put the money in your pocket or bank account and use it, as long as you have it available when the tenant moves out.

However, several cities require landlords to pay or credit tenants with interest on security deposits. A few cities require that the funds be kept in separate interest-bearing accounts.

Here are a few things you should keep in mind about local requirements for interest payments on security deposits:

1. All cities that require landlords to pay interest on security deposits have rent control except Santa Cruz and Watsonville.

2. All cities that require landlords to pay tenants interest during the tenancy allow the landlord to

---

[7]*Korens v. R.W. Zukin Corp.*, 212 Cal. App. 3d 1054, 261 Cal. Rptr. 137 (1989).

either pay it directly to the tenant or credit it against the rent.

3. For those cities that require landlords to put deposits in separate accounts:

• Only one account is required for all the landlord's deposits. You don't have to open one for each tenant's deposit.

• All security deposits, including last month's rent, if collected, must be placed in the separate account.

The chart below summarizes the features of all California cities' deposit laws:

Some landlords have found that it is good public relations to pay tenants interest on their deposits, even if there is no local law in requiring it. This, of course, is up to you.

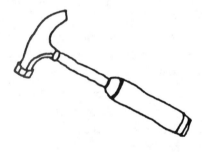

G. Insurance as a Back-Up to Deposits

This isn't a book on how to buy landlord's insurance, but because insurance can compensate you for some damages caused by tenants, it is appropriate to mention insurance here. After all, the legal limits as to how much you can charge for deposits are so strict

that you may want to get all the additional protection possible.

There are basically two broad types of policies to protect yourself from damage caused by your tenant:

1. Landlord's insurance, which protects you from:

• losses from fire and water damage, including lost rents while the property is being rebuilt or repaired

• personal liability for injury to a tenant or someone else and illegal acts by you and your employees.

You will need landlord's insurance for many reasons (discussed in Chapter 12). You may also wish to include earthquake coverage in such a policy.

2. Renter's insurance, often called a "Tenant's Package Policy," which covers:

• the tenant's liability to third parties—for example, injuries to guests that result from the tenant's neglect, such as a wet and slippery floor in the tenant's kitchen

• damage to the tenant's own property caused by fire and water damage

• certain types of damage to your building caused by the tenant's acts.

Our lease and rental agreements (see Clause 17 in Chapter 2.C) give the tenant the option of purchasing renter's insurance or assuming financial liability for damages the tenant or a guest causes. Our move-in letter (Chapter 7) highlights some of the risks tenants face unless they purchase insurance.

One advantage of requiring insurance is that if there is a problem caused by a tenant which is covered by the tenant's policy, your premium rate won't be affected even though your landlord's policy also covers the damage.

CITIES REQUIRING INTEREST OR SEPARATE ACCOUNTS FOR SECURITY DEPOSITS

City	Ordinance	Interest-Bearing Account	Payments During Tenancy	Other Features
Berkeley	Rent Stabilization and Eviction for Good Cause Ordinance, § 7	Required. Account must be insured by FSLIC (Federal Savings & Loan Insurance Corp.)	All interest produced must be paid in December of each year and when deposit refunded at end of tenancy.	
Cotati	Municipal Code §19.12.150	Required. Account must be "insured."	All interest produced must be paid when deposit refunded at end of tenancy.	
East Palo Alto	Ordinance 17-83, § 7	Required. Account must be insured by FSLIC if account at savings and loan or FDIC (Federal Deposit Insurance Corp.) if account at bank.	All interest produced must be paid in December of each year and when deposit refunded at end of tenancy.	
Hayward	Ordinance 83-023, § 13	Not required.	Landlord must pay 6.5% annual interest rate on deposits held over a year, with payments made within 20 days of tenant's move-in "anniversary date" each year, and when deposit refunded at end of tenancy.	Violation can subject landlord to liability for three times the amount of unpaid interest owed.
Los Angeles	Ordinance No. 166368	Not required.	Landlord must pay 5% annual interest rate on deposits held over a year. Payments need only be made every five years and when deposit refunded at end of tenancy.	
San Francisco	Administrative Code, Chapter 49. (Not part of city's rent control law.)	Not required.	Landlord must pay 5% annual interest on deposits held over a year with payments made on tenant's move-in "anniversary date" each year, and when deposit refunded at end of tenancy.	Ordinance does not apply to government-subsidized housing but may apply in other situations, even though property not subject to rent control.
Santa Cruz	Municipal Code §§ 21.02.010-21.02.090	Not required.	Landlord must pay 5% annual interest rate on deposits held over a year, with payments made on tenant's move-in "anniversary date" each year, and when deposit refunded at end of tenancy.	Santa Cruz has no rent control law.
Santa Monica	City Charter Article XV111, Chapter 14	Required. Account must be insured by FSLIC or FDIC.	Landlord need not pay tenant any of the interest, but failure to do so is a "factor" in the city denying an individual landlord's requested rent increase (or granting a tenant's requested rent decrease).	Landlord cannot raise deposit during tenancy, even if rent is raised, unless tenant agrees.
Watsonville	Municipal Code §§ 5.40.01-5.40.08	Not required.	Landlord must pay 5% annual interest rate on deposits held over six months, with payment or a rent credit on January 1st, and when deposit refunded at end of tenancy	Watsonville has no rent control law.
West Hollywood	Municipal Code Section 6408(B)	Not required.	Landlord must pay 5.5% annual interest rate on deposits, with payments made only on tenant's move-in "anniversary date" every five years, and when deposit refunded at end of tenancy.	

How does a tenant's policy help you if the place is damaged? Well, if damage is caused by fire or water (for example, the tenant leaves something burning on the stove which causes a kitchen fire), his policy, not yours, will be responsible. But what if a tenant simply moves out and destroys your property? In that case, a tenant's policy will not pay off if it's clear the tenant committed the vandalism.[8]

H. When Rental Property Is Sold

When rental property is sold, what should the landlord do with the deposits already collected? After all, when the tenant moves out, she'll quite naturally want her deposit back. Who owes her the money? The responsibility can be shifted to the new owner, if the seller either:

- refunds the deposits to the tenants, or
- transfers the deposits to the new owner.[9]

1. Seller Refunds the Deposit to Tenants

The first option is for the seller to refund the deposits (including last month's rent), less proper deductions to each tenant, with a detailed itemization of the reason for and amount of each deduction as you would with any security deposit. We don't recommend this, because you're refunding the deposit before the tenant moves out—and thus before you're aware of any necessary deductions for cleaning and damages. This makes little sense, and requires the new owner to ask tenants for new deposits in the middle of their tenancy. (You could, of course, inspect the premises before refunding the deposit, but

this would be inconvenient for both landlord and tenant).

2. Seller Transfers Deposit to New Owner

We recommend this second option which requires the seller to:

1. Transfer the deposit to the new owner (less any lawful deductions for back rent owed and for any necessary cleaning and damages in excess of ordinary wear and tear that you know about at the time of transfer), plus any interest in cities that require payment of interest on deposits (see Section F, above), and

2. Give the tenant a written notice of the change of ownership, itemizing all deductions and giving the new owner's name, address and phone number. The notice should be sent by first-class mail (preferably certified, return-receipt requested) or personally delivered.

The procedure for transferring the money to the new owner depends on whether you have established a separate account for tenants' deposits. If you have a separate account, you can simply make the change at the bank by transferring the account to the new buyer. If you have mixed the deposit money with your own, be sure to include a provision in the real property sales contract that itemizes the deposits for all the units and says the buyer acknowledges receipt of them (perhaps through a credit against the sale price) and that he specifically agrees to take responsibility for the repayment of all deposits.

A sample notice to the tenant is shown below, and a blank tear-out form is in the Appendix.

As we stated earlier, you'll probably have no idea of whether cleaning or damage deductions should be made. However, this type of notice can be used to deduct any back rent the tenant owes at the time of transfer. (Chapter 20 provides detailed instructions on how to itemize deductions and figure out rent due.)

---

[8]Since it often isn't clear as to whether the tenant's conduct was due to deliberate vandalism, as opposed to carelessness and neglect, tenant's insurance companies often will pay at least part of a claim disputed in this respect. It may be difficult to determine whether a stranger, as opposed to the tenant, entered and caused the damage.

[9]CC § 1950.5 (f).

SAMPLE NOTICE OF SALE OF REAL PROPERTY AND OF TRANSFER OF SECURITY DEPOSIT BALANCE

Notice of Sale of Real Property and of Transfer of Security Deposit Balance
Civil Code Section 1950.5(g)(1)

To: _____Robert Fisher_____,
              (name)

Tenant(s) in possession of the premises at:

_____123 Main Street_____,
              (street address)

City of ____Placerville____, County of ____El Dorado____, California.

The real property described above was sold on ___June 1 , 19___

to _____Jake Brumer_____
              (name of new owner)

___456 Gold Street, Placerville, California___
              (street address)

whose telephone number is _____(916) 555-1234_____.
                              (phone number)

Your security deposit, less any deductions shown below, has been transferred to the new owner, who is now solely responsible to you for it.

Deposit Amount: $___500.00___

Deductions:
    Unpaid Back Rent: $___125.00___
    Other Deductions: $____-0-____
    Total Deductions: $___125.00___

Net Deposit Transferred
to New Owner: $___375.00___

Explanation of Deductions:
__back rent balance due__ $___125.00___
__for month of June 19__

_____

Please contact the new owner, whose address and phone number are listed above, if you have any questions.

Date: ___June 15, 199___   *Laurel Meyer*_____
                                  Owner/Manager

If you don't properly transfer the deposit to the new owner and notify the tenants as required, the new owner will still be liable (along with you) to the tenants for any untransferred portion of the deposit. (One exception to this rule applies if the new owner can convince a judge that after making reasonable inquiry when buying the property, she erroneously concluded that the deposits were in fact transferred, or that the seller refunded them to the tenants before selling.) Also, the new owner can't increase the tenant's deposits to make up for your failure to transfer the money. The new owner, if stuck with this situation, will be able to sue you for any funds he's out by virtue of your failure to transfer and notify.[10]

SAMPLE CONTRACT PROVISION TRANSFERRING TENANTS' DEPOSITS

1. Where Tenants' Deposits To Be Transferred to Buyer at Later Date

As part of the consideration for the sale of the property described herein, Seller shall transfer to Buyer all security, as that term is defined by Section 1950.5 of the Civil Code, deposited with Seller by tenants of the premises, after making any lawful deductions from each tenant's deposit, in accordance with Subdivision (g) of Section 1950.5. Seller shall notify Buyer and each tenant of the amount of deposit remaining on account for each tenant, and shall notify each tenant of the transfer to Buyer. Thereafter, Buyer shall assume liability to each tenant for the amount transferred after such lawful deductions.

2. Where Tenants' Deposits Already Transferred to Buyer

As part of the consideration for the sale of the property described herein, Buyer acknowledges transfer from Seller of all security, as that term is defined by Section 1950.5 of the Civil Code, deposited with Seller by tenants of the premises, after making any lawful de-

ductions from each tenant's deposit, in accordance with Subdivision (g) of Section 1950.5. Seller shall notify Buyer and each tenant of the amount of deposit remaining on account for each tenant, and shall notify each tenant of the transfer to Buyer. Thereafter, Buyer shall assume liability to each tenant for the amount transferred after such lawful deductions.

I. If You're Purchasing Rental Property

When buying rental property, make sure the seller follows one of the two legal options outlined above, and that all tenants have been notified of the transfer. (To doublecheck, you might want to ask the seller to use the foregoing transfer forms and provide you with copies of each proposed notice.)

Some other key points when you're buying rental property:

- Make sure you know the total dollar amount of security deposits. For a multi-unit building, it could be tens of thousands of dollars. If it is substantial, and the seller is not transferring security deposit funds to you, you may want to negotiate an appropriate reduction in the sales price.

- You may not require the tenant to pay you an additional security deposit to replace any amount the seller failed to transfer, except for a legitimate deduction the seller made and of which the tenant has been notified. For example, if the seller deducted $125 for unpaid back rent, you can require the tenant to pay you an additional deposit of this amount.

- If you want to change the rental agreement or lease, you must use a 30-day notice (for month-to-month rental agreements) or wait until the end of the lease term. (See Chapter 14 for raising rents and changing other terms of tenancy.)

---

[10]CC § 1950.5(i).

Property Managers

If you've had enough of fielding tenants' repair requests, collecting rent and looking after all the other day-to-day details of running a rental property business, you've probably thought about hiring a property manager.

You may not have a choice: State law requires that a manager reside on the premises of any apartment complex with sixteen or more units.[1] But you may want to hire a resident manager even if you have a smaller number of units. If you own several apartment complexes (large or small), you may want to use a property management firm.

This chapter reviews the nuts and bolts of hiring and working with a manager or property management firm, including:

- how to select a manager or management company and delegate responsibilities

- contracts with managers

- your legal obligations as an employer

- how to protect yourself from liability for a manager's illegal acts

- how to fire or evict a manager.

A. Hiring Your Own Manager

Many owners of small (less than 16-unit) apartment complexes do much of the management work themselves, hiring their own resident managers as needed. When a small landlord does hire a manager, it's typically a tenant who lives in a multi-unit building. The tenant gets reduced rent in exchange for collecting rents, relaying complaints and keeping the building and yard clean. Or, the landlord collects the rent directly, leaving the manager mostly in charge of low-level maintenance and overall supervision of the tenants and premises.

1. Selecting the Right Manager

The person you hire to manage your property should be honest and responsible and have a good credit history. Look for someone who communicates well—both with you and other tenants. If you select a manager from current tenants, pick one who pays rent on time and who you think will be meticulous about keeping records, particularly if collecting rent will be part of the job.

Avoid anyone who harbors biases based on race, national origin, religion, sex, sexual preference or other group characteristics; this is especially important if the manager will be showing apartments, taking rental applications or selecting tenants. A manager who will be collecting overdue rents and serving three-day notices to pay rent or quit should not be fearful of minor confrontations with tenants.

Finally, if you want to delegate routine maintenance, make sure the person you choose knows how to do minor repairs, such as unclogging toilets, unsticking garbage disposals and replacing light switches.

2. Setting the Manager's Duties

The manager's duties will depend largely on the number of units to be managed, your own needs and the manager's abilities. Delegate more responsibilities if you live far away from the property or don't want to be involved in day-to-day details such as showing

---

[1] Cal. Code of Regulations, Title 25, § 42.

vacant units, collecting rents and keeping the premises clean. The Residential Rental Property Management Agreement (Section B, below) includes a list of duties you may want to delegate.

B. Avoiding Legal Problems

To avoid legal trouble down the road, when you hire a resident manager, follow the guidelines in this section.

1. Use Separate Employment and Rental Agreements

When you decide to hire a tenant as a manager, you and the manager should sign two separate agreements:

- a month-to-month rental agreement that can be terminated by either party on 30 days' written notice,[2] and

- an employment agreement that can be terminated at any time for any reason by either party.

An exception to this rule: A single agreement is appropriate when you have a special manager's unit set up both as an office and residence. (See Section F, Firing or Evicting a Manager.)

If you have separate employment and rental agreements with a tenant-manager, the manager will pay the full rent and receive a separate salary. And if you fire a tenant-manager, there will be no question that he is still obligated to pay the full rent, as he has done all along. And because your obligations as an employer are the same whether you compensate the

manager with reduced rent or a paycheck (you must still pay Social Security and payroll taxes, for example), the paperwork is no more difficult than using the rent-reduction method.

EXAMPLE

Louise uses two agreements with her new tenant-manager Sydney: a month-to-month rental agreement under which Sydney pays $600 rent each month, and a management agreement under which Louise pays Sydney $50 each week and which can be terminated without reason at any time by either party.

On January 1, Sydney pays his $600 rent to Louise. On January 7, Louise pays Sydney his weekly $50 and gives him a written notice saying his services as a manager are no longer required, but that he may stay on as a tenant. Louise no longer pays Sydney his weekly $50, and Sydney knows that in February he'll have to pay the regular rent of $600.

Why Not Use an Oral Agreement?

Landlords and resident managers often agree orally on the manager's responsibilities and compensation, never signing a written agreement.

Even though oral agreements are usually legal and binding, they are not advisable. Memories fade, and the parties may have different recollections of what they agreed to. If a dispute arises between you and the manager, the exact terms of an oral agreement are difficult or impossible to prove if you end up arguing about them in court. It is a far better business practice to put your understanding in writing.

Example: Theresa agrees to collect rents and do routine repairs for her landlord, Larry, in exchange for reduced rent: $400 per month for a $600 apartment. Theresa neglects the repair part of the agreement, and Larry decides to fire and evict her. Theresa fights the eviction in court and says she never agreed to do repairs. Larry will have to try to prove that Theresa really did agree to do repairs and so is legally obligated to pay the unreduced $600 rent.

---

[2]As discussed in Chapter 2, the law allows landlords and tenants to agree to as little as seven days' written notice. Although setting such a short notice period isn't recommended for regular tenants, you may wish to include a reduced notice provision in a manager's rental agreement. It will come in handy if you want to fire the manager and terminate the tenancy on short notice if his continued presence would cause problems.

Giving a resident manager reduced rent in exchange for management services, on the other hand, isn't a good idea. If the manager doesn't properly perform his duties and you terminate the employment, you may run into problems when you insist that the ex-manager go back to paying the full rent.

If the ex-manager refuses to pay the full rent, your only alternative is to initiate an eviction lawsuit (see Section F, below). The lawsuit is almost sure to be complicated by the fact that the amount of rent due depends on whether the manager's employment was properly terminated and whether he owes any extra rent as a result of not performing his duties.

EXAMPLE

Boris and Thomas sign an agreement under which Thomas collects rents and handles routine repairs, in exchange for $200 off the monthly rent of $600. When Thomas turns out to be an incompetent repairperson, Boris fires him as of the end of the month, and the next month demands the full $600 rent. Thomas refuses to pay more than $400, claiming he was fired unjustly. Although Boris is willing to keep Thomas as a regular tenant, he wants him to pay the rent. When Thomas won't pay it all, Boris serves him with a three-day notice demanding the $200. Thomas still refuses to pay, so Boris files an eviction lawsuit.

Boris could have avoided all this by having a separate employment agreement with Thomas covering management responsibilities (collecting rent and handling routine repairs), compensation ($200 per month) and termination policy (termination of management duties at any time with or without cause).

Below is an example of a sound written agreement that spells out the manager's responsibilities, hourly wage or salary, hours and payment schedule. A blank tear-out form, which you can modify to fit your exact needs, is in the Appendix.

To protect yourself from liability for your manager's illegal activities in carrying out his responsibilities, also prepare a more detailed set of instructions clarifying duties and basic legal guidelines. We show you how in Section D, below.

2. Meet Your Obligations as an Employer

Whether or not you compensate a tenant-manager with reduced rent or a regular salary, the law requires you to provide employee benefits. You are also responsible for a certain amount of paperwork and recordkeeping. If you don't pay Social Security and meet your other legal obligations as an employer, you may face financial or even criminal penalties.

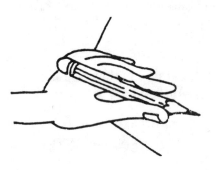

> ### *Help with Paperwork*
>
> *If you hate paperwork, consider hiring a payroll service. It will handle virtually all the details of employing a manager—for example, withholding Social Security and unemployment taxes—for a relatively small fee, such as $20 to $50 per month. To get cost quotes, check the yellow pages under Payroll Service or Bookkeeping Service.*

Income Taxes. The IRS considers the manager's compensation—whether in the form of payments or reduced rent—as taxable income to the manager. For that reason, your manager must fill out a federal W-4 form (Employee Withholding Allowance Certificate) when hired. You must deduct state and federal taxes from each paycheck, turn over withheld funds each quarter to the IRS and the California Franchise Tax Board and give the manager a W-2 form (Wage and Tax Statement) at the end of the year.

For details on reporting and deduction requirements, contact the IRS (800-TAX-FORM) and the California Franchise Tax Board (800-852-5711).

Social Security. Every employer must pay to the IRS a Social Security "payroll tax," currently equal to 7.65% of the employee's gross (before deductions) compensation. You must also deduct an additional 7.65% from the employee's wages and turn it over (with the payroll tax) to the Social Security Administration quarterly.

If you compensate your manager with reduced rent, you must still pay the Social Security payroll tax. For example, an apartment owner who compensates a manager with a rent-free $500/month apartment must pay 7.65% of $500, or $38.25, in payroll taxes each month. The manager is responsible for paying another 7.65% ($38.25) to Social Security.

Contact the IRS for deduction requirements and forms.

Minimum Wage. However you pay your manager—by the hour, or with a regular salary—you should monitor the number of hours worked to make sure you're complying with state and federal minimum wage laws.

If the total number of hours a manager works, multiplied by the minimum hourly wage, exceeds the rent reduction or other fixed rate of pay, you are in violation of minimum wage laws. For example, a manager who works four 20-hour weeks during the month must receive at least $4.25/hour (as of July 1991), or $340. A landlord who pays less—even if it's in the form of a rent reduction—will run afoul of the minimum-wage laws.[3] California minimum wage laws also require employers to pay time-and-a-half if an employee works more than eight hours a day or forty hours a week.

To make sure you comply with minimum wage laws, the agreement with your manager should limit the total number of hours worked each month, or provide for additional payment if the manager works more hours than anticipated.

For information on minimum wage laws, contact a local office of the State Department of Industrial Relations, Labor Standards Enforcement Division.

Disability and Workers' Compensation Insurance. As an employer, you must provide disability and workers' compensation insurance. If you don't, and a manager is injured on the job—for example, by falling down the stairs while performing maintenance, or even by a violent tenant—you could face serious legal problems. You could be sued by the State Department of Industrial Relations and possibly by the injured manager. If you lose such a lawsuit, the court judgment will not be covered by any other kind of landlord's insurance.

Contact the local office of the State Employment Development Department for information about disability insurance payments and your insurance agent regarding workers' compensation insurance.

Unemployment Taxes. A manager who is laid off, quits for good reason, or is fired for anything less than gross incompetence or dishonesty is entitled to unemployment benefits. These benefits are financed by state payroll taxes paid by employers. Failure to pay unemployment taxes will lead to legal problems if a former manager applies for benefits, and possibly before. The California Employment Development Department (EDD) may impose tax and penalty assessments (without first filing a lawsuit) against employers who don't pay required payroll taxes. Contact the local office of the EDD for the appropriate instructions and forms.

---

[3]If you compensate your manager by a rent reduction, you can count only up to two-thirds of the "fair market rental value" of the apartment for the purpose of complying with minimum-wage laws. (Labor Code § 1182.8.) For example, if the rent is normally $500, and you charge the tenant-manager only $100/month, only $333 of the $400 rent reduction may be counted for minimum-wage purposes. This is another reason why compensation by rent-reduction is not a good idea.

SAMPLE RESIDENTIAL RENTAL PROPERTY MANAGEMENT AGREEMENT

Residential Rental Property Management Agreement

1. This Agreement is between _____Jacqueline La Mancusa_____, Owner of residential real property at _____1704 Donner Avenue_____, _____Bakersfield_____, California, and _____Bradley Marsh_____, Manager of the property. Manager is currently renting unit number ___5___ of the property under a separate written rental agreement.

2. Manager shall be resident manager of the premises, beginning _____April 10,_____.
                                                       (date)

Manager's duties are set forth below:

RENTING UNITS

	answer phone
x	show vacancies
x	accept rental applications
	select tenants
x	accept initial rents and deposits
	other (specify):

VACANT APARTMENTS

x	inspect apartment when tenant moves in
x	inspect apartment when tenant moves out
	vacuum carpets
	shampoo carpets
	clean refrigerator
	clean plumbing fixtures
	wash windows
	clean stove and oven
	clean cabinets and closets
	clean sink, showers, bathroom
	wash and polish floors
	clean ceramic tiles
	clean light fixtures
	clean tops of doorways, windows and woodwork
	other (specify):

RENT COLLECTION

x	collect rents when due
x	sign rent receipts
x	maintain rent-collection records
x	collect late rents and charges
x	inform Owner of late rents
x	prepare Three-Day Notices To Pay Rent or Quit
x	serve Three-Day Notices To Pay Rent or Quit
x	serve rent-increase and tenancy-termination notices
x	deposit rent collections in bank
	other (specify):

MAINTENANCE

	vacuum and clean hallways and entry ways
x	replace light bulbs in common areas
	drain water heaters
x	clean stairs, decks, facade and sidewalks
x	clean garage oils on pavement
x	mow lawns
x	trim shrubs
	clean up garbage on grounds
	other (specify):

REPAIRS

x	accept tenant complaints and repair requests
x	inform Owner of maintenance and repair needs
x	maintain written log of tenant complaints
	handle routine maintenance and repairs, including:
x	plumbing stoppages
x	garbage disposal stoppages/repairs
x	faucet leaks/washer replacement
x	toilet-tank repairs
	toilet-seat replacement
x	stove burner repair/replacement
x	stove hinges/knobs
x	dishwasher repair
x	light switch and outlet repair/replacement
	heater thermostat repair
	window repair/replacement
	painting
x	replacement of keys
	other (specify):

3. Manager shall be available to tenants during the following days and times (*specify*):

<u>   Monday through Friday 3:00 p.m.-6 p.m.   </u>.

4. Manager shall be compensated as follows (*check box which applies*):

(x) $<u>   250   </u> per month, payable

___ once a week on <u>   </u>

<u> x </u> once a month on <u>   the 1st of the month   </u>

___ twice a month on the ____ and _____ days of the month.

or

( ) $ _____ per hour, plus overtime pay as required by law for time spent performing specifically assigned duties, payable

___ once a week on _____

___ once a month on _____

___ twice a month on the _____ and _____ days of the month.

5. If the hours required to carry out any duties may reasonably be expected to exceed <u>   4   </u> hours in any day or <u> 12 </u> hours in any week, Manager shall notify Owner and obtain Owner's consent before working such extra hours, except in the event of an emergency. Extra hours worked due to emergency must be reported to Owner within 24 hours.

6. Owner will reimburse Manager for the cost of materials, not to exceed $<u>   200   </u> for any repair unless authorized in advance by Owner.

7. This Agreement may be terminated by Owner or Manager at any time by written notice to the other.

8. This Agreement does not affect any provision of the rental agreement between Owner and Manager.

9. Owner and Manager additionally agree that: <u>   </u>
<u>   </u>.

10. All agreements relating to Manager's responsibilities are incorporated in this Agreement. Any modifications to the agreement must be in writing.

Dated: <u>   April 3 , 199   </u>   *Jacqueline La Mancusa* <u>   </u>
                                              Owner

Dated: <u>   April 3 , 199   </u>   *Bradley Marsh* <u>   </u>
                                              Manager

C. Management Companies

Property management companies generally take care of renting units, collecting rent, taking tenant complaints, arranging repairs and maintenance and evicting troublesome tenants. Property management companies are often used by owners of large apartment complexes and by absentee owners too far away from the property to be directly involved in everyday details.

A management company acts as an independent contractor, not an employee. Typically, you sign a contract spelling out the management company's duties and fees. Most companies charge a fixed percentage—typically five to ten percent—of the total rent collected. This gives the company a good incentive to keep the building filled with rent-paying tenants. (Think twice about companies that charge a fixed percentage of the rental value of your property, regardless of whether you have a lot of vacancies or turnover.)

Hiring a management company has a number of advantages. Compared to a tenant-manager, management company personnel generally develop a more professional, less emotional relationship with tenants, and are also usually better informed about the law. Another advantage is that you eliminate much of the paperwork associated with being an employer. Because you contract with a property management firm as an independent contractor, and it hires the people who actually do the work, you don't have to worry about Social Security, unemployment or workers' compensation.

The primary disadvantage of hiring a management company is the expense. For example, ten percent of the $700 rents collected each month from tenants in a 20-unit complex amounts to $1,400 a month or $16,800 per year.

If you hire a management company to manage your property, you still must have an on-site manager if your building has more than sixteen units. If your rental property has only a few units, or you own a number of small buildings spread over a good-sized geographical area, the management company probably won't hire resident managers, but will simply respond to tenant requests and complaints from its central office.

Management companies have their own contracts, which you should read thoroughly and understand before signing. Be sure you understand how the company is paid and its specific responsibilities.

Questions To Ask When You Hire
a Management Company

- *Who are its clients: owners of single-family houses, small apartments or large apartment complexes? Look for a company with experience handling property like yours.*
- *Is it located fairly close to your property?*
- *Are employees trained in landlord-tenant law? Can they consult an attorney qualified in landlord-tenant matters?*
- *If your property is under rent control, are company personnel familiar with the rent control law?*
- *Can you terminate the management agreement without cause on reasonable notice?*

D. An Owner's Liability for a Manager's Acts

A landlord is legally responsible for the acts of a manager or management company, who is considered the landlord's "agent." For example, you could be sued and found liable if your manager:

- refuses to rent to a qualified tenant who is a member of a minority group or has children (see Chapter 9)

- makes illegal deductions from the security deposit of a tenant who has moved out, or does not return the departing tenant's deposit within the two weeks allowed by law (see Chapters 5 and 20)

- ignores a dangerous condition such as sub-standard wiring which results in an electrical fire causing injury or damage to the tenant (see Chapter 11)

- libels a tenant or invades her privacy by flagrant and damaging gossip, trespass or harassment (see Chapter 13).

In short, a landlord who knows the law but has a manager (or management company) who doesn't could wind up in a lawsuit brought by prospective or former tenants. And many insurance companies do not pay for any loss or defend any lawsuit based on a manager's intentional misconduct, such as purposeful discrimination or retaliation against a tenant.

Here's how to minimize your liability for your manager's mistakes or illegal acts:

1. Limit the authority you delegate to your manager. If you specify the manager's responsibilities in writing, you reduce (but do not eliminate) your liability for manager misconduct that exceeds the authority you delegated. For example, a landlord who instructs a manager in writing only to accept rental applications, with the landlord actually selecting the tenant, is less likely to be held liable for a manager who, without authority, rents an apartment in a discriminatory fashion.

2. Make sure your manager is familiar with the basics of landlord-tenant law. If you delegate more duties to your manager, such as authority to select tenants or serve three-day notices or 30-day notices, provide some legal guidelines. You might also give your manager this book to read and refer to. Written guidelines not only help the manager avoid legal trouble, but also demonstrate that you acted in good faith, which could be very useful should a tenant sue you based on your manager's misconduct. Your guidelines should dovetail with the manager's responsibilities laid out in the Residential Rental Property Management Agreement.

Below is a sample set of instructions for a manager with fairly broad authority. Obviously, if your manager is given more limited authority, your instructions should also be more limited.

The High Cost of a Bad Manager

If tenants complain about illegal acts by a manager, pay attention. The owners of a Fairfield, California apartment complex learned this lesson the hard way—by paying more than half a million dollars to settle a tenants' lawsuit.

The tenants, mostly single mothers, were tormented by an apartment manager who spied on them, opened their mail and sexually harassed them. They were afraid to complain, for fear of eviction. When they did complain to the building's owners, they refused to take any action—and the manager stepped up his harassment in retaliation.

Finally, tenants banded together and sued, and the details of the manager's outrageous and illegal conduct were exposed. The owners settled the case before trial, in July 1991. When this book went to press, they had already agreed to pay more than $575,000 to the women. With attorneys fees, the total was expected to approach $690,000.

SAMPLE INSTRUCTIONS TO MANAGER

Dear New Manager:

Welcome to your new position as resident manager. In performing your duties under our management agreement, please keep the following in mind:

1. Discrimination in rental housing on the basis of race, religion, sex, sexual preference, marital or familial status, age, national or ethnic origin, and any other unreasonable or arbitrary basis is illegal—whether you are accepting rental applications for vacant apartments or dealing with current residents. Your duties, in the event of a vacancy, are to advertise and accept rental applications in a nondiscriminatory manner. This includes allowing all individuals to fill out applications and offering the unit on the same terms to all applicants. After you have collected all applications, please notify me at the phone number listed below. I will arrange to sort through the applications and make the final decision as to who occupies units.

2. Do not issue any rent-increase or termination notices without my prior approval, unless a tenant's rent is more than five days past due and he or she is not withholding rent because of dissatisfaction with the apartment—for example, the tenant has made no complaints in the previous six months. In that case, you may, without prior approval from me, serve the tenant a Three-Day Notice To Pay Rent or Quit, using the blank forms I have given you. However, if you have any reason to think that the tenant may assert that the failure to pay rent is based on any defects in the rental unit, please contact me immediately. Do this even if you are convinced that the tenant's complaints are unfounded.

3. Treat all tenants who complain about defects, even trivial defects or ones you believe to be nonexistent, with respect. Enter all tenant complaints into the log book I have supplied to you. Respond to tenant complaints about the building or apartment units immediately in emergencies, and within 24 hours in non-emergencies. If you cannot correct or arrange to correct any problem or defect yourself, please telephone me immediately.

4. Except in serious life- or property-threatening emergencies, never enter (or allow anyone else to enter) a tenant's apartment without consent or, in his or her absence, unless you have given the proper notice. Proper notice is presumed to be 24 hours' notice, preferably in writing. You may enter in the tenant's absence during ordinary business hours to do repairs or maintenance work, provided you have given the tenant a 24-hour notice

(preferably in writing and delivered personally, but posted on the door if necessary) and the tenant hasn't objected. Please call me if you have any problems gaining access to a tenant's apartment for maintenance or repairs.

5. When a tenant moves in, and again when he or she moves out, inspect the unit. If possible, do this with the tenant. On each occasion, both you and the tenant should complete and sign a Landlord/Tenant Checklist form. Also take a series of Polaroid pictures.

6. If you think a tenant has moved out and abandoned the apartment, do not enter it. Telephone me first.

7. Once a tenant has vacated an apartment and given you the key, itemize all cleaning costs and costs necessary to repair damages in excess of ordinary wear and tear. Give me a copy of this itemization, along with a notation of the amount of any back rent, the before and after Landlord/Tenant Checklist forms and the departing tenant's forwarding address. Please make sure I see this material within a week after the tenant moves out, preferably sooner. I will mail the itemization and any remaining security deposit balance to the tenant within the required two-week period.

8. If you have any other problems or questions, please do not hesitate to call me. Leave a message on my answering machine if I am not at home.

Sincerely,

_____
Owner

_____
Address

_____
Phone

_____

I have received a copy of this memorandum and have read and understood it.

Dated: _____   _____
                                                        Manager

Anti-discrimination training. You may wish to have your manager attend anti-discrimination training sessions given by local fair-housing groups. This will help the manager avoid illegal discrimination and shows that you are making efforts to comply with anti-discrimination laws.

3. Make sure your landlord's insurance covers illegal acts of your employees. No matter how thorough your precautions, you may still be liable for your manager's illegal acts—even if your manager commits an illegal act in direct violation of your instructions. To really protect yourself, purchase a good landlord's insurance policy. (We show you how in Chapter 12.)

4. Keep an eye on your manager and listen to your tenants' concerns and complaints. If you suspect problems—for example, poor maintenance of the building or sexual harassment—do your own investigating. Try to resolve problems and get rid of a bad manager before problems accelerate and you end up with an expensive tenants' lawsuit.

E. Notifying Tenants of the Manager

You are legally required to give tenants either your name and address or those of someone who is authorized to accept legal documents for you. (CC §§ 1961-1962.7.) This information must be in writing if the tenant has a written lease or rental agreement, and available on demand if the rental agreement is oral. It is included in our lease and rental agreements (see Clause 2, Chapter 2).

If you want to authorize the manager to receive all legal papers from tenants—termination of tenancy notices or court documents in an eviction lawsuit, for example—notify the tenants that they can serve the manager with such documents. Two sample disclosure notices are shown below.

SAMPLE DISCLOSURE NOTICES

Notice: Address of Manager and Owner of Premises

Muhammad Azziz, 1234 Market Street, Apartment 1, San Jose, CA, is authorized to manage the residential premises at 1234 Market Street, San Jose, CA. If you have any complaints about the condition of your unit or common areas, please notify Mr. Azziz immediately. He is authorized to act for and on behalf of the owner of the premises for the purpose of receiving all notices and demands from you, including legal papers (process).

Notice: Address of Owner of Premises

Rebecca Epstein, 12345 Embarcadero Road, Palo Alto, CA, is the owner of the premises at 1234 Market St., San Jose, CA. If you have any complaints about the condition of the unit or common areas, please notify Ms. Epstein immediately.

If you violate this disclosure law, the law deems your manager to be your agent for the purpose of service of legal notices—whether you like it or not. Also, the law allows the tenant to serve legal notices by certified mail (no return receipt required) rather than by personally delivering them to the manager. This means that a current or former tenant can serve lawsuit papers on you simply by mailing them, by certified mail, to your manager.

EXAMPLE

Three of your tenants have written rental agreements that don't give your name and address or name anyone to receive legal notices on your behalf. Three other tenants have oral agreements with your manager, Mike, who refused to disclose your name and address, which is not posted on the premises.

The tenants sue you over housing code violations, including defective heaters and a leaking roof that Mike never told you about. They serve the lawsuit papers (summons and complaint) on Mike, who is your agent for service of process because you didn't comply with the disclosure law. Mike throws the papers away without telling you about them, and neither you nor he appears in court. All the tenants win because you were properly served—through your agent—and didn't appear in court.

F. Firing or Evicting a Manager

If you fire a manager, you may also want him to move out of your property, particularly if he occupies a special manager's unit or the firing has generated (or resulted from) ill will. How easy it will be to get the fired manager out depends primarily on whether or not you have separate management and rental agreements.

1. Separate Management and Rental Agreements

If you and the tenant-manager signed separate management and rental agreements, firing the manager will not affect the tenancy. The ex-manager will have to keep paying rent but will no longer work as manager.

To evict the former manager, you will have to give a normal 30-day written termination notice, subject to any just-cause eviction requirements in rent control cities. (See Chapter 18.) All rent control cities do allow eviction of fired managers, though some cities impose restrictions on it. If the tenant has a separate fixed-term lease, you cannot terminate the tenancy until the lease expires.

2. Single Management/Rental Agreement

What happens to the tenancy when you fire a manger depends on the kind of agreement you and the manager had.

a. If the Manager Occupied a Special Manager's Unit

If you fire a manager who occupies a specially constructed manager's unit (such as one with a reception area or built-in desk) which must be used by the manager, your ability to evict the ex-manager depends on:

- the terms of the management/rental agreement, and

- local rent control provisions.

If the agreement says nothing about the tenancy continuing if the manager quits or is fired, termination of the employment also terminates the tenancy. That means you can evict the ex-manager without a separate tenancy-termination notice. In that case, no written notice is required to terminate the tenancy, unless one is required under the agreement.[1]

---

[1]See CCP § 1161(1).

The just-cause eviction provisions of any applicable rent control law, however, may still require a separate notice, or otherwise restrict your ability to evict a fired manager.

b. If the Manager Didn't Occupy a Manager's Unit

If the manager was simply compensated by a rent reduction, and there is no separate employment agreement, there may be confusion as to whether the rent can be "increased" after the manager is fired. (This is one reason we recommend against this kind of arrangement.)

If an ex-manager refuses to pay the full rent, you will have to serve a Three-Day Notice To Pay Rent or Quit, demanding the unpaid rent. (See Chapter 16.) If she still won't pay, you'll have to follow up with an eviction (unlawful detainer) lawsuit.

3. Eviction Lawsuits

If you want want to evict a former manager, we recommend that the eviction lawsuit be handled by an attorney who specializes in landlord-tenant law.

Eviction lawsuits against former managers can be extremely complicated. This is especially true if the management agreement requires good cause for termination of employment or a certain period of notice. (Our form agreement requires neither.) Such lawsuits can also be complicated where a single combined management/rental agreement is used or if local rent control laws impose special requirements.

Handling Requests for References

If another landlord asks you for a reference for someone you employed but later fired as manager, just follow this bit of folk wisdom: If you can't say something good, don't say anything at all. In light of the potential for being named in a slander suit, it's best to simply decline to give any information about a former manager (or tenant) rather than say anything negative. Besides, if you politely say, "I would rather not discuss Mr. Jones," the caller will get the idea.

Getting the Tenant Moved In

Legal disputes between landlords and tenants have gained a reputation for being almost as strained and emotional as divorce court battles. Many disputes are unnecessary and could be avoided if—right from the very beginning—both landlord and tenant understood their legal rights and responsibilities. A clearly written lease or rental agreement, signed by all adult occupants, is the key to starting a tenancy. (See Chapter 2.) But there's more to getting new tenants moved in. You should also:

- Inspect the property, fill out a Landlord/Tenant Checklist and take pictures of the unit.

- Prepare a move-in letter highlighting important terms of the tenancy.

- Collect rent and security deposit checks.

A. Inspect and Photograph the Unit

It is absolutely essential for you and prospective tenants (together, if at all possible) to check the place over for damage and obvious wear and tear, by filling out a Landlord/Tenant Checklist form and taking photographs of the rental unit.

1. Filling Out the Landlord/Tenant Checklist

A Landlord/Tenant Checklist, inventorying the condition of the rental property, is an excellent device to protect both you and your tenant when the tenant moves out and wants the security deposit returned. Without some record as to the condition of the unit, you and the tenant are all too likely to get into arguments about things like whether the kitchen linoleum was already stained or the bedroom mirror was already cracked at the time the tenant moved in.

The checklist, coupled with a system to regularly keep track of the rental property condition, can also be useful if tenants withhold rent, claiming the unit needs substantial repairs. (See Chapter 11 for instructions and forms to periodically update

the safety and maintenance of your rental properties.)

HOW TO FILL OUT THE CHECKLIST

A sample Landlord/Tenant Checklist is shown here and a blank tear-out copy is included in the Appendix.

You should fill out the checklist together. If you can't do this together, complete the form and then give it to the tenant to review. The tenant should make any changes and return it to you.

The checklist is in two parts. The first side covers the general condition of each room. The second side covers the condition of any furnishings provided, such as a living room lamp or bathroom shower curtain.

If your rental property has rooms or furnishings not listed on the form, you can note this in "Other Areas," or cross out something that you don't have and write it in. If you are renting out a large house or apartment or providing many furnishings, you may want to attach a separate sheet.

If your rental unit does not have a particular item listed, such as a dishwasher or kitchen broiler pan, put "N/A" (not applicable) in the "Condition on Arrival" column.

Mark "OK" in the space next to items which are in satisfactory condition.

Make a note—as specific as possible—on items that are not working or are in bad condition. For example, don't note just "needs fixing" if a bathroom sink is clogged; it's as easy to write "clogged drain," so later the tenant can't claim to have told you about the leaky faucet.

The last two columns—*Condition on Departure* and *Estimated Cost of Repair or Replacement*—are for use when the tenant moves out and you need to make deductions from the security deposit for items that need to be repaired, cleaned or replaced. (See Chapter 20 for details on recordkeeping and security deposits.)

After you and the tenants agree on all of the particulars, you all should sign and date the form on both sides as well as any attachments. Keep the original for yourself and attach a copy to the tenant's lease or rental agreement. (See Clause 11 of our form agreements.)

Be sure the tenant also checks the box on the bottom of the first page of the checklist stating that the smoke detector—required for new occupancies by state law—was tested in his presence and shown to be in working order. This section on the checklist also requires the tenant to test the smoke detector monthly and to replace the battery when necessary. By doing this, you'll limit your liability if the smoke detector fails and results in fire damage or injury. (See Chapter 11 for details on the landlord's responsibility to provide smoke detectors and maintain the property and Chapter 12 for a discussion of landlord's liability for injuries to tenants.)

Be sure to keep the checklist up to date if you repair, replace, add or remove items or furnishings after the tenant moves in. Both you and the tenant should initial and date any changes.

2. Take Pictures of the Property

Taking photos or videotapes of the unit before the tenant moves in is another excellent way to avoid disputes over a tenant's responsibility for damage and dirt. When the tenant leaves, you'll be able to compare "before" and "after" photographs. This will help if a tenant sues you for not returning the full security deposit. Nothing is better in the defense of a tenant's security deposit lawsuit than a landlord's pictures showing that the unit was immaculate when the tenant moved in and a mess when she moved out. Photos/videos can also help if you have to sue a former tenant for cleaning and repair costs above the deposit amount.

It's best to take "before" photographs with a Polaroid or other camera that develops pictures automatically; the tenant can then date and sign or initial the pictures on the spot. If possible, you should repeat this process with after pictures, to be signed or initialled by the tenant as part of your established move-out procedure (described in Chapter 20).

B. Send New Tenants a Move-In Letter

A move-in letter should dovetail with the lease or rental agreement (see Chapter 2) but cover day-to-day issues, such as how and where to report maintenance problems (covered in detail in Chapter 11). It should also spell out the role of the manager, if any. A move-in letter can be changed from time to time as necessary. A sample is shown below for month-to-month tenancies with a resident manager. You should tailor this letter to your particular needs (for example if your property is subject to local rent control).

SAMPLE LANDLORD-TENANT CHECKLIST—General Condition of Rooms

LANDLORD-TENANT CHECKLIST—General Condition of Rooms
(see reverse side for furnished property)

1234 Fell Street   Apt. 5   San Francisco
Street Address   Unit Number   City

	Condition on Arrival	Condition on Departure	Est. Cost of Repair/Replacement
Living Room			
Floors & Floor Coverings	OK		
Drapes & Window Coverings	OK		
Walls & Ceilings	OK		
Light Fixtures	OK		
Windows, Screens & Doors	back door scratched		
Front Door & Locks	OK		
Smoke Detector	OK		
Fireplace	N/A		
Other			
Other			
Kitchen			
Floors & Floor Coverings	cigarette burn hole (1)		
Walls & Ceilings	OK		
Light Fixtures	OK		
Cabinets	OK		
Counters	discolored		
Stove/Oven	OK		
Refrigerator	OK		
Dishwasher	N/A		
Garbage Disposal	N/A		
Sink & Plumbing	OK		
Smoke Detector	OK		
Other			
Other			
Dining Room			
Floors & Floor Covering	OK		
Walls & Ceiling	OK		
Light Fixtures	OK		
Windows, Screens & Doors	OK		
Smoke Detector	OK		
Other			
Other			

Bathroom(s)	Bath 21	Bath 2 N/A	Bath 1	Bath 2	
Floors & Floor Coverings	OK				
Walls & Ceilings	OK				
Windows, Screens & Doors	OK				
Light Fixtures	OK				
Bathtub/Shower	tub chipped				
Sink & Counters	OK				
Toilet	OK				
Other					
Other					

Bedroom(s)	Bedroom 1	Bedroom 2	Bedroom 3	Bedroom 1	Bedroom 2	Bedroom 3	
Floors & Floor Coverings	OK	OK					
Windows, Screens & Doors	OK	door scratch					
Walls & Ceilings	OK	OK					
Light Fixtures	dented	OK					
Smoke Detectors	OK	OK					
Other							
Other							

Other Areas			
Furnace/Heater	OK		
Air Conditioning	N/A		
Lawn/Ground Covering	N/A		
Garden	N/A		
Patio, Terrace, Deck, etc.	N/A		
Other			
Other			

Use this space to provide any additional explanation: _____

_____

_____

☑ Tenants acknowledge that all smoke detectors were tested in their presence and found to be in working order, and that the testing procedure was explained to them. Tenants agree to test all detectors at least once a month and to report any problems to Owner/Manager in writing. Tenants agree to replace all smoke detector batteries as necessary.

SAMPLE LANDLORD-TENANT CHECKLIST—Furnishings

LANDLORD-TENANT CHECKLIST—Furnishings

	Condition on Arrival			Condition on Departure			Est. Cost of Repair/Replacement
Living Room							
Coffee Table	2 scratches on top						
End Tables	N/A						
Lamps	OK						
Chairs	OK						
Sofa	OK						
Other							
Other							
Kitchen							
Broiler pan	N/A						
Ice Trays	OK						
Other							
Other							
Dining Area							
Chairs	OK						
Stools	N/A						
Table	leg bent slightly						
Other							
Other							
Bathroom(s)	Bath 1	Bath 2		Bath 1	Bath 2		
Dresser Tables	N/A						
Mirrors	OK						
Shower Curtain	OK						
Hamper	N/A						
Other							
Other							
Bedroom(s)	Bedroom 1	Bedroom 2	Bedroom 3	Bedroom 1	Bedroom 2	Bedroom 3	
Beds (single)	OK	N/A					
Beds (double)	N/A	OK					
Chairs	OK	OK					
Chests	N/A	N/A					
Dressing Tables	OK	N/A					
Lamps	OK	OK					
Mirrors	N/A	N/A					
Night Tables	N/A	N/A					
Other							
Other							
Other Areas							
Bookcases	N/A						
Desks	N/A						
Pictures	hallway picture frame chipped						
Other							
Other							

Landlord-Tenant Checklist completed on moving in on _____ February 14, _____, 19_____, and approved by:

_____Ira Eppler_____ and _____Chloe Gustafson_____
Owner/Manager   Tenant

_____Heather Crouse_____
Tenant

_____
Tenant

Landlord-Tenant Checklist completed on moving out on _____, 19_____, and approved by:

_____ and _____
Owner/Manager   Tenant

_____
Tenant

_____
Tenant

SAMPLE MOVE-IN LETTER

Dear Mr. O'Hara:

Welcome to Happy Hill Apartments. We hope you will enjoy living here.

It is our job to provide you with a clean, undamaged, pleasant place to live. We take our job seriously. This letter is to explain what you can expect from the Management and what we'll be looking for from you.

Rental Agreement: Your signed copy is attached. Please let us know if you have any questions. A few things we'd like to highlight here:

• There is no grace period for the payment of rent (see Clause 5 for details, including late charges). Also, we don't accept post-dated checks.

• If you want someone to move in as a roommate, please contact us. If your rental unit is big enough, we will arrange for the new person to fill out a rental application and, if it's approved, for all of you to sign a new rental agreement.

• To terminate your month-to-month tenancy, you must give at least 30 days' written notice to Management. Management may also terminate the tenancy, or change its terms, on 30 days' written notice.

(or, if the tenant has a fixed term lease:)

• You occupy the premises under a fixed-term lease. You are responsible for all rent payments through the lease term, even if you move out before the lease expires. During the lease term, your rent cannot be increased, nor can other terms of your tenancy be changed.

• Your security deposit is only to be applied, by the owner, to costs of cleaning, damages or unpaid rent after you move out. You may not apply any part of the deposit, during your tenancy, toward any part of your rent in the last month of your tenancy. (See Clause 7 of your rental agreement.)

Manager: Sophie Beauchamp (Apartment #15, phone 555-1234) is your resident manager. You should pay your rent to her and promptly let her know of any maintenance or repair problems (see below) and any other questions or problems. She's in her office every day from 8 A.M. to 10 A.M. and from 4 P.M. to 6 P.M.

Check-In Sheet: By now, Sophie Beauchamp should have taken you on a walk-through of your apartment to check the condition of all walls, drapes, carpets, appliances, etc. These are all listed on the Landlord-Tenant Checklist, which you should have carefully gone over and signed. When you move out, we will ask you to check each item against its original condition as indicated on the Checklist.

Maintenance/Repair Problems: You have a right to expect repairs to be made promptly. To help us accomplish this, the Management will give you

Maintenance/Repair Request forms to report to the manager any problems in your apartment or the building or grounds, such as a broken garbage disposal. Keep several forms handy. (Extra copies are available from the manager.)

Except in an emergency, all requests for repairs should be made on this form during normal business hours. In case of emergency, call the manager at 555-1234.

Semi-Annual Safety and Maintenance Update: It's our goal to keep your unit and the common areas in excellent condition. To help us do this, we'll ask you to fill out a form every six months, to report any potential safety hazards or maintenance problems that otherwise might be overlooked. Please take the time to fill this out and send it back with your rent check.

Annual Safety Inspection: Once a year we will inspect the condition and furnishings of your rental unit and update the Landlord-Tenant Checklist.

Insurance: Clause 17 of your rental agreement makes you responsibile for losses not covered by landlord's insurance, which typically covers damage to the building. We highly recommend that you purchase insurance because tenants face many of the same risks that homeowners do:

• You could lose valuable property through theft or fire.

• You could be sued if someone is injured on the premises you rent.

• If you damage the building itself—say you start a fire in the kitchen and it spreads to other apartments—you could be responsible for large repair bills.

Contact your insurance agent for more information on renter's insurance.

8. Moving-Out: It's a little early to bring up moving out, but please be aware we have a list of items that should be cleaned before we conduct a move-out inspection. If you decide to move out, please ask the manager for a copy of our Move-out Sheet, explaining what is required and describing our procedures.

9. Telephone Number Changes: Please notify us if your home or work phone number changes, so we can reach you if an emergency occurs during the day.

Please let us know if you have any questions.

Sincerely,

Tony Giuliano, Owner

C. Cash Rent and Security Deposit Checks

You don't want to get stuck with a tenant who's going to bounce checks to you. And if the new tenant's first rent or deposit check bounces, you might have to undertake time-consuming and expensive legal proceedings to evict a tenant who's paid you nothing.

To avoid this, never sign a rental agreement, let a tenant move furniture into your property or give him a key until you have the tenant's cash, or a certified check or money order for the first month's rent and security deposit. An alternative is to cash a tenant's check at the bank before the move-in date. (While you have the tenant's first check, photocopy it for your records; the information on it can be helpful if you ever need to bring legal action.)

Responsible tenants, who prefer to plan ahead, will pay the rent and sign the lease at least several days before the move-in date; you can give the tenant a copy of the lease and the keys when the check clears or you receive cash or certified funds.

Clause 4 of our Lease and Rental Agreement forms require tenants to pay rent on the first day of the month, with rent to be pro-rated between a move-in date (if it's other than the first) and the end of that month. For example, with a monthly rent of $900 due on the first of June, a tenant who moves in on the 21st should pay ten days' pro-rated rent of $300, before the July rent is due July 1.

As a general rule, if the pro-rated rent for that first partial month is less than half a month's rent, you should request a more substantial amount up front. The reason for this is simple. A few tenants might impress you in person and look good on their applications, but yet are unable to come up with all the rent when due. Such individuals often look for rentals that require only a few hundred dollars up front; they don't worry about how they'll pay the rent later, hoping to find roommates by the time the rent comes due. You stand to lose heavily if you allow a person like this to move in on $300 pro-rated rent for the last ten days of the month and hope he'll come up with the regular $900 monthly rent on the first of the following ,month. If he doesn't come up with the full rent, and it takes you up to a month to evict him, you're out a month's rent plus eviction costs, a sum larger than any security deposit—which should be used to compensate you for the damage and mess this tenant may leave behind.

Insisting on a substantial up-front payment helps ferret out such individuals. There are a few ways to do this:

1. Require the pro-rated rent of less than half a month plus the next month's entire rent, plus the security deposit. (The deposit can be either two or three times the monthly rent amount, depending on whether the rental unit is furnished or unfurnished; see Chapter 5.) For example, your tenant who moves in on June 21 and pays $300 for the rent through June 30 should also be asked to pay in advance the $900 rent for July and the security deposit.

2. Insist on an entire month's rent up front and then pro-rate the second month. For example, the tenant who moves in on June 21 would first pay the full $900 rent for July. Then come July 1, the $300 rent for June 21 through 30 is due.

3. Simply require rent payments on the day of the month that the tenant moved in, so that a tenant who moves in on the 21st will always pay rent on the 21st.

We recommend the first way—accepting the pro-rated rent if it is more than half a month's rent or, if it is less than that, the pro-rated amount plus another month's rent. It's easier and keeps the rent due on the convenient and customary first of the month.

Lawyers, Legal Research, Eviction Services and Mediation

Generally California landlords can deal with most routine legal questions and problems without a lawyer. Just the same, there are times when good advice from a specialist in landlord-tenant law will be helpful, if not essential—for example in complicated evictions or lawsuits by tenants alleging that dangerous conditions or wrongful acts caused injury.

This chapter recommends a strategy to most efficiently and effectively use legal services:

- First, keep up-to-date on landlord-tenant law so that you can anticipate and avoid many legal problems.
- Second, use mediation services to settle disputes and head off lawsuits.
- Third, consider typing services as an alternative to lawyers in standard eviction cases.
- Fourth, know the best way to go about hiring a lawyer and negotiating fees.

Related Topics

To avoid legal problems in the first place, follow these guidelines:

- Screen tenant applicants carefully (Chapter 1).
- Use a clear, unambiguous written rental agreement or lease (Chapter 2).
- Make sure your manager knows landlord-tenant law (Chapter 6).
- Clarify tenants' responsibilities and grievance/repair procedures with a move-in letter (Chapter 7).
- Establish a system for reporting and handling repairs (Chapter 11).

A. Legal Research Tools

Using this book is a good way to educate yourself about the laws that affect your business—but one book is not enough by itself. At one time or another, you'll need to do some further research in the law library.

1. Local Ordinances

If you are a landlord in a city with a rent control ordinance, you need a copy of the ordinance, as well as all rules issued by the rent board covering rent increases and hearings.

Even if your rental property is not in a rent control area, you should be aware of any local ordinances that affect your business—for example, if your city requires dead-bolt locks in all rental units, or requires that you pay interest on tenants' security deposits.

2. State Laws

It's essential that you also have current copies of the California statutes that regulate the landlord-tenant relationship. They are collected in volumes called codes.

The California Civil Code (CC) contains most of California's substantive landlord-tenant law, primarily in Sections 1940 through 1991. It includes laws governing minimum building standards, payment of rent, change and termination of tenancy, privacy, security deposits and abandoned property, to name a few.

The California Code of Civil Procedure (CCP) is a set of laws explaining how people enforce legal rights in civil lawsuits. Eviction lawsuit procedures are contained in Sections 1161 through 1179 of the Code of Civil Procedure. Also of interest are the small claims court procedures, covered in Sections 116.110 through 116.950.

These codes are available in many public libraries and all county law libraries (found in county courthouses). However, because it's so important that you have immediate access to the laws that affect your business, we recommend that you buy copies of your own. They are sold in a number of different editions and are available at any law bookstore. In addition, Nolo Press sells inexpensive paperback versions (see back of this book for order information).

Remember that you'll need a new volume every year—the state legislature tinkers with landlord-tenant laws every session. You simply can't rely on an old set of statutes.

3. Court Decisions

Sometimes it isn't enough to read a statute—you also need to read the decisions of appeals courts, which explain what the statute means. These decisions are written by higher courts that hear appeals of decisions in trial courts, and state why the appeals court agrees or disagrees with the ruling of the trial court. Sometimes these case decisions are extremely important. For example, Civil Code Sections 1941 through 1942 set minimum housing standards. The 1974 case of *Green v. Superior Court* interpreted those statutes to allow tenants in substandard housing to withhold rent—without paying to make repairs themselves— even though no law specifically provides for this type of rent withholding. (See Chapter 11 for a discussion of this issue.)

The best way to learn of the existence of written court decisions which interpret a particular law is to first look in an "annotated code." An annotated code is a set of volumes of a particular code, such as the Civil Code or Code of Civil Procedure, that contains not only all the laws (as do the regular codes), but also a brief summary of many of the court decisions interpreting each law. These annotated codes— published by West Publishing Company (*West's Annotated California Codes*—blue volumes) and by Bancroft-Whitney (*Deering's California Codes*— brown volumes)—can be found in any county law library or law school library in the state. Some public libraries also have them.

These annotated codes have comprehensive indexes by topic, and are kept up-to-date each year with paperback supplements ("pocket parts") stuck in a pocket inside the back cover of each volume. To keep up to date on new laws and court decisions, look at these pocket parts each year (they're published in January and February), for Civil Code Sections 1940-1991 and Code of Civil Procedure Sections 1161 through 1179.

If a case summarized in an annotated code looks important, you may want to read the actual court opinion. To find it, you'll need the title of the case, the year of the decision, and the "citation" following each brief summary of the court decision. The citation is a sort of shorthand identification for the set of books, volume, and page where the case can be found.

One set of volumes, the *Official Reports of the California Courts of Appeal*, shows decisions of the lower appellate courts, which include the Courts of Appeal (one for each of six districts in the state) and the Superior Court Appellate Department (one for each county). The Courts of Appeal hear appeals of cases brought in Superior Court (involving more than $25,000). Courts of Appeal decisions are abbreviated "Cal. App.," "Cal. App. 2d," and "Cal. App. 3d," representing the first, second and third series of volumes. Superior Court Appellate Departments hear appeals of cases brought in Municipal Court (involving $25,000 or less), and those decisions are listed in the "Supplement" of each volume of the official reports. These cards are therefore abbreviated "Cal. App. 2d Supp." and "Cal. App. 3d Supp."

A second set of volumes, the *Official Reports of the California Supreme Court*, lists decisions of the California Supreme Court, the state's highest court, which reviews selected cases of the Courts of Appeal. Supreme Court decisions are abbreviated "Cal.," "Cal. 2d," or "Cal. 3d," representing the first, second and third series of volumes.

California appellate and Supreme Court decisions are also published by the West Publishing Company in the *California Reporter* (abbreviated "Cal. Rptr.") and *Pacific Reporter* (abbreviated "P." or "P.2d," respectively for the first and second series).

SAMPLE CASE CITATIONS

case name | volume number | 3rd series of Official Reports of the California Supreme Court | page number | volume number | the case also appears in *Calif. Reporter*, the unofficial reports | page number | volume number | the case is also listed in 2nd series of *Pacific Reporter* | page number | year of decision

Green v. Superior Court, 10 Cal. 3d 616, 11 Cal. Rptr. 704, 517 P.2d 1168 (1974)

case name | 3rd series of Official Reports of the California Courts of Appeal, Volume 137, page 770 | the case is also listed in *Calif. Reporter*, the unofficial reports, Volume 187, page 242 | year of decision

Glaser v. Myers, 137 Cal. App 3d 770, 187 Cal. Rptr. 242 (1982)

CALIFORNIA'S TRIAL AND APPELLATE COURTS

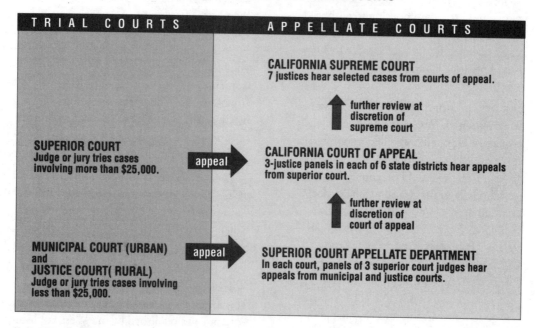

Note. Small Claims Court is a division of Municipal Court. A defendant who loses in Small Claims Court can request a new trial in Superior Court. (From there, no further appeal is allowed, escept at the Court of Appeal's discretion.)

Legal Research Help

We don't have space here to show you how to do your own legal research in anything approaching a comprehensive fashion.

To go further, we recommend two excellent resources. The first is Legal Research: How To Find and Understand the Law, *by Steve Elias, which gives easy-to-use, step-by-step instructions on how to find legal information. The other is* Legal Research Made Easy: A Roadmap Through the Law Library Maze *by Robert C. Berring, videotape presentation on the subject. Both are published by Nolo Press. (See order information at the back of this book.)*

B. Mediating Disputes with Tenants

Mediation is a technique where a neutral third party helps people settle differences themselves, without going to court. Unlike a judge in court or an arbitrator in a formal hearing, a mediator does not impose a decision on the parties, but facilitates a compromise. Generally, mediation works well in situations where people want to settle their disputes so they can work together in the future. In a landlord-tenant context, mediation can be extremely helpful in areas such as disputes about noise, the necessity for repairs, a tenant's decision to withhold rent because defects have not been repaired, rent increases, privacy and security deposits. Many large landlords find that an established mediation procedure is an invaluable way to head off lawsuits.

At the mediation session, each side gets to state his or her position, which often cools people off considerably and frequently results in a compromise. If the dispute is not resolved easily, however, the mediator may suggest ways to resolve the problem, or may even keep everyone talking long enough to realize that the real problem goes deeper than the one being mediated. For example, if a tenant has threatened rent withholding because of a defect in the premises, you may learn that the tenant's real grievance is that your manager is slow to make repairs. This may lead to the further discovery that the manager is angry at the tenant for letting his kids pull up his tulips.

At any rate, mediation often works, and if it doesn't, you haven't lost much. If mediation fails, you can still fight it out in court.

Mediation is most effective when there's an established procedure tenants and landlords can use. Here's how to set one up:

1. Find a mediation group that handles landlord-tenant disputes. There are many mediation programs throughout the state, and almost all California cities receive federal funds to arrange for mediators to handle disputes between landlords and tenants. For more information, call city hall, or the rent board in rent-controlled cities, and ask for the staff member who handles "landlord-tenant mediation matters" or "housing disputes." That person should refer you to the public office or private agency that attempts to informally resolve landlord-tenant disputes before they reach the court stage. Many mediation groups are city- or county-funded, and do not charge for their services.

You can also contact one of the respected mediation organizations, such as the American Arbitration Association, or a neighborhood dispute resolution center, such as San Francisco's Community Boards Program, and arrange for this group to mediate landlord-tenant disputes.

2. Explain procedures for lodging complaints to every tenant. A move-in letter (see Chapter 7) would be a good place to do this. Make sure tenants know they can request mediation for disputes which escalate to the point where normal face-to-face compromise techniques prove to be of no avail, whether over privacy, rent withholding because of allegedly defective conditions or whatever. Emphasize the fairness of the mediation process.

3. If possible, split the cost (if any) of a mediation. (If this isn't acceptable to the tenant, and you pay the total mediation cost, make sure your tenant realizes that the mediator has no power to impose a decision.)

C. Non-Lawyer Eviction Services

Filing and following through with an eviction lawsuit involves filling out a number of legal forms. And once the forms are filed with the court, they must then be served on the tenant—a task that isn't always easy. You can do it yourself, using *The Landlord's Law Book Volume 2: Evictions,* or can hire a lawyer. There is also a third route: getting help with the paperwork, filing and service from an eviction service run by non-lawyers, known as "legal typing services" or "independent paralegals." They exist in most metropolitan areas.

For a flat fee that is usually much lower than what lawyers charge, and often at a faster pace, eviction services take the basic information from you, prepare most of the initial paperwork, file the necessary papers in court, and have the tenant served with the Summons and Complaint.

Typing services aren't lawyers. They can't give legal advice about the requirements of your specific case and can't represent you in court—only lawyers can. You must decide what steps to take in your case, and the information to put in the needed forms.

A non-lawyer eviction service can, however:

- provide written instructions and legal information needed to handle your own case

- provide the appropriate eviction forms and fill them out according to your instructions

- type your papers so they'll be accepted by the court

- arrange for filing the eviction forms in court and serving them on the tenant.[1]

Most typing services handle only routine cases. If the tenant contests the eviction suit—which happens less than one-fourth of the time, the eviction service won't be able to help you in court. At this point, you must represent yourself in court or hire your own lawyer to take over. The eviction service may have a lawyer on its staff who you can hire or may refer you to a lawyer.

To find an eviction service, check with a landlords' association or look in the telephone book under "Eviction Services." Many typing services advertise in local throwaway papers like the *Classified Flea Market.* You can also get a list of California typing services from the National Association for Independent Paralegals, at 800-542-0034.

Be sure the eviction service or typing service is reputable and experienced, as well as reasonably priced. (The cost should not exceed $100 for the service, plus another $100 for court filing fees and sheriff's fees.) Ask for references and check them. As a general matter, the longer a typing service has been in business, the better. The National Association for Independent Paralegals will mediate complaints about any member typing service.

---

[1] In the case of *People v. Landlords' Professional Services,* 215 Cal. App. 3d 1599 (1989), the court ruled that an eviction service whose nonlawyer employees gave oral legal advice was unlawfully practicing law. The court, however, said eviction services could legally give customers forms and detailed self-help legal manuals, fill out the forms as directed by the customer and file and serve the papers.

D. Finding a Lawyer

Throughout this book, we point out specific instances when an attorney's advice or services may be useful, including complicated eviction, discrimination and personal injury lawsuits.

Finding a good, reasonably priced lawyer is not always an easy task. If you just pick a name out of the telephone book, you may get an unsympathetic lawyer, or one who will charge too much, or one who's not qualified to deal with your particular problem. If you use the attorney who drew up your family will, you may end up with someone who knows nothing about landlord law. This sorry result is not necessarily inevitable—there are competent lawyers who charge fairly for their services.

As a general rule, experience is most important. You want a lawyer who specializes in landlord-tenant law. The best way to find a suitable attorney is through some trusted person who has had a satisfactory experience with one. Your best referral sources are other landlords in your area and your local landlords' association.

The worst referral sources are:

- Heavily advertised legal clinics, which are less likely to offer competitive rates for competent representation in this specialized area. While they may offer low flat rates for routine services such as

drafting a will, it's less common to see legal clinics charge reasonable flat fees for other specific services. It is not unusual for legal services to advertise a very low basic price and then add to it considerably, based on the assertion that your particular problem costs more.

- Referral panels set up by local bar associations. While they sometimes do minimal screening before qualifying the expertise of lawyers in landlord/tenant law, usually the emphasis is on the word "minimal." You may get a good referral from these panels, but they sometimes refer people to inexperienced practitioners who don't have enough clients and who use the panel as a way of generating needed business.

Once you get a good referral, call the law offices that have been recommended and state your problem. Find out the cost of an initial visit. You should be able to find an attorney willing to discuss your problems for $75. If you feel the lawyer is sympathetic to your concerns and qualified to handle your problem, make an appointment to discuss your situation.

Beware of lawyers who advertise "free consultations." As your own business experience doubtless tells you, the world provides little or nothing of value for free. This is doubly true when it comes to buying legal help. Lawyers who will see you for nothing have every motive to think up some sort of legal action which requires their services. If you insist on paying fairly for an attorney's time, you are far more likely to be advised that no expensive legal action is needed.

Here are some things to look for in your first meeting:

- Will the lawyer answer all your questions about fees, her experience in landlord-tenant matters, and your specific legal problem? Stay away from lawyers who make you feel uncomfortable asking questions.
- Is the lawyer willing to assist you when you have specific questions, billing you on an hourly basis

when you handle your own legal work—such as evictions? Is she willing to answer your questions over the phone and charge only for the brief amount of time the conversation lasted? Or does she insist on a more time-consuming (and profitable) office appointment? If the lawyer tries to dissuade you from representing yourself in any situation, or won't give any advice over the phone despite your invitation to bill you for it, find someone else. There are plenty of lawyers who will be very happy to bill you hourly to help you help yourself.

• If you want someone to represent you in an eviction lawsuit, does the lawyer charge a flat fee, or an hourly fee with a maximum? Most evictions, especially for nonpayment of rent, are routine and present little trouble, even when contested by the tenant. Many attorneys charge reasonable flat fixed rates, such as $250 to $350, to handle eviction lawsuits. If the lawyer's hourly rate exceeds $100, with no upper limit, you can do better elsewhere.

• If your property is in a rent-controlled city, does the lawyer practice in or near that city and know its rent-control laws and practices?

• Does the lawyer represent tenants, too? Chances are that a lawyer who represents both landlords and tenants can advise you well on how to avoid many legal pitfalls of being a landlord.

E. Paying a Lawyer

If you do need a lawyer, find one who does not object to your doing as much legal work as you want and who will charge a reasonable hourly rate for occasional help and advice. While this isn't impossible, it may be difficult, because some lawyers may not want to accept piecemeal work.

Most lawyers charge $100 to $200 an hour. How you pay your lawyer depends on how often you need legal services.

1. Large Landlord with Regular Legal Needs

If you own more than a dozen rental units, and do not wish to handle all your own evictions from start to finish (even if uncontested), you will probably want to work out a continuing relationship with the lawyer, and you should have more than enough leverage to set up a relatively economical arrangement. There are several ways to go:

• Pay the attorney a modest monthly retainer to work with you and represent you in court in routine eviction cases as needed. (Other types of cases, such as where a tenant sues for damages, are so time-consuming that representation is not included in such retainer agreements.) You can usually get a lot of service for a reasonable pre-established rate.

• Negotiate a fee schedule for various kinds of routine services based on the lawyer handling all your work. As you will probably provide a fair amount of business over the years, this should be substantially below the lawyer's normal hourly rate.

• Do the initial legal work in evictions and similar procedures yourself, but turn over to a lawyer cases which become hotly contested or complicated. If this is your plan, look for a lawyer who doesn't resent your doing some of your own legal work and who won't sock you with a high hourly rate for picking up a case you began.

2. Small Landlord with Occasional Legal Needs

If you are a very small landlord, you expect (and hope) that you will have little continuing need for a lawyer. The drawback to needing only occasional legal help is that a lawyer has little incentive to represent you for a reasonable fee when you get into occasional legal hot water. But it's possible to find a lawyer who specializes in landlord-tenant law who will charge you the same prices larger landlords get.

And who knows, the lawyer may hope that you will expand your business and become a more profitable client in the future.

Note on attorney fees clause in lawsuits. If your lease or written rental agreement has an attorney fees provision (as ours does, Clause 20), you are entitled to recover your attorneys' fees if you win a lawsuit based on the terms of that agreement. There's no guarantee, however, that a judge will award attorney fees equal to your attorney's actual bill, or that you will ultimately be able to collect the money from the tenant or former tenant. Also, as discussed in Chapter 2, an attorney fees clause in your lease or rental agreement works both ways. Even if the clause doesn't say so, you're liable for the tenant's attorney fees if you lose.[2] (Landlord's insurance does not cover such liability where the lawsuit is unrelated to items covered by the policy, such as eviction lawsuits by the landlord and security-deposit refund suits by the tenant.)

---

[2]CC § 1717.

Discrimination

At one time, a landlord could refuse to rent to someone, or evict a month-to-month
tenant on 30 days' notice, simply because he didn't like the color of the tenant's skin, religion or national origin. All sorts of groups, including blacks, Asians, Jews, Hispanics, unmarried couples, gays, families with children and the disabled, were routinely subjected to discrimination.

Fortunately, the days of legal discrimination are long gone. Several federal and California civil rights laws provide severe financial penalties for landlords who discriminate on the basis of race, religion, sex, age and a number of other categories. And just to be sure all bases are covered, the California Supreme Court has ruled that almost any unreasonable discrimination in housing is illegal.[1]

This chapter reviews information you need to avoid illegally discriminating:

- Illegal types of discrimination and major laws and court cases, including recent developments in the field such as expanded protection for families with children

- Legal reasons to turn down prospective tenants such as a bad credit history or too many tenants for the size of the premises

- Tenants' legal remedies, in state and federal courts, for discrimination

- Special rules applying to landlords who share their premises with tenants.

A. Forbidden Types of Discrimination

As a group, landlords have a mediocre record when it comes to treating prospective tenants fairly and objectively. Legislatures responded by first outlawing discrimination on the basis of race. Over the last 30 years, Congress, state legislatures and the courts have steadily expanded the scope of anti-discrimination rules. Essentially, any discrimination that is not rationally related to a legitimate business reason is now against the law. Courts can assess substantial financial penalties for unlawful discrimination, and can order a landlord to rent housing to a person who was discriminated against.

Even an innocent owner whose agent or manager discriminates without the owner's knowledge can be sued and found liable. (To protect yourself, make sure your manager knows the law. See Section E, below, and Chapter 6.)

It is illegal for a landlord to refuse to rent to a tenant, or to engage in any other kind of discrimination (such as requiring higher rent or larger deposits) on the basis of a group characteristic, such as nationality, race or religion. But these aren't the only ways a landlord can be legally liable for unlawful discrimination. A landlord's attempted or actual termination of a tenancy for a discriminatory reason, or discrimination in providing services, such as the use of pool, meeting room or other common area, is illegal and can provide the discriminated-against tenant with a defense to an eviction lawsuit as well as a basis for suing the landlord for damages. (See Section C, below.)

EXAMPLE 1

An owner, Osgood, rents apartments in his six-unit apartment building without regard to racial or other unlawful criteria. His tenants include a black family and a single Latin-American woman with children. Osgood sells his building to Leo who immediately gives only these two tenants 30-day notices. Unless Leo can come up with a valid non-discriminatory reason for evicting these minority tenants, they can successfully defend an eviction lawsuit Leo brings on the basis of unlawful discrimination. The tenants can also sue Leo for damages in state or federal court.

---

[1] *In re Cox*, 3 Cal. 3d 205 (1972) and *Marina Point, Ltd. v. Wolfson*, 30 Cal. 3d 72 (1982).

EXAMPLE 2

Now, let's assume that Leo, having lost both the eviction lawsuits and the tenants' suits for damages against him, still tries to discriminate by adopting a less blatant strategy— adopting an inconsistent policy of responding to late rent payments. When Leo's white tenants without children are late with the rent, he doesn't give them a Three-Day Notice To Pay Rent or Quit until after a five-day grace period, while non-white tenants receive their three-day notices the day after the rent is due. In addition, Leo is very slow when non-white tenants request repairs. These more subtle means of discrimination are also illegal, and Leo's tenants have grounds to sue him for damages on account of emotional distress, plus punitive damages of up to three times that amount and attorney fees. Leo's tenants also have grounds to defend any eviction lawsuit Leo brings against them.

Many local ordinances, including some rent control ordinances, also prohibit discrimination on the basis of age (children) and sexual orientation. Although these ordinances tend to duplicate the categories of discrimination which courts have ruled are forbidden by California's Unruh Civil Rights Act, they can strengthen the basis for a tenant's lawsuit.[2]

1. Race

Landlords who turn away prospective tenants on the basis of race don't come out and admit what they're doing. Commonly, a landlord falsely tells a person who's a member of a racial minority that no rentals are available, or that the prospective tenant's income and credit history aren't good enough. Local fair-housing groups uncover this discriminatory practice by having "testers" apply to landlords for vacant housing. Typically, a tester who is black or Hispanic will fill out a rental application, listing certain occupational, income and credit information. Then, a white tester will apply for the same housing, listing

information very similar to that given by the minority applicant.

A landlord who offers to rent to a white tester having the same qualifications as a minority applicant who is rejected without valid reason is probably discriminating. Landlords should be aware that such incidents have resulted in hefty lawsuit settlements.

Another common type of racial discrimination occurs when a minority individual first phones the property owner or manager to ask about an advertised rental unit. Often, he or she will be encouraged to come over to look at the property, only to be treated coldly or rudely when the owner or manager sees the applicant is a member of a minority group.

Needless to say, this type of outrageous discriminatory conduct can get an owner sued.

2. Ethnic Background and National Origin

Discrimination on the basis of ethnic background and national origin is practiced—and detected—in ways similar to discrimination based on race.

While no law expressly prohibits discrimination based on immigration status—for example, requiring certain persons to prove their immigration status before renting to them—a court would probably rule that this practice is illegal discrimination based on national origin. Unless a landlord asked every applicant to show an immigration card or proof of citizenship (birth or naturalization certificate), he could be heading for trouble. Since no law requires landlords to verify their tenants' immigration status, asking about this is not a good idea.

3. Religion

Fortunately, religious discrimination is rare, although a few smaller landlords rent only to members of their own religion. This is illegal.

---

[2]*McHugh v. Santa Monica Rent Control Board*, 49 Cal. 3d 348 (1989).

ILLEGAL DISCRIMINATION

State law, and in some cases federal law, absolutely forbids discrimination on the following grounds, regardless of a landlord's claim of a legitimate business need.

Discrimination	Federal Civil Rights Act of 1866 (1)	Federal Fair Housing Act (2)	Unruh Act (CA) (3)	Fair Employment & Housing Act (CA) (4)	Court Decisions (see footnote number)	Local Ordinances
Race	X	X	X	X		X
Ethnic background		X	X	X		
National origin		X	X	X		
Religion		X	X	X		X
Sex		X	X	X		X
Marital status			X	X	(5)	X
Age and families with children		X	X		(6)	X
Disability		X	X			X
Sexual orientation			X		(7)	X
Receipt of public assistance			X		(8)	

(1)   42 United States Code § 1982.

(2)   42 United States Code §§ 3601-3619.

(3)   CC §§ 51-53.

(4)   Government Code Sections 12955-12988. For specific prohibition of discrimination on the grounds of marital status, see *Atkisson v. Kern County Housing Authority*, 58 Cal. App. 3d 89 (1976); and *Hess v. Fair Employment and Housing Comm.*, 138 Cal. App. 3d 232 (1982).

(5)   *Hess v. Fair Employment and Housing Commission*, 138 Cal. App. 3d 232 (1982).

(6)   *Marina Point, Ltd. v. Wolfson*, 30 Cal. 3d 72 (1982) construes the Unruh Act to prohibit discrimination against families on the sole basis that they have children.

(7)   *Hubert v. Williams*, 133 Cal. App. 3d Supp. 1 (1982).

(8)   59 Ops. Cal. Atty. Gen. 223. However, a landlord may legally refuse to rent to a tenant who fails to meet minimum-income criteria, so long as the same test is applied equally to all applicants regardless of their source of income. *Harris v. Capital Growth Investors XIV*, 52 Cal. 3d 1142 (1991).

4. Sex

Sex discrimination sometimes takes the form of refusing to rent to single women with a certain income, but renting to men with similar incomes, though this is rare. Sex discrimination also sometimes takes the form of sexual harassment—refusing to rent to a person who resists a landlord's or manager's sexual advances, or making life difficult for a tenant who has resisted such advances.

5. Marital Status

In California, it is illegal to discriminate against couples because they are married or unmarried. The California Fair Employment and Housing Commission has ruled that a landlord may not discriminate on this basis—for example, by refusing to rent to unmarried couples—even if the discriminatory practice is based on a sincere religious belief.[3]

6. Age and Families with Children

State and federal law, plus ordinances in several California cities, forbid discrimination against families with children—commonly called age discrimination—except in housing reserved exclusively for senior citizens.[4]

Landlords often try to disguise discrimination against families with children by restricting the number of occupant children to one or two per bedroom, supposedly to prevent "overcrowding," or by refusing to allow two children of the opposite sex to share a bedroom. The California Department of Fair Employment and Housing considers these practices to be illegal if the landlord appears to be using them as an excuse to discriminate. (See Section B.2 below

---

[3]As of this writing, this ruling is being appealed.

[4]CC § 51.3 defines senior-citizen housing as that reserved for persons 62 years of age or older, or a complex of 150 or more units (35 in non-metropolitan areas) for persons older than 55 years. The federal law definition is almost identical (42 USC § 3607).

for discussion of overcrowding.) It's also illegal to only allow children on ground floors or to designate certain apartments as separate adult units and family units.

7. Disability

It is illegal to refuse to rent to a physically disabled person on the same terms as if they were not disabled. In addition, you must rent to an otherwise qualified blind, deaf or physically disabled person with a properly trained dog, even if you otherwise ban pets.

Landlords should not ask prospective tenants whether they have disabilities or illnesses, including AIDS, and should not ask to see medical records. However, a landlord may turn away a person with a history of disruptive or abusive behavior, even if it is the result of a physical or mental illness.

The federal Fair Housing Act also requires that landlords make reasonable accommodations for the disabled such as permitting a disabled tenant to modify her quarters at her own expense—for example, allowing a tenant with limited hand strength to install lever doorknobs. Reserving a parking space near the apartment of a tenant who has difficulty walking would be another reasonable accomodation.

8. Sexual Orientation

It is illegal to discriminate on the basis of someone's sexual orientation. This includes homosexuality.

9. Smoking

Discrimination against smokers is not specifically prohibited by any civil rights law, and no California court has ruled that such discrimination is arbitrary so as to be prohibited by the Unruh Act.

Recent court decisions have given a narrow definition to "arbitrary" discrimination against a category of individuals (such as smokers) not listed in the Unruh Act when the landlord has a valid purpose to discriminate. In light of this, we think a court would probably allow landlords to refuse to rent to smokers, for the reason that tobacco smoke may damage walls, carpets and drapes.

10. Waterbeds

State law forbids an owner of property built after January 1973 from refusing to rent to a tenant simply because she has a waterbed.[5] However, the landlord may insist on strict standards, discussed under Clause 18 in Chapter 2 on leases and rental agreements.

11. Public Assistance

You may not refuse to rent to a person simply because he is receiving public assistance. You may, however, refuse to rent to persons whose incomes fall below a certain level, as long as you apply that standard across the board. For example, if you require all prospective tenants to have a $1,000 monthly income before you will consider renting to them, the fact that this excludes welfare recipients who receive only $700 a month does not constitute illegal discrimination under the Unruh Act.[6]

However, you would be guilty of unlawful discrimination if you normally rented to tenants regardless of income, but set an income requirement for public assistance recipients, or if you refused to rent to a person who qualified under your guidelines, solely because he received welfare.

12. Other Arbitrary Discrimination

After reading the above list outlining the types of discrimination forbidden by California and federal law, you may assume that it is legal to discriminate for any reason not mentioned by name in a state or federal law. For example, because none of the civil rights laws specifically prohibits discrimination against men with beards or long hair, you might conclude that such discrimination is permissible. This is not true.

Even though California's Unruh Civil Rights Act contains only the words "sex, race, color, religion, ancestry, or national origin" to describe types of discrimination that are illegal, the courts have ruled that these categories are just examples of illegal discrimination. The courts have construed the Unruh Act to forbid all forms of arbitrary discrimination which bear no relationship to a landlord's legitimate business concerns. In fact, it was on this basis that the California Supreme Court ruled that landlords can't discriminate against families with children. That court has also stated that discrimination against other groups, such as "Republicans, students, welfare

---

[5]CC § 1940.5.

[6]In *Harris v. Capital Growth Investors XIV*, 52 Cal. 3d 1142 (1991), the California Supreme Court ruled that a landlord who insisted a tenant's monthly income equal three times the rent did not unlawfully discriminate in violation of the Unruh Act.

recipients," or "entire occupations or avocations, for example, sailors or motorcyclists"[7] is also illegal.

However, discrimination on the basis of economic factors bearing a legitimate relationship to the landlord's business is not illegal. The court also approved a landlord's insistence that all tenants have a monthly income equal to three times the rent.[8]

EXAMPLE

Bill refuses to rent his $600/month apartment to a person whose monthly household income is less than $1,500. This is legal. However, Bill cannot apply different minimum-income standards on the basis of a prohibited category of discrimination such as race, sex or marital status. Bill should resist the temptation to lower his $1,500/month standard to $1,200 for the benefit of a single person.

B. Legal Reasons to Discriminate

Only arbitrary discrimination in rental housing is illegal. Landlords may choose among prospective tenants based on valid business criteria, such as ability to pay the rent.

You may legally refuse to rent to prospective tenants with bad credit histories, unsteady employment histories or even low incomes you reasonably regard as insufficient to pay the rent. Why? Because these reasons for tenant selection are reasonably related to your legitimate business interests. And if a person who fits one or more obvious "bad tenant risk" criteria happens to be a member of a minority group, you are still on safe legal ground as long as:

- You are not applying a generalization about people of a certain group to an individual, and
- You can document your legal reasons for not renting.

You could, for example, legitimately refuse to rent to a prospective tenant because he has a violent criminal record, uses illegal drugs or wants to run a business from his home, whether it be typesetting or prostitution.

But pay attention to the fact that judges, tenants' lawyers and fair housing groups know full well that some landlords try to make up legal reasons to discriminate, when the real reason is that they just don't like people with a particular racial, ethnic or religious background. So, if you refuse to rent to a person who happens to be black, gay, female, who has children, or speaks only Spanish, be sure you document your legitimate business reason specific to that individual (such as insufficient income or a history of eviction for nonpayment of rent).

Here are some of the common legal reasons you may discriminate based on your business interests.

1. Credit Record and Income

You can legitimately refuse to rent to a prospective tenant who has a history of nonpayment of rent or who you reasonably believe would be unable to pay rent in the future.

Here's some advice on how to avoid charges of discrimination when choosing tenants on the basis of income or credit history:

---

[7]See *Marina Point, Ltd. v. Wolfson*, 30 Cal. 3d 72, 180 Cal. Rptr. 496 (1982).

[8]*Harris v. Capital Growth Investors XIV*, 52 Cal. 3d 1142 (1991).

1. Do a credit check on every prospective tenant and base your selection on the results of that credit check. Regular use of credit reporting agencies is the best way to protect yourself against an accusation that you're using a bad credit history as an excuse to illegally discriminate against certain prospective tenants. If you won't rent to someone evicted by a previous landlord for nonpayment of rent (information commonly found in credit reports) be sure you apply this policy to all tenants, and that your decision is based on reliable information. (Chapter 1 shows you how to use credit reports and other sources to find out whether a prospective tenant has ever been evicted.)

2. Avoid point systems that rank prospective tenants on the basis of financial stability. Some landlords evaluate prospective tenants by giving each one a certain number of points at the outset, with deductions for bad credit and other references and additional points for extremely good ones. Points are also awarded based on length of employment and income. The person with the highest score gets the nod.

Point systems give the illusion of objectivity, but because the weight given each factor is subjective, they're really about the same as just picking someone who looks good and can leave you equally as open to charges of discrimination.

3. If you use the approach of refusing to rent to a person whose income is less than three or even two times the rent, be sure to apply it to all applicants without exception.[9]

4. Don't give too much weight to years spent at the same job, which can arguably discriminate against certain occupations.

---

[9]*Harris v. Capital Growth Investors XIV*, 52 Cal. 3d 1142 (1991)., 259 Cal. Rptr. 586 (1989).

Note on Low-Income Tenants

Many tenants with low incomes may qualify for federally subsidized housing assistance, the most common being the Section 8 program of the federal Department of Housing and Urban Development (HUD). ("Section 8" refers to Section 8 of the United States Housing Act of 1937, 42 USC 1437f.) That program subsidizes tenants' rents by paying part of the rent directly to the landlord. The local housing authority, landlord and tenant enter into a one-year agreement, which includes a written lease supplied by the county housing authority. The tenant pays up to 30% of his monthly income to the landlord, and the housing authority pays the landlord the difference between the tenant's contribution and what it determines is the market rent each month.

Section 8 offers several advantages to the landlord:
- *The larger part of the rent is paid on time every month by the housing authority, and the tenant's portion is low enough so that he doesn't have too much trouble paying on time either.*
- *If the tenant doesn't pay the rent and you have to evict him, the housing authority guarantees the tenant's unpaid portion, and also guarantees payment for damages to the property by the tenant, up to a certain limit.*

Section 8's disadvantages are that:
- *The housing authority's determination of what is market rent is often low.*
- *The landlord is locked into a tenancy agreement for one year, and can't terminate the tenancy except for nonpayment of rent or other serious breach of the lease. (Evictions based on grounds other than nonpayment of rent are difficult.)*

You have the right to refuse to rent on a Section 8 basis without violating any anti-discrimination laws. Call the housing authority in the county where your property is located if you wish to participate in the Section 8 program. They will refer eligible applicants to you and will prepare the necessary documents (including the lease) if you decide to rent to a particular tenant.

5. Don't discriminate against married or unmarried couples by counting only the man's income.[10] Always consider the income of persons living together, married or unmarried, in order to avoid the accusation of marital status or sex discrimination.

State and federal laws prohibiting discrimination against women do allow you to consider one spouse's income alone if only one spouse signs the rental agreement or lease. It's in your best interest to have all tenants sign a lease or rental agreement, (as we recommend in Chapter 2), because if you need to bring an eviction suit for nonpayment of rent, you can get a judgment for rent against both of them, which means you can try to collect from two people rather than just one.[11] (See Chapter 10 for the legal responsibilities of tenants and co-tenants.)

2. Occupancy Limits

The fact that discrimination against families with children is illegal does not mean you have to rent a one-bedroom apartment to a family of five. You can legally establish reasonable space-to-people ratios, but you cannot use overcrowding as a euphemism for refusing to rent to tenants with children, if you would rent to the same number of adults.

A few landlords have adopted criteria that for all practical purposes forbid children under the guise of preventing overcrowding—for example, allowing only one person per bedroom, with a couple counting as one person. Under these criteria, a landlord would rent a two-bedroom unit to a husband and wife and their one child, but would not rent the same unit to a mother with two children. Although the courts have not yet ruled on this practice, which has the effect of

keeping all (or most) children out of a landlord's property, chances are they will soon find these policies illegal.[12] At the least, it's strong evidence of an intent to discriminate.

The state Fair Employment and Housing Commission has ruled that a Los Angeles apartment owner who limited occupancy to one person per bedroom—when state health and safety laws would have allowed as many as ten people in a two-bedroom apartment there—had clearly intended to exclude children. The tenants who had been denied an apartment and complained to the state were awarded $2,500 each.

The Fair Employment and Housing Commission is the judicial and enforcement arm of the California Department of Fair Employment and Housing (DFEH). The DFEH (one of the places a tenant can complain about discrimination, see Section C below) will investigate a complaint for possible filing with the Commission based on a "two-plus-one" rule: If a landlord's policy is more restrictive than two persons per bedroom plus one additional occupant, it is suspect. Thus, a landlord is asking for trouble when she insists on two or fewer people in a one-bedroom unit, four or fewer in a two-bedroom unit, six or fewer in a three-bedroom unit and so on. However, a landlord who draws the line at three people to a one-bedroom, five to a two-bedroom, and seven to a three-bedroom unit will be on a safe ground in this regard. However, the Department will not penalize a landlord whose standards are more restrictive if the landlord has a reasonable percentage of children in the complex (compared to the community), a good history of renting to families with children and a legitimate

---

[10] CC § 1812.30.

[11] State law does allow a landlord, in collecting a judgment for back rent against a married individual, to collect from the community property of both spouses, or even the separate property of the non-signing spouse. (CC §§ 5120.110 and 5120.140.) Still, it's easier to collect, and to avoid complex post-judgment proceedings by getting a judgment against both spouses based on their both having signed the lease or rental agreement.

[12] One court has already ruled against a landlord who did not permit more than four persons to occupy three-bedroom apartments, *Zakaria & Lincoln Property Co.*, 185 Cal. App. 3d 500, 229 Cal. Rptr. 669, (1986). In *Smith v. Ring Brothers Management Corp.*, 183 Cal. App. 3d 649, 228 Cal. Rptr. 525 (1986), another court held that a rule precluding a two-child family from occupying a two-bedroom apartment violated a local ordinance similar to state law.

reason for the restrictive standards, such as concern with preventing excessive wear and tear.

Until the courts spell out just what type of occupancy standards a landlord can legitimately apply, we suggest that you apply this "two (per bedroom) plus one" rule, to avoid any possible legal trouble.

Most important, maintain a consistent occupancy policy. If you allow three adults to live in a two-bedroom apartment, you had better let a couple with a child live in the same type of unit, or you leave yourself open to charges that you are illegally discriminating.

Finally, do not inquire as to the age and sex of any two children who will be sharing the same bedroom. This is their parents' business, not yours.

Children born to tenants. In a non-rent controlled city, you can evict tenants with month-to-month rental agreements by giving a 30-day notice, provided you do not have an illegal discriminatory motive. Be careful, though, if your reason for evicting is that a tenant has given birth. You should not evict for this reason unless the new arrival results in overcrowding under the two-plus-one rule. You also should realize that any tenants, particularly ones who are expecting a child, are likely to be upset if you ask them to move. They may scrutinize your rental policies and practices toward families with children, and may initiate a complaint with the Department of Fair Employment and Housing or even file a lawsuit.

You may be within your rights to insist on a reasonable rent increase after a child is born, provided:

- Your tenant has only a month-to-month rental agreement rather than a lease fixing rent for a specific period.

- Your property is not subject to rent control. (Some cities, including San Francisco, rule out childbirth as a rationale for a rent increase.)

- The rent increase is reasonable and truly based on the number of occupants in the property.

3. Animals

You can legally refuse to rent to people with pets, or restrict the types of pets you accept—provided this rule is applied to all tenants alike. However, it is not legal to refuse to rent on this basis if the animal is a properly trained dog for a blind, deaf or physically disabled person.

C. Legal Penalties for Discrimination

A landlord who unlawfully discriminates against a tenant or prospective tenant may end up in state or federal court or before a state or federal housing agency facing allegations of discrimination.

Showing you how to defend a housing discrimination lawsuit is beyond the scope of this book. With the exception of a suit brought in small claims court, you should see an attorney if a tenant sues you or files an administrative complaint against you for discrimination.

State and federal court and housing agencies which find that discrimination has taken place have the power to:

- Order a landlord to rent a particular piece of property to the person who was discriminated against.

- Order the landlord to pay the tenant for "actual" or "compensating" damages, including any higher rent the tenant had to pay as a result of being turned down, and damages for humiliation, emotional distress or embarrassment.

- Make the landlord pay punitive damages (extra money as damages for especially outrageous discrimination) and the tenant's attorney fees.

Under the Federal Fair Housing Act, which covers discrimination based on sex, race, religion, disability, family status and national or ethnic origin, punitive damages are limited to $1,000. For racial discrimination, however, higher punitive damages are allowed under the Civil Rights Act of 1866.[13] The state's Fair Employment and Housing Commission's power to award punitive damages is limited to $1,000 per violation.

Under California's Unruh Civil Rights Act, triple actual damages may be awarded in a lawsuit for a violation of discrimination laws, and at least $250 must be awarded if you go to court. Small claims courts can award damages of up to their maximum jurisdictional amounts of $5,000. For more information on small claims courts, see *Everybody's Guide to Small Claims Court* by Ralph Warner (Nolo Press).

A tenant may complain about illegal discrimination by filing a lawsuit in state or federal court, or by filing an administrative complaint with the U.S. Department of Housing and Urban Development (HUD) or the California Department of Fair Employment and Housing (DFEH).

Commonly, the federal courts require that the tenant first file a complaint with HUD. Similarly,

HUD usually, but not always, requires that the tenant first file a complaint with the state agency. If you wish to know more about complaint procedures, contact HUD or the DFEH.

The HUD Equal Opportunity office for California is located at 450 Golden Gate Ave., San Francisco. Phone: 415-556-0800. See the list below of local offices of the DFEH. Discrimination on other grounds not prohibited by federal law, such as marital status or sexual orientation, can generally be taken only to the state court or to California's Department of Fair Employment and Housing.

California Department of Fair Employment and Housing Offices

Bakersfield
1001 Tower Way, #250
805-395-2728

Fresno
1900 Mariposa Mall, Ste. 130
209-445-5373

Los Angeles
322 West First St., Rm. 2126
213-620-2610

Oakland
1330 Broadway, Ste. 1326
415-464-4095

Sacramento
2000 "O" St., #120
916-445-9918

San Bernardino
1845 S. Business Center Dr., #127
714-383-4711

San Diego
110 West C Street, Ste. 1702
619-237-7405

San Francisco
30 Van Ness Ave.
415-557-2005

San Jose
111 No. Market St., Ste. 810
408-277-1264

Santa Ana
28 Civic Ctr. Plaza, Rm. 538
714-558-4159

Ventura
5720 Ralston St., #362
805-654-4513

---

[13]*Morales v. Haines* 486 F.2d 880 (7th Cir. 1973); *Lee v. Southern Home Sites Corp.*, 429 F. 2d 290 (5th Cir. 1970).

D. Owner-Occupied Premises

A resident-owner who shares a house or apartment with only one paying tenant, sharing common kitchen and bathroom facilities, is not subject to the anti-discrimination rules that affect other landlords. California and federal civil rights laws apply only to housing rental operations that are considered to be a "business."

That means roommate or house-sharing ads with all sorts of restrictions like, "Young, female, nonsmoking vegetarian who reads Asimov wanted to share house" are legal.

What is owner-occupied and what isn't is not always obvious. Renting out a single apartment or house, or even half of an owner-occupied duplex, does constitute the operation of a business to which anti-discrimination laws apply.[14]

And when an owner-occupant (or tenant) rents *two* rooms or portions of a dwelling (such as in a

single-family house with three or more bedrooms), California's civil rights laws apply.[15] If a landlord in this situation discriminates on the basis of race or religion, there could well be cause for legal action. (We haven't, however, heard of any lawsuits challenging people's rights to choose only nonsmoking, vegetarian, single mothers or some other narrowly restricted group in shared-housing situations.)

E. Managers and Discrimination

If you hire a manager, particularly one who selects tenants, make certain that she fully understands laws against housing discrimination. (See Chapter 6 on landlord liability for a manager's conduct and strategies for avoiding problems in this area.)

Even properly instructing your manager about illegal discrimination, however, will not necessarily protect you if she violates the law. You must take precautions to ensure that your manager doesn't discriminate.

One way to do this is to prepare a written policy statement as to the law and your intention to abide by it. Require that your manager post this in the building office or somewhere on the premises and give it to all prospective tenants. It might look like this:

---

[14]An owner-occupant of a duplex, or triplex or larger complex, is governed by civil rights laws in the renting of the other unit(s) in the building, even though he or she lives in one of the other units, because the owner-occupant is renting out property for use as a separate household, where kitchen or bathroom facilities aren't shared with the tenant. See *Swann v. Burkett*, 209 Cal. App. 2d 686 (1962) and 58 Ops. Cal. Atty. Gen. 608 (1975).

[15]Government Code Section 12927(c).

SAMPLE STATEMENT ON EQUAL OPPORTUNITY IN HOUSING

```
FROM:  Shady Dell Apartments

TO:    All Tenants and Applicants


It is the policy of the owner and manager of Shady Dell Apartments to
provide equal opportunity in housing. We comply with all federal, state
and local laws prohibiting discrimination. In short, we rent our units
without regard to a tenant's race, ethnic background, sex, religion,
marital or family status, physical disability or sexual orientation. If
you have any questions or complaints regarding our rental policy, the
following agencies will provide you with information on fair-housing
laws:


California Department of Fair          U.S. Department of Housing & Urban
Employment & Housing                   Development
```
(fill in address and phone number of office nearest you)   *(fill in address and phone number of office nearest you)*

If despite your best efforts, you think your manager may use unlawful discriminatory practices to select or deal with tenants, you should immediately resume control of tenant selection yourself. Remember, if there is trouble, you will end up paying for it. If you aren't sure what your manager is doing, you might even wish to do some investigating. When you have a vacancy, have someone you suspect the manager might discriminate against apply for a vacancy. How does your manager treat them? Would you want to defend a lawsuit brought by the prospective tenant?

F. Insurance Coverage for Discrimination Claims

Your landlords liability policy will protect you for suits based on claims of illegal discrimination only if it covers illegal acts by you and your employees beyond the standard fire and personal liability protections (discussed in Chapter 12). Even then, there's some uncertainty over whether the law requires insurance companies to cover you for your intentional acts. In other words, if you set out to intentionally discriminate and someone you illegally discriminate against successfully sues you, your insurance company may resist paying a lawyer to defend you in court and/or paying off the judgment against her.

Co-Tenants, Sub-Tenants and Guests

Conscientious landlords go to a lot of trouble to screen prospective tenants. All those sensible precautions, however, may do you no good if unapproved tenants move in, in addition to, or in place of, the people you chose. You may have trouble getting the new tenants to pay rent or pay for damage to the unit. And if worst comes to worst, you may have a tough time evicting them.

Fortunately, you can usually avoid these problems, and others, by spelling out co-tenants' and sub-tenants' rights and responsibilities in your lease or rental agreement.

Common Definitions

Co-tenants. Two or more tenants who rent the same property under the same lease or rental agreement, both being jointly liable for the rent and other terms of the agreement. Roommates and couples who move in at the same time are generally co-tenants. (See Section A.)

Sub-tenant. Someone who rents all or part of the premises from a tenant (not the landlord). The tenant continues to exercise some control over the rental property, either by occupying part of the unit or intending to retake possession at a later date. (See Section B.)

Sublease. A written or oral agreement by which a tenant rents to a sub-tenant. (See Section B.)

Roommates. Two or more unrelated people living under the same roof and sharing rent and expenses. (See Section C.)

Assignment. The transfer by a tenant of all his rights of tenancy to another who is the "assignee." (See Section D.)

 Our form agreements (Chapter 2) spell out these respective rights and responsibilities by:

- Limiting the number of people who can live in the rental property (Clause 9)

- Allowing only the persons whose names appear on the lease or rental agreement, along with their minor children, to live in the property (Clauses 1 and 9)

- Requiring the landlord's written consent in advance for any sublet, assignment of the lease or rental agreement, or for any additional people to move in (Clause 10)

- Allowing tenants' guests to stay no more than 10 days in a six-month period (Clause 9)

A. Renting to More than One Tenant

When two or more people rent property together, and all sign the same rental agreement or lease (or enter into the same oral rental agreement where they move in at the same time), they are co-tenants. Each co-tenant shares the same rights and responsibilities under the lease or rental agreement. Neither co-tenant may terminate the other's tenancy.

1. Co-Tenants' Responsibilities

In addition to having the same rights and responsibilities, each co-tenant is independently obligated to abide by the terms of the agreement. All co-tenants are legally responsible to the landlord.

a. Paying Rent

All co-tenants, regardless of agreements they make among themselves, are liable for the entire amount of the rent.

EXAMPLE

James and Helen sign a month-to-month rental agreement for an $800 apartment. They agree between themselves to each pay half of the rent. After three months, James moves out without notifying Helen or the owner, Laura. As one of two co-tenants, Helen is still legally obligated to pay all the rent (although she might be able to recover James's share by suing him in small claims court).

Laura has three options if Helen can't pay the rent:

1. Laura can give Helen a Three-Day Notice To Pay Rent or Quit, and follow through with an unlawful detainer (eviction) lawsuit if Helen fails to pay the rent or move within the three days.

2. If Helen offers to pay part of the rent, Laura can legally accept it, but Helen is still responsible for the entire rent. (It's common for roommate co-tenants to offer only "their portion" of the rent, when in fact they're all jointly liable for it all.) See Chapter 3 for a detailed discussion of accepting partial rent payments.

3. If Helen wants to stay and find a new co-tenant, Laura can't unreasonably withhold her approval (see Section D, below). She should, however, have the new co-tenant sign a rental agreement (see Section C, below.)

b. Violations of the Lease or Rental Agreement

In addition to paying rent, each tenant is responsible for any co-tenant's action that violates any term of the lease or rental agreement—for example, if one co-tenant seriously damages the property, or moves in an extra roommate or a pit bull, contrary to the lease or rental agreement. The landlord may hold all co-tenants responsible and terminate the entire tenancy with the appropriate three-day notice, even though some of the co-tenants objected or weren't consulted by the prime offender.

If you have to evict a tenant for a breach other than for nonpayment of rent (in which case you would evict all the tenants), you must decide whether to evict only the offending co-tenant or all of them. Your decision will depend on the circumstances. You obviously don't want to evict an innocent co-tenant who has no control over the troublemaker who just brought in a pit bull—assuming the innocent one can still shoulder the rent after his roommate is gone. On the other hand, you may wish to evict all co-tenants if they each share some of the blame for the problem.

2. Disagreements Among Co-Tenants

Usually, co-tenants orally agree between themselves to split the rent and to occupy certain parts of the property, such as separate bedrooms. Not infrequently, this sort of arrangement goes awry. If the situation gets bad enough, the tenants may start arguing about who should leave, whether one co-tenant can keep the other out of the apartment or who is responsible for what part of the rent.

The best advice we can give landlords who face serious disagreements between co-tenants is not to get involved, as a mediator or otherwise. If one or more co-tenants approach you about a dispute, explain that they must resolve any disagreements between themselves. Remind them that they are each legally obligated to pay the entire rent, and that you are not affected by any agreement they have made among themselves.

If one tenant asks you to change the locks to keep another co-tenant out, tell the tenant that you cannot legally do that. If the tenant fears violence from a co-tenant, refer her to the local superior court, where the tenant can seek a restraining order. A landlord may not lock out one tenant unless a court has issued an order that the tenant stay out.

B. Sub-Tenants and Sublets

A sub-tenant is a person who rents all or part of the property from a tenant and does not sign the rental agreement or lease with the landlord. A sub-tenant is someone who either:

- rents (sublets) an entire dwelling from a tenant who moves out temporarily—for the summer, for example; or

- rents one or more rooms from the tenant, who continues to live in the unit.

If a tenant moves out permanently and transfers all his rights under the lease or rental agreement to someone else, that new tenant is not a sub-tenant; he is an "assignee." See Section D, below, on assignments.

1. Sub-Tenants' Responsibilities

The tenant functions as the sub-tenant's landlord. The sub-tenant is responsible to the tenant for whatever rent they've agreed on between themselves. The tenant, in turn, is the one responsible to the landlord for the rent. Even a tenant who has temporarily moved out and sublet the property is liable to the landlord—this is true even if the landlord, for convenience, accepts rent from the sub-tenant. Doing so does not make the sub-tenant the landlord's tenant.

A sub-tenant has an agreement only with the tenant. This is true even if the sub-tenant is approved by the landlord. Because the sub-tenant does not have a separate agreement with the landlord, he does not have the same legal rights and responsibilities as a tenant (described in Section A, above) .

The sub-tenant's right to stay depends on the tenant's right to stay. So if you can legally evict the tenant, then you can evict the sub-tenant. (See Section C.2, below.) For example, if the lease or rental agreement prohibited the tenant from subleasing without the landlord's consent and the tenant brought in a sub-tenant anyway, the tenant would be in breach of the lease. The landlord could evict the tenant for this breach, and since the sub-tenant's right to stay depends on the tenant's right to stay, the landlord could evict the sub-tenant also.

See Section C below for a discussion of how a sub-tenant can gain the same legal rights as a tenant.

2. If a Tenant Wants To Sublet

Our lease and rental agreement require the tenant to obtain the landlord's written consent in advance in order to sublet or bring in additional people to live in the unit.[1] (See Chapter 2, Clause 10.) This will let you control who lives in your property.

Suppose you wish to accommodate a tenant who wants to sublet her apartment for six months while she is out of the area, and you approve of the proposed sub-tenant. You may want to insist on signing a written agreement with the new person for the six-month period that the original tenant plans to be away. That makes the new person a regular tenant who is liable to you for the rent, not a sub-tenant who is liable to someone else (the tenant). You should also get the original tenant to sign a document, such as the sample below, stating that he agrees to terminate his tenancy.

---

[1]If you want to collect damages against a tenant with a lease or rental agreement who leaves early, you cannot unreasonably withhold your consent to sublet. See Chapter 19 for a discussion of this concept of the landlord's obligation to mitigate damages.

SAMPLE TERMINATION OF TENANCY AGREEMENT

Termination of Tenancy Agreement

I, _____ name of tenant _____, agree that my

tenancy at _____ address _____,

entered into on _____ date of original agreement _____, 19 ____, will

terminate _____ effective date of termination _____ 19 ____.

Date: _____ date _____   *signature of tenant* _____
                                     Tenant

This will terminate the tenancy so that you can rent the property to the new tenant. Then, when the first tenant returns and the second leaves, you can again rent to the first, using a new agreement.

If the original tenant is uneasy about you renting to the sub-tenant directly, and asks you how he will get the unit back if the new tenant is reluctant to leave at the end of six months, as long as your lease or rental agreement prohibits subletting, your answer should be a polite version of, "That's your problem." Think of it this way. By asking you the question, your tenant admits that he doesn't completely trust the new tenant, even though he selected her. You don't want to be in the middle of this type of situation. It's better that the original tenant bear the brunt of any problem—if there is one—than you.

If, on the other hand, you want to hold the original tenant's place and allow him to come back after the six months, you just may consent to the sublet. Although the sub-tenant won't be liable to you for the rent, you can still evict her if the rent isn't paid. If the rent continues to be paid but the sub-tenant won't leave after the six months, it's up to the tenant to evict the sub-tenant.

C. When a Tenant Brings in a Roommate

Suppose love (or loneliness) strikes your tenant and he wants to move in a roommate? Assuming your lease or rental agreement restricts the number of people who can occupy the unit (as ours does in Clause 9), the tenant must get your written permission for additional tenants.

1. Giving Permission for a New Roommate

Obviously, your decision to allow a new co-tenant should be based on whether or not you believe the new person will be a decent tenant. If your tenant proposes to move in a new person who has a good credit record and isn't otherwise objectionable, and there is enough space in the unit, you may want to allow the new roommate. (See Chapter 9.B, for overcrowding standards which you may lawfully impose.) If the new occupant is a spouse, and there's no problem with overcrowding, be careful before you say no. Refusal to allow your tenant to live with her spouse could be considered illegal discrimination based on marital status.

San Francisco's Master Tenants

A San Francisco ordinance has created the legal category of "master tenant" in shared housing situations. A master tenant (or tenants) is the person who signs the lease or rental agreement with and is responsible to the landlord. This master tenant then has the legal authority to rent to others, unless, of course, the lease or rental agreement (as ours do) prohibits subletting without the landlord's prior written consent. Oddly, the master tenant can charge other tenants (who have not signed the lease or rental agreement) more rent than he himself pays (up to the rent control level) and can evict other tenants whenever he pleases, with no need to demonstrate just cause for eviction under the city rent control ordinance. (See Chapter 4 for a discussion of just cause provisions.)

We do not believe that it's wise for a San Francisco landlord to get into a master tenant/sub-tenant situation for two reasons: First, a sub-tenant is responsible only to the master tenant for rent, and not to the owner. As a property owner, you are better protected when all occupants of the property are jointly liable to you, as co-tenants on the same lease, for all the rent. Second, the law in this area is complicated by conflicting rent board rules.

You should insist that all co-tenants sign a lease or rental agreement with you, and if one or more leaves, deal directly with their replacements.

a. Raising the Rent

When an additional tenant comes in, it is perfectly reasonable for you to raise the rent (or the security deposit), if it is allowed under local rent control laws. To accomplish this, have both the original and new occupants sign a new lease or rental agreement at the higher rent, as co-tenants. (Failing that, if it's a month-to-month rental agreement, you could increase the rent by a 30-day notice, if you don't care

about the new occupant being a sub-tenant who is not liable to you directly.) Obviously, more people living in a residence means more wear and tear and higher maintenance costs in the long run. Also, a rent increase when an additional tenant moves in should cause little hardship to the current occupants, who will now have someone else to pay part of the rent. The new rent should be in line with rents for comparable units occupied by the same number of persons.

If the existing tenant has a fixed-term lease, you will have to change the lease to raise the rent. As long as the lease allows a set number of tenants and requires your permission before the tenant moves in new people, you can legally withhold your permission until the lease is changed to provide a reasonable rent increase. If the property is subject to rent control, however, you may need to petition the local rent control board for permission to increase the rent based on an increased number of occupants. (For more on rent control, see Chapter 4).

b. Prepare a New Rental Agreement or Lease

If you allow a new person to move in, make sure he becomes a full co-tenant by preparing a new lease or rental agreement for signature by all tenants. Do this before the new person moves in to avoid the possibility of a legally confused situation.

EXAMPLE

Chung, the landlord, rents to Suzy. Olaf moves in later without signing a rental agreement or lease. Because Olaf has not entered into a contract with Chung, he starts with no legal rights or obligations to Chung. His obligations to Suzy, as her sub-tenant, depend on their agreement regarding the rent and Suzy's right to live in the apartment. Suzy is completely liable for the rent and for all damage to the premises, whether caused by Olaf or herself, because she, not Olaf, entered into a contract with Chung. Olaf would only be liable for damage he negligently caused, if Chung could prove that Olaf was the one who caused the damage.

2. Guests and New Occupants You Haven't Approved

Our form rental agreement and lease allow guests to stay overnight up to ten days in any six-month period without your written permission. (See Clause 9.) The value of this clause is that a tenant who tries to move someone in for a longer period has violated the lease or rental agreement, which gives you grounds for eviction (discussed below).

If a tenant simply moves a roommate in on the sly—despite the fact that your lease or rental agreement prohibits it—or it appears that a "guest" has moved in clothing and furniture and begun to receive mail at your property, take decisive action right away. If you don't take action, the roommate will turn into a sub-tenant—one you haven't screened or approved of.

A sub-tenant, despite not having all the rights of a tenant, is entitled to the same legal protection, if you try to evict, to which a tenant is entitled. Such an individual must be:

- served a separate Three-Day Notice To Pay Rent or Quit
- named in an eviction lawsuit
- served with legal papers.

This is a lot more hassle in the event of an eviction, and a tremendous hassle if you never learn the sub-tenant's name. (For details on the eviction process, see Chapter 18 and *Landlord's Law Book, Volume 2: Evictions.*)

One option is to make the roommate or guest a tenant by preparing a new lease or rental agreement. You may also increase the rent or the security deposit, unless that's prohibited by any applicable rent control ordinance. If you do not want to rent to the guest or roommate and if that person remains on the premises, make it clear that you will evict all occupants based on breach of the occupancy terms of the lease.

If your tenant has a month-to-month tenancy in an area where there is no rent control, and the tenant is not renting under a federal housing program, you can always give the tenant a 30-day notice to leave, without giving any reason. (We discuss terminations of tenancy in Chapter 18.)

 If you live in a rent control area requiring just cause for eviction, see Chapters 4 and 18.C. Generally, moving in an illegal tenant should qualify as just cause to get rid of the tenant under most rent control ordinances, because it is a significant violation of the terms of the tenancy. However, you can't evict a tenant until you first give him notice of the problem—in this case, the additional person—and a chance to cure it—get the new person to leave.

Note on discrimination against guests: You cannot legally object to a tenant's frequent overnight guests based on your religious or moral views. (See Chapter 9.) It is illegal to discriminate against unmarried couples, including gay or lesbian couples, in California.

D. If a Tenant Leaves and Assigns the Lease to Someone

A lease or rental agreement gives a tenant certain rights—the most important, obviously, is to live in the premises. If the tenant permanently gives or sells all these rights to someone else, it's called an "assignment," because the tenant has legally assigned all her rights to someone else. For example, a tenant who signs a year lease may leave after six months and assign the rest of the term to a new tenant.

The lease and rental agreement at the back of this book (Clause 10) forbid assignments without the owner's consent.

Assignments aren't quite as bad as sublets, however, as far as a landlord is concerned. The new occupant (assignee) is responsible to the landlord for everything the original tenant was liable for—even without an agreement between the assignee and the landlord.[2] Someone who sublets, however, is responsible only to the first tenant and not the landlord.

Nevertheless, even if your lease or rental agreement allows a tenant to assign his rights, it's better to have the new tenant sign a new lease or written rental agreement. That will make your legal relationship with the new tenant clear.

If you unreasonably withhold your consent for a tenant to assign her rights—for example, six months left under a year-long lease—you may lose your right to recover the rest of the rent due under the lease. A landlord is obligated to limit his loss by renting to a suitable new tenant as soon as possible. (This is discussed in detail in Chapter 19.) If you turn down an acceptable prospect found by the tenant, you won't be able to sue the original tenant for not paying the rent for the rest of the lease term.

---

[2]CC § 822.

The Landlord's Duty To Repair and Maintain the Property

The tenant's responsibility to pay rent depends on the landlord's fulfilling his legal duty to maintain the property and keep it in good repair. Obviously, then, keeping up rental property should be something every landlord takes seriously.

This chapter describes the specific housing standards and laws landlords must follow and outlines strategies for dealing with tenants who threaten to or withhold rent because of the property's condition. It also provides practical advice on how to stay on top of your repair and maintenance needs and minimize financial penalties and legal problems.

Related Topics

- Lease and rental agreement provisions on landlords' and tenants' responsibilities for repair and maintenance: Chapter 2

- Delegating maintenance and repair responsibilities to a manager: Chapter 6

- Highlighting repair and maintenance procedures in a move-in letter: Chapter 7

- Landlords' liability for a tenant's injuries from defective housing conditions: Chapter 12

- How to avoid illegal retaliatory evictions after tenants complain about housing conditions or withhold rent: Chapter 15

- Evicting a tenant who damages the property: Chapter 18

A. State and Local Housing Standards

Several state and local laws set housing standards for residential rental property. These laws require landlords to put their rental apartments and houses in good condition before renting them and keep them that way while people live there. Here is a list of the laws you need to know about:

California's State Housing Law—also known as the State Building Standards Code.[1] This law lists property owners' general obligations to keep residential property in livable condition. It refers, in turn, to very specific housing standards contained in the Uniform Housing Code enforced by local governments.

Local ordinances. Most cities and counties have adopted and enforce the Uniform Housing Code (UHC), which contains very specific housing standards—for example, regarding the heating system. The UHC is available in most libraries and may be purchased from the International Conference of Building Officials, 5360 South Workman Mill Road, Whittier, CA 90601, 213-699-0541. A few cities, including Los Angeles, have enacted ordinances with additional requirements. Check with the building inspector or health department of the city or county where you own rental property to see which local laws apply to your property.

Civil Code Section 1941.1. This state statute lists the minimum legal requirements for a rental dwelling to be "tenantable," or legal to rent to tenants. If you don't meet these requirements—for example, if the property has a leaking roof—a tenant may well be excused from paying all or part of the rent. (See Section F, below.) Many of the Section 1941.1 requirements overlap those set forth in the State Housing Law and local ordinances. (For example, Civil Code Section 1941.1 requires only that "hot water" be available, while the UHC requires that the water heater be able to heat the water to 120° Fahrenheit.)

Health and Safety Code Section 13113.7. This statute requires all units in multi-unit buildings to have smoke detectors.

---

[1]Health and Safety Code Sections 17900 through 17995, including regulations contained in Title 25 of the California Code of Regulations.

Housing Standards Under State Law

Rental housing standards set out in Civil Code Section 1941.1 and in the State Housing Law as set out in the Uniform Housing Code (UHC) include:

- A structure that is weatherproof and waterproof; there must be no holes or cracks through which wind can blow, rain can leak in or rodents can enter (CC § 1941.1).

- A plumbing system in good working order (free of rust and leaks), connected to both the local water supply and sewage system or septic tank. The landlord is not responsible for low pressure, contamination or other failures in the local water supply—his obligation is only to connect a working plumbing system to the water supply (CC § 1941.1).

- A hot water system capable of producing water of at least 120° Fahrenheit (CC § 1941.1 and UHC).

- A heating system that was legal when installed (CC § 1941.1), and which is maintained in good working order and capable of heating every room to at least 60° Fahrenheit (UHC).

- An electrical system that was legal when installed, and which is in good working order and without loose or exposed wiring (CC § 1941.1). There must be at least two outlets, or one outlet and one light fixture, in every room but the bathroom (where only one light fixture is required). Common stairs and hallways must be lighted at all times (UHC).

- A lack of insect or rodent infestations, rubbish or garbage in all areas (CC § 1941.1). With respect to the living areas, the landlord's obligation to the tenant is only to rent out units that are initially free of insects, rodents and garbage. If the tenant's housekeeping attract pests, that's not the landlord's responsibility. However, the landlord is obliged to keep all common areas clean and free of rodents, insects and garbage at all times.

- Enough garbage and trash receptacles in clean condition and good repair to contain tenants' trash and garbage without overflowing before the refuse collectors remove it each week (CC § 1941.1).

- Floors, stairways, and railings kept in good repair (CC § 1941.1).

Each rental dwelling must, under both the UHC and the State Housing Law, have the following:

- A working toilet, wash basin and bathtub or shower. The toilet and bathtub or shower must be in a room that is ventilated and allows for privacy.

- A kitchen with a sink, which cannot be made of an absorbent material such as wood.

- Natural lighting in every room through windows or skylights having an area of at least one-tenth of the room's floor area, with a minimum of 12 square feet (three square feet for bathroom windows). The windows in each room must be openable at least halfway for ventilation, unless a fan provides for ventilation.

- Safe fire or emergency exits leading to a street or hallway. Stairs, hallways and exits must be litter-free. Storage areas, garages and basements must be free of combustible materials.

- Health and Safety Code § 13113.7 requires smoke detectors in all multi-unit dwellings, from duplexes on up. Apartment complexes must also have smoke detectors in the common stair wells .

Illegal clauses in leases or rental agreements. A landlord cannot escape his duty to keep rented property in good repair and properly maintained by trying to make it the tenant's responsibility. However, the tenant and landlord can agree that the tenant is solely responsible for repairs and maintenance in exchange for lower rent.[2] (We discuss how in Chapter 2.) But any lease or written rental agreement provision by which a tenant agrees to give up his rights to a habitable home or allegedly pays less than the normal rent in exchange for assuming the landlord's duties of maintenance and repair is illegal and unenforceable.[3] (See Section F, below, for a discussion of a tenant's rights to withhold rent and sue when a landlord fails to keep the rental property in a habitable condition.)

B. Enforcement of Housing Standards

The State Housing Law and local housing codes are enforced by the building department of the city (the county, in unincorporated areas). Violations creating immediate health hazards, such as rats or broken toilets, are handled by the county health department.

---

[2]CC § 1942.1. Also see *Knight v. Hallsthammar*, 29 Cal. 3d 46 (1981).

[3]Also see *Green v. Superior Court* (1974) 10 Cal. 3d 616.

Fire hazards, such as trash in the hallways, are also dealt with by the local fire department.

If you establish a system for tenants to regularly report on maintenance and repair needs and if you respond quickly when complaints are made (we show how in Section J below), you may never have to deal with these local agencies.

1. Inspections by Local Agencies

A local building, health or fire department usually gets involved when a tenant complains. The agency inspects the building and requires the owner to remedy all violations found, including any the tenant didn't complain about.

In some cases, a tenant's complaint about a single defect can snowball, with the result that several agencies require the landlord to make needed repairs. For example, say a tenant complains to the health department about a lack of heat. During its inspection, the health department observes an unsafe stove and an unventilated bathroom. The health department notifies the fire department about the stove and the building department about the bathroom which then do their own inspections.

Some cities don't wait for tenants to complain. They routinely inspect rental property for compliance with local law.

State and local agencies don't enforce Civil Code Section 1941.1 which requires a rental unit to be "tenantable." It is enforced by the tenant through the withholding of rent and other remedies, described in Section F below.

2. Failure To Comply With Repair Orders

If you fail to make any repairs demanded by local officials, the city or county may bring a lawsuit, or even criminal charges, against you. Violations of the State Housing Law are misdemeanors, punishable by a fine of up to $1,000 ($5,000 for a second offense within five years) and up to six months' imprisonment.[4] For very serious violations due to "habitual neglect of customary maintenance" that endanger "the immediate health and safety of residents or the public," the maximum penalty is a $5,000 fine and up to a year in jail or both, for each violation. (In 1987, a Los Angeles slumlord with a history of failing to make needed repairs was sentenced to two years in jail.[5])

You may be required to pay "relocation benefits" to tenants who must move in order for you to effect repairs.[6] (The tenant's right to move out is discussed in Section H below.) You may even be disallowed from claiming state income-tax write-offs associated with the property, including interest, taxes and depreciation on the building.[7]

In addition to penalties assessed by governmental agencies, the tenant may sue you if you don't make necessary repairs. (Section I below discusses lawsuits by tenants for defective conditions.) Tenants can even ask the court to appoint a receiver, who would be authorized to collect rents, manage the property and supervise the necessary repairs.[8]

A tenant may also withhold rent if you fail to make necessary repairs. In fact, if you haven't made repairs within 60 days after being ordered to by a government agency, the tenant is automatically entitled to withhold rent. See Sections F and G below.

The Los Angeles Rent Escrow Account Program

Under the Rent Escrow Account Program (REAP), Los Angeles tenants may in some circumstances pay rent directly into a city-managed escrow account if the owner fails to make repairs ordered by the local building or health department within 60 days after receiving written notice to repair.

If the repairs aren't completed on time, the Department of Housing Preservation and Production requests the owner to appear at an informal conference to explain the delay. If the Department of Housing isn't satisfied, a REAP advisory committee, consisting of representatives of the housing, building and fire departments, can recommend that the City Council impose a rent escrow. A landlord can appeal this recommendation to a hearing officer. If the hearing officer also recommends imposition of the escrow, the matter then goes to the City Council for the ultimate decision.

If the City Council orders it, tenants may pay their rents into the city escrow program. As long as tenants do so, they cannot be evicted for nonpayment of rent. (Needless to say, a 30-day notice of termination of tenancy would seem retaliatory at this stage, and Los Angeles's rent control law requires a landlord to show just cause for eviction.) Also, a landlord whose building has been put under REAP is prohibited from passing on the costs of repairs in the form of higher rents, as is normally allowed under the city's rent control ordinance.

With city authorization, repairs can be paid for by the escrow program administrator out of the escrow. However, taxes and mortgage payments cannot be made out of the escrow. After all required repairs have been made, any money left over is returned to the landlord, minus an administrative fee.

Obviously, the best way to avoid REAP is to quickly respond to repair orders by local authorities. Failing that, be cooperative and conciliatory at the informal conference, stressing your willingness to make needed repairs. If any of the problems were caused by tenants, you should point that out. If your building is recommended for REAP and you believe some of the defects were caused by tenants, you should see an attorney about appealing for a formal hearing before a hearing officer.

---

[4]Health and Safety Code §§ 17995 -17995.5.

[5]*People v. Avol*, Los Angeles County Superior Court No. CR-A23579 (1987).

[6]Health and Safety Code § 17980.7.

[7]California Revenue and Taxation Code §§ 17299 and 24436.5.

[8]Health and Safety Code § 17980.7.

C. Maintenance of Appliances and Other Amenities

State and local housing laws deal with basic living conditions only—heat, water and weatherproofing, for example. They do not deal with "amenities"—other facilities that are not essential but make living a little easier. Examples are drapes, washing machines, swimming pools, saunas, parking places, intercoms and dishwashers. The law does not require the landlord to furnish these things, but a landlord who does might be required to maintain or repair them—not by state and local housing laws, but by her own promise to do so.

The promise might be express or implied. When the lease or rental agreement says that the landlord will repair certain things or maintain them a certain way, the promise is express. When the landlord (or a manager or agent) says or does something that seems to indicate the landlord would be responsible for repairing or maintaining something, the promise is implied. Here are some typical examples of implied promises.

EXAMPLE 1

Tina sees Joels ad for an apartment, which says "heated swimming pool." After Tina moves in, Joel stops heating the pool regularly, because his utility costs have risen. Joel has violated his implied promise to keep the pool heated. (Joel should avoid ad language that commits him to such things.)

EXAMPLE 2

When Joel's rental agent shows Tom around the building, she goes out of her way to show off the laundry room, saying, "Here's the laundry room—it's for the use of all the tenants." Tom rents the apartment. Later the washing machine in the laundry room breaks down, but Joel won't fix it. Joel has violated his implied promise to maintain the laundry room appliances in working order.

EXAMPLE 3

Tina's apartment has a built-in dishwasher. When she rented the apartment, neither the lease nor the landlord said anything about who was to repair the dishwasher if it broke. The dishwasher has broken down a few times and whenever Tina asked Joel to fix it, he did. By doing so, he has established a "usage" or "practice" that the landlord—not the tenant—is responsible for repairing the dishwasher.

If you violate an express or implied promise relating to the condition of the premises, the tenant may sue you for money damages, usually in small claims court. The tenant cannot repair the appliance and deduct the cost from the rent (see Section E below). Whether the tenant may legally use rent withholding in this situation is not yet clear. However, if the breach of promise really cuts into what the tenant had a right to expect, and affects the habitability of the unit, a court may allow a tenant to withhold rent.[9]

Rent control note. A decrease in promised services may be considered an illegal rent increase. (See Chapter 14.F.)

D. The Tenant's Responsibilities

State law also requires tenants to use rented premises properly and keep them clean. Specifically, Civil Code Section 1941.2 requires the tenant to:

Keep the premises as "clean and sanitary as the condition of the premises permits." For example, a tenant whose kitchen had a rough, unfinished wooden floor that was hard to keep clean would not be able to keep the floor bright, shiny and spotless.

Properly operate gas, electrical and plumbing fixtures. Examples of abuse include overloading an electrical outlet, flushing large foreign objects down

---

[9]In *Secretary of HUD v. Layfield,* 88 Cal. App. 3d Supp. 28 (1979), a court allowed rent withholding because of the landlord's failure to provide security, even though the lease had no express promise of security.

the toilet and allowing bathroom fixtures to become filthy.

Refrain from damaging or defacing the premises or allowing anyone else to do so.

Use living and dining rooms, bedrooms and kitchens for their proper respective purposes. For example, the living or dining room should not regularly be used as makeshift bedrooms.

If a tenant violates these requirements, the landlord is still responsible for the condition of the premises and can still be prosecuted for violating housing standards. But the tenant cannot withhold rent or sue the landlord if the tenant has contributed to the poor condition of the premises.[10]

EXAMPLE

Lance complains to his landlord, Gary, about a defective heater. When Gary's repairperson goes to fix the heater, he is confronted by an overwhelming smell of garbage and mildewed laundry. Lance cannot sue Gary for failing to fix the heater until and unless Lance cleans house, even though the foul smell didn't cause the heater to break. Lances failure to keep the place clean and sanitary obviously inter–feres substantially with his landlord's attempt to fix the heater.

To protect a landlord against a tenant's careless damage to the property, our form lease and rental agreements make the tenant financially responsible for repair of damage caused by the tenant's negligence or misuse. (See Clause 17, Chapter 2.) That means, where the tenant or his friends or family cause damage—for example, a broken window, a toilet clogged with children's toys or a refrigerator that no longer works because the tenant defrosted it with a carving knife—it's the tenant's responsibility to make the repairs or to reimburse the landlord for doing so.

EXAMPLE

By his own sorrowful admission, Terry, angry over the loss of his job, puts his fist through a window. As as result, a cold wind blows in, cooling off Terry, if not his temper. Terry can't withhold rent to make his landlord fix the window, since Terry caused the problem in the first place. However, under state and local law, Terry's landlord is still responsible for fixing the window, after which he can and should bill Terry for the repair.

If a tenant refuses to repair or pay for the damage he caused, the landlord can sue the tenant, perhaps in small claims court, for the cost of the repairs. If the tenancy is from month to month in a non-rent-controlled area, you may also want to consider a 30-day termination notice. If the damage is very severe, such as numerous broken windows or holes in the wall, you can use a three-day notice and sue for eviction on the basis that the tenant has "committed waste" to the property. (See Chapter 18.B and *The Landlord's Law Book, Volume 2: Evictions.*)

You could also evict based on the tenant's breach of the lease or rental agreement provision forbidding damage to the premises (Clause 17), but you would have to give the tenant a chance to correct the problem. On the other hand, if you proceed under the theory that the tenant has committed waste, your three-day notice need not give this option—ex-

---

[10]CC §§ 1929 and 1942 (c).

cept in some rent-controlled cities.[11] In any eviction case based on a three-day notice, you must also be able to establish that the damage was truly caused by the tenant's neglect, or you will lose the case and have to pay the tenant's court costs and attorney fees.

Common Myths About Responsibilities for Repairs

Paint. *No law requires a landlord to repaint the interior every so often. So long as the paint isn't actually flaking off, it should comply with the law. If you fail to remove flaking paint and an injury results—for example, a child becomes ill from eating lead-based paint chips— a court may find you liable because of your carelessness. (We discuss negligence in Chapter 12.)*

Drapes and Carpets. *As for carpets and drapes, so long as they're not sufficiently damp or mildewy to constitute a health hazard, and so long as carpets don't have dangerous holes that could cause someone to trip and fall, the landlord isn't legally required to replace them.*

Windows. *Quite a few landlords think a tenant is responsible for all broken windows. This is not true. A tenant is responsible only if she or her guest intentionally or carelessly broke the window. If the damage was outside the tenant's control, however— for example, because a burglar, vandal or neighborhood child broke a window—the landlord is responsible for fixing the window.*

E. The Tenant's Right To Repair and Deduct

Under certain circumstances a tenant can, without the landlord's permission, have a defect repaired and withhold the cost of the repairs from the following month's rent.[12] (A tenant can also just move out of an untenantable premise—see Section H.)

This is commonly called the "repair-and-deduct" remedy. It is subject to the following restrictions:

- The defect must be related to "tenantability." In other words, the problem must be at least somewhat serious and directly related to health or safety. Examples are broken heaters, stopped-up toilets and broken windows.

- The defect or problem must not have been caused by the careless or intentional act of the tenant or a guest. Thus, a tenant cannot use this remedy to replace a window he broke himself.

- The amount the tenant withholds must be less than one month's rent.

- The tenant can use this remedy no more than twice in any 12-month period.

- Before having the repair done, the tenant must give the landlord or manager "reasonable" notice of the problem, either orally or in writing.

Of all these rules, the rule that the tenant give "reasonable" notice is the one most open to interpretation. According to Civil Code Section 1942 (b), reasonable notice is presumed to be 30 days. But it can be a lot less for an urgent problem, such as a defective heater in winter, a leaky roof during the rainy season or a stopped-up toilet any time.

---

[11]CCP § 1161(4).

[12]CC § 1942.

EXAMPLE 1

Phil complains to his landlord, Linton, that the kitchen sink faucet drips slightly. Under their rental agreement, the landlord is responsible for the water bill. Since Linton pays for the water, and since Phil can close his bedroom door at night to block out the noise, the dripping faucet isn't a serious problem. Phil must give Linton 30 days to change the faucet washer before he can have a plumber do it and deduct the cost from his rent.

EXAMPLE 2

In July, Pam tells her landlord, Lorraine, that she was treated to some April showers in her living room three months earlier, due to a leaky roof. Unless it suddenly starts raining regularly in the middle of summer, this problem, though serious, isn't urgent. Pam must wait at least 30 days before she can take the repair into her own hands.

EXAMPLE 3

On a cold Monday in January, Frank tells his landlord, Regina, that the heater no longer works. By Wednesday night, Regina still hasn't fixed the heater. In the meantime, Frank and his family must sleep in a 45-degree apartment. So, on Thursday, after only two days, Frank has the heater fixed at a cost of $100. In February, Frank deducts this amount from his rent. Regina sues to evict Frank for non-payment of rent. The judge decides that two days' notice was reasonable under the circumstances, and Regina loses. She must pay not only her court costs and attorney fees, but Frank's as well.

If it comes to a fight, reasonable notice will be defined by a judge, not by the landlord. And going to court over this sort of dispute, unless the tenant's behavior was truly outrageous, is not a productive way to arrive at a decision.

A landlord's best bet is to set up a good responsive maintenance system and stick to it. We discuss this in more detail in Section J, below. And remember, in deciding whether the tenant acted unreasonably, consider how much it would have cost you to make the same repair. Obviously, a tenant who pays $200 for a simple toilet repair that should have cost only $40 is acting more unreasonably than one who paid $80 for a repair you could have accomplished for $50.

F. The Tenant's Right to Withhold Rent When the Premises Aren't Habitable

The repair-and-deduct remedy isn't the only legal way a tenant can withhold part or all of the rent from a landlord who doesn't properly maintain residential property. A tenant can also legally refuse to pay all or part of the rent if the unit falls short of the minimum requirements for a habitable dwelling, as set forth in Civil Code Section 1941.1. In addition, one court decision seems to have expanded tenants' rights by allowing them to withhold rents for reasons not even addressed by Civil Code Section 1941.1.[13]

1. What Justifies Rent Withholding

Under California law, every landlord makes an implied promise that a dwelling will be fit for human habitation—whether or not that promise is written down in a lease or rental agreement.[14] If the landlord does not keep the place in a habitable condition at all times, he is said, in legalese, to have "breached the implied warranty of habitability." That breach justifies the tenant's withholding of rent.

For a tenant to legally withhold rent, the problems must not have been caused by the tenant, and the following must be true:

- The defects must be serious ones that threaten the tenant's health or safety.

- The tenant must have given the landlord reasonable notice of the problem.

[13]For example, in *Secretary of HUD v. Layfield*, 88 Cal. App. 3d Supp. 28 (1979), an appellate court ruled that a tenant could withhold rent if the landlord failed to provide adequate security patrols, even though there is no law requiring security guards.

[14]*Green v. Superior Court*, 10 Cal. 3d 616 (1974).

a. Severity of Problems

A tenant can withhold rent only if the premises have "substantial" defects. Examples of substantial defects are a bathroom ceiling that has collapsed and not been repaired, rats, mice and cockroaches infesting the building, several rooms lacking heat in the winter or lack of hot water. Fairly trivial defects, such as leaky water faucets or cracked windows or plaster, aren't enough to violate the implied warranty of habitability.

EXAMPLE

Wilbert rents a two-bedroom apartment from Molly for $600 a month. Because the toilet makes an occasional running sound until Wilbert jiggles the handle, Wilbert withholds an entire month's rent. Molly gives Wilbert a three-day notice and follows this with an eviction lawsuit. The judge decides that because the problem wasn't substantial, Wilbert had no right to withhold the rent, and gives Molly a judgment for the $600 rent, court costs and possession of the property. (Because Molly handled her own suit, he is not eligible for attorney fees.)

b. Notification of the Landlord

A tenant who wants to withhold rent must first notify the landlord or manager of the problem. There are, however, no precise notice requirements—for example, that the notice be in writing or delivered a certain way. There is also no definite rule as to how much time the landlord has to fix the problem after receiving notice of it, except that 60 days is too long under any circumstances.[15] In other words, the tenant can give the notice orally or in writing, but before withholding rent on account of a defect, she must give the landlord a "reasonable" time to respond. If the question ends up in court, what's reasonable will be defined by a judge.

Some tenants make false claims to try to get out of paying some rent or avoid being evicted. For ex-

ample, a tenant who is simply unable to pay the rent calls the health department to complain about—and exaggerate the effect of—a minor plumbing problem that she previously tolerated and never complained about to the landlord. The best way to thwart these kinds of tenants is to establish and follow a good maintenance and inspection system. (See Section J, below.)

2. How Much Rent a Tenant Can Legally Withhold

If the landlord does not fix a serious problem within a reasonable time, the tenant can withhold rent. But how much? Theoretically, the tenant can withhold as much rent as the defect lowers the value of the property. But as a practical matter, the tenant can withhold as much rent as the landlord—or a judge, if the case gets to court—will allow under the circumstances. A judge will make a decision based on what she thinks is the rental value of the premises, in light of the seriousness of the defect.

Judges use various criteria to determine what's a reasonable amount of rent to withhold. For example, if a particular defect makes one or more rooms unlivable—such as a bad roof leak during the rainy season—the judge will probably pro-rate the rent based on the reduced number of livable rooms or floor space.

---

[15]CC §§ 1942.3 and 1942.4.

EXAMPLE

For $900 a month, Lou rents a two-bedroom house to Ken. The house is heated by two wall heaters, one in the kitchen and one in a bedroom, which is somewhat isolated in a separate wing. In late November, the bedroom heater stops working. This leaves one end of the house, including one of the two bedrooms and a bathroom, chilly and uncomfortable. On December 1, the heater is still not fixed, so Ken refuses to pay Lou any rent. Lou finally fixes the heater on December 15 and demands the rent. Ken claims he only owes $450, half the rent for December. Lou takes the $450, but insists on the other $450, giving Ken a three-day notice to pay up or get out, followed by an unlawful detainer (eviction) lawsuit when Ken doesn't respond.

After hearing the case, the judge decides that since half the house was livable for the first half of December, Ken should also pay half of that half-month's rent, or $225, in addition to what he already paid. However, because Ken was correct in withholding rent, he wins the suit and can stay in his apartment if he pays Lou the $225, and Lou must pay Ken's court costs and attorney fees. However, if Ken doesn't pay the additional $225, Lou wins, getting a judgment for the $225, possession of the property, and court costs.

In other situations, the judge might base a decision on the testimony of a person in the real estate industry who knows about what the property, with all defects, would rent for to an informed tenant. Or, a judge may even guess at an amount due the tenant as compensation for the inconvenience or annoyance of putting up with a problem—such as water leaking into the living room during winter months—and subtract that from the monthly rent.

If you do end up in court, be prepared to prove the following:

- The claimed defect was not so serious or substantial as to render the property untenantable.

or

- Even if the defect was substantial, you were never given adequate notice and a chance to fix it. (It is at this point that you should present your detailed complaint procedure to the court and show, if possible, that the tenant didn't follow it.)

or

- Assuming there was a substantial defect which wasn't fixed within a reasonable time (perhaps you were away and your manager screwed up), this defect justifies only the withholding of a small amount of rent because it didn't inconvenience the tenant much. For example, although an inoperable heater is a substantial defect, it won't cause the tenant too much discomfort in the summer; or perhaps a tenant who used a portable electric heater instead wasn't badly inconvenienced.

Court fights over rent withholding are covered in Section G.2 below.

G. The Landlord's Options if a Tenant Withholds Rent

When confronted with a tenant who withholds all or part of the rent, whether justifiably or not, most landlords almost reflexively turn to a lawyer to bring an eviction lawsuit. But even if the landlord eventually gets the tenant evicted, it is often only after considerable cost. In most eviction suits, the lawyers are the only clear winners. Even if the landlord gets a judgment for unpaid rent and attorney fees, these amounts often turn out to be uncollectible.

If you feel your tenant improperly deducted the costs of repairs from the rent or withheld rent—perhaps by giving you little or no notice—try working things out with the tenant. Failing that, if you feel strongly enough about it, sue the tenant for the deducted part of the rent, in small claims court or in a municipal court eviction lawsuit.

1. Working Out a Compromise

If you think the tenant is wrong, but sincere, and is not simply trying to make up an excuse for not paying rent, you may want to go along with the tenant's withholding or repair-and-deduct proposal. If, for example, the tenant uses the repair-and-deduct remedy, but you feel you were never given adequate notice, and could have had the problem fixed for $50 less than the tenant paid, it may make sense to drop the matter. Trying to evict the tenant will cost far more, and you may not win the suit.

This isn't to say you should roll over and accept any silly scheme a tenant invents. Set up a meeting with the tenant to review your repair procedures. Listen to any grievance the tenant has, and make sure that the next time there is a problem, you will be notified promptly. Obviously, if a tenant persists in being unreasonable, you will eventually have to get more assertive.

Or you may want to try to work out a compromise with the tenant. A compromise would certainly include repairing any defect having to do with any of the tenantability factors listed in Section A. You might also give the tenant a pro-rated reduction in rent for the period between the time the tenant notified you of the defect and the time it was corrected.

For example, suppose a leaky roof during a rainy month deprives a tenant of the use of one of his two bedrooms. If the tenant gave the landlord notice of the leak, and the landlord did not take care of the problem quickly, the tenant might be justified in deducting $300 from the $800 rent for that month. However, if the tenant didn't tell the landlord of the problem until the next month's rent was due, a compromise might be reached where the tenant bears part of the responsibility, by agreeing to deduct only $100 from the rent.

The first step in working towards a compromise with the rent-withholding tenant is to call him. Dropping over unannounced to talk may threaten the tenant and put him in a defensive posture. If you're reluctant to call, you might want to try a letter. See the sample letter below.

If you can't work something out with the tenant, consider mediation, where a neutral third party can help you arrive at a solution. Many cities have agreements with local nonprofit organizations which conduct mediation between landlords and tenants. These organizations can be extremely helpful in resolving disputes over the amount of rent (if any) it is reasonable to withhold, the condition of the premises or the need for repairs. (We discuss mediation in some detail in Chapter 8.)

Many organizations that offer mediation also conduct arbitration, if the parties can't reach an agreement. In arbitration, a neutral third party makes a decision—just like a judge in court, but after a much less formal hearing. In binding arbitration, the parties agree in advance, in writing, to abide by the decision. If you and the tenant agree to binding arbitration, an informal hearing is held. Each person tells his or her side of the story, and an arbitrator reaches a decision, which is enforceable in court.

SAMPLE LETTER SUGGESTING COMPROMISE ON RENT WITHHOLDING

May 3, 199_

Tyrone McNab
Villa Arms, Apt. 4
123 Main Street
Monterey, California

Dear Mr. McNab:

I am writing you in the hope we can work out a fair compromise to the problems that led you to withhold rent. You have rented a unit at the Villa Arms for the last three years and we have never had a problem before. Let's try to resolve it.

To review briefly, on May 1, Marvin, my resident manager at Villa Arms, told me that you were refusing to pay your rent because of several defective conditions in your apartment. Marvin said you had asked him to correct these problems a week ago, but he hasn't as yet attended to them. Marvin states that you listed these defects as some peeling paint on the interior wall of your bedroom, a leaky kitchen water faucet, a running toilet, a small hole in the living room carpet and a cracked kitchen window.

I have instructed Marvin to promptly arrange with you for a convenient time to allow him into your apartment to repair all these problems. I am sure these repairs would already have been accomplished by now except for the fact that Hank, our regular repairperson, has been out sick for the last ten days.

Because of the inconvenience you have suffered as a result of the problems in your apartment, I am prepared to offer you a pro-rated rebate on your rent for ten days, this being the estimated length of time it will have taken Marvin to remedy the problems from the day of your complaint. As your monthly rent is $450, equal to $15 per day, I am agreeable to your paying only $300 rent this month.

If this is not acceptable to you, please call me at 555-1234 during the day. If you would like to discuss any aspect of the situation in more detail, I would be pleased to meet with you at your convenience. I will expect to receive your check for $300, or a call from you, before May 10.

Sincerely,

Sandra Schmidt

2. Court Fights Over Rent Withholding

Rent withholding almost always comes before a judge in the context of an unlawful
detainer (eviction) lawsuit. In response to the tenant's failure to pay rent, the landlord serves a Three-Day Notice To Pay Rent or Quit, and when the tenant fails to do either, files suit.

A tenant normally has the burden of convincing a judge that the withholding was reasonable, unless the landlord took more than 60 days to fix any defect that a local health or building-inspection department official insisted be repaired following an inspection.[16] In this case, the burden falls on the landlord to prove the tenant was wrong to withhold rent.

Here's how judges typically rule on rent withholding:

- If the judge rules that the tenant had no right to withhold any rent at all, the landlord will win a judgment for the unpaid rent, court costs (and attorney fees if the rental agreement had an attorney fees clause) and possession of the property, and the tenant's eviction will be ordered.

- If the judge decides that the tenant had the right to withhold rent and withheld the correct amount, she will rule for the tenant, who will be able to stay in the property. In addition, the landlord will be responsible for paying the tenant's court costs, and attorney fees if the lease or rental agreement has an attorney fees clause.

- If the judge decides that the tenant had a right to withhold rent, but not as much as he did, it's a little more complicated. The judge will normally order the tenant to pay the difference, sometimes giving the tenant up to five days to do so. If the tenant pays the landlord within the time the judge allows, he gets to stay, wins the lawsuit, and can even get a judgment against the landlord re-

quiring him to pay court costs.[17] (This is because the tenant had a valid complaint, even if he did withhold too much rent, and the tenant shouldn't be penalized for having been unable to guess the right amount of rent to withhold.)

- On the other hand, if the tenant doesn't pay the difference between how much rent he withheld and what he should have withheld, the landlord will then win a judgment for that amount, possession of the property, court costs, and attorney fees, if the lease or rental agreement has an attorney fees clause and the landlord was represented by an attorney. (See Chapter 18 for more on eviction lawsuits.)

⚠️ **Retaliatory eviction and rent increases are illegal.** Occasionally, a landlord, faced with a troublesome tenant who seems to be unreasonably asserting his legal remedies to the letter of the law—whether in the form of a complaint to local officials or the deduction of repair costs from the rent—gives the tenant a 30-day notice terminating the tenancy or raising the rent. A tenant can defend against this sort of eviction or rent increase on the basis that the landlord is illegally retaliating against him for exercising his rights.[18] (For a detailed discussion of retaliatory evictions, see Chapter 15.)

---

[16]CC §§ 1942.3 and 1942.4.

[17]See CCP § 1174.2 and *Strickland v. Becks*, 95 Cal. App. 3d Supp. 18, 157 Cal. Rptr. 656 (1979). This rule also applies to attorney fees if the applicable lease or rental agreement has an attorney fees clause. This is because CC § 1717(a) says that attorney fees provided for in a written contract are considered "costs of suit," and so are treated the same way as costs in this respect.

[18]CC § 1942.5. Also, in the cases of *S.P. Growers Assn. v. Rodriguez*, 17 Cal. 3d 719 (1976) and *Vargas v. Municipal Court*, 22 Cal. 3d 902 (1978), the California Supreme Court upheld the right of a tenant who sued a landlord to defend a subsequent eviction on the basis that it was motivated by the landlord's intent to retaliate against the tenant for having brought suit

H. The Tenant's Right To Move Out

In several circumstances, tenants have the right to move out because of defective conditions in the premises.

1. Asking Tenants To Move So Repairs Can Be Made

If local authorities sue a landlord who fails to repair code violations in a reasonable time, and a court rules that the property's conditions "substantially endanger the health and safety of residents," and the landlord must ask tenants to move in order to make repairs, the landlord must:

- Provide the tenant with comparable temporary housing nearby, or if that's not possible, pay her the difference between the old rent and the tenant's new rent elsewhere, for four months.

- Pay the tenant's moving expenses, including packing and unpacking costs.

- Insure the tenant's belongings in transit, or pay for the replacement value of property lost, stolen or damaged in transit.

- Pay the tenant's new utility connection charges.

- Give the tenant the first chance to move back into the old place when repairs are completed.[19]

2. The Tenant's Right To Move Out of Untenantable Premises

If there is a problem that allows a tenant to use the repair-and-deduct remedy (Section E, above), the tenant also has the option of simply packing up and leaving without further notice if the landlord fails to fix the problem in a reasonable time.[20] The tenant is not responsible for payment of any rent from the time the repair should have been made, even if due

under a long-term lease. In addition, the tenant is entitled to a pro-rated refund of any rent paid in advance, that covers the time during which the unit was in disrepair, and compensation for living in substandard housing.

EXAMPLE

On January 1, Lionel leases his house to Lisa for a year, and Lisa pays the first month's rent of $900. On February 1, Lisa pays the rent again, but the next day, the water heater springs a leak. Lisa tells Lionel about the problem, but Lionel does nothing. Several more anguished calls from Lisa, who has no hot water, produce no action. After fifteen days, Lisa simply packs up and leaves. She is probably acting reasonably and legally under the circumstances.

Not only is Lisa relieved of any further obligation under the lease, but she's also entitled to a refund of $450, representing the pro-rated rent for the second half of the month, plus her security deposit (less any lawful deductions). In addition, Lisa is entitled to a further rent reduction on account of having no hot water for the half month she was there. If Lionel and Lisa can't agree on this figure, a judge will have to decide when Lisa takes Lionel to small claims court.

I. The Tenants' Right To Sue for Defective Conditions

A landlord who fails to maintain property can also be sued by a tenant. By failing to repair defective conditions, the landlord breaches an implied term of the lease or rental agreement—that is, to provide a habitable dwelling. The tenant, whether he remains in the property or moves out, can sue the landlord for the following:

- Partial or total refund of rent paid while conditions were substandard;

- The value, or repair costs, of property lost or damaged as a result of the defect—for example, furniture ruined by water leaking through the roof;

---

[19]Health and Safety Code § 17980.7.

[20]CC § 1942.

- Compensation for personal injuries—including pain and suffering—caused by the defect;
- Attorney fees, if the lease or rental agreement has an attorney fees clause (as our form agreements do—see Chapter 2).

A landlord is not protected from liability by a provision in a lease or rental agreement in which the tenant purports to give up the right to sue the landlord. These clauses are illegal and will not be enforced by courts.

A landlord may not retaliate against a tenant who files a lawsuit and stays in the property. (See Chapter 15 for a discussion of retaliatory eviction.) It may seem inconsistent for a tenant to take the extreme step of suing his landlord and expect to remain on the property. Nevertheless, a tenant who sues and stays is exercising a legal right, and retaliation, such as with a 30-day rent increase or termination notice, is illegal and will give the tenant yet another ground on which to sue.[21]

J. Avoiding Repair and Maintenance Problems

A landlord's best defense against rent-withholding hassles is to establish a clear, easy-to-follow procedure for tenants to ask for repairs, to respond quickly when complaints are made and to make annual safety inspections. We recommend that you:

1. Use the written Landlord/Tenant Checklist form in Chapter 7 to check over the premises before new tenants move in.

2. Give tenants a form (Maintenance/Repair Request, discussed below) to report immediately plumbing, heating, weatherproofing or other defects or safety problems—both in the tenant's unit and in common areas such as hallways and parking garages.

3. Twice a year, give your tenants a checklist on which to report any potential safety hazards or maintenance problems that might have been overlooked. See the Semi-Annual Safety and Maintenance Update, described below.

4. Keep a written log (or have your property manager keep one) of all complaints (including those made orally) and correspondence and how and when they were handled.

5. Notify the tenant in writing if repairs will take more than 48 hours, excluding weekends.

6. Once a year, inspect all rental units, using the Landlord/Tenant Checklist as a guide. See Annual Safety Inspection, described below.

7. Give every tenant a copy of your complaint procedure and safety and maintenance system. This should be part of a move-in letter, described in Chapter 7.

8. Place conspicuous notices about your complaint procedures in several places around your property.

9. Remind tenants of your policies and procedures to keep your building in good repair as part of every written communication. Be sure to include a brief review of the complaint procedure.

For example, at the bottom of all routine notices, rent increases and other communications, a landlord might remind tenants of the following:

"It is the policy of the management to properly maintain your apartment unit. If you have any questions or complaints regarding your unit or the building, please direct them to the manager between 9 A.M. and 6 P.M., Monday through Saturday, either by calling 555-9876 or by coming to the office with a completed Maintenance/Repair Request form. In case of emergency during non-business hours, call 555-6789."

This system gives you a several benefits. First, it allows you to fix little problems before they grow into big ones. Specifically, it helps you communicate with tenants who do have legitimate problems and creates

---

[21]See CC § 1942.5.

a climate of cooperation and trust that can work wonders in the long run.

And at least as important, it provides you with an excellent defense when it comes to those few unreasonable tenants who seek to withhold rent for no adequate reason other than their disinclination to pay. (In addition, if you need to establish that the repair problem is phony, you may want to have the repairperson who looked at the "defect" come to court to testify about it.) You may still have to go to court to evict them, but your carefully documented procedures will help you accomplish this with a minimum of time and expense.

If you regularly solicit comments about the condition of your rental property, a tenant who doesn't report a problem can't, legally, later refuse to pay the rent because of your failure to repair that problem. If you make it your normal business practice to save all repair requests from tenants, the absence of a request is evidence that the tenant has made no complaints.

Finally, this kind of repair and recordkeeping system can also help keep down your potential liability to your tenants in lawsuits based on injuries suffered as a result of allegedly defective conditions on your property—both because there are less likely to be injuries in the first place if your property is well maintained, and because in many situations an injured person must prove not only that they were hurt, but that you were negligent (unreasonably careless). This can be difficult to do if you adopt an extremely responsive repair scheme and stick to it. (Landlord liability for injuries is discussed in Chapter 12.)

EXAMPLE

Geeta owns a 12-unit apartment complex and encourages her tenants to request repairs in writing, using the Maintenance/Repair Request Form shown below. Most tenants use the form. One month, Ravi doesn't pay his rent, even in response to Geeta's three-day notice. When Geeta files an eviction suit, Ravi claims he withheld rent because of a leaky roof and defective heater Geeta supposedly refused to repair. At trial, Geeta testifies that she routinely saves all tenants' filled-out forms for at least one year, and that she has no record of ever receiving a complaint from Ravi, even though she supplied him with blank forms. The judge has reason to doubt Ravi ever complained, and rules in Geeta's favor.

1. Resident's Maintenance/Repair Request Form

One way to assure that defects in the premises will be reported by conscientious tenants—while helping to refute bogus tenant claims about lack of repairs—is to provide all tenants with a Maintenance/Repair Request form. Give each tenant two or three copies when they move in, explain how the form should be used to request specific repairs, and make it clear that more copies are available. If you have a resident manager, make sure she keeps an ample supply in her office.

Here is a sample Maintenance/Repair Request form and a tear-out copy is in the Appendix.

SAMPLE RESIDENT'S MAINTENANCE/REPAIR REQUEST

Resident's Maintenance/Repair Request

Date: _August 28, 199_

Address: _392 Main St., #401, Modesto_

Resident's Name: _Mary Griffin_

Phone (Home): _555-1234_

Phone (Work): _555-5678_

Problem: _Garbage disposal doesn't work_

Comments (including best time to make repairs): _Best times are after 6 PM or Saturday morning_

I authorize entry into my unit to perform the maintenance or repair requested above, in my absence, unless stated otherwise above.

Mary Griffin
Resident

- -

FOR MANAGEMENT USE

Work done: _Fixed garbage disposal (removed spoon)_

Time spent: _1/2_ hours

Date completed: _August 9_ , 19 ____

Unable to complete on _____, 19 ____ because:

Hal Ortiz
Owner/Manager

You should respond quickly to all complaints about defective conditions. This doesn't mean you have to jump through hoops to fix things that don't need fixing or to engage in heroic efforts to make routine repairs when fixing them in the normal course of business would be adequate. It does mean prompt action under the circumstances. If you're unable to take care of a repair right way, and it isn't of such a serious nature as to require immediate action, let the tenant know, in writing, why you won't be able to act immediately. Here's a sample Time Estimate for Repair and a tear-out copy is in the Appendix.

SAMPLE TIME ESTIMATE FOR REPAIR

Time Estimate for Repair

Stately Manor Apartments

October 10, 199

Jane Walker

123 Main Street, Apt. 12

San Jose, California

Dear Resident:

Thank you for promptly notifying us of the following problem with your unit:

Fixing the pilot light on your gas stove.

We expect to have the problem corrected on ___October 13___, 19 ___,
due to the following:

New pilot light element is out of stock locally, but has been ordered and will be delivered then.

We regret any inconvenience this delay may cause. Please do not hesitate to point out any other problems that may arise.

Sincerely,

Fred Tebbetts

Owner/Manager

If a tenant threatens to withhold rent, respond promptly in writing (see sample letter, below), telling him either:

a. When the repair will be made and the reasons why it is being delayed; or

b. That you do not feel there is a legitimate problem and that the complaint is simply a ploy to justify rent withholding. At this point, you might also consider suggesting that you and the tenant mediate the dispute. (See Section G.1.)

 Don't retaliate against complaining tenants. When landlords are confronted by tenants asking that repairs be made, they sometimes—especially when they feel the particular tenant is unreasonable or otherwise unpleasant—look around for some tenant misconduct to justify not making the repair. This is a mistake, unless the tenant's failure to maintain the property is fairly outrageous. It can result in legal problems which are out of proportion to the maintenance problem. A landlord's tit-for-tat response may escalate into rent withholding on the part of the tenant, necessitating a nasty eviction lawsuit. Even if a landlord is legally right and is judged so in court, the time and expense involved are unlikely to be worth it.

The better response is usually to fix the problem and try to work out a clear maintenance plan with the tenant for the future. If this fails, you may want to think about trying to get rid of the tenant. This is fairly easy to do, unless you are in a jurisdiction containing a rent control law with a just-cause-for-eviction provision or have a long-term lease. Still, you must be careful that your move to end the tenancy cannot be legally interpreted as retaliating against the tenant for making a legitimate complaint. See Chapter 15 for rules on retaliatory evictions.

SAMPLE LETTER WHEN TENANT THREATENS TO WITHHOLD RENT

Robin Lee
123 Davis Place
Venice, California

July 21, 199_

Bruce Moore
456 Springsteen Square
Apartment 7
Los Angeles, California

Dear Mr. Moore:

This is in response to your letter of July 19, in which you suggested the possibility of withholding your next month's rent if the bathroom toilet is not repaired.

I have ordered the replacement parts necessary to prevent the stopper from improperly seating and allowing water to run from the tank to the bowl. An order was necessary through ABC Plumbing Supply because I have been assured that the part is not available locally. I expect to receive the part within one week. Until then, the toilet still flushes and is usable, despite the running sound it makes.

As you will recall, I came to check the toilet on three occasions and found it perfectly operable. I suspect that the stopper only occasionally does not seat properly into the hole separating the toilet tank from the bowl. In any event, a jiggle on the flush handle when the toilet makes a running sound will correct the problem on the few occasions when the stopper fails to seat. The problem is a minor one which does not result in your unit being considered uninhabitable, and therefore does not justify rent withholding under California law. Accordingly, should you withhold rent on this basis, I will have no choice but to give you a three-day notice to pay rent or leave the premises, followed by an eviction suit if you fail to comply.

Sincerely,

Robin Lee
Owner/Manager

Privacy note. To gain access to make repairs, the landlord can enter the rental premises only with the tenant's consent, or after having given reasonable notice, presumed to be 24 hours. See Chapter 13 for rules and procedures for entering a tenant's home to make repairs and how to deal with tenants who make access inconvenient for you or your maintenance personnel.

2. Semi-Annual Safety and Maintenance Update

Another way to encourage your tenants to report needed repairs is to give them a Semi-Annual Safety and Maintenance Update on which to list any problems. Insisting that tenants return this Update twice a year should help you in court against a tenant raising a false "habitability" defense, particularly if the tenant did not note any problems on his most recently completed Update.

Here is a sample Semi-Annual Safety and Maintenance Update and a blank tear-out copy is in the Appendix.

3. Annual Safety Inspection

Some landlords perform annual "safety inspections" as part of their system for repairing and maintaining the property. For example, you might make sure that items listed on the Semi-Annual Safety and Maintenance Update—such as smoke detectors, heating and plumbing systems and major appliances—are safe and in working order.

A landlord cannot insist on such inspections against the tenant's will, even if a lease or rental agreement clause so provides. This is because the law does not allow the landlord to enter the dwelling against the tenant's will—even on 24 hours' notice—solely to perform inspections.[22] Any lease or rental agreement provision allowing for this is illegal and unenforceable.[23] Also, evicting a tenant because she refused to allow such an inspection would constitute illegal retaliatory eviction.[24]

However, most tenants will not object to yearly safety inspections if you're courteous about it—giving 24 hours' notice and trying to conduct the inspection at a time convenient for the tenant. If you encounter hesitation, just point out that you take your responsibility to maintain the property very seriously. Remind her that you'll be checking for plumbing, heating, electrical and constructional problems that she might not notice, which could develop into bigger problems later if you're not allowed to check them out.

---

[22]CC § 1954.

[23]CC § 1953(a)(1).

[24]CC § 1942.5(c).

SAMPLE SEMI-ANNUAL SAFETY AND MAINTENANCE UPDATE

Semi-Annual Safety and Maintenance Update

Please complete the following checklist and note any safety or maintenance problems in your unit or on the premises.

Please describe the specific problems and the rooms or areas involved. Here are some examples of the types of things we want to know about: garage roof leaks, excessive mildew in rear bedroom closet, fuses blow out frequently, door lock sticks, water comes out too hot in shower, exhaust fan above stove doesn't work, smoke alarm malfunctions, peeling paint and mice in basement. Please point out any potential safety and security problems in the neighborhood and anything you consider a serious nuisance.

Please indicate the approximate date when you first noticed the problem and list any other recommendations or suggestions for improvement.

Please return this form with this month's rent check. Thank you.

The Management

Name: _Mary Griffin_

Address: _392 Main St., #401_

_____Modesto, California_

Please indicate (and explain below) problems with:

Floors and floor coverings

Walls and ceiling

Windows, screens and doors

Window coverings (drapes, mini-blinds, etc.)

Electrical system and light fixtures

Plumbing (sinks, bathtub, shower or toilet)   Water pressure low in shower

Heating or air conditioning system

Major appliances (stove, oven, dishwasher, refrigerator)   Exhaust fan doesn't work

Basement or attic

Locks or security system   Front door lock sticks

Smoke detector

Fireplace

Cupboards, cabinets and closets

Furnishings (table, bed, mirrors, chairs)

Laundry facilities

Elevator

Stairs and handrails

Hallway and common areas

Garage

Patio, terrace or deck

Lawn, fences and grounds   Shrubs near back stairway need pruning

Pool and recreational facilities

Roof, exterior walls, and other structural

Driveway and sidewalks

Neighborhood

Nuisances   Tenant in #501 often plays stereo too loud

Other

Specifics of problems: _____

_____

_____

Other Comments: _____

_____

_____

February 1, 199 _____   *Mary Griffin* _____
Date   Tenant

- -

FOR MANAGEMENT USE

Action/Response: Fixed shower, exhaust fan and sticking front door
   lock on February 15. Pruned shrubs on February 21. Spoke with
   tenant in 501 about keeping stereo low on February 2.

_____

_____   _____
Date   Owner/Manager

Landlord's Liability for Dangerous Conditions

As a property owner, you are responsible for keeping the premises safe for tenants and guests. You must also be sure that conditions on the property don't bother neighbors. If you fall short in either of these obligations, you could be faced with a lawsuit from an injured tenant or angry neighbor.

Landlords may be liable for physical injuries caused by faulty premises, such as a broken step, inadequate lighting or substandard wiring. Tenants can sue for medical bills, lost earnings and pain and suffering in small claims court (up to $5,000), municipal court (up to $25,000) or superior court (where the sky's the limit).

A tenant or a neighbor may sue the landlord for damages for maintaining a legal nuisance—a serious and persistent condition that adversely affects the tenant's (or neighbor's) enjoyment of the property—even if no physical injury occurs. For example, a tenant, plagued by the stench of garbage scattered about because the landlord hasn't provided enough garbage cans for the apartment building, can sue the landlord for the annoyance and inconvenience of putting up with the smell. A tenant or neighbor—or a group of them—may sue a landlord who does nothing to evict a drug-dealing tenant.

We don't have the space here to show you how to fight a personal injury or nuisance lawsuit brought by a tenant. If you are sued, unless the suit is filed in small claims court, you'll need a lawyer. (See Chapter 8 for advice on choosing a lawyer. For advice on small claims court, see *Everybody's Guide to Small Claims Court*, by Ralph Warner (Nolo Press).)

We do, however, give you an overview of the legal and practical issues involved, which will help you reduce the likelihood that you will be sued or found liable.

Related Topics

- Lease and rental agreement provisions on landlords' and tenants' responsibilities for damage to premises, repairs and liability-related issues: Chapter 2

- How to minimize your liability for your manager's mistakes or illegal acts: Chapter 6

- Landlord's liability for intentional discrimination: Chapter 9

- How to comply with state and local housing laws and avoid safety and maintenance problems: Chapter 11

- Liability for invasion of privacy: Chapter 13

- Liability for retaliatory conduct against the tenant: Chapter 14

- Liability for illegal evictions: Chapter 17

A. Legal Standards for Liability

As a general rule, a landlord is liable to a tenant for any injury caused by a defect in the premises, unless the tenant caused the defect and the landlord didn't know about it.

An injured tenant may sue a landlord under several different legal theories. This section briefly discusses the most important ones, which landlords need to know about to protect themselves from lawsuits.

1. Negligence: The Landlord's Careless Acts

Negligence is the most common legal theory under which tenants or guests injured by a housing defect sue landlords. Negligence is behavior that is unreasonable, considering all the circumstances. If someone is injured or property is damaged as a result of your unreasonable acts, you are liable.[1]

What is unreasonable? If someone sues a landlord alleging an injury caused by a landlord's negligence, some of the issues considered by the judge or jury would be:

- whether or not the landlord could have foreseen such an injury

- the severity of the foreseeable injury

- whether the landlord knew (or should have known) of the dangerous condition

- how difficult it would have been to fix the dangerous condition

A tenant can prove a landlord was negligent by showing, for example, that the landlord ignored tenant complaints about a dangerous condition that subsequently caused injury.

Even absent tenant complaints, a tenant could show negligence with evidence that a landlord did not discover or fix defects that he could have discovered from a reasonable inspection.

A landlord who fails to exercise reasonable care is liable for an injury or loss occurring on the property whether the victim is a tenant or a visitor,[2] whether the injury occurred in an apartment or in a common area, such as a stairway or courtyard.

Here are some examples of injuries, for which courts have held a negligent landlord liable:

- Tenant falls off stairway due to a defective handrail.[3]

- Tenant trips over a rock on a common stairway not properly maintained by the landlord.[4]

- Tenant injured or property damaged by fire resulting from defective heater or wiring.[5]

Landlords are also legally responsible for the acts of a property manager or management company (discussed in Chapter 6), and may even be held liable for the acts of outside contractors whose actions result in common areas being maintained in an unsafe condition. So if a manager carelessly causes an injury, the landlord may end up footing the bill.

EXAMPLE

Mal is the on-site manager of an apartment building with several long corridors, through which the tenants and their guests must pass to get to their apartments. After a number of bulbs in hallway ceiling light fixtures burn out, several tenants ask Mal to replace them. Despite repeated tenant complaints, as well as recent muggings in nearby buildings, Mal doesn't get around to replacing the bulbs. One evening, Vinny, a visitor, is severely beaten and robbed while walking through a poorly lit hallway to his friend's apartment.

Mal, as well as the building's owner, Layne, will almost surely be held liable for the full extent of Vinny's injuries. Having been informed of the problem, Mal and Layne might have prevented (or at least discouraged) the attack with proper maintenance of the lighting system. Had there been no complaints preceding the attack, Mal and Layne might still be found liable, on the theory that it was negligent under the circumstances not to make regular inspections to make sure hallway lighting was adequate.

---

[1]CC § 1714.

[2]The California Supreme Court ruled that a landlord has the same duty of care to maintain the property regardless of whether the person injured is a tenant, guest or visitor. *Rowland v. Christian,* 69 Cal. 2d 108, 70 Cal. Rptr. 97 (1968).

[3]*Brennan v. Cockrell,* 35 Cal. App. 3d 796, 111 Cal. Rptr. 122l (1973).

---

[4]*Henrouille v. Marin Ventures,* 20 Cal. 3d 512, 143 Cal. Rptr. 247 (1978).

[5]*Evans v. Thompson,* 72 Cal. App. 3d 978, 140 Cal. Rptr. 525 (1977), and *Golden v. Conway,* 55 Cal. App. 3d 948, 128 Cal. Rptr. 69 (1976).

Landlord liability for injuries to tenants by third parties and issues involving drug-dealing tenants are discussed in Sections B and C below.

Fences

It is negligent for a landlord not to fence off a dangerous condition on the property, such as a swimming pool, from children. One court ruled, however, that a landlord did not have to fence off property against busy thoroughfares.[6]

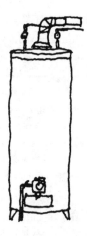

a. Negligence Per Se: Landlord Liability for Violating a Law

When a tenant is injured because the landlord violated a law designed to protect tenants, the landlord is presumed to be negligent. Lawyers call this "negligence per se."

Probably the most common example of landlords' negligence per se is failure to install smoke alarms when required by state or local law. For example, a tenant who suffers injury or damage as the result of a fire that would have been extinguished

sooner, but wasn't because the landlord violated a law requiring smoke detectors in the building, does not have to convince a court that the landlord was negligent. The law assumes the landlord was negligent because he violated the law.

A number of cities and counties now require smoke detectors and fire extinguishers in all rental units. And all multiple-unit dwellings, from duplexes on up, offered for rental after January 1987, must be equipped with smoke detectors.[7] Violation is a criminal offense. The ordinances of many cities and counties also require rental units to be equipped with deadbolt locks.

Illegal Lease/Rental Agreement Provisions

Landlords used to be able to protect themselves from most suits brought by tenants by putting a clause in all leases and rental agreements which freed the landlord of responsibility for injuries suffered by a tenant, even those caused by the landlord's negligence. Often called an "exculpatory clause," this provision is no longer legal or enforceable.[8] (See Chapter 2.E.)

---

b. Defenses to Negligence Charges

Even if a landlord has been negligent in failing to correct a problem that caused harm to a tenant or guest, there are still a few defenses and partial defenses available in some situations.

Comparative negligence. If the injured tenant or visitor was also guilty of negligence—for example, if he was drunk, or didn't watch his step when he tripped on a rock on the landlord's poorly maintained common stairway—the landlord's liability is proportionately reduced. For example, if a judge or jury ruled that a tenant who had suffered $10,000 in damages was equally (50%) as negligent

---

[6]*Brooks v. Eugene Berger Management Corp.*, 215 Cal. App. 3d 1611, 264 Cal. Rptr. 756. (1989).

[7]Health & Safety Code § 13113.7.

[8]CC § 1953.

as the landlord, the tenant would recover only $5,000.

Assumption of risk. A person who knows the danger of a certain action and decides to take the chance anyway is said to "assume the risk" of injury. If he is injured as a result, he is not entitled to recover anything, even if another person's negligence contributed to the injury.

EXAMPLE

A tenant falls and is injured when he takes a shortcut over a sidewalk that has fallen into disrepair and is littered with broken pieces of cement. The tenant knew that the sidewalk was dangerous. The tenant sues the landlord claiming the landlord was negligent not to fix the sidewalk. Because he knew the possible risk, the tenant might not win a lawsuit against a landlord based on the landlord's negligence.

2. Liability for Hidden Defects in the Property

A landlord is liable for injuries suffered by a tenant— or others—due to defects in the property. Even a landlord who has exercised all reasonable precautions to keep the property safe is liable for tenants' personal injuries. It doesn't matter that the injury occurs through no fault of the landlord whatsoever or even if the defect was hidden.

a. The Theory of Strict Liability

This liability without fault is called "strict" liability. To prevail in a case based on strict liability, a plaintiff (the person suing) does not have to prove that the defendant (the person sued) was negligent. All the injured person must prove is that a defect in the property caused the injury. The rationale behind the rule is that an injured tenant would find it impossible to prove that a landlord knew or should have known of a defect. The landlord, as the owner of the premises, is made responsible for anything that

happens on the property to injure an innocent tenant or third party.

Landlords are strictly liable for defects in the premises as a result of a California Supreme Court case, *Becker v. IRM Corp.*[9] In the *Becker* case, the Court ruled that the owner of a 36-unit apartment complex was liable to a tenant seriously injured by a shower door made of dangerous untempered glass. The landlord was liable even though untempered glass appears no different from tempered safety glass used in modern shower doors, and even though the landlord could not have known about the untempered glass. When the landlord purchased the building, shower doors on only five of the apartment units contained safety glass. Those in the other units contained untempered glass—which no one but a glass expert could tell was unsafe.

Under standard negligence rules, the landlord would not have been liable. He did not act unreasonably (negligently) by failing to replace the untempered glass doors with safety glass. The landlord never knew about the kinds of glass installed in his units; the previous owner didn't tell him, and no tenant had ever complained—until, of course, one was seriously injured in the accident that made this hidden defect apparent.

The *Becker* strict liability rule does not mean that a landlord is liable every time a tenant is injured. Strict liability applies only to defects in the property.

EXAMPLE

Tanya is injured when the defective heater in her apartment catches fire. Under the theory of strict liability, her landlord is responsible for Tanya's injury, even though the landlord had no knowledge of the defect and even though a contractor, rather than the landlord or his employee, had installed the heater.

---

[9]38 Cal. 3d 454, 213 Cal. Rptr. 213 (1985).

b. Defenses in Strict Liability Cases

A landlord sued for an injury caused by a defect in the premises may be able to defend the lawsuit based on the tenant's assumption of the risk (see Section 1.b, above) or misuse of the premises. For example, if the tenant overloaded or otherwise misused an appliance that caused a fire, the landlord may not be held liable. But if the misuse was foreseeable, the landlord may still be liable.[10] It is very hard to make generalizations about strict liability, because every case depends on its own unique circumstances.

Property Exempt from Strict Liability Rule

One California appellate court has ruled that strict liability does not apply to owners who rent out their own single-family residence on a temporary basis, or when the defect is apparent. In that case, a tenant was hurt because of a stairway handrail that ended slightly short of a stairway, in violation of the Uniform Building Code.[11] This case, which flies in the face of the Becker case by limiting strict liability to larger landlords, may not be followed by other courts. Because a lower-ranking court of appeal may not legally overrule a Supreme Court case, trial courts may either wind up being more confused or simply ignore the case as an aberration.

---

[10]In strict liability cases against manufacturers, the manufacturer has been found liable when the consumer misused the product in a way that the manufacturer should have foreseen. The same rule will probably be applied to landlords.

[11]*Vaerst v. Tanzman*, 222 Cal. App. 3d 1535, 272 Cal. Rptr. 503 (1990).

3. Breach of Warranty and Fraud

A landlord who makes an express promise in a written lease or rental agreement, such as to provide heightened security, is very likely to be held liable to any tenant injured if the promise isn't kept. Even without such a written provision, a landlord who advertises or tells tenants or prospective tenants about some special feature of the property, such as a security system, is likely to be held liable for a tenant's injury.

EXAMPLE

A landlord advertises the elaborate security measures of an apartment complex, including special locks, private security-guard patrols and 24-hour television monitoring in halls and lobby. The landlord will probably be liable to a tenant who is attacked or robbed if the security precautions aren't as good as advertised or are cut back because there has been a complete absence of violent incidents or burglaries. In some situations, the landlord would probably not be held liable absent the claims of special security devices in the first place.

4. The Landlord's Reckless or Intentional Acts

A landlord who injures someone as the result of an intentional or reckless act is liable for the injury or property damage. "Reckless," generally, means extremely careless regarding an obvious defect or problem. When a landlord has been aware of a long-existing and dangerous defect, but neglected to correct the problem, the landlord is guilty of recklessness, not just ordinary carelessness.

Intentional injuries are rarer, but they do occur. For example, if the landlord or manager intentionally inflicted emotional distress on the tenant, the tenant may sue for compensation for emotional upset and mental suffering.[12] How much will a tenant win? Whatever the jury decides the tenant deserves.

In such cases, a judge or jury may award "punitive" damages—extra money over and above the amount required to compensate the victim. Punitive damages are designed to punish a person guilty of injuring someone through reckless or intentional conduct, with an eye toward preventing similar conduct in the future.[13] Punitive damages are not covered by any type of insurance, and a landlord who is hit with a punitive damages award will always have to pay for it out of his own pocket.

B. Injuries to Tenants by Third Parties

A landlord's duty to keep premises safe includes taking reasonable measures to protect tenants and visitors from assault. If a landlord's or manager's negligence results in injury to a tenant or visitor from an intentional or criminal act, the landlord may be liable.

Remember, you are not negligent if you did everything a reasonable person would do, under the circumstances, to prevent injury. Generally, if a tenant is injured by a violent act that you could neither foresee nor prevent, you will not be legally liable.

EXAMPLE

Pat, a tenant in a small apartment complex, goes downstairs to the well-lit and locked laundry room accessible only by keys issued to each tenant. Pat does not lock the door. While she is loading her wash, a stranger bursts in, followed by another person wielding a gun. A gunfight ensues in the laundry room and Pat is injured by a stray bullet. Pats landlord will probably not be held responsible for Pat's injuries because the owner took the security precaution of keeping the laundry room locked, the lighting was good, and no other violent incidents had occurred there that would have made the owner realize greater precautions were necessary.

Here are some cases in which landlords have been held liable for tenants' injuries and property damage caused by other tenants or third parties on the property. All involved situations that the landlord might have guarded against. (See Section C for related cases of landlord liability involving drug-dealing tenants.)

- Tenant's visitor killed in dim, empty parking area with broken security system and a history of violent crimes.[14]

- Tenant robbed and assaulted in dimly lit common area where landlord knew or should have known about earlier robberies and assaults. [15]

- Tenant raped as a result of poor security or lighting in common areas, or after complaining of defective locks in apartment.[16]

- Tenant's visitor bitten by another tenant's vicious dog. The landlord was found to be liable for doing nothing about the dog, even though he knew it

[12]*Stoiber v. Honeychuck,* 101 Cal. App. 3d 903 (1980).
[13]CC § 3294.

[14]*Gomez v. Ticor,* 145 Cal. App. 3d 622, 193 Cal. Rptr. 622 (1983).

[15]*Penner v. Falk,* 153 Cal. App. 3d 858, 200 Cal. Rptr. 661 (1984), and *Isaacs v. Huntington Memorial Hospital,* 38 Cal. 3d. 112, 211 Cal. Rptr. 356 (1985).

[16]*Olar v. Schroit,* 202 Cal. Rptr. 457 (1984), *Kwaitkowski v. Superior Trading Corp.,* 123 Cal. App. 3d 324, 176 Cal. Rptr. 494 (1981), and *O'Hara v. Western Seven Trees Corp.,* 75 Cal. App. 3d 798, 142 Cal. Rptr. 487 (1977).

was vicious.[17] The dog's owner was also held to be liable.

C. Liability for Drug-Dealing and Problem Tenants

A landlord can also be liable for damage or injury caused by problem tenants. In general, a landlord who fails to evict a tenant who seriously and continuously disturbs other tenants or neighbors can be sued for damages. These days, a problem of this sort is more often due to a tenant who deals or uses illegal drugs.

Trafficking in illegal drugs, most notably cocaine, has turned some formerly placid neighborhoods into battle zones. Drug dealing has hurt landlords and law-abiding residents alike. It causes lower rents and property values for owners and reduces safety and security for tenants and neighbors. To combat this seemingly intractable problem, the law is making landlords who rent to dealers liable for the interference with neighbors' enjoyment of their property.

The legal theory boils down to this: Landlords have a responsibility to keep their properties safe. That means it's up to the landlord to keep dealers out or, failing that, to kick them out pronto when they are discovered. When they allow drug-dealing tenants to annoy, frighten or even prey upon other tenants and neighbors, law-abiding tenants may start withholding rent, and neighbors or the government may bring costly lawsuits against the landlord.

1. Rent Withholding

Although no statute specifically allows it, one court has said that tenants may withhold rent if the landlord fails to protect their security.[18] (See Chapter 11.F, for details on rent withholding.) A landlord who does nothing about a tenant's drug-dealing is certainly open to this accusation.

Even if the landlord tried to evict the complaining tenants for nonpayment of rent, a court could well rule that the tenants were within their rights to withhold rent until the property again became reasonably safe and peaceful.

2. Lawsuits Against Landlords

Tenants and others who become victims of the crime that surrounds a drug dealer's home may also sue a landlord who does nothing to stop drug dealing on his property.

In recent years, exasperated neighbors have brought individual lawsuits against such landlords in small claims court—and won. Clusters of such claims can quickly add up to tens of thousands of dollars.

In 1989, 19 neighbors plagued by the crime, noise and fear generated by a crack house in Berkeley won small claims court judgments of $2,000 each (the California small claims maximum has since risen to $5,000) against an absentee owner who had ignored their complaints for years. In San Francisco, a similar rash of small claims suits cost a landlord $35,000. Soon after the verdicts, both landlords evicted the troublesome tenants.

In another example, a group of San Francisco neighbors successfully sued the city Housing Authority for allowing drug dealing and related crime to flourish on its property. They won a total of $25,500.[19]

---

[17]*Ucello v. Landenslayer*, 44 Cal. App. 3d 504, 118 Cal. Rptr. 741 (1975). For more on landlord liability for tenants' dogs, see *Dog Law*, by Mary Randolph (Nolo Press).

[18]*Secretary of HUD v. Layfield*, 88 Cal. App. 3d. Supp. 28 (1979).

[19]*San Francisco Chronicle*, November 2, 1990.

Many cities are also passing new laws aimed at getting drug dealing tenants evicted. The laws both make it easier for landlords to evict and punish landlords who sit by while drug dealing goes on in their property. In Los Angeles, for example, the police department can notify landlords when tenants are arrested or convicted of drug-related offenses. In Pasadena, a landlord who refuses to evict the tenants after a request from the city can be fined up to $5,000.

Local governments are also rigorously enforcing laws that allow them to sue landlords to have premises declared a public hazard or nuisance. Cities don't even have to pass any new laws. Under state law, cities and counties can bring suit to have a drug-dealer-infested building declared a public nuisance.[20]

Landlords can even lose their property altogether. Federal or local law enforcement authorities can take legal action to have housing used by drug dealers seized and turned over to the government, even if the owner's part in the crime is just to ignore it. In 1988, the San Mateo County district attorney brought just such a suit against the owner of a 60-unit drug haven in the city of East Palo Alto. The owner was fined $35,000 in civil penalties and had to shut the building down and pay tenants' relocation expenses.

3. Avoiding Problems

Given the risks of having a drug-dealing tenant, it makes sense for a landlord to do everything reasonably possible to avoid renting to drug dealers.

Screen prospective tenants carefully (as discussed in Chapter 1). Include a provision in leases or rental agreements that states that use of illegal drugs by tenants or their guests won't be tolerated. (See Clause 15, Chapter 2.)

Keep an eye on your property and listen carefully to complaints from other tenants or neighbors. If you suspect a problem, don't wait for neighbors or the city to sue you before you act. It's much cheaper to prevent a lawsuit than to fight one.

Start out by giving the tenant a stern written warning such as the one shown in Chapter 18.C. A written warning can lay the groundwork to show that you weren't negligent because you tried to correct the problem and build a case for eviction.

4. Getting Rid of a Tenant Who Deals Drugs or Disturbs Others

A landlord who inadvertently rents to a tenant who later becomes a serious disturbance to neighbors or other tenants—by dealing drugs or other outrageous behavior—will want to evict that person.

If a local rent control law or the lease requires it, however, you must have a reason to evict a tenant. Chapter 18.B.3 discusses how to evict a drug-dealing tenant.

D. Avoiding Liability for a Tenant's Injury

There are specific steps you can take to protect yourself from lawsuits and at the same time make your tenants' lives safer and hopefully happier.

---

[20]Health and Safety Code § 11570.

- To protect yourself from charges of negligence, regularly look for dangerous conditions on the property and fix them promptly.

- Adopt a policy of soliciting and responding quickly to tenant complaints about potential safety problems and nuisances. Back your policy up with a good recordkeeping system. (See Chapter 11.)

- Install and maintain basic security features: deadbolt locks, smoke detectors, fire extinguisher, window locks, outside lighting.

- Scrupulously keep up to date on, and comply with, all state and local safety laws.

- If you promise safety features (a locked gate to the pool, for example) or a security system, keep your promises to the letter. If something breaks, fix it fast.

- Be aware of threats to tenants' safety and security from third parties or other tenants. If a tenant is a serious nuisance to other residents or neighbors, evict him.

- Get liability insurance.

See Chapter 6 for how to protect yourself from your manager's mistakes and illegal acts.

E. Liability Insurance

Given today's litigious world, even the most conscientious landlord faces the possibility of losing her property as the result of lawsuits by tenants and others. Aside from avoiding problems (see Section D, above), the best way to minimize your potential financial loss is to purchase liability insurance.

A landlord can suffer financial ruin as the result of a tenant's or guest's injury. Not only will you have to compensate an injured person from having to pay judgments and settlements to tenants, but you'll almost inevitably run up legal fees if you must defend a personal injury lawsuit.

Liability insurance pays for injuries suffered by others as the result of defective conditions on the property, and the costs of defending personal injury lawsuits. Liability insurance is usually included in a fire and building insurance policy that covers damage to the property caused by fire, storms and vandalism, and various other rental property owners' insurance, such as protection from illegal acts by you or your manager or employees.

Insurance policies do not cover liability for punitive damages awarded in a lawsuit, or for intentional acts, such as beating up a tenant. (Illegal discrimination or retaliation are also treated by some insurers as being an intentional act not covered by the policy, but most liability insurers will at least pay for the defense of such lawsuits.) However, punitive damages are almost never awarded in landlord-tenant cases based on accidental injuries. Also, as a general rule, a landlord won't be liable for punitive damages if he refrains from extreme neglect and intentional wrongs against tenants and others.

When choosing insurance, always deal with insurance agents and brokers with good reputations in your community. Get recommendations from people who own property similar to yours, or from real estate people with several years experience—they will know who comes through and who doesn't.

Here are some tips when choosing liability and building insurance:

- Purchase high levels of liability coverage. Typical coverage is $300,000 for each occurrence, but buying more coverage is a very good idea. Personal injury damage awards, especially in large metropolitan areas, can be very high, and a million dollars' coverage does not cost a great deal more than $100,000 coverage.

- Make sure the liability policy covers not only physical injury but also libel, slander, unlawful and retaliatory or discriminatory eviction, wrongful arrest and invasion of privacy suffered by tenants and guests.

- Purchase non-owned auto liability insurance to protect yourself from accidents and injuries caused by your manager or other employee while running errands for you in their own automobile.

- Keep your fire insurance coverage equal to the value of your property. This may well be more than your bank or mortgage company requires you to purchase.

- Depending on where your property is located, you may want extended building insurance coverage for damage caused by flood, wind, hailstorms and earthquakes. Earthquake coverage should include liability coverage for injuries to tenants and others by inadequately secured falling structures and fixtures. Earthquake insurance on the building itself often has a very high deductible, in the tens of thousands of dollars, so as to cover only major damage, but it still is a good option if your building is highly susceptible to earthquake damage.

Landlords' Right of Entry and Tenants' Privacy

Next to disputes over rent or security deposits, the most emotional misunderstandings between landlord and tenants commonly involve conflicts between a landlord's right to enter the property—to maintain, repair, show for sale or rent, or just plain inspect it—and a tenant's right to be left alone to enjoy his home. What is so unfortunate is that many of these problems are unnecessary—they could easily be avoided if landlord and tenant understood and followed existing legal rules and common sense.

We can't help you if one of your tenants turns paranoid every time you want to inspect the furnace or fix the plumbing. We can make sure you know your legal rights and responsibilities, as well as offer you several management strategies that have worked well for other landlords.

The tenant's duty to pay rent is conditioned on the landlord's proper repair and maintenance of the premises. (See Chapter 11.) This means that, of necessity, a landlord must keep fairly close tabs on the condition of the property. For this reason, and because it makes good sense to allow landlords reasonable access to their property, the law clearly recognizes the right of a landlord to enter the premises under a number of defined circumstances.

This doesn't mean a landlord can enter a tenant's home at any time for any reason. Once you rent residential property in California, you must respect it as your tenant's home. You may enter it only under certain circumstances, which we discuss below. If you don't follow the legal rules regarding a tenant's privacy rights, the tenant could sue you or withhold rent. And an owner can be held liable for his property manager's disrespect of the tenant's right of privacy even if the owner never even knew about the manager's conduct.

Related Topics

- Recommended lease and rental agreement clauses for landlord's access to rental property and illegal provisions regarding landlord's rights of entry and inspection: Chapter 2

- How to make sure your manager doesn't violate tenants' right of privacy: Chapter 6

- Tenants' right of privacy and landlord's policy on guests: Chapter 10

- Procedures for respecting tenants' right of privacy while handling tenant complaints about safety and maintenance problems and conducting an annual safety inspection: Chapter 11

- Privacy issues regarding evictions: Chapter 15

- Entering premises which have been abandoned by a tenant: Chapter 19

A. The Landlord's Right of Entry

State law allows a landlord to legally enter rented premises while a tenant is still in residence in four broad situations:[1]

1. To deal with an emergency

2. When the tenant gives permission

3. To make needed repairs (or assess the need for them)

4. To show the property to prospective new tenants or purchasers.

A landlord's right to entry cannot be expanded, or the tenant's privacy rights waived or modified, by any provision in a lease or rental agreement.[2]

In most instances—except emergencies, abandonment (that is, when the tenant moves out with-

---

[1]CC § 1954.

[2]CC § 1953(a)(1).

out notifying the landlord) and invitation by tenant—a landlord can enter only during normal business hours and then only after reasonable notice, presumed to be 24 hours. A few clarifying points:

- Notice need not be in writing, but it's a good idea to give written notice—if the tenant later claims that you didn't follow legal procedures regarding right to entry, your copy of a written notice that you posted on the tenant's door is proof that you notified him in advance of your intention to enter.

- Normal business hours, customarily, are 9 A.M. to 5 P.M., Monday through Friday, but the statute doesn't give specific hours and days. You may want to change the permissible hours of entry to fit your particular needs. Our form lease and rental agreement define normal business hours as 9 A.M. to 6 P.M. Monday through Friday, and 9 a.m. to noon Saturday. (See Clause 14, Access for Inspection and Emergency, in our tear-out lease/rental agreement forms, Chapter 2.)

1. Entry in Case of Emergency

A landlord or manager can enter the property without giving notice to respond to a true emergency that threatens injury or property damage if not corrected immediately. For example, a fire, gas or serious water leak is a true emergency which, if not corrected, will result in damage, injury or even loss of life.

Here are some examples of situations in which it would be legal for the landlord or his manager to enter without giving the tenant notice:

- A tenant tells your on-site manager she hears screams coming from the apartment next door. After calling the police, your manager uses her pass key to enter and see what's wrong.

- Your manager sees water coming out of the bottom of a tenant's back door, but the tenant has changed the locks. It's okay to break in, to find the water leak.

- Smoke is pouring out the tenant's window. You call the fire department and use your master key—or break in if necessary—to check out the fire.

On the other hand, a landlord's urge to repair an important but non-life- or property-threatening defect (say a stopped-up drain) isn't a true emergency that allows entry without proper notice.

To facilitate your right of entry in an emergency, you are entitled to have a key to the premises, including keys to any locks the tenant may add. To avoid misunderstandings in this area, we recommend that you state this right in the lease or rental agreement (Clause 14 in our sample agreement forms in Chapter 2).

Don't change locks. It is unwise to change a lock installed by a tenant, even if you immediately give the tenant a key. This invites a lawsuit and false claims that you tried to lock the tenant out or stole the tenant's possessions.

But what if the tenant installs a security system or burglar alarm? If these systems involve alterations to the property—even cutting a hole in a door for a deadbolt lock—they can be restricted with a lease provision that forbids alterations without the landlord's consent. (Clause 16 of our form lease and rental agreement.)

Clause 14 also requires the tenant to provide instructions on how to disarm any burglar alarm system, if the landlord so requests. Not all landlords will want to know how to disarm tenant-installed security systems, given the idiosyncrasies of all the alarm systems on the market. In addition, if a tenant's goods are stolen and the alarm doesn't function, a landlord may wish he did not know the code or have the key.

The decision is yours. If an emergency occurs and you have to enter and shut off the alarm, but don't know how, rest assured. All you really need to know is the name and phone number of the alarm company, which is commonly printed on the alarm box itself. Call the alarm company and explain the situation.

If you do have to enter a tenant's apartment in an emergency, be sure to leave a note explaining the circumstances and the date and time you entered.

2. Entry With the Permission of the Tenant

A landlord can always enter rental property, even without 24 hours' notice, if the tenant agrees without pressure or coercion. If problems are only occasional and you have no special needs of entry, you can probably rely on a friendly telephone call to the tenant asking for permission to enter. (Don't be too insistent, lest the tenant claim you coerced this permission out of him.)

If the tenant agrees, but has been difficult and not always reliable in the past, you might even want to cover yourself by documenting his apparent willingness by sending him a confirmatory thank-you note afterwards, and keeping a copy for yourself. If this is met with unease or outright hostility, you should send a formal 24-hour notice. (See Section 3, below.)

If you have a maintenance problem that needs regular attending to—for example, a fussy heater or temperamental plumbing—you might want to work out a detailed agreement with the tenant covering entry.

3. Entry To Make Repairs

State law allows you and your repairperson to enter the tenant's home "To make necessary or agreed repairs, decorations, alterations, or improvements [and to] supply necessary or agreed services...." [3] In this situation, however, you must enter only during normal business hours and must give the tenant "reasonable notice." It is always wise to give your

tenant at least 24 hours' notice if possible. However, if there is a good reason—for example, a repairperson is available to make urgently-needed repairs on a few hours' notice—you can legally give a reasonable but shorter notice. Under the statute, the 24-hour notice period is presumed to be reasonable, but it is not absolutely required.

EXAMPLE

If Marcus, a landlord, arranges to have a repairperson inspect a wall heater at 2 P.M. on Tuesday, he should notify his tenant, Georgia, on or before 2 P.M. on Monday. But if Marcus can't reach Georgia until 6 P.M.—for example, she can't be reached at home or at work—less than 24 hours' notice is probably okay. Of course, if Georgia consents to Marcus's plan, the notice period is not a problem (see Section 2, above).

If you can't reach the tenant at home or at work to give 24 hours' notice of your intention to enter, it is a good idea to post a note detailing your plan on the tenant's front door, keeping a copy for your own records. Now, if the tenant doesn't receive the notice, it's because she didn't return home and you couldn't reach her at work, in which case, a 24-hour notice would have been impractical anyway.

In many situations, the 24-hour notice period will not be a problem, as your tenant will be delighted that you are making needed repairs and will cooperate with your entry requirements. However, as every long-time landlord knows, some tenants are uncooperative when it comes to providing reasonable access to make repairs, at the same time that they are extremely demanding that repairs be made. If you must deal with a tenant who is a stickler for her legal right of privacy, your best bet is to give at least 24 hours' notice of your intent to enter rather than try to shorten this period.

Here is a sample letter:

---

[3]CC § 1954.

SAMPLE LETTER REQUESTING ENTRY

November 19, 199_

Elliot Faust
123 Parker Street
Apartment 4
Berkeley, CA

Dear Mr. Faust:

Pleased be advised that in response to your complaint regarding the heater in your apartment, the management has arranged to have it repaired tomorrow, on Tuesday, November 20, at 2:00 P.M. We attempted to give you telephoned notice to this effect today between 9:00 A.M. and 5:00 P.M. Because we were unable to reach you at home or work, I am leaving this note on your door.

Sincerely,

Melba Tharpe, Manager

A fill-in-the-blank notice for entry to make repairs (or to show property) is shown in Section 4 below, and a tear-out form is in the Appendix.

Problems may arise if the repairperson shows up late—for example, if he's supposed to come at 4 P.M. and doesn't show up until 8 A.M. the next morning. A tenant who has been seriously inconvenienced is likely to be hostile and to stand on her rights. If it isn't possible to get the repairperson to come on time in the first place, call the tenant and explain the problem, and ask permission to enter later on. If the tenant denies permission, you'll have to give a second 24-hour notice.

Entry To inspect for needed repairs. As a general rule, the landlord may not insist on entering rented property simply to inspect it. A lease or rental agreement provision that allows this may be of no legal effect, as an unlawful waiver by the tenant of his or her right to privacy. On the other hand, since the law allows entry to keep the property maintained and repaired, occasional periodic inspections—such as one every six or twelve months to see whether anything needs to be repaired or improved—are probably okay, provided the tenant is given at least 24 hours' notice. But a landlord wishing to conduct an inspection should back off if the tenant objects. (See Chapter 11.J for a discussion of annual safety inspections.)

 Don't use the right to inspect improperly. A landlord can't use his right to access to harass or annoy the tenant. Repeated inspections, even when 24-hour notice is given, are an invitation to nonpayment of rent or a lawsuit. To clear up any uncertainty in this regard, your rental agreement or lease should spell this out, as do our sample agreements (see Clause 14, Chapter 2). Also, we recommend an annual safety inspection (see Chapter 11), to be mentioned in a move-in letter in (Chapter 7).

Waterbed exception. If the tenant has a waterbed, a landlord may inspect its installation periodically to make sure it complies with the standards a landlord may legally impose.[4]

4. Entry To Show Property

You may enter rented property to show it to prospective tenants toward the end of a tenancy or to prospective purchasers if you wish to sell the property. You must, however, comply with the business hours and reasonable notice provisions discussed above.

Below is a sample fill-in-the-blank notice that can be used for this type of situation, as well as for entry to make repairs. The Appendix includes a tear-out form to make extra copies.

a. Showing Property to Prospective New Tenants

A landlord who doesn't plan to renew a tenant's about-to-expire lease, or who has given or received a 30-day notice terminating a month-to-month tenancy, may show the premises to prospective new tenants during the last few weeks of the outgoing tenant's stay. It is not a good idea, however, to show property if a dispute exists over whether the current tenant has a right to stay. If there's a chance the dispute will end up in court as an eviction lawsuit, the current tenant may be able to hang on for several weeks or even months. Insisting on showing the property in this situation only causes unnecessary friction, and you will be unable to tell the new tenants when they can move in.

Our contracts include a clause to protect you from liability if you must delay a new tenant's move-in date after you've signed a lease or rental agreement. (Clause 12 in Chapter 2.)

---

[4]CC § 1940.5(g).

SAMPLE NOTICE OF INTENT TO ENTER DWELLING UNIT

Notice of Intent to Enter Dwelling Unit
Civil Code § 1954

To: _Anna Rivera_____,
(name)

Tenant(s) in possession of the premises at

_123 Market Street, Apt. # 14_____,
(street address)

City of _Los Angeles_____, County of _Los Angeles_____, California.

PLEASE TAKE NOTICE that on _____, 19____,

(   ) at approximately ___:___ AM/PM

(X) during normal business hours,

the undersigned owner, or the owner's agent, will enter the said premises for the following reason:

(X) To make or arrange for the following repairs or improvements:
_fix garbage disposal_____

_____

_____

(   ) To exhibit the premises to: (   ) a prospective tenant or purchaser, (   ) workers or contractors regarding the above repair or improvement,

(   ) Other: _____

If you wish to be present, you may make the appropriate arrangements. If you have any questions or if the above-stated date or time is inconvenient, please notify the undersigned at
_(213) 555-7899_____.
(phone number)

Date: _January 5, 199_____   _Marlene Morgan_____
                                                              Owner/Manager

b. Showing Property to Prospective Buyers

You may also show potential buyers or mortgage companies your property—whether a rented single-family house, condominium unit or a multiple-unit building. Remember that 24 hours is presumed to be reasonable notice to your tenant.

Problems usually occur when an overeager real estate salesperson shows up on the tenant's doorstep without warning or calls on very short notice and asks to be let in to show the place to a possible buyer. In this situation, the tenant is within his right to say politely but firmly, "I'm busy right now—try again in a few days after we've set a time convenient for all of us." Naturally, this type of misunderstanding is not conducive to good landlord-tenant relations, not to mention a sale of the property. Make sure the real estate salespeople you deal with understand the law and respect your tenant's rights to advance notice.

Selling a house occupied by a tenant isn't easy on anyone. At times, you will want to show the place on short notice. And you may even want to have an occasional open house on weekends. Your tenant, on the other hand, is liable to feel threatened by the change in ownership. From her point of view, any actions you take to show the house to strangers may seem like an intolerable intrusion.

Obviously, the best way to achieve your ends is with the cooperation of the tenant. One good plan is to meet with the tenant in advance and offer a reasonable rent reduction in exchange for cooperation—for example, two open houses a month and showing the unit on two-hour notice, as long as it doesn't occur more than three times a week. However, you should realize that this type of agreement is in force only so long as the tenant continues to go along with it. Technically, any written agreement changing the rent is really an amendment to the rental agreement, and rental agreement clauses under which tenants give up their privacy rights are void and unenforceable if it comes to a court fight. This may be one situation when an informal understanding that the rent be lowered so long as the tenant agrees to the frequent showings may be better than a written agreement.

c. Putting For Sale or For Rent Signs or Lockboxes on the Property

Occasionally, friction is caused by landlords who put For Sale or For Rent signs on tenants' homes, such as a For Sale sign on the lawn of a rented single-family house. Even if a landlord is conscientious about giving 24 hours' notice before showing property, putting a sale or rental sign on the property is virtually an invitation to prospective buyers or renters to disturb the tenant with unwelcome inquiries.

Be particularly careful with "For Sale" signs. Tenants who like where they are living often justifiably feel threatened and insecure about a potential sale. A new owner may mean a rent increase or eviction notice if the new owner wants to move in herself. In this situation, if your tenant's privacy is ruined by repeated inquiries, the tenant may resort to rent withholding or sue you for invasion of privacy, just as if you personally had made repeated illegal entries.

Keep in mind that in the age of computerized multiple-listing services, many real estate agents commonly sell houses and other real estate without ever placing a For Sale sign on the property, except when an open house is in progress. If you or your real estate agent must put up a sign advertising sale or rental of the property, make sure it clearly warns against disturbing the occupant and includes a telephone number to call. A good compromise is a sign which says Shown by Appointment Only or Do Not Disturb Occupant. If your real estate agent refuses to accommodate you, find a new one that will respect your tenants' privacy and keep you out of a lawsuit.

Don't use a lockbox. Under no circumstances should an owner of occupied rental property which is listed for sale allow the placing of a key-holding "lockbox" on the door. This is a metal box that attaches to the front door and contains the key to that door. It can be opened by a master key held by area real estate salespeople. Since a lockbox allows a salesperson to enter in disregard of the 24-hour notice requirement, it should not be used—period. A lockbox will leave you wide open to a tenant's lawsuit for invasion of privacy, and possibly liable for any property the tenant claims to have lost.

5. Entry After the Tenant Has Moved Out

To state the obvious, a landlord may enter the premises at any time after the tenant has moved out. It doesn't matter whether the tenant left voluntarily after giving back the key, or involuntarily after the sheriff or marshall evicted the tenant following a successful eviction lawsuit.

In addition, a landlord who believes a tenant has abandoned the property—that is, skipped out without giving any notice or returning the key—may legally enter. Chapter 19 explains the legal procedure for entry if you are not absolutely sure your tenant has left permanently.

> *What To Avoid To Comply With the Law on Tenants' Privacy*
>
> *Don't:*
> - *Enter tenant's home without giving 24 hours' notice—except in the true emergency.*
> - *Conduct too-frequent inspections.*
> - *Enter tenant's home alone without witnesses.*
> - *Enter a tenant's home against his wishes.*

B. What To Do When Tenants Are Unreasonable

Occasionally, a landlord who gives reasonable notice of her intent to enter the tenant's home for legitimate purposes is still adamantly refused entry by the tenant. If you repeatedly encounter unreasonable refusals to let you or your employees enter the premises during normal business hours for one of the reasons listed earlier in this chapter, you can legally enter anyway, provided you do so in a peaceful manner. However, for practical reasons, a wise landlord faced by a tenant who is unreasonably asserting her right to privacy will not enter alone. It's just common sense to bring someone along who can later act as a witness in case the tenant claims some of her property is missing.

Another problem landlords face is that some tenants have their locks changed. No statute or court decision addresses whether a tenant is within her rights to change the locks without giving the landlord an extra key. This would seem to be illegal because it restricts your right of access in a true emergency or when you have given proper notice. As noted above, our lease and rental agreements require landlord key access, as well as notice of any change of locks or the installation of any burglar alarms. (See Clause 14, Chapter 2.)

If you have a serious conflict over access with an otherwise satisfactory tenant, a sensible first step is to meet with the tenant to see if the problem can be resolved. If you come to an understanding, follow up with a note to confirm your agreement. Here's an example:

"This will confirm our conversation of __(date)__ regarding access to your apartment at __(address)__ for the purpose of making repairs. The management will give you 24 hours' advance written notice, and will enter only during business hours or weekdays. The person inspecting will knock first, then enter with a passkey if no one answers."

If this doesn't work, try mediation by a neutral third party. (See Chapter 8.)

If attempts at compromise fail, you can evict the tenant. You can give the tenant a 30-day notice to leave if the tenancy is one from month-to-month in a non-rent controlled city. If you rent under a lease or in an area requiring just cause for eviction, you can use a three-day notice to shape up or leave, if the lease or rental agreement contains an appropriate right-of-entry provision.[5] The cause justifying eviction is the tenant's breach of that provision (Clause 14 in our written lease and rental agreements, Chapter 2).

If you contemplate an eviction lawsuit against the tenant, make sure you can document your position. Keep copies of any correspondence and notes of your conversations with the tenant.

C. Tenants' Remedies if a Landlord Acts Illegally

Conscientious landlords should be receptive to a tenant's complaint that her privacy is being violated and work out an acceptable compromise.

If you violate a tenant's right to privacy, and you can't work out a compromise, the tenant has several options.

Withholding rent because the landlord has denied tenant "quiet enjoyment" of premises. A tenant may withhold a portion of the next month's rent, claiming you have violated her right to quiet enjoyment of the property.[6] (See Clause 15 of our form lease/rental agreement, Chapter 2.) "Quiet enjoyment" of rental real property means that a tenant has the same right to enjoy her home free from interference by her landlord (or anyone else) as does a homeowner. If the tenant withholds rent, you have two choices:

- Accept a tenant's nonpayment of whatever part of the rent she felt she deserved as compensation for your invasion or privacy, or

- Bring an eviction suit based on nonpayment of rent.

Chapter 11 includes a detailed discussion of rent withholding, specifically as it relates to habitability. The basic issues are the same for invasion of privacy.

Suing the landlord in court. A tenant can also bring a lawsuit, asking for money damages. It's easy for a tenant to press her claim for $5,000 or less in small claims court without a lawyer. She can sue for a larger amount in regular municipal or superior court.

Depending on the circumstances, the legal theories by which a tenant can sue her landlord for unlawful entry include:

- Trespass

- Invasion of privacy

- Breach of implied covenant of quiet enjoyment[7]

---

[5]As we explain in Chapter 18 and in *Volume 2: Evictions*, you're much better off giving a month-to-month tenant a 30-day termination notice stating no reason (at least in non-rent-controlled cities where you don't need "just cause" for eviction), rather than using a three-day notice that gives the tenant the chance of contesting the reason for eviction stated on the notice.

---

[6]*Guntert v. Stockton*, 55 Cal. App. 3d 131 (1976).

[7]*Guntert v. Stockton*, 55 Cal. App. 3d 131 (1976).

- Intentional infliction of emotional distress[8]
- Negligent infliction of emotional distress.

Moving out without liability for further rent. Finally, you should know that repeated abuses by a landlord of a tenant's right of privacy give a tenant under a lease a legal excuse to break it by moving out, without liability for further rent. Also, unlawful entry into a tenant's home—even by the landlord—can be considered a criminal trespass.

D. Other Types of Invasions of Privacy

Entering a tenant's home without consent isn't the only way a landlord can interfere with the tenant's privacy. Here are a few other common situations, with advice on how to handle them.

1. Allowing Others To Enter

Occasionally a landlord or resident manager will be faced with a very convincing stranger who will tell a heart-rending story: "I'm Nancy's boyfriend and I need to get my clothes out of her closet now that I'm moving to New York," or, "If I don't get my heart medicine which I left in this apartment, I'll die on the spot," or "I'm John's father and I just got in from the North Pole, where a polar bear ate my wallet and I have no other place to stay." The problem arises when you can't contact the tenant at work or elsewhere to ask whether it's okay to let the desperate individual in.

A story may be legitimate—still, it doesn't make sense to expose yourself to the potential liability involved should you get taken in by a clever con artist. There is always a chance that the person is really a smooth talker who your tenant has a dozen good reasons to want kept out.

Never let a stranger, including the police (unless they have a search warrant or need to enter to prevent a catastrophe, such as an explosion), into your tenant's home without your tenant's permission. A landlord may not, for example, consent to a warrantless police search of premises occupied by a tenant.[9]

If you do let a stranger in, your tenant can sue you for any damage or loss incurred. Even if you have been authorized to allow a certain person entry, it is wise to ask the stranger for identification. Although this no-entry-without-authorization policy may sometimes be difficult to adhere to in the face of a convincing story, stick to it. You have much more to lose in admitting the wrong person into the tenant's home than you would have to gain by letting in someone who's "probably okay."

2. Giving Information to Strangers

As a landlord, you may be approached by strangers, including creditors, banks and perhaps even prospective landlords, to provide credit or other information on your tenant. Resist your natural urge to be helpful, unless the tenant has given you written permission to release this sort of information. You have nothing to gain, and possibly a lot to lose, if you give out information that your tenant feels constitutes a serious violation of her privacy. And if you give out incorrect information—even if you believe it to be accurate—you can really be in a legal mess if the person to whom you disclose it relies on it to take some action that negatively affects your tenant.

---

[8]In a suit by a tenant alleging that a landlord was guilty of the intentional infliction of emotional distress, the court ruled that it was necessary to prove four things: (a) outrageous conduct on the part of the landlord; (b) intention to cause or reckless disregard of the probability of causing emotional distress; (c) severe emotional suffering; and (d) actual suffering or emotional distress. *Newby v. Alto Riviera Apartments,* 60 Cal. App. 3d 288 (1976) .

---

[9]*People v. Escudero,* 23 Cal. 3d 800, 806 (1979); *People v. Roman,* 227 Cal. App. 3d 674, 278 Cal. Rptr. 44 (1991) .

If you tell others that a tenant has filed for bankruptcy (and this isn't true), and the tenant is damaged as a result—for example, his credit rating is adversely affected or he doesn't get a job—the tenant has grounds to sue.

Some landlords feel that they should communicate information to prospective landlords, especially if the tenant has failed to pay rent, maintain the premises or has created other serious problems. If you do give out this information, make sure you are absolutely factual and that the information you provide has been requested. If you go out of your way to give out negative information—for example, you try to blackball the tenant with other landlords in your area—you definitely risk legal liability for libelling your tenant and interfering with her contractual rights.

 Beware of gossipy managers. A number of landlords we know have had serious problems with on-site managers who have gossiped about tenants who, for example, paid rent late, were served with a three-day notice, had overnight visitors or drank too much. This sort of gossip may seem innocent, but if flagrant and damaging can be an invasion of privacy for which you can be liable. So, impress on your managers their duty to keep confidential all sensitive information about tenants.

EXAMPLE

Your resident manager, Moe, tells Jerry that his ex-girlfriend Wendy "went out for the evening with the same guy she's had over here every other night." As a result, Jerry makes Wendy's life miserable for the next few weeks—or months. Wendy sues Moe—and you—for invading her privacy and subjecting her to Jerry's abuse.

3. Calling or Visiting Tenants at Work

Should you need to call your tenant at work (say when his Uncle Harry shows up and asks to be let into his apartment), try to be sensitive to whether it's permissible for him to receive personal calls. While some people work at desks with telephones and have bosses who don't get upset about occasional personal calls, others have jobs that are greatly disrupted by any phone call. A general rule seems to be that the more physical the type of the work, the more tyrannical employers are about prohibiting personal phone calls at work.

Under no circumstances should you continue to call a tenant at work who asks you not to do so. This is especially true when calling about late rent payments or other problems.

Never leave specific messages with your tenant's employer, especially those that could reflect negatively on her. A landlord who leaves a message like "Tell your deadbeat employee I'll evict her if she doesn't pay the rent" can expect at least a lot of bad feeling on the part of the tenant, and, at worst, a lawsuit for slander or invasion of privacy.

As for visiting the tenant at work—say to collect late rent—this is something you should avoid unless invited. What it boils down to is that no matter what you think of your tenant, you should respect the sensitive nature of the tenant's relationship with her employer.

There may be times you'll need to contact the tenant at work if you can't find the tenant at home after repeated tries—for example, to serve notice of a rent increase (Chapter 14) or an eviction notice (Chapter 18).

4. Undue Restrictions on Guests

A few landlords, overly concerned about tenants moving new occupants into the property, go a little overboard in keeping tabs on the tenants' legitimate guests who stay overnight or for a few days. Often their leases, rental agreements or rules and regulations require a tenant to "register" any overnight guest.

Our form agreements limit guests' visits to no more than 10 days in any 6-month period, to avoid having a guest turn into an illegal sub-tenant. While landlords should be concerned about persons who begin as guests becoming permanent unauthorized residents (see Chapter 10), it is overkill to require a tenant to inform his landlord of a guest whose stay is only for a day or two. Keep in mind that just because you rent your tenant her home, you don't have the right to restrict her social life or pass upon the propriety of her visitors' stays. Extreme behavior in this area—whether by an owner or a management employee—can be considered an invasion of privacy for which you may be held liable.

5. Spying on a Tenant

As a result of worrying too much about a tenant's visitors, a few landlords have attempted to interrogate tenants' visitors, knock on their tenants' doors at odd hours or too frequently to see who answers, or even peek through windows. Needless to say, this sort of conduct can render a landlord liable for punitive damages in an invasion of privacy lawsuit. As far as talking to tenants' guests is concerned, engaging in anything more than pleasant hellos or non-threatening small talk is legally out of bounds. If you think your tenant's activity with respect to guests-cum-residents, or anything else, is a problem, make an appointment with the tenant and ask to talk about it.

Raising Rents and Changing Other Terms of Tenancy

A landlord's freedom to raise rent or change other terms of the tenancy depends primarily on whether the tenant has a lease or a rental agreement (written or oral) for a month-to-month or other periodic tenancy. For the most part, a lease fixes the terms of tenancy for the length of the lease, while the terms of a periodic tenancy can be changed by giving the tenant proper written notice.

This chapter explains the rules for raising rents and changing other terms of a month-to-month or other periodic tenancy. These rules normally don't apply to long-term leases—the rent may be increased only when the lease expires.

Related Topics

- Legal rules regarding when, where and how rent is due; late charges and returned check charges; partial and late rent payments: Chapter 3

- Local rent control ordinances, including property covered, administration and hearings, registration requirements, rent formulas, security deposits, vacancy decontrol and just cause evictions: Chapter 4

- Landlord liability for retaliatory rent increases: Chapter 15

- Legal rules and procedures for terminating tenancies: Chapter 18

A. Basic Rules To Change or End a Tenancy

If you rent using a rental agreement (whether oral or in writing) for a month-to-month or other periodic tenancy, you or your tenant can terminate the tenancy by giving written notice to the other (except, of course, in some cities which have rent control ordinances requiring the landlord to have "just cause" to evict. (See Chapter 4.H.)

The length of the notice period is normally determined by the interval between rent payments (one month, two weeks, etc.), unless the rental agreement specifies a longer or shorter notice period necessary to terminate the tenancy. In other words, a landlord can normally terminate a month-to-month tenancy on 30 days' written notice, a week-to-week tenancy on seven days' notice, etc. The same rule applies when the landlord wants to change the terms of a tenancy.[1] To increase the rent or otherwise change the terms of the tenancy, the landlord must normally give a month-to-month tenant 30 days' written notice.[2]

If the tenant has a fixed-term lease—one that expires on a particular future date—you cannot raise the rent during the lease term, unless the lease allows it. (This type of provision is rarely seen in residential leases, which customarily are for terms of six or twelve months.) However, at the end of the term, the rent can be increased.

---

[1] CC § 827.

[2] This period can be reduced to as low as seven days if there's a clause to that effect in the rental agreement. (See Chapter 2.D.) Some rental agreements call for a notice period of 60 or even 90 days.

Rent Increases and Long-Term Leases

What happens when a lease ends? Strictly speaking, the tenant must move, unless you either enter into a new lease with her, or continue to accept monthly rent. (See Chapter 19.)

If the tenant stays and you continue to accept monthly rent, even though no new agreement is signed, the tenancy becomes a periodic one with the rent due at the same interval as called for under the lease (usually once a month). You can now raise the rent, change one or more of the terms of the tenancy, or terminate the now month-to-month tenancy by giving the tenant a written 30-day notice, following the same rules discussed in this chapter for periodic tenancies.

Why do you have to change the terms of the lease by written notice if the lease has run out? Because state law provides that when a lease ends, all its terms continue in effect except those which have to do with the lease term itself.[3]

Example: Les rents a house from Owsley under a one-year lease that runs from January through December. The lease provides that the $900 monthly rent is payable on the first day of the month, and that no pets are allowed. The lease expires on December 31, and Owsley elects to continue the tenancy by accepting another $900 from Les in the next month of January. The tenancy is now month-to-month, with all other terms the same, the rent still being $900, with no pets allowed. If Owsley wants to raise the rent or change the terms of what is now essentially a written month-to-month rental agreement, he'll have to give Les a 30-day notice to that effect.

Once again, end-of-lease rent increases, as well as your right to insist the tenant leave at the end of the lease term, are subject to local rent-control ordinances which may restrict rent increases even after a lease expires, and cities with just cause eviction provisions may allow the tenant to stay on, even though the lease has expired. (See Chapter 4.)

B. Rent Increase Rules

The rules for increasing rent vary, depending on whether or not your property is under rent control.

1. No Rent Control

In areas without rent control, there is no limit to the amount a landlord can increase the rent of a month-to-month or other periodic tenant. Similarly, there is no restriction on the period of time between rent increases. You can legally raise the rent as much and as often as good business dictates. Of course, common sense should tell you that if your tenants do not perceive your increases as being fair, you may end up with vacant rental units or a hostile group of tenants looking for ways to make you miserable.

You can't, however, legally raise a tenant's rent as retaliation—for example, in response to a legitimate complaint or rent-withholding action (see Chapters 11 and 15) or as a discriminatory action (see Chapter 9). One way to protect yourself from charges that ordinary rent increases are retaliatory or discriminatory is to adopt a sensible rent-increase policy and stick to it. For example, many landlords raise rent once a year in an amount that more or less reflects the increase in the Consumer Price Index.

Other landlords use a more complicated formula which takes into account other rents in the area, as well as such factors as increased costs of maintenance or rehabilitation. They make sure to inform their tenants about the rent increase in advance and apply the increase uniformly with all their tenants. Usually, this protects the landlord against any claim of a retaliatory rent increase by a tenant who has coincidentally made a legitimate complaint about the condition of the premises.

---

[3]CC §1945.

EXAMPLE

Lois owns two multi-unit complexes. In one of the complexes, Lois raises rents uniformly, at the same time, for all tenants. In the other apartment building (where she fears tenants hit with rent increases all at once will organize and generate unrest), Lois does things differently: She raises each tenant's rent in accordance with the Consumer Price Index on the yearly anniversary of the date each tenant moved in. Either way, Lois is safe from being judged to have retaliatorily increased rents, even if a rent increase to a particular tenant follows on the heels of a complaint.

Of course, any rent increase given to a tenant who has made a complaint should be reasonable—in relation to the previous rent, what you charge other similarly-situated tenants, and rents for comparable property in the area—or you are asking for legal trouble.

EXAMPLE

Lonnie has no organized plan for increasing rents in his 20-unit building, but simply raises them at random. On November 1, he raises the rent for one of his tenants, Teresa, without remembering her recent complaint about her heater. Teresa was the only one to receive a rent increase in November. In this situation, Teresa has a strong retaliatory rent-increase case against Lonnie, simply because an increase which seemed to single her out happened to coincide with her exercise of a legal right. If the increase made her rent higher than those for comparable units in the building, she will have an even better case.

For a discussion of landlord liability for retaliatory rent increases and tenant lawsuits against the landlord, see Chapter 15.

2. Rent Control

In cities with rent control, rent increases are governed by additional limitations. If your property is located in a city with rent control, you should check that city's ordinance to see whether it applies to your property. (See Chapter 4 for a detailed discussion of rent control.) Your property might not be covered, since quite a few cities exempt single-family homes, duplexes and so forth; some cities with "vacancy de-control" provisions in their rent control ordinances exempt a previously-controlled rental after the tenant voluntarily leaves or is evicted for cause, etc.

If a rent-control ordinance does affect your property, check it for the following:

The maximum yearly rent increase. The ordinance may allow periodic increases of either a fixed percentage or a percentage tied to a consumer price index, or the local rent board may establish the amount of the increase each year, in which case you will have to inquire. In cities that keep track of permissible rent control levels by requiring the landlord to register the property, state law requires the rent board, on request, to notify the landlord and tenant of the permissible rent.[4]

Whether the landlord must obtain permission from a rent board for a higher increase than set out by the ordinance or board. This is generally required in "moderate" and "strict" rent-controlled cities. In some cities with mild rent control, a landlord can raise rents as much as she wants, with the tenant having the burden to object to increases above the approved formula increase.

Whether the ordinance requires that a rent increase notice contain specific information, such as a reason for the increase, in addition to normal state law notice requirements. You may also want to contact a local landlords association, or perhaps a lawyer who routinely represents landlords and is familiar with requirements of the locality's rent control law.

---

[4]CC §1947.8.

C. Preparing a Notice To Raise Rent

A notice raising the rent of a tenant who occupies a unit under an oral or written rental agreement with a periodic tenancy—for example, month-to-month or week-to-week—must be in writing and must clearly state the following:

1. The name of the tenant

2. The full address of the property, including street, city and county

3. The amount of the new rent

4. The amount of the new security deposit (if increased)

5. When the change is to go into effect. This can normally be no sooner than 30 days for a month-to-month tenancy, unless a rental agreement clause allows for a shorter time. But it can be longer, even if the lease or rental agreement doesn't require this. You can give a tenant as much notice as you want.

6. Pro-rated rental rate (see Section E)

7. The date the rent increase notice is given

8. The signature of the owner or manager.

In Section D, you'll find a sample rent-increase notice prepared on a form we call Notice of Change of Terms of Tenancy. A tear-out, fill-in-the-blanks version of this form can be found in the Appendix at the back of the book.

Deposits. We noted in Chapter 5 that if you wish to raise the amount of a tenant's deposit when you raise the rent, you must specifically state that you are doing this. To accomplish this, check the box marked "Other" on the Notice of Change of Terms of Tenancy form and indicate the amount of the new deposit. We discuss the maximum amount you can charge for a deposit for furnished and unfurnished units in Chapter 5.

D. How the Notice Is Served on the Tenant

The law is very strict on how a notice changing the terms of tenancy must be served on a tenant. It is not enough that you mail the notice or simply post it on the door, unless the tenant admits to receiving it— something you can never count on. Here are the three legal methods of service for a 30-day notice.

1. Personal Service

The best type of service of the 30-day notice is to simply hand your tenant the notice. Handing the notice to any other person, such as someone who lives with your tenant but is not listed as a co-tenant on the written rental agreement, is not sufficient, except as described next under the heading "Substituted Service."

For personal service to be legally effective, it is not necessary that your tenant accept the notice in her hand, and you or your manager (or whoever serves the notice) should not attempt to force the tenant to take the notice. It is enough that you make some sort of personal contact with your tenant and offer her the notice. If your tenant refuses to accept the notice, simply lay it down at her feet and walk away. Service is legally effective.

SAMPLE NOTICE OF CHANGE OF TERMS OF TENANCY

Notice of Change of Terms of Tenancy

To: _____ Duc Mihn _____ ,
                        (name)

Tenant(s) in possession of the premises at:

_____ 1234 Market Street, Apartment #5 _____ ,
                        (street address)

City of ___ Sacramento ___, County of ___ Sacramento ___, California.

The terms of tenancy under which you occupy these premises are changed as follows:

(x)   The monthly rent will be increased to $___700___, payable in advance.

(x)   Other: _The amount of the security deposit is raised to $1,400, an_
        _increase of $100_____ .

The change in terms of tenancy shall be effective

(x)   ____ on March 1, 19 ____ .
                    (date)

(   )   On the 30th day following service on you of this notice. If the change of terms of
        tenancy is an increase in rent, the amount due on the next following due date, pro-rated
        at the current rental rate prior to the 30th day, and pro-rated at the increased rate
        thereafter, is $_____ .

Date: ____ January 17, 19 _____

                                    Dana Wickham _____
                                    Owner/Manager

2. Substituted Service on Another Person

If the tenant to whom you're attempting to give the notice never seems to be home, and you know where he works, you must try to personally serve him at his place of employment. If you are unable to locate the tenant at his workplace, the law allows you to use "substituted service" in lieu of personally giving the notice to the tenant.

Substituted service simply means that you give the 30-day notice to a "substitute" person of "suitable age and discretion," preferably an adult,[5] at your tenant's home or business, with instructions to that person to give the notice to the tenant. This must be followed with a mailed notice to the tenant's home to be effective.

To serve the notice this way, you must:

- Try to personally serve the tenant at his home, but not succeed.

- Try to personally serve him at work, but not succeed.

- Leave a copy of the notice with an adult at home or work.

and

- Mail another copy to the tenant at home by ordinary first-class mail.[6]

Substituted service requires two notices. Service of the notice is not legally complete until you both leave a copy with the substitute and mail a second copy to the tenant at home.

[5]However, if no adult is available, giving the notice to a teenage resident of the tenant's household is sufficient. *Lehr v. Crosby*, 123 Cal. App. 3d Supp. 1 (1981).

[6]CCP §1162(2).

In late November, Lola , having rented an apartment to Raphael on a month-to-month basis for three years at a rent of $650 a month (payable on the first day of each month), wants to raise Raphael's rent to $725, effective January 1 of the following year. This means Lola's rent-increase notice must be served on or before December 1 (30 days before January 1). On November 30, Lola gives up trying to personally serve the notice on Raphael who never seems to be home, at least according to Raphael's teenage daughter, who always answers the door. Lola then simply gives the notice to the daughter. Come January, Raphael ignores the notice, claims he never received it, and refuses to pay the increased rent. Raphael is right (technically, at least), as he was never properly served. However, had Lola given the notice to Raphael's daughter in late November and promptly followed through by mailing a second copy of the notice to Raphael, the rent increase would have been legally effective.

3. Posting and Mailing Service

If you can't find a tenant on whom you wish to serve the 30-day notice, and you can't find anyone else at home or work (or if you don't know where the tenant is employed), you may serve the notice using a procedure known as "posting and mailing." (People in the business call it "nail and mail.") To do this, you tack or tape a copy of the notice to the front door of the rental unit and mail a second copy to the tenant at that address. In order to serve the notice this way, you must do the following, in the order indicated:

- Try to personally serve the tenant at home, and not succeed.

- Try to serve her at work and not succeed.

- Post a copy of the notice on the front door of the property.

- Mail another copy to the tenant at home by first-class mail.[7]

[7]CCP §1162(3).

Again, service of the notice is not complete until you have followed through by mailing a second copy of the notice.

EXAMPLE

Carl, wants to give his tenant Sue a notice increasing Sue's rent by $50 a month. Unfortunately, Carl can never find Sue (or anyone else) at home, and doesn't know where she works. Since that leaves no one on whom to personally or substitute-serve the rent-increase notice, Carl is left with the posting-and-mailing alternative. To accomplish this, Carl can tape one copy to the door of the property and mail a second copy to Sue at that address by regular first-class mail.

4. Effect of Improper Service

Once the tenant acknowledges receiving the notice, or pays the increased rent, she gives up the right to complain about any legal insufficiency in the manner the 30-day notice was served, and the rent increase becomes effective, even if the service of the notice is technically improper. This is true regardless of the tenant's reason for acquiescing to the increase—it doesn't matter if she didn't know the notice had to be served a certain way, was too concerned about maintaining good relations with her landlord to raise the issue or simply didn't care.

EXAMPLE

On May 25, Natalie prepares a notice telling her tenant Linda her rent will be increased from $775 to $875 a month, effective July 1. Natalie mails the notice by ordinary first-class mail. Linda pays the increased rent on July 1, and every month after, but learns in December that the law requires the notice to have been served by personal, substituted or posting and mailing service. Linda demands that Natalie give her back the $100 increase she paid during each of those months. Natalie doesn't have to give a refund, since Linda, by paying the increase, gave up her right to insist on technically-legal service of the notice.

 Avoid informal rent increases. In practice, rents are often increased by a simple agreement between the landlord and tenant, or even a simple acquiescence on the tenant's part, even though this rent increase procedure does not comply with legal requirements. Many landlords do not give tenants proper written notice, but merely tell them of the increase. If the tenant responds by paying the increased rent, for even a month, he has given up the right to object to the increase. In effect, the tenant's failure to assert his right not to pay the increase is an implied agreement that the rent has been increased. Even if you know your tenants well and believe they will go along with a rent increase, we believe it is a poor business practice to rely on oral notice alone. As a courtesy, you may wish to tell your tenant of the increase personally, perhaps explaining the reasons—although reasons aren't legally necessary, except in areas covered by rent control. (See Chapter 4.) However, you should also follow up with a proper written notice. Good business practice requires written notice and documentation of all important decisions.

Here is a checklist which should help you follow correct procedures when you are about to raise your tenant's rent:

Checklist to Raise Rent

- *Determine that your tenancy is from month-to-month or some other shorter period. As part of doing this, make sure your agreement doesn't require a 60- or 90-day notice period. (No increases are allowed during the term of a lease unless specified in the lease.)*
- *Find out if any local rent control laws prevent or limit your proposed increase.*
- *Decide when you want the increase to take effect. At least 30 days' notice is required for month-to-month tenancy, unless your rental agreement calls for a shorter notice period.*
- *Fill out the blank Notice of Change of Terms of Tenancy at the back of this book. Sign the notice and make a copy for your files.*
- *Give the notice personally to the tenant or use substituted or posting-and-mailing service.*

E. When the Rent Increase Takes Effect

One of the legal misconceptions tenants are prone to make is the belief that a rent increase must take effect at the beginning of a rental term. This is not true. The increase may take effect 30 days after you serve the tenant with a 30-day notice of the increase. For example, in the case of a month-to-month tenancy, where the rent is paid in advance on the first day of each month, a 30-day notice can increase the rent effective June 10, if served 30 days earlier on May 10.[8] However, if you increase rent in the middle

---

[8]See CC § 827.

of a month, the rent for that month must be pro-rated, and the calculations are a little tricky. For this reason, many landlords find it easier to raise the rent as of the first of the full month after the notice is properly given, even though this may mean you give the tenant more than 30 days' notice.

If you do wish to pro-rate, here is the proper way to do it. Assume you wish to raise the rent of a tenant who has a written rental agreement with rent payable on the first of each month by giving notice on the 10th of the month. Assuming you, in fact, give the tenant a notice on the 10th of May, increasing the rent from $500 to $550, the rent increase is effective June 9 (May has 31 days, but it's best to use a 30-day month, no matter how many days the month has). This would mean that the tenant would owe rent pro-rated at $500/month from June 1 through June 8, plus rent pro-rated at $550 per month from the 9th through the 30th. Remember, the rent is due on the first of the month, because rent is payable in advance. This works out to $537.10. Again, it may be more trouble figuring out how this number is calculated than it's worth.

F. Changing Terms Other Than Rent

If you rent to tenants under a periodic tenancy, the law allows you to change the terms of the agreement other than the amount of rent. Any rental agreement provision can be modified or even added in this way, as noted in Clause 3 of our form rental agreement. (See Chapter 2.) For example, the landlord could, with a 30-day notice, impose a pool fee, change the rules or fees for parking or reduce the number of people allowed to live in a unit Similarly, a landlord who originally allowed her month-to-month tenant to have a pet could give her a 30-day notice imposing a new provision forbidding pets. (At least one city, Los Angeles is an exception because it forbids landlords from adding a no-pets clause to a rental agreement.)

The same form you use to raise the rent can be used to change terms other than rent. (See Notice of Change of Terms of Tenancy in Section C.) But instead of checking "The monthly rent will be increased to $ _____ , payable in advance," check "Other" and write in the change you wish to make. For example:

- "Tenant is prohibited from keeping pets in or on the premises."

- "Tenant may only park one motor vehicle in the parking lot behind 111 Navelier St."

- "Tenant must pay $25 per month for use of the swimming pool. Payment to be made with the monthly rent."

Just as some cities' rent control ordinances regulate the amount by which landlords can raise rents, some ordinances also prevent a landlord from otherwise changing the terms of the tenancy, particularly by reducing services while keeping the rent the same. For example, San Francisco's rent control ordinance was interpreted to prevent several landlords from taking back their tenants' rights to park in previously allowed parking spaces or to begin charging parking fees. If your property falls under a rent control ordinance, check to see if it restricts changes in terms other than rent. Also prohibited by local rent control laws, as well as by state law,[9] are changes in rental agreement terms that purport to have the tenant give up legal rights. In other words, the illegal and unenforceable rental agreement and lease terms discussed in Chapter 2.E, are no more effective if accomplished by a Notice of Change of Terms of Tenancy than they would be if included in the original lease or rental agreement.

There is a tear-out Notice of Change of Terms of Tenancy in the Appendix. The notice should specify the following information:

1. The tenant's name

2. The full address of the property, including street, city and county

3. The change of terms, spelled out as carefully as if you were inserting it as an additional clause in a rental agreement for the first time.

4. When the change of terms is effective, giving at least 30 days' notice in the case of a tenancy from month to month

5. The date the notice is given

6. The signature of the owner or manager.

A sample notice follows. It should be served in the same manner as a notice increasing the rent, namely by personal service (or substituted or posting-and-mailing service, if necessary).

---

[9] CC §1953(b).

SAMPLE NOTICE OF CHANGE OF TERMS OF TENANCY

Notice of Change of Terms of Tenancy

To: _____ Jean Friedman _____,
              (name)

Tenant(s) in possession of the premises at:

_____ 456 Main Street, Apartment 7 _____,
                      (street address)

City of ___ Los Angeles ___, County of ___ Los Angeles ___, California.

The terms of tenancy under which you occupy these premises are changed as follows:

(   )   The monthly rent will be increased to $_____, payable in advance.

(x)   Other: <u>Tenant shall not allow more than three persons to reside in</u>
          <u>the premises without Owner's written permission</u>   .

The change in terms of tenancy shall be effective

(x) ___ on March 1, 19 ___ .
              (date)

(   )   On the 30th day following service on you of this notice. If the change of terms of tenancy
is an increase in rent, the amount due on the next following due date, pro-rated at the current
rental rate prior to the 30th day, and pro-rated at the increased rate thereafter, is $_____.

Date: ___ January 31, 19 ___

                                        Felicia Alou _____
                                        Owner/Manager

Retaliatory Rent Increases and Evictions

It is illegal for a landlord to retaliate against a tenant "for having lawfully and peaceably exercised *any rights under the law*," whether by reducing services, giving or even threatening to give a 30-day rent-increase or termination notice or doing anything else that works to the tenant's disadvantage.[1] The general idea is that tenants should not be punished by landlords just because they are invoking their legal rights or remedies.

Our goal in this chapter is twofold. First, we want you to clearly understand how the law defines retaliatory evictions and retaliatory rent increases. Second, and more important, we want you to know how to anticipate and avoid the legal problems that can be created by the few tenants who will try to maneuver you into the position of appearing to violate their rights.

Unfortunately, this chapter is essential reading for all landlords, even those of you (the great majority, certainly) who have no intention of ever illegally retaliating against any tenant for exercising her legal rights. The problem is that the laws have been written so broadly that all sorts of innocently motivated conduct can form the basis for either a lawsuit against the landlord for damages, or a successful defense against a landlord's unlawful detainer action.

In other words, a well-meaning ignorance of the law can cause you many problems, especially if you are dealing with a dishonest tenant who is determined to misuse the law to try to avoid paying rent. If you know your legal rights and learn to take sensible advance steps to nullify and counter a tenant's hostile urges, you should have few legal problems.

 If you own property in areas with rent control laws which contain just cause for eviction provisions, you should refer to Chapter 4. This is not to say that retaliatory rent increases and terminations are legal in rent control areas. To the contrary, most rent control ordinances have anti-retaliation provisions which are even stricter than state law; in fact, some local ordinances even provide criminal penalties. It's just that the question of whether rent increases and terminations are retaliatory, and therefore illegal, seldom comes up in most rent control areas, where more stringent local laws restrict rent increases and terminations of every kind, retaliatory or not.

A. Types of Retaliation That Are Prohibited

As we've discussed in preceding chapters, residential tenants have a number of legal rights and remedies. Because tenant-protection laws would be meaningless if a landlord could legally retaliate against a tenant who asserts her legal rights, the law forbids such retaliation. For example, the right of a month-to-month tenant to complain to the local fire department about a defective heater would be worth little if the landlord, angry about the complaint, could retaliate against her with an immediate 30-day termination or rent increase notice. Recognizing this, the California legislature and courts have made it illegal for a landlord to attempt to penalize a tenant in any way simply because she has attempted to vindicate a legal right that works to the landlord's disadvantage.

---

[1]CC § 1942.5

Tenants' Rights

Under the theory that to be forewarned allows you to be forearmed, we list some key tenants' rights here and give a few examples where landlords are commonly accused of retaliating against the tenant:

For tenants on a fixed-term lease: the right to refuse to pay a rent increase before the end of the lease term—unless the lease calls for periodic rent increases. Chapter 14.

For month-to-month tenants: the right to insist on a written notice of 30 days before submitting to any change in terms of tenancy: Chapter 14.

The right to be free from discriminatory treatment based on factors such as race, religion, sex, disability and marital status, and to complain to administrative agencies, or even courts, when she (the tenant) feels her rights are being violated: Chapter 9.

The right to live in premises free of defects that might endanger a tenant's health or safety, including the right to complain to local authorities or to withhold rent in appropriate cases, or even to file a lawsuit against a landlord who fails to keep the premises in proper repair: Chapter 11.

The right to privacy and freedom from having the landlord enter the property when he feels like it: Chapter 13.

The right to engage in political activity of any kind, including the right to organize or take part in a tenants' organization or other tenant protests. A tenant who actively campaigns for local candidates whom property owners find obnoxious, or who campaigns for a rent control ordinance, has an absolute right to do so without fear of intimidation.

The above list is for illustration only. There are many more situations in which a tenant can assert a particular right and the landlord's subsequent efforts to evict the tenant or raise the rent on account of it will be considered illegal. This is true no matter how unpleasantly conveyed, ill-founded or just plain wrong the tenant's gripe is. After all, the issue isn't whether the tenant had a good reason to act as he did, but whether his act was the exercise of a legal right and whether the landlord's subsequent act was a form of retaliation. Thus, tenants have prevailed on retaliatory eviction grounds in situations as diverse as the tenant's refusal to lie for the landlord at a trial and the tenant's calling the police for a crime committed by a manager.[2]

B. Proving Retaliation

Both landlords and tenants commonly have misconceptions about the timing and proof required for tenants to raise the defense of retaliation.

1. Retaliation for Complaints to Government Agencies

It is illegal to retaliate against a tenant who has made a complaint about housing conditions, either to the landlord or to a health or building inspection department, no matter how unfounded or frivolous the tenant's complaint may have been. If the tenant has withheld rent to protest bad housing conditions, or makes use of the "repair-and-deduct" remedy, it is considered a form of illegal retaliation to follow this with a 30-day termination or rent increase notice.

If a tenant whose rent is paid up complains to a government agency about defects in the premises, and if the landlord subsequently raises rent, decreases services or evicts the tenant within 180 days, retaliation is presumed. If the tenant goes to court, the landlord must prove that the action was not retaliatory.[3] After 180 days, the tenant can still sue, but retaliation is no longer presumed.

---

[2]See *Barela v. Superior Court*, 30 Cal. 3d 244, 178 Cal. Rptr. 618 (1981) and *Custom Parking, Inc. v. Superior Court*, 138 Cal. App. 3d 90, 187 Cal. Rptr. 674 (1982).

[3]CC § 1942.5(a).

Aside from limitations in any applicable rentcontrol ordinance, a landlord can legally raise the rent or terminate the tenancy at any time, if there is a legitimate non-retaliatory reason. But if challenged, the landlord will have to prove that his actions were not retaliatory.

2. Retaliation for Other Acts

If the tenant asserts any other legal right—that is, other than complaining to a government agency about defects in the premises—the tenant must prove retaliation is the motive for any rent increase, decrease in services or eviction which follows. Under both statutory and common law, the tenant may raise the defense of retaliation or sue the landlord for retaliatory eviction at any time, and it doesn't matter whether or not the tenant is paid up in rent.[4] (Even so, as time goes on, it becomes harder for the tenant to establish that the landlord still has a retaliatory motive.)

A landlord's conduct can be proof of his motive. In deciding whether a landlord acted with a retaliatory motive, judges look at such things as:

- how soon the landlord responded with a rent increase or termination notice after the tenant exercised a legal right

- how the landlord treated the complaining tenant as compared to other tenants who didn't exercise their rights in the same way

- the overall reasonableness of the landlord's conduct

- whether the landlord appears to have had a legitimate reason for the actions.

How retaliation cases are fought out in court—either by a tenant defending an eviction lawsuit or by a tenant suing a landlord—are discussed in Section D below.

---

[4]CC § 1942.5(c). Also, see *Glaser v. Meyers*, 137 Cal. App. 3d 770 (1982).

C. Avoiding Charges of Retaliation

Sometimes it seems that every time a tenant can't or won't pay a legitimate rent increase, they will claim you are guilty of retaliatory misconduct. The same sort of unreasonable reliance on tenant protection laws can occur when you seek to terminate the tenancy for a perfectly legitimate reason and the tenant doesn't want to move. How do you cope with this sort of cynical misuse of the law? As with most things legal, there is no single answer. However, if you are prepared to plan ahead, you should be able to minimize any legal problems.

You start with a great advantage when faced with a tenant who attempts to defeat your legitimate rent increase or tenancy termination with phony retaliation claims. As a business person, you have an opportunity to plan ahead—anticipate that some tenants will adopt these tactics and prepare to meet them. The tenant, on the other hand, must react on an ad hoc basis and often has just a superficial knowledge of the law.

How exactly do you plan ahead? First, realize that some tenants affected negatively by any course of action you plan, such as a rent increase or eviction notice—no matter how legal and justified—are likely to strike back, often more by reflex than by thought. Second, try to anticipate what they will do and be prepared to avoid or counter their tactics. Here are a number of proven landlord techniques:

1. Set up clear, easy-to-follow procedures for tenants to ask for repairs and respond quickly when complaints are made, coupled with annual safety inspections. (We show you how in Chapter 11.) This sort of policy will go a long way toward demonstrating that a complaint is phony—for example, if a tenant faced with a rent increase or tenancy termination suddenly complains to an outside agency about some defect in the premises they rent, without talking to you first. Also, if your periodic inquiries result in complaints from several tenants, but you only evict one tenant, you can show you don't have a policy of retaliating against tenants who do complain.

2. Do not announce your intention to terminate a tenancy in advance. Telegraphing your intentions gives the tenant a chance to lodge a complaint. For example, suppose you tell the tenant on the 25th that you're going to give him a 30-day notice on the 31st. His complaint to the health department on the 28th —over a trivial defect—will be followed by your written notice dated the 31st. The short timespan between his complaint and your 30-day notice will appear to substantiate the tenant's claim of your supposed retaliatory intent. Similarly, if you and a tenant are at loggerheads, and no compromise seems possible, move quickly. Don't give the tenant time to create a raft of phony retaliatory eviction defenses.

If you genuinely want to work things out with the tenant, extend the notice period—but do this after the established date of the notice to avoid any attempts of phony retaliation.

3. Even though the law (in non-rent control areas) says that a landlord doesn't need a reason to terminate a tenancy, be prepared to demonstrate that you do have a good reason to evict the tenant. In other words, in anticipation of the possibility that a tenant may claim that you are terminating her tenancy for retaliatory reasons, you should be prepared to prove that your reasons were valid and not retaliatory. When you think of it, this burden isn't as onerous as it might first appear. From a business point of view, few landlords will ever want to evict an excellent tenant. And assuming there is a good reason why you want the tenant out—for example, the tenant repeatedly pays his rent late in violation of the rental agreement—you only need document it. (See Chapter 18, for legitimate reasons for terminating tenancies.)

4. Have legitimate business reasons for any rent increases or other changes in the conditions of the tenancy, and make the changes reasonable. The best answer to a charge of retaliation is proof that your act was based on legitimate business reasons and was wholly independent of any exercise by tenants of their rights. Chapter 14 discusses how to adopt a sensible rent-increase policy.

5. If a tenant withholds rent or makes a complaint for even an arguably legitimate reason at about the time you were going to raise the rent or give the tenant a 30-day notice anyway, wait. First take care of the complaint. Next, let some time pass. Then, do what you planned to do anyway (assuming you can document a legitimate reason for your action); however, if the landlord disagrees with the right of the tenant to withhold rent, he can give the tenant a three-day notice to pay rent or quit, with an eye toward suing the tenant on the basis of rent nonpayment. (See Chapter 16 for a discussion of three-day notices.)

The delay may cost you a few bucks, or result in some inconvenience, or even cause you to lose some sleep while you gnash your teeth, but all of these are preferable to being involved in litigation over whether or not your conduct was in retaliation for the tenant's complaint.

EXAMPLE

A tenant, Fanny, makes a legitimate complaint to the health department about a defective heater in an apartment she rents from Abe. Even though Fanny does so without having had the courtesy to tell Abe or his manager first, Fanny is still within her legal rights to make the complaint. About the same time Fanny files the complaint, neighboring tenants complain to Abe, not for the first time, about Fanny's loud parties that last into the wee hours of the morning. Other tenants threaten to move out if Fanny doesn't. In response to the neighboring tenants complaints, Abe gives Fanny a 30-day notice. She refuses to move and Abe must file an unlawful detainer complaint. Fanny responds that the eviction was in retaliation for her complaint to the health department. A contested trial results. Perhaps Abe will win in court, but in this situation, there is a good chance he won't.

Now, let's look at how you might better handle this problem:

Step 1. Fix the heater.

Step 2. Write the tenant, reminding her of your established complaint procedures. Tell her that you consider this sort of repair a routine matter which didn't necessitate a complaint to a public agency.

Here is a sample letter:

SAMPLE LETTER REMINDING TENANT OF COMPLAINT PROCEDURE

February 1, 19_

Fanny Hayes
123 State Street, Apt. 15
San Diego, CA

Dear Ms. Hayes:

As you know, Ms. Sharon Donovan, my resident manager at Sunny Dell
Apartments, repaired the heater in your unit yesterday, on January 31.

Ms. Donovan informs me that she never received a complaint from you nor
any request to repair the heater, and that she learned about the problem
for the first time when she received a telephone call to that effect from
Cal Mifune of the San Diego County Health Department. Apparently, you
notified the Health Department of the problem without first attempting to
resolve it with Ms. Donovan.

While you certainly do have a legal right to complain to a governmental
agency about any problem, you should be aware that the management of
Sunny Dell Apartments takes pride in its quick and efficient response to
residents' complaints and requests for repairs.

In the future, we hope that you'll avail yourself of our complaint
procedure if you have a problem with any aspect of your apartment. Simply
fill out a Maintenance/Repair Request form, available from Ms. Donovan
during her office hours of 9:00 A.M. to 6:00 P.M., Monday through
Saturday. In case of an urgent request during the evening or on Sundays,
you may call me at 555-1234.

Sincerely,

Abe Horowitz, Owner

Step 3. Carefully document the noise complaints of the neighbors. If possible, get them in writing. Feel out the neighbors about whether they would testify in court if necessary.

Step 4. Write the tenant about the neighbors' complaints.[5] The first letter should be conciliatory. Offer to meet with the tenant to resolve the problem, but also remind the tenant of the rental agreement (or lease) provision banning illegal conduct, and that excessive noise after a certain hour is a violation of city or county ordinances. If the first letter doesn't work, follow up with another letter, even if you don't think this will do any good either. These letters will help you greatly should a court fight develop later.

Below are two sample letters. Also, see Chapter 18C for a fill-in-the-blank warning letter you can send a tenant in response to complaints from neighbors or other residents. The form warning letter in Chapter 18 may be useful in many types of situations—not just those where a tenant claims retaliation.

Step 5. If possible, wait a few months, during which you should carefully document any more complaints before giving the tenant a 30-day notice.

This sort of preparatory work may influence the tenant not to claim you are guilty of retaliatory conduct. However, even if it does not, and you do end up in court, you should win easily.

D. Liability for Illegal Retaliation

Here are the methods by which a tenant can assert that a landlord is guilty of unlawful retaliatory conduct. We believe you need to know what they are so you can avoid being accused of such conduct.

1. The Tenant's Defense to an Eviction Lawsuit

A tenant who believes her landlord has illegally retaliated against her for having exercised a legal right can use what is called an "affirmative defense" in an eviction lawsuit.[6] (See Chapter 18 for details on eviction lawsuits.) It comes up when a landlord goes to court to enforce a 30-day termination notice after the tenant refuses to move out, or to sue for nonpayment of rent because the tenant refuses to pay a rent increase she claims is retaliatory. The tenant says in effect, "Even if the landlord serves me with the proper 30-day notice or an otherwise valid termination of tenancy (or rent increase), the landlord's action is invalid because she was retaliating against me for exercising a legal right."

---

[5]In several cities with rent control ordinances that require just cause for eviction, you are required to give the tenant a preliminary written notice to cease whatever conduct you claim violates the lease or rental agreement. Only if the tenant fails to comply can you legally give him a three-day or 30-day notice to terminate the tenancy. If you rent in one of these areas, you'll need to modify the following letter to comply with the requirements of your rent control ordinance. (See Chapter 18.C.3.)

[6]In an eviction lawsuit, the tenant has the burden of proving that the landlord's motive was to retaliate against her. *Western Land Office v. Cervantes,* 175 Cal. App. 3d 724, 220 Cal. Rptr. 784 (1985). However, this opinion suggests that if a tenant exercise a right under the law, and the landlord serves her with a termination or rent increase notice within six months, the landlord must state on the notice a justification or reason for the termination or rent increase.

FIRST SAMPLE LETTER REGARDING NEIGHBORS' COMPLAINTS

February 15, 19_

Fanny Hayes
123 State Street, Apt. 15
San Diego, CA

Dear Ms. Hayes:

I am writing this letter to inform you that several of your neighbors have complained to Ms. Sharon Donovan, Sunny Dell Apartments' resident manager, on several occasions during late January and early February, when you apparently hosted several parties in your apartment. In addition to complaints regarding shouting and the playing of loud music until 2:00 A.M., it appears that several party guests littered beer cans and other debris in the balcony outside the entrances to your apartment and those of several other units.

It is very important to the management of Sunny Dell Apartments that our residents be able to enjoy the peace and quiet of their homes. While we have no objections to our residents hosting occasional parties, we would hope that such events would be conducted with due regard for other residents, some of whom are elderly people quite easily agitated by excessive noise and litter.

Accordingly, we request that when you host parties in your apartment, you keep the noise within reasonable levels, particularly after 10:00 P.M., and that you restrain your guests from littering the common areas. Thank you for your cooperation.

Sincerely,

Abe Horowitz, Owner

SECOND SAMPLE LETTER REGARDING NEIGHBORS' COMPLAINTS

February 25, 19_

Fanny Hayes
123 State Street, Apt. 15
San Diego, CA

Dear Ms. Hayes:

On February 15, I wrote to inform you that several of your neighbors had complained about loud music until the early hours of the morning from frequent parties you have in your apartment. I also called your attention to complaints regarding litter scattered about by your party guests.

Since then, I have received several more similar complaints regarding parties given within the past two weeks. Some of the persons complaining have indicated their intention to move should this conduct continue. You appear intent on ignoring both my warnings to you and complaints made directly to you by your neighbors. For example, I am told that on February 20, you refused to reduce the volume of very loud music played at 1:30 A.M. until the police were called to ask you to do so, and that the next morning your neighbors discovered 15 empty beer cans and bottles scattered about the entrance to your apartment.

Please be advised that Clause 15 of your rental agreement makes illegal conduct in and about the premises a violation of the agreement and that the making of excessive noise during late hours is rendered unlawful by city ordinance. Accordingly, this sort of behavior is of the type for which your tenancy may be terminated. Should I receive any more complaints of similar conduct by you or your guests, I will have no choice but to have Ms. Donovan give you a 30-day notice of termination of tenancy.

Sincerely,

Abe Horowitz, Owner

Let's take two examples to show how this works.

EXAMPLE 1

On March 1, Abe gives his tenant, Fanny, a 30-day notice to move, effective April 1. Come April 1, Abe refuses to accept Fanny's offer of another month's rent of $400, telling her he expects her to move. Fanny refuses, claiming that Abe's notice was motivated by Fanny's January 25 complaint to the Health Department about the heater. If Abe wants to make Fanny move, he'll have to bring an eviction lawsuit, serving Fanny with a "summons" and "complaint." Fanny will then file an "answer" which states the "affirmative defense" that the notice was retaliatory. In this situation, the case will go to trial about May 10.

If Abe can convince the judge his real reason for giving Fanny the 30-day notice was her repeated loud parties that other tenants complained about, and that his motive wasn't to retaliate against Fanny, the judge will award Abe the pro-rated rent through May 10 ($400 for April, plus $133.33 for May 1-10), possession of the property, court costs, and attorney fees if Abe hired an attorney and the lease or rental agreement contains an attorney fees clause. Only then will Fanny have to move.

If the judge thinks Abe's motive was to retaliate, Fanny can stay, getting a judgment against Abe for court costs and for attorney fees (if either party is entitled to them in the lease or rental agreement). However, once it's settled that Fanny stays, her rent for April and May ($800 total) will come due. If Fanny doesn't pay the rent, Abe can legitimately serve her a Three-Day Notice To Pay Rent or Quit, and sue again if the rent still remains unpaid.

EXAMPLE 2

On September 1, Dolores gives her tenant Kit a 30-day notice increasing Kit's rent from $500 to $550 per month. On October 1, Kit hands Dolores a check for $500, refusing to pay the $50 increase on the basis that it was retaliatory. Kit, who began organizing a building tenants' union in July, is convinced the increase is Dolores's way of striking back. Dolores accepts the $500, but then gives Kit a three-day notice to pay the $50 or vacate. When Kit does neither, Dolores files suit based on nonpayment of rent, Kit answers with a retaliatory rent increase defense, and the case goes to trial about November 15.

If Dolores wins, the judge will award her the unpaid $50 for October, plus the pro-rated rent of $275 through November 15, court costs, attorney fees if appropriate, and of course, possession of the property; Kit will have to move.

If Kit wins, the judge will order Dolores to pay Kit's court costs and attorney fees, if applicable. Since the decision is in Kit's favor, the judge has clearly decided the rent increase was retaliatory; thus, the proper rent is $500 after all. Of course, now that it's November, and the case is over, with Kit staying on, he'll owe Dolores the $500 rent in November.

Although the above examples show both the tenants and the landlords fighting bitter court battles to the very end, the examples are intended only to show what the law provides for when taken to this extreme. This isn't to say that both parties can't try to compromise at any stage. Always keep in mind that a landlord's victory can sometimes be hollow. If after spending hundreds (or even thousands) of dollars on lawyers and filing fees and going without rent while the lawsuit is pending, the landlord winds up with an empty apartment and a court judgment that is uncollectible because the tenant skipped town or is judgment proof (has no assets), the landlord has not gained much.

2. Tenant Lawsuits Against the Landlord

It's also important for all landlords to realize that a tenant who feels the landlord has illegally retaliated against her doesn't have to sit back and wait for the landlord to take the matter to court. The tenant can initiate a lawsuit. Many tenants' attorneys advise their clients to do just this in order to put the landlord at a psychological disadvantage. In effect, the tenant asks the court to rule that the landlord's conduct was retaliatory, and to bar the landlord from bringing an eviction suit.

The tenant can also ask for money. A tenant who sues a landlord and convinces a judge or jury that the landlord illegally retaliated against her for exercising a legal right can obtain a judgment for damages for emotional distress, mental pain and suffering, punitive damages, court costs and attorney fees, even if the lease or rental agreement doesn't have an attorney fees clause.[7] Potential liability in these suits can and does reach tens of thousands of dollars.

The defense of this sort of lawsuit is well beyond the scope of this book, and a lawyer is strongly advisable. If you have a good landlord's insurance policy which protects you from so-called "illegal acts," this will cover you in this situation (except for the deductible amount and punitive damages), and you can turn your legal defense over to the insurance company. See Chapter 12 on landlord liability for tenantability-related defects, where landlord insurance is discussed in more detail. If you have no insurance, see Chapter 8 on how to find, compensate and work with a lawyer.

It's also important to realize that a tenant doesn't have to bring a lawsuit before the landlord does in order to be able to obtain money damages. If the landlord brings an eviction suit, and the tenant defends on the basis of retaliation and wins, the tenant, bolstered by her victory, can bring another suit for damages. In fact, the tenant who won the preceding eviction suit on the basis that the landlord illegally retaliated may be able to apply the rulings from the first lawsuit to the second one, so as to prevent the landlord from again denying and litigating the issue of retaliation. In other words, the only issue in the second suit will be how much the landlord owes the tenant. This is one more illustration of how important it is to not engage in retaliatory behavior or, in spite of these efforts, to win or settle any eviction suit where the tenant defends on the basis of retaliatory eviction.

---

[7] See also CC § 1942.5(f). *Newby v. Alto Rivera Apartments,* 60 Cal. App. 3d 288, 131 Cal. Rptr. 547 (1976).

The Three-Day Notice To Pay Rent or Quit

A landlord who is serious about having tenants pay their rent on time must be prepared to use the tools the law provides for enforcing payment. Ultimately, the landlord's most powerful weapon to assure payment of rent is her right to file an eviction lawsuit against tenants who don't pay. Although we reserve discussion of how to bring an eviction lawsuit for the second volume, there is one preliminary aspect of a rent-nonpayment suit which must be outlined here. This is the requirement that a landlord give the tenant three days' written notice to pay the rent or quit (leave). This chapter show you how to give that notice.

Related Topics

- Laws regarding how much rent you can charge, where, how and when rent is due, and accepting partial rent payments: Chapter 3

- How to end a tenancy with a 30-day notice and various other types of three-day notices: Chapter 18

A. When To Use a Three-Day Notice

Many landlords resist handing out three-day notices. After all, preparing and serving a three-day notice involves at least a little bit of trouble, and it's easy to conclude that it is the first step in what is sure to be a nasty court eviction battle, something almost every landlord dreads.

First, you should realize that serving a Three-Day Notice To Pay Rent or Quit does not necessarily lead to a lawsuit. A three-day notice is a tool designed to get the tenant to pay rent, not to evict her. Remember, an eviction lawsuit is generally something the tenant wants to avoid at least as much as you do. In fact, most tenants who receive a three-day notice do pay up within the three days.

In a few cases, tenants don't pay, which means the three-day notice becomes the first step in a court action. If this occurs, the judge will likely scrutinize the notice carefully. If the notice contains certain errors, you will lose an eviction lawsuit, perhaps having to pay the tenant's attorney fees. In other words, even though a three-day notice doesn't necessarily lead to an unlawful detainer suit, you usually don't know in advance whether a particular notice will be the first step in a lawsuit. It may be; you should therefore take pains to be sure all notices you prepare and serve are legally correct.

B. How To Determine the Amount of Rent Due

The most common type of defect in a three-day notice involves the landlord demanding more rent than is due, or demanding improper extras, such as late charges, check-bounce fees, interest, utility charges or even past due installments promised by the tenant towards a security deposit.

These are costly mistakes: If the three-day notice demands the wrong amount, it does not legally terminate the tenancy. To win an eviction lawsuit against a tenant who fails to pay rent, the judge has to rule that the tenancy was properly terminated by your having served a valid three-day notice on the tenant, followed by the tenant's nonpayment within the three days. A tenancy isn't legally terminated unless the three-day notice to which a tenant fails to respond stated the proper rent amount and was legally correct in other respects. For example, a three-day notice demanding $1,450 from a tenant who owes only $1,400 isn't legally sufficient to terminate the tenancy even though the tenant does owe the $1,400, and a judge won't allow an eviction based on the incorrect rent amount.

To avoid making a mistake in your three-day notice, you should keep the following rules in mind:

Do not demand anything other than past due rent in a three-day notice. Do not include late charges, fees of any kind, interest, utility charges or anything else in a three-day notice—even if a written lease or rental agreement says you're entitled to payment for such items. Does this mean that you cannot legally collect these charges? No. It simply means you can't legally include them in the three-day notice or recover them in an eviction lawsuit. You can deduct these amounts from the security deposit or sue for them later in small claims court. See Chapter 20.

Rent control note. If your three-day notice demands more rent than was legally due under the local rent control ordinance, the notice is defective. You can't evict a tenant for refusal to pay a rent increase that was illegal under a rent control ordinance, even if the tenant also refuses to pay the part of the rent that is legal under the ordinance. A three-day notice is also defective under a rent control ordinance if the landlord at any time collected rents in excess of those allowed under the ordinance and failed to credit the tenant with the overcharges, even though she now charges the correct rent and seeks to evict only on nonpayment of the legal rent. Since the previously collected excess rents must be credited against unpaid legal rent, any three-day notice that doesn't give the tenant credit for previous overcharges is legally ineffective because it demands too much rent. Check your local rent control ordinance for any special requirements on three-day notices.

Rent is almost always due in advance for the entire rental period. (See Clause 4 of our form lease and rental agreements, Chapter 2.) For example, rent is due in advance on November 1 for the period November 1 through November 30. In other words, the amount of rent due is not apportioned on the basis of the date the three-day notice is served, but is due for the whole month, on the first or other rent payment date. The only time rent must be appor-

tioned as part of a three-day notice is when the tenancy terminates in the middle of the rental period, usually because of an earlier 30-day notice. For example, if the landlord gives a 30-day notice on November 15, the tenancy should terminate on December 15. This means that on December 1, only 15 days' rent is due if the rental period begins on the first of the month. If the tenant fails to pay on the first, the landlord should serve a three-day notice demanding only pro-rated rent for the 15-day period. To do this, you must first arrive at a daily rental amount. This is easy. The daily rental is always taken to be the monthly rental divided by 30, even in months with 28, 29 or 31 days.

If the tenant has paid you part, but not all, of the rent due, your demand for rent must reflect the partial payment. See Chapter 3.F, for a discussion of accepting partial rent payments after a three-day notice.

You do not have to credit any part of a security deposit to the amount of rent you ask for in the three-day notice. In other words, you have a right to wait until after the tenant has moved, to see if you should apply the deposit to cover any necessary damages or cleaning. See Chapter 20.

Here are a few examples of how rent is calculated in various situations:

EXAMPLE 1

Richard has been paying $500 rent to his landlord Loretta on the first of each month, as provided by a written rental agreement. On October 6, Richard still hasn't paid his rent, and Loretta serves him with a three-day notice to pay the $500 or leave. (Although Loretta has, in effect, given Richard the benefit of a five-day grace period, she didn't have to, and could have given Richard the notice on October 2.) Even though the rental agreement provides for a $10 late charge after the second day, Loretta should not list that amount in the three-day notice.

EXAMPLE 2

Dan's rent of $750 is due the 15th of each month for the period of the 15th through the 14th of the next month—in advance of course. Dan's check for the period from October 15 through November 14 bounces, but his landlord Len doesn't discover this until November 15. Now, Dan not only refuses to make good on the check, but also refuses to pay the rent due for the November 15 through December 15 period. It's now November 20. What should Len ask for in his three-day notice? Dan owes Len $750 for October 15-November 14 (the rent which was to have been covered by the bounced check), plus $750 for the period November 15-December 14. The three-day notice should demand payment of $1,500. Len should not add check-bouncing charges or late fees to the amount in the three-day notice. And even though Dan promises to leave in a few days, Len should demand rent for the entire period of November 15 through December 14.

EXAMPLE 3

Laurie gives Dean a 30-day notice on June 10, after Dean paid his June rent (due on June 1) nine days late. Because the 30-day notice will terminate Dean's tenancy on July 10, Dean will only owe rent for the first ten days of July due on the first day of that month. In this situation, rent should be apportioned if it is necessary to send a three-day notice. In other words, if Dean doesn't pay up on July 1, the three-day notice Laurie gives Dean on July 2 should demand this 10 days' rent, or 1/30th of the monthly rent ($350/30 =$11.66/day) for each of these days, a total of 10 x $11.66, or $116.60.

EXAMPLE 4

Renee is a month-to-month tenant who pays her landlord $600 rent on the first of each month. On June 30, she gives her landlord a 30-day notice saying she'll be leaving at the end of July. Her letter also says "Please consider my $600 security deposit as the last month's rent for the month of July." Renee's landlord has no obligation to let Renee do this, and can serve her a three-day notice demanding July's rent of $600 on July 2, the day after it's due. As a practical matter, however, he might be wiser to ask Renee for permission to inspect the property to see if it is in good enough condition to justify the eventual return of the security deposit. If so, there is little to be gained by filing a three-day notice and then suing for unpaid rent, since by the time the case gets before a judge, the need to return the security deposit (this must be done within 14 days after Renee leaves) will cancel it out.

To summarize, to issue a correct three-day notice, demand only rent, due in advance and not pro-rated (except where the tenancy terminates in the middle of a rental period because of the service of an earlier 30-day notice), and give credit for partial rent payments, but not for any part of the security deposit.

Note on habitability defenses. In arriving at the amount of rent due, you do not have to anticipate a claim by your tenant that she doesn't owe the entire rent because the property was "untenantable" for all or part of the time for which you claim rent. In other words, ask for the entire amount due under the terms of the lease or rental agreement. If the tenant doesn't pay (or the two of you don't work out a compromise settlement and you file an unlawful detainer lawsuit), it's up to the tenant to assert her habitability defense in court. However, if you expect a tenant to raise a habitability defense in court, we strongly urge you to read Chapter 11 before proceeding.

On the other hand, if a tenant has deducted from the rent the actual cost of repairs of a habitability-related defect, and notified you of that earlier, you should give the tenant credit for the cost of repair, if the deduction is legitimate and proper. (See Chapter 11.)

C. How To Fill Out a Three-Day Notice

A sample Three-Day Notice To Pay Rent or Quit appears below, and a blank tear-out form is included in the Appendix. You may tear out the form or use a copy, following the instructions that follow the sample form.

Pay close attention to the directions. Any mistake in the notice, however slight, may give your tenant (or her attorney) an excuse to contest or delay any eviction lawsuit you may ultimately bring if the tenant doesn't pay up in response to your notice. At worst, a mistake in the three-day notice may render your unlawful detainer lawsuit "fatally defective"—which means you lose, must pay the tenant's court costs and attorney fees (in addition to your own), and have to start all over again with a correct three-day notice.

For example, if you just demand the rent and do not set out the alternative of the tenant leaving, your notice is fatally defective. The notice must also include a statement that you will pursue legal action (or declare the lease or rental agreement "forfeited") if the tenant does not pay the entire rent or move.

DIRECTIONS FOR COMPLETING THE THREE-DAY NOTICE TO PAY RENT OR QUIT

Step 1.   Fill in the Tenant's Name

The first blank is for the name(s) of the tenant(s) to whom the three-day notice is addressed. Although this is technically not required, it is so customary to put the tenant's name on a three-day notice that to omit it could invite a delaying tactic from a tenant's attorney on the theory that the tenant might not have known it was for her. Be sure to list the names of the tenant(s) whose names are listed on a written lease or rental agreement, or with whom you orally entered into a rental agreement, plus the names, if known, of any other adult occupants of the property. (See Section D.3, Whom To Serve.)

Step 2.   Fill in the Address

List the street address, city and county. In addition, be sure to list the apartment number if your tenant lives in an apartment complex or in a condominium unit.

In the unlikely event the unit has no street address, you should use a legal description of the premises available from your deed to your property, along with an ordinary, understandable description of where the place is located—for example, "the small log cabin behind the third hill going north on River Road from Pokeyville." You can retype the notice to make room for the legal description or staple a separate property description as an attachment to the notice and type "the property described in the attachment to this notice" in place of the address.

Step 3.   Fill in the Rent Due

The next space is for you to fill in the amount of rent due. It is mandatory to state this figure accurately (see Section B above). Although it is not legally required to indicate the rental period(s) for which the rent is due, it is customary, and some judges who are used to seeing it may question, or even reject, notices that don't include the dates.

Step 4.   Sign and Date the Notice

The ultimatum language—that the tenant either pay the rent within three days or move out, or you'll bring legal action—and the "forfeiture" language are already included in the printed form. All you need to add are your signature and the date you signed it. The date is not legally required, but it helps to clarify when the rent was demanded. The date should not be the same day the rent was due, but at least one day later.

Be sure to make several copies for your records (the original goes to the tenant).

SAMPLE THREE-DAY NOTICE TO PAY RENT OR QUIT

Three-Day Notice To Pay Rent or Quit

To: _____ Tyrone Jones _____ ,
        (name)

Tenant(s) in possession of the premises at:

_____ 123 Market Street, Apartment 4 _____ ,
        (street address)

City of ___ San Diego ___, County of ___ San Diego ___, California.

Please take notice that the rent on these premises occupied by you, in the amount of $ __400__ ,

for the period from _____ August 1, 19 _____ to _____ August 31, 19 _____ ,

is now due and payable.

You Are Hereby Required to pay this amount within THREE (3) days from the date of service on you of this notice or to vacate and surrender possession of the premises. In the event you fail to do so, legal proceedings will be instituted against you to recover possession of the premises, declare the forfeiture of the rental agreement or lease under which you occupy the premises, and recover rents, damages and costs of suit.

Date: ____ August 5, 19 ____

Charles Austen _____
Owner/Manager

....

Proof of Service

I, the undersigned, served this notice, of which this is a true copy, on _____ , one of the occupants listed above as follows:

☐ On _____ , 199____, I delivered the notice to the occupant personally.

☐ On _____ , 199____, I delivered the notice to a person of suitable age and discretion at the occupant's residence/business after having attempted personal service at the occupant's residence, and business if know. On _____ , 199____, I mailed a second copy to the occupant at his or her residence.

☐ On _____ , 199____, I posted the notice in a conspicuous place on the property, after having attempted personal service at the occupant's residence, and business, if known, and after having been unable to find there a person of suitable age and discretion. On _____ , 199____, I mailed a second copy to the occupant at the property.

I declare under penalty of perjury under the laws of the State of California that the foregoing is true and correct.

Dated: _____ , 199____   _____

Step 5. Complete the Proof of Service Box on Your Copy of the Notice

At the bottom of the Three-Day Notice To Pay Rent or Quit is a "Proof of Service" which indicates the name of the person served, the manner of service and the date(s) of service. You or whoever served the notice on the tenant should fill out the Proof of Service on your copy of the three-day notice and sign it. You do not fill out the Proof of Service on the original notice that is given to the tenant. If more than one person is served with the notice, there should be a separate Proof of Service (on a copy of the notice) for each person served. Save the filled-out Proof(s) of Service on the copies of the three-day notice—you'll need these if you end up filing an eviction lawsuit.

D. Serving the Three-Day Notice on the Tenant

The law is very strict about when and how you give the three-day notice to your tenant(s).[1] Even a slight departure from the rules may result in your losing any eviction lawsuit you bring if it is contested.

1. When To Serve the Notice

The Three-Day Notice To Pay Rent or Quit can be given to your tenant on any day after the rent was due, but not on the day it is due. For example, if the rent for a particular month is due on the first day of each month, if you give the notice to the tenant on that day, it will have no legal effect. Of course, if you allow a several-day grace period (remember, you don't legally have to, before serving the notice), you will have no problem.

If the rent comes due on a Saturday, Sunday or holiday, rent is due on the next business day.[2] The three-day notice cannot be given until the next day after that. This is one of the many technicalities of eviction law that is not corrected by the passage of time after the lawsuit is filed. Bizarre as it sounds, if you gave the notice only a day prematurely, but the tenant still didn't pay the rent during the two to three weeks he contested the lawsuit, you may still lose the case anyway. The moral is simple—count your days carefully.

EXAMPLE

When Tara didn't pay her $400 rent to her landlord Helga on Friday, January 1, Helga prepared a Three-Day Notice to Pay Rent or Quit, giving it to Tara the next day. Unfortunately for Helga, the rent wasn't actually due until January 4, even though Tara's lease said it was due on the first, because January first, New Year's Day, was a legal holiday, as were January 2nd and 3rd, Saturday and Sunday. Oblivious to all this, Helga waited the three days, and, as Tara still hadn't paid the rent, filed her eviction lawsuit on January 6. Tara contested it, and the case finally went to court on February 5. Even though Tara clearly owes Helga the rent for January, and now for February, Helga loses the lawsuit because Helga gave Tara the three-day notice before the rent was legally past due. Now Helga will have to pay Tara's court costs as well as her own. Assuming Tara has still not paid the rent, Helga can, of course, serve a new three-day notice and begin the eviction procedure again.

---

[1] See *Lydon v. Beach*, 89 Cal. App. 69 (1928) (notice can be served only after rent falls due), and CCP § 1162 (manner of service).

---

[2] Although Civil Code Section 7 defines "holidays" to include Sundays and special legal holidays, Section 12a of the Code of Civil Procedure (which governs Three-Day Notices To Pay Rent or Quit) defines "holiday" to include Saturdays also. Legal duties—including the payment of rent—which fall on such a holiday need not be performed until the next business day. CC § 11, CCP §12a.

2. Who Should Serve the Three-Day Notice?

Anyone over the age of eighteen can legally give or serve the three-day notice on the tenant. However, if you have to bring an eviction lawsuit against the tenant, that person may have to come to court to testify that he or she gave the tenant the notice, so make sure you pick someone who will be available.

You can legally serve the notice yourself, but it's often a better business practice to have it served by someone else. Many owners have their managers serve all three-day notices. That way, if the tenant refuses to pay the rent and contests the resulting eviction suit by falsely claiming he didn't receive the notice, you will not have to rely on your own testimony that you served the notice. Instead, you can present the testimony of someone not a party to the lawsuit who is more likely to be believed by a judge. Of course, you must weigh this advantage against your time, trouble or expense getting someone else to serve the three-day notice and, if necessary, appear in court.

3. Whom To Serve

If you rented your property to just one tenant, whose name alone appears on any written rental agreement or lease, you should serve that person with the three-day notice.

If you rented to more than one tenant, it's a good idea to serve separate copies of the three-day notice on each, even though it is legally sufficient for a landlord to serve just one of several co-tenants who are all listed on a written lease or rental agreement.[3] We recommend serving everyone to minimize the possibility that a non-served tenant will try to defend against any subsequent eviction lawsuit on the ground that he didn't receive the notice.

You normally have no obligation to serve the three-day notice on occupants who are not named in the written rental agreement or lease and with whom you've had no dealings in renting the property. However, if the tenant has rented to a sub-tenant (even illegally) and left, so that only one or more sub-tenants live there, you must serve the sub-tenants, in addition to the tenant.[4] (Serve the non-resident tenant by substituted service (see Section 4, below). However, if the person has been living in your property for some time—for example, the lover or roommate of one of your tenants—and you have had contact with the person and treated them as a tenant (perhaps you even accepted rent from them), you should serve them with a three-day notice as well. We discuss who is and who is not a tenant in Chapter 10.

4. How the Notice Is Served on the Tenant

The law is very strict on how the three-day notice must be served on the tenant.[5] It is not enough that you mail the notice or simply post it on the door. Here are the three legal methods of service for a three-day notice:

Personal service. The best way to serve the three-day notice is to simply hand your tenant the notice. It isn't necessary that the tenant take the notice in his hand; if he refuses to do so, it may be dropped at his feet. Giving the notice to any other person, such as someone who lives with your tenant but is not listed as a co-tenant on the written rental agreement, is not sufficient, except as described next under the heading "Substituted Service."

Substituted service on another person. If the tenant you're attempting to give the three-day notice to never seems to be home, and you know where she works, you should try to personally serve her at the

---

[3]*University of Southern California v. Weiss*, 208 Cal. App. 2 d 759, 25 Cal. Rptr. 475 (1962).

[4]*Chinese Hospital Foundation Fund v. Patterson*, 1 Cal. App. 3d 627, 632, 8 Cal. Rptr. 795 (1969); see CCP § 1161(2).

[5]CCP § 1162.

place of employment. If you are unable to locate the tenant at either place, the law allows you to use substituted service in lieu of personally giving the notice to the tenant. That means you can leave a copy of the notice with an adult at the tenant's home or workplace and mail a second copy to the tenant at home. The first day of the notice's three-day period is the day after both these steps are accomplished.

Substituted service rules are contained in Chapter 14.D.

EXAMPLE

Andy should have paid his rent on the first of the month. By the fifth, you're ready to serve him with a Three-Day Notice to Pay Rent or Quit. When you try to personally serve it on him at home, a friend of Andy's answers the door, saying Andy's not home. You can't serve the notice on Andy's friend yet because you still have to try Andy's workplace—the one listed on the rental application Andy filled out when he moved in. You go to Andy's workplace only to find that Andy called in sick that day. You could either give the notice to one of Andy's co-workers, or go back and give it to his friend at home, with instructions to give it to Andy when they see him. After that, you mail another copy of the notice to Andy at home by ordinary first-class mail. Service is complete only after all this has been done.

Posting and mailing service. If you can't find the tenant on whom you wish to serve the three-day notice, and you can't find anyone else at home or work (or if you don't know where the tenant is employed), you may serve the three-day notice through a procedure known as "posting and mailing." To do this, attach a copy of the three-day notice to the tenant's front door, and mail another copy, following the instructions in Chapter 14.D.

EXAMPLE

Lana 's rent is due on the 15th of each month, but she still hasn't paid you by the 20th. You can never find her (or anyone else) at home, and you don't know where she works. Since that leaves no one whom to personally or substitute serve the three-day notice, that leaves you with the posting-and-mailing alternative. You can tape one copy to the door of the property and mail a second copy to her at that address by regular first-class mail. Begin counting the three days with the next day after both of these tasks are accomplished.

5. Counting the Three Days After Service

The date of service is the date you hand the tenant the notice, if you use personal service. If you left the three-day notice with someone else at the tenant's home (or office) or posted a copy on the premises and mailed another copy, the date of service is the date you took that action. It doesn't matter that the tenant didn't actually receive the notice until later.[6]

To count the three days, do the following:

- Ignore the date of service and start counting on the next day.
- Count three days.
- If the third day falls on a Saturday, Sunday or holiday, ignore that day and move on to the next business day.

---

[6]*Walters v. Meyers*, 226 Cal. App. 3d Supp. 15 (1990). There is, however, some contradictory case law on this issue. An appeals court in Santa Clara County has ruled that posting-and-mailing service isn't effective, and that the notice's three-day period doesn't begin running, until the first day after the tenant actually receives the notice. *Davidson v. Quin*, 138 Cal. App. 3d Supp. 9, 188 Cal. Rptr. 421 (1982).This could cause problems where the tenant claims he never received the notice or received it several days after the posting and mailing. Although this ruling defies common sense, it is legally binding in Santa Clara County. It is not binding in other counties, but judges in other counties may follow the ruling, so avoid posting-and-mailing service if other methods are possible. Otherwise, try to talk to the tenant—before you file an eviction lawsuit—and pin her down as to having received the notice. (Don't ask, "Did you get my three-day notice?" Ask, "When are you going to pay the rent I asked for in the three-day notice I left you?")

EXAMPLE 1

You serve the tenant with a three-day notice on Wednesday. To count the three days, do not count Wednesday; begin with Thursday. This makes Saturday the third day. But Saturday is a holiday, and so is Sunday. So the third day is Monday. Therefore, the tenant has until the end of Monday to comply. If you file your eviction lawsuit before Tuesday, it may be thrown out of court if the tenant raises the issue.

EXAMPLE 2

You serve the tenant on Friday. Saturday is the first day, Sunday is the second day and Monday is the third day. Neither of the weekend days extends the three-day period.

If the tenant pays before the end of the three days, the notice is cancelled and she doesn't have to leave. After three days, you may refuse the tenant's rent and proceed with an eviction suit. If you accept rent (even a partial payment) after the three-day period, however, you waive your right to evict for the late payment.[7]

E. If the Tenant Still Won't Pay (or Leave)

Although one of the main purposes behind a Three-Day Notice To Pay Rent or Quit is to get the tenant to pay, you may be faced with a tenant who still won't or can't pay the rent within the three days. As we'll see in Chapter 17, it is illegal to harass the tenant in any way, even if she has no valid reason for not paying. Threatening or physically evicting a tenant or cutting off his or her utilities is illegal and may subject you to severe liability. The only legal way to evict a nonpaying tenant who won't move voluntarily is to file an eviction lawsuit, go to court and obtain a judgment that the sheriff or marshal evict the tenant. Eviction lawsuits are discussed in Chapter 18 and in detail in the second volume.

---

[7]*EDC Associates, Ltd. v. Gutierrez*, 153 Cal. App. 3d 169 (1984).

Landlord No-No's: Self-Help Evictions, Utility Terminations and Taking Tenants' Property

As any experienced landlord will attest, there are occasional tenants who do things so outrageous that the landlord is tempted to bypass normal legal protections and take direct and immediate action to protect his property. For example, after numerous broken promises to pay rent, a landlord may consider changing the locks and putting the tenant's property out in the street. Or, in a situation where the landlord is responsible for paying the utility charges, he may be tempted to simply not pay the bill in the hopes that the resulting lack of water, gas or electricity will hasten the tenant's departure. When you realize how long a legal eviction can sometimes take, these actions can almost seem sensible.

If you are tempted to take the law into your own hands to force or scare a troublesome tenant out of your property, heed the following advice: *Don't do it!* Only the sheriff, marshal or constable is legally allowed to physically evict a tenant, and then only after the landlord has obtained a court order allowing the eviction to take place.[1] (We show you how to do this in *Volume 2, Evictions.*) Evictions, or attempted evictions, by anyone else are illegal and may result in arrest, a lawsuit by the tenant for a great deal of money, or both. Obtaining such a court order and having the appropriate law enforcement officials carry out the eviction certainly entails some trouble, expense and delay. This is a cost of the property rental business that can be minimized by proper selection of tenants and good management techniques, but can never be completely eliminated.

If you are sued by a tenant who you forcibly evicted or tried to evict, the fact that the tenant didn't pay rent, left your property a mess, verbally abused you, or otherwise acted outrageously, will not be a valid defense. You will very likely lose the law-

suit, and it will cost you far more than evicting the tenant using normal court procedures.

This chapter discusses the rules regarding forcible evictions, other coercive attempts to get tenants out and the taking of tenants' belongings, all of which are illegal.

Related Topics

- How to anticipate and avoid liability for retaliatory rent increases and evictions: Chapter 15
- The legal rules and procedures for evicting a tenant: Chapter 18

A. Forcible Evictions

It is illegal for a landlord (or anyone else) to forcibly enter a tenant's residence or to peaceably enter the residence and then force or threaten the tenant out.[2] It's just as illegal for a landlord to knock on the tenant's door, be invited in and then threaten to bodily evict the tenant, as it is for a landlord to kick down the door or break a window to enter the property. Or, to take another example, if a landlord simply tells a tenant: "I want you out," while accompanied by sufficiently numerous or large persons apparently capable of accomplishing the task, the landlord is courting serious legal trouble.

A landlord foolish enough to evict, or try to evict, by force or threat can be sued by the tenant under all sorts of legal theories, including trespass, assault, battery (if physical force is used against the tenant), and even intentional infliction of emotional distress.[3] Enough said, we hope.

See Chapter 13 for a discussion of a landlord's rights of entry and tenant remedies if a landlord acts illegally and invades a tenant's privacy.

---

[1] There is one exception to this. Civil Code Section 1946.5 and Penal Code § 602.3 allow an owner-occupant of a house who is renting to no more than one roomer or lodger, to insist—without going to court—that the local police evict the lodger for nonpayment of rent after three days, or for refusing to leave after expiration of a 30-day notice.

[2] CCP §§1159 and 1160.

[3] *Newby v. Alta Rivera Apartments*, 60 Cal. App. 3d 288 (1976).

B. Locking or Driving the Tenant Out Without Force

It is illegal for a landlord to use any of the following nonviolent methods to evict or drive out a tenant:[4]

- Locking the tenant out by changing the locks in his absence, attaching a "bootlock" to the door or nailing the door shut

- Removing doors or windows in the hope that the tenant will move out because of the resulting drafty and unsecured dwelling

- Removing any of the tenant's property, or even the landlord's furniture rented as part of furnished premises

- Shutting off any of the utilities (including gas, electricity, water or elevator service), or causing them to be shut off by nonpayment where the landlord pays for the utilities.

Reminder. Even if your lease or rental agreement form contains a provision that purports to allow the landlord to break into the tenant's home, change the locks, recover property, shut off the utilities or otherwise legally forgo the requirements of a lawful eviction, it is completely void and of no effect. (See Chapter 2.E.)

---

[4]CC § 789.3.

It's possible that not all utility cut-offs violate this law. For example, suppose a landlord who pays for the tenant's utilities properly gives a month-to-month tenant a 30-day notice of change of terms of tenancy which requires the tenant to put the utilities in his own name and pay for them. (This may not be permissible in certain rent-controlled cities.) If the tenant refuses, and the landlord stops paying for the utilities, so as to result in a shutoff, the landlord's intent is not to illegally evict the tenant, but to enforce a proper change in terms. Still, this course is risky, since a judge may feel differently. Also, if it turns out that for any reason the change in the terms of the rental agreement is not effective— for example, the 30-day notice was defective or found to be retaliatory in a later court action—the utility shutoff is at least a breach of contract for which the landlord can still be held liable.

In a lawsuit by a tenant against a landlord accused of unlawful lock-out, property removal or utility shutoff, a court may award the tenant all of the following:

- The tenant's "actual damages." This can include damages for inconvenience, emotional distress or humiliation, loss of property illegally removed by the landlord (or stolen or damaged by third persons after the landlord put the property outside), and loss of use of the premises. Examples include tenant losses for such things as meat spoiling in the refrigerator after the electricity is turned off or motel bills if the tenant has to find a temporary place to live because the utilities were turned off.

- Punitive damages of up to $100 for each day, or fraction of a day, that the tenant is unable to stay in the premises or goes without utilities or without property removed by the landlord, with a minimum punitive damages liability of $250.

- Additional punitive damages if the landlord's conduct is especially outrageous, such as beating up the tenant or taking his property. In 1988, a jury awarded 23 tenants of a San Francisco residential hotel $1.48 million from their landlord, who had cut off water, entered tenants' rooms without notice and threatened the tenants, most of whom were elderly or disabled.[5]

- A court-ordered award of attorney fees, even if the lease or rental agreement has no attorney fees clause.

- A restraining order, injunction or other court order preventing the landlord, under penalty of contempt of court, from using any other illegal means to attempt to get the tenant out.

A tenant can bring suit in small claims court (for up to $5,000), or retain a lawyer and sue in municipal court (for up to $25,000), or superior court (over $25,000).

As with suits for forcible eviction, a landlord cannot defend a suit for wrongful lock-out, property removal or utility shutoff on the basis that the tenant didn't pay the rent, promised to leave but didn't or did something else even more outrageous. The legal system takes the view that a landlord (or a tenant, for that matter), when faced with the tenant's (or landlord's) wrong, cannot take the law into his own hands, then later excuse himself because of the other's original misconduct. The place for the landlord to complain is in a separate suit against the tenant.

C. Seizing the Tenant's Property

You cannot take and sell a tenant's personal belongings without a court order if she fails to pay the rent. While state law allows a way to get such a court order, it is is of almost no practical value to a landlord.[6] First of all, the law applies mainly to persons residing in hotels and motels. Second, to obtain such an order, you must convince a judge that your tenant is about to destroy or remove his property—property on which you may have a lien in an actual innkeeper situation—from the premises. Even when the law applies, it requires that the tenant be given a hearing in court, separate from any hearing on the impending eviction case. Needless to say, the trouble and expense of doing this (not to mention the problems of getting a judge to sign the order) by far exceed any benefit you could obtain from being able to take the tenant's property. And even if you get the property, it's not likely to benefit you much; the tenant will probably be entitled to get most of it back.

D. Effect of Landlord's Forcible Eviction on a Tenant's Liability for Rent

Among the things that clearly excuse a tenant from paying the rent is eviction from the property or other interference with her right to "quiet enjoyment" of the premises. The tenant can also sue a landlord who interferes with his tenant's use of the property by forcibly evicting her, locking her out, removing her property or shutting off her utilities. And if the landlord himself sues to evict the tenant, it will be unclear how much rent the tenant still owes. Here's an example, based on an actual case handled by one of the authors:

---

[5]The trial judge had tripled the amount based on the San Francisco rent control law. The landlord appealed the verdict, however, and the appellate court ruled that the San Francisco rent control ordinance does not allow tripling awards for mental anguish. *Balmoral Hotel Tenants Association v. Lee*, 226 Cal. App. 3d. 686, 276 Cal. Rptr. 640 (1990). Still, after the appeal, the judgment stood at a hefty half-million dollars.

---

[6] CC §§1861-1861a, known as California's Baggage Lien Law.

EXAMPLE

Albert, exasperated at Rosie's repeated excuses for not coming up with the $850 monthly rent for July and August, entered Rosie's apartment on August 6, changed the locks, put Rosie's property and furniture in the hallway and shut off the utilities. Rosie and her two children stay with friends until her lawyer gets a court order letting Rosie move back in on August 10. Rosie's lawyer got the court order as part of a lawsuit against Albert for actual and punitive damages (including punitive damages of $100 per day for each of the five days when she was locked out). Albert sees a lawyer, who advises him to do what he should have done in the first place—file an unlawful detainer suit after service of the proper Three-Day Notice To Pay Rent or Quit.

On August 12, Albert prepares and serves the three-day notice, which demands the full $1,700 rent for July and August. Rosie defends on the basis that the lock-out reduced the rent actually due by an amount equal to five days' pro-rated rent, so that only $1,558 was due. At the unlawful detainer trial a month later, the judge rules that the three-day notice was defective because it erroneously demanded $1,700. Since it was defective, it didn't legally terminate Rosie's tenancy. Accordingly, Rosie wins, getting a judgment against Albert for attorney fees under the attorney fees clause in her rental agreement. Albert has to start all over again with a new and correct three-day notice and unlawful detainer lawsuit. He eventually gets Rosie out in October. Rosie, of course, hasn't paid any rent all this time and Albert still has to defend against Rosie's lawsuit. In the end, Albert loses a few thousand dollars, when you add up the judgment against him, attorney fees and lost rent.

Terminating Tenancies

A landlord who wants to be rid of a troublesome tenant (particularly one who pays the rent in response to a three-day notice), generally will have to use a 30-day termination notice or a three-day notice that orders the tenant out. This chapter shows you how to legally terminate your tenant's tenancy by properly serving the appropriate termination notice. See *Landlord's Law Book, Volume 2: Evictions,* for details on the specific legal process for filing an unlawful detainer lawsuit to evict the tenant.

TERMINATION NOTICES AT A GLANCE

Kind of Termination Notice	When Used
30-Day Notice (no reason given)	To end month-to-month tenancy in non-rent control city. See Section A.
30-Day Notice (with reason for termination)	To end month-to-month tenancy in cities that require just cause for eviction, and in government-subsidized tenancies. See Section C.3.
Three-Day Notice (conditional)	To end month-to-month or fixed-term tenancy when tenant has violated a term of the tenancy but must be given a chance to correct it. See Section B.1 (or Section C.2 for cities that require just cause for eviction).
Three-Day Notice (unconditional)	To end month-to-month or fixed-term tenancy when tenant has violated a term of the tenancy which cannot be corrected in three days. May be preceded by warning letter demanding the tenant comply with terms of tenancy or face eviction notice. See Section B.2 (or Section C.2 for cities that require just cause for eviction).
Three-Day Notice for Nonpayment of Rent	To end month-to-month or fixed-term tenancy when tenant has paid rent late, primarily used in hope that tenant will stay and pay the rent. See Chapter 16.

Be meticulous in preparing notices. Landlords must strictly comply with all of the law's requirements when it comes to preparing and serving termination notices.[1] If you make even a small mistake in a required notice, or the tenant doesn't receive the notice, the eviction itself might be invalid and you may have to start the process over. Follow our directions carefully. If you're unsure about notice requirements or have any doubt about the language or validity of your termination notice, consult an attorney specializing in landlord-tenant law.

---

[1]*Kwok v. Bergren,* 130 Cal. App. 3d 596, 599-600 (1982).

Related Topics

- Lease and rental agreement provisions on grounds and procedures for ending tenancies: Chapter 2

- Evicting a manager: Chapter 6

- Highlighting termination rules and procedures in a move-in letter to the tenant: Chapter 7

- How to find and use legal help for evictions: Chapter 8

- Illegal reasons and procedures for terminating a tenancy: Chapters 9 (discrimination), 15 (retaliation) and 17 (forcible evictions)

- Starting the tenancy termination process for non-payment of rent: Chapter 16

- Termination of month-to-month rental agreements and fixed-term leases by the tenant, including situations when the tenant leaves before the end of the term: Chapter 19

A. The 30-Day Notice in Cities That Don't Require Just Cause for Eviction

As a general rule, a landlord may give a tenant with a month-to-month tenancy a 30-day termination notice for any reason, or for no reason at all.[2]

There are, however, some important restrictions on the use of 30-day notices:

Rent control cities that require just cause for eviction. In the cities of Berkeley, Beverly Hills, Cotati, East Palo Alto, Hayward, Los Angeles, San Francisco, Santa Monica, Thousand Oaks and West Hollywood, the 30-day termination notice must state the reason for termination. See Section C, below.

Subsidized housing. When the landlord receives rent or other payments from a federal, state or local program to assist low-income tenants, the form lease drafted by the government agency usually lists acceptable reasons for termination. You must state one of these reasons in the 30-day notice when terminating housing-authority-assisted ("Section 8") tenancies or Housing and Urban Development (HUD)-assisted tenancies.[3] (See Chapter 9.B for information on Section 8 tenancies.)

Discrimination. Even if just cause for eviction isn't required, you can't evict because of race, religion, sex, marital status, having children, sexual preference or other arbitrary reasons. (See Chapter 9 on discrimination.)

Retaliatory eviction. You can never legally terminate a tenancy to retaliate against a tenant for exercising any right under the law, such as the tenant's right to complain about housing conditions or to organize other tenants into a tenants' union. (See Chapter 15 for details on illegal retaliation.)

1. When To Use a 30-Day Notice

Your reason for terminating a tenancy can become relevant, even though legally you aren't required to have one, if a tenant accuses you of discrimination or retaliation. In any eviction lawsuit based on termination by a 30-day notice, if the tenant claims your motive is to retaliate or discriminate, you will have to counter with the true non-retaliatory, non-

---

[2]As noted in Chapter 2.E, if a rental agreement so specifies, or rent is paid at a shorter interval, a periodic tenancy can be ended with less than 30 days' notice.

[3]"Section 8" refers to Section 8 of the United States Housing Act of 1937 (42 U.S.C. Section 1437f), a federal law providing government housing assistance to low-income families. Another federal law providing government housing assistance is Section 236 of the National Housing Act of 1949 (12 U.S.C. Section 1517z-1). Allowable reasons for eviction are contained in the standard-form leases the housing authority or HUD requires the landlord to use. See also Title 24, Code of Federal Regulations, Sections 450 et seq., 882 et seq. For additional information about the more stringent requirements for eviction from government-subsidized rentals, see the following cases: *Appel v. Beyer*, 39 Cal. App. 3d. Supp. 7 (1974); *Gallman v. Pierce*, 639 F. Supp. 472 (ND. Cal. 1986); *Mitchell v. Poole*, 203 Cal. App. 3d Supp. 1 (1988); *Gersten Companies v. Deloney*; 212 Cal. App. 3d 1119 (1989).

discriminatory reason for eviction. Make sure your reason for evicting any tenant is related to the smooth and peaceful operation of your rental business and cannot possibly be construed as either discriminatory or retaliatory.

Here are some valid reasons to give a 30-day notice in non-rent control cities:

- Your tenant is repeatedly late with the rent. You've given Three-Day Notices To Pay Rent or Quit several times, and the tenant has come through with the rent before the end of the third day. Your warnings to pay rent on time in the future have had no effect.

- The tenant has given you a number of bad checks. You've used three-day notices and the checks were made good, but it keeps happening.

- Your tenant repeatedly disturbs other tenants or neighbors by having loud and boisterous parties or playing a stereo at unreasonable levels. Other tenants are complaining to you.

- Your tenant is using illegal drugs in or about the property or, even worse, dealing in them. (We discuss evicting drug-dealing tenants in Section B.3, below.)

- The tenant has damaged the property—for example, by causing holes in the wall or cigarette burns in the carpet.

- The tenant is extremely obnoxious or vulgar to you, your manager or other tenants.

- Your tenant repeatedly violates a clause of your rental agreement, such as the "no pets" provision or a valid limit on the number of people living in the premises.

- You want the property vacant to remodel it.

- You're selling your rental property (a single-family dwelling, for example), and the new buyers want the tenants out before escrow closes.

- You want to move in yourself or want to rent the property to a close friend or relative.

In some of these cases, you can also use a three-day notice. Section B.5 below discusses why you're usually better off using a 30-day notice—when you have a choice.

2. Preparing the 30-Day Notice

A sample 30-day notice appears below and a blank tear-out form is in the Appendix.

As you can see, filling in this notice normally requires little more than: (1) the name of the tenant, (2) the address of the rental property, (3) the date and (4) your signature.

Be sure to make at least two copies for your records. The original goes to the tenant. Fill in the Proof of Service (indicating how, when and by whom the notice was served) on the copy after giving the original to the tenant. See Chapter 16.C for directions on completing the Proof of Service.

 If you are in a rent control city that requires that you state a reason for terminating a tenancy, you must follow the instructions in Section C.3, below.

Rental Agreement Requires Less Than 30-Days' Notice

If your rental agreement has a provision reducing the notice period required to terminate a tenancy to as low as seven days (see Chapter 2.C), you will have to modify our form slightly. Simply delete the "30" every place it appears and fill in the lesser number of days— for example, "seven."

If you collect rent once a month, be sure that a seven-day notice doesn't terminate the tenancy during a period for which you've already collected rent in advance. For example, if you collected the rent for August on August 1, serving a seven-day notice any sooner than August 24 would be an illegal attempt to end the tenancy before the end of the paid-for rental period, August 31.

SAMPLE 30-DAY NOTICE OF TERMINATION OF TENANCY (NON-RENT CONTROL CITY)

30-Day Notice of Termination of Tenancy

To: _____ _Jerry Hodges_ _____ ,
          (name)

Tenant(s) in possession of the premises at:

_____ 123 Market Street, Apartment 4 _____ ,
          (street address)

City of ___ San Diego ___, County of ___ San Diego ___, California.

    YOU ARE HEREBY NOTIFIED that effective 30 DAYS from the date of service on you of this notice, the periodic tenancy by which you hold possession of the premises is terminated, at which time you are required to vacate and surrender possession of the premises. If you fail to do so, legal proceedings will be instituted against you to recover possession of the premises, damages and costs of suit.

Date: ___ November 14, 19 ___   _Carlos Luiz_ _____
                                    Owner/Manager

....

Proof of Service

    I, the undersigned, served this notice, of which this is a true copy, on _____, one of the occupants listed above as follows:

☐ On _____, 199____, I delivered the notice to the occupant personally.

☐ On _____, 199____, I delivered the notice to a person of suitable age and discretion at the occupant's residence/business after having attempted personal service at the occupant's residence, and business if known. On _____, 199____, I mailed a second copy to the occupant at his or her residence.

☐ On _____, 199____, I posted the notice in a conspicuous place on the property, after having attempted personal service at the occupant's residence, and business, if known, and after having been unable to find there a person of suitable age and discretion. On _____, 199____, I mailed a second copy to the occupant at the property.

☐ On _____, 199____, I mailed the notice by certified mail addressed to the occupant at his or her place of residence.

    I declare under penalty of perjury under the laws of the State of California that the foregoing is true and correct.

Dated: _____, 199____   _____

3. Serving the 30-Day Notice

As with a Three-Day Notice To Pay Rent or Quit (see Chapter 16), you must follow specific procedures when serving a 30-day notice.

a. When To Serve a 30-Day Notice

A 30-day notice can be served on the tenant on any day of the month. For example, a 30-day notice served on March 17 terminates the tenancy effective 30 days later, on April 16. This is true even when rent is paid for a period running from the first to the last day of each month.

Simply count 30 days, regardless of whether the month has 28, 29 or 31 days. If the 30th day falls on a Saturday, Sunday or holiday, the tenant has until the close of the next business day (usually Monday) to move.

It's usually best to serve the 30-day notice shortly after you receive and cash the tenant's rent check for the month. If the tenant paid rent on time, the 30-day notice will usually be given toward the beginning of the month, and the last day of legal tenancy will fall several days into the next month. The advantage is that you will already have the rent for almost all the time the tenant can (legally) remain on the premises. If the tenant refuses to pay any more rent (for the day or two in the next month), you can just deduct it from the security deposit. (Chapter 20 shows how.)

EXAMPLE

Cleve is habitually late with his rent, usually paying on the third day after receiving your three-day notices. You decide it's time for a change of tenants. On October 2, you knock on Cleve's door and ask for the rent. If you luck out and get him to pay, cash the check. (You may even want to do it at his bank so that you get your money immediately.) After the check clears, promptly serve Cleve his 30-day notice. The last day of his tenancy will be in early November and on November 1, he'll only owe you a few days' rent. Since you can't bring an eviction lawsuit asking for this amount without a three-day notice (which really isn't worth the trouble), you can deduct this amount from the security deposit when Cleve leaves.

Of course, if Cleve doesn't pay his rent on the second day of October, you can use a Three-Day Notice To Pay Rent or Quit. If he still doesn't pay within three days, you can sue for nonpayment of rent. (See *Landlord's Law Book, Volume 2: Evictions.*)

If a 30-day notice terminates the tenancy in the middle of a month or rental period, the tenant will owe rent only for the period that ends on the 30th day.

EXAMPLE

Because of her constant loud parties, you serve your tenant, Rhoda, with a 30-day notice on August 13. The last day of the tenancy should be the 30th day after that, or September 12. On September 1, Rhoda owes you rent only for those first 12 days of September. The rent for each day is the monthly rent, $600, divided by 30, or $20. The rent for the first 12 days of September is 12 x $20, or $240.

Don't accept rent for a period beyond the 30-day period—if you do, you cancel the 30-day notice and will have to start all over again with a new one.[4] It is especially important to pro-rate rent accurately. Don't accept any rent at all if you collected "last month's rent" from the tenant.

---

[4]*EDC Associates, Ltd. v. Gutierrez,* 153 Cal. App. 3d 167, 171 (1984); *Highland Plastics, Inc. v. Enders,* 109 Cal. App. 3d Supp. 1, 11 (1980).

EXAMPLE

Because of her frequent late rent payments, you gave Sujata a 30-day notice on January 22, terminating her tenancy effective February 21. The rent is $1,200 per month, due on the first of the month. When Sujata moved in, you accepted $1,200 as "last month's rent." You are legally bound to use it for the last month's rent. Sujata's last month's rent (and more) is already paid. If you accept any rent at all on February 1, Sujata will be able to claim that you voided the 30-day notice by accepting rent beyond the notice period. Your best bet is to hold onto the last month's rent of $1,200, of which $840 is the actual rent for the first 21 days in February. The remaining $360 is handled like a security deposit, which you would have been wiser to call it in the first place. (See Chapter 5.E on security deposits.)

Many tenants served with a 30-day notice in the middle of a month or rental period will not be eager to pay rent for part of the next month. Their attitude may be, "You're evicting me anyway, so I'm not giving you anything." If you expect this reaction, talk to your tenant in advance and try to settle the issue amicably. If your efforts fail, you have two choices:

- Take the unpaid rent for that last portion of the month out of the security deposit; or

- Wait until the second day of the new 30-day period (the day after the tenant should have paid the rent) and serve the tenant with a Three-Day Notice To Pay Rent or Quit which demands payment for the pro-rated rent due. If the tenant refuses to pay or leave after the three days, you can file an unlawful detainer lawsuit based on nonpayment of rent. (You can't sue for this pro-rated rent in an eviction lawsuit based on the 30-day notice unless you also use a Three-Day Notice To Pay Rent or Quit.)

EXAMPLE

In the second example above, Rhoda owed $240 in pro-rated rent for the first 12 days of September. On September 1, Rhoda refuses to pay. On September 2, you serve Rhoda a three-day notice demanding that she pay the $240 rent or leave. If she ignores it, you can file a lawsuit based on her refusal to pay on September 6 without having to wait until the day after the 30-day period (September 13) to sue. If you decide to do this, refer to *The Landlord's Law Book: Volume 2: Evictions*.

If you give the 30-day notice on the last day of the month, or the first day of a 31-day month, so that the tenancy expires neatly at the end of the following month, you can avoid calculating pro-rated rent. Unfortunately, this requires that you give the tenant the 30-day notice on or before the rent for the entire last month is due, thus giving the tenant an opportunity to refuse to pay for an entire month. If the security deposit more than covers this amount, you may want to risk this.

b. Who Should Serve the 30-Day Notice?

The 30-day notice may be served by any person over age 18, including you. See Chapter 16.D.2, for some of the pros and cons of serving the notice yourself.

c. Whom To Serve

You should try to serve a copy of the 30-day notice on each tenant to whom you originally rented the property. However, as with a Three-Day Notice To Pay Rent or Quit, service of a 30-day notice on one of several co-tenants who are listed together on a written lease or rental agreement is legally sufficient. (See Chapter 16.D.3, for more on this.)

d. How To Serve the Notice

A 30-day notice may be legally be served in any of the three ways a Three-Day Notice To Pay Rent or Quit can be served:

- Personal service

- Substituted service on another person plus mailing or

- Posting and mailing.

These methods are explained in Chapter 16.D.4.

In addition, the 30-day termination notice may be served by certified mail, return receipt requested.[5]

B. The Three-Day Notice in Cities That Don't Require Just Cause for Eviction

Sometimes you may wish to use a three-day notice to terminate a tenancy, especially if the tenant has a fixed-term lease that doesn't expire for some time, as opposed to a month-to-month tenancy, in which a 30-day notice may be used. There are basically three types of three-day notices:

- Three-Day Notice To Pay Rent or Quit

- Three-Day Notice To Perform Covenant or Quit

- Three-Day Notice To Quit

1. The Three-Day Notice To Perform Covenant or Quit

If a tenant violates a lease or rental agreement clause, you can serve a three-day notice demanding that the tenant leave or correct the violation.[6] If the violation could be corrected within a reasonable period of

time, the notice must give the tenant the option to correct the violation. If the violation is not correctable, the notice need only tell the tenant to leave within three days. (See Section B.2, below.)

But tenants generally fail to respond to three-day notices that do give this option—other than Three-Day Notices To Pay Rent or Quit—so these notices are primarily a means for terminating a tenancy, with an eye toward initiating an eviction lawsuit.

Most lease or rental agreement violations are considered correctable. Those which are not considered correctable and for which the landlord therefore may serve an unconditional Three-Day Notice To Quit include: subletting, extensively damaging the premises, causing a nuisance (repeatedly disturbing other tenants or neighbors) or having used the premises for an illegal purpose. The tenant who violates a no-pets clause can correct the violation by getting rid of the pet; a tenant who refuses to pay an installment toward a security deposit which he agreed in the lease to pay can correct the violation by paying the installment.

Always give the tenant the benefit of the doubt on this one—if you're unsure, give the tenant the option of correcting the problem. If the tenant refuses to leave after getting your three-day notice and you have to file an eviction lawsuit, you don't want your case thrown out of court because you should have given the tenant the option in the notice but didn't.

Your Three-Day Notice To Perform Covenant or Quit should contain all of the following:

1. The tenant's name.

2. A description of the rental property—the street address, apartment number (if any), city and county.

3. A very specific statement as to how the tenant violated a particular provision of the rental agreement or lease. State that the tenant failed to "perform the covenant" (abide by a provision) of the lease, and cite the specific clause.

---

[5]Unlike 30-day notices changing terms of tenancy (covered in Chapter 14), certified mail service is specifically allowed for 30-day termination notices. CC §§ 827 and 1946.

[6]CCP 1161(3).

THREE-DAY NOTICES AT A GLANCE

Kind of Termination Notice	When Used
Three-Day Notice To Pay Rent or Quit	Requires the tenant who is late in paying the rent to pay the rent or move within three days. Failure to do so allows landlord to bring eviction lawsuit against the tenant. (See Chapter 16.)
Three-Day Notice To Perform Covenant or Quit	Requires the tenant who has violated a lease or rental agreement provision to correct the problem (perform covenant) or move (quit) within three days. For example, if the tenant's lease forbids pets, this type of three-day notice requires the tenant to get rid of her pet or move within three days. If the tenant does correct the problem within the three-day period, the tenancy continues. If the tenant does not correct the problem within three days, the landlord may bring an eviction lawsuit. This lawsuit is very similar to a lawsuit based on a Three-Day Notice To Pay Rent or Quit after the tenant has failed to pay. (See Section B.1.)
Three-Day Notice To Quit	Simply orders the tenant to leave and does not give the tenant the alternative of stopping his misbehavior. This type of notice can be used only if the tenant has sublet the premises, contrary to a lease or rental agreement provision; seriously and repeatedly disturbed neighbors or other tenants; seriously damaged the property; used the property for an illegal purpose; or violated the lease or rental agreement in a manner that cannot be corrected within three days. (See Section B.2.)

4. A demand that the covenant be "performed" (for example, by getting rid of the pet) within three days, or that the tenant leave the premises within three days if the violation is noncorrectable.

5. A statement that you will pursue legal action (or declare the lease or rental agreement "forfeited") if the tenant does not cure the violation or move within the three days.

6. Your signature, or that of your manager's. The date is optional.

Make at least two copies for your records.

Fill in the Proof of Service on the copy after giving the original to the tenant. See Chapter 16.C for directions on completing the Proof of Service.

A sample Three-Day Notice To Perform Covenant or Quit is shown below. A blank tear-out form is included in the Appendix.

SAMPLE THREE-DAY NOTICE TO PERFORM COVENANT OR QUIT

Three-Day Notice To Perform Covenant or Quit

To: _____ Glen Cagney _____ ,
                                  (name)

Tenant(s) in possession of the premises at:

_____ 123 Main Street, Apartment 4 _____ ,
                                  (street address)

City of ____ San Jose ____ , County of ____ Santa Clara ____ , California.

    YOU ARE HEREBY NOTIFIED that you are in violation of the lease or rental agreement under which you occupy these premises because you have violated the covenant to:

_____ refrain from keeping a pet on the premises _____

_____

in the following manner:

_____ by having a dog and two cats on the premises (Clause 13). _____

    YOU ARE HEREBY REQUIRED within THREE (3) DAYS from the date of service on you of this notice to remedy the violation and perform the covenant or to vacate and surrender possession of the premises.

    If you fail to do so, legal proceedings will be instituted against you to recover possession of the premises, declare the forfeiture of the rental agreement or lease under which you occupy the premises, and recover damages and court costs.

Date: ____ November 6, 19 ____   *Larry Smith* _____
                                        Owner/Manager

....

Proof of Service

    I, the undersigned, served this notice, of which this is a true copy, on _____ , one of the occupants listed above as follows:

☐ On _____ , 199____ , I delivered the notice to the occupant personally.

☐ On _____ , 199____ , I delivered the notice to a person of suitable age and discretion at the occupant's residence/business after having attempted personal service at the occupant's residence, and business if known. On _____ , 199____ , I mailed a second copy to the occupant at his or her residence.

☐ On _____ , 199____ , I posted the notice in a conspicuous place on the property, after having attempted personal service at the occupant's residence, and business, if known, and after having been unable to find there a person of suitable age and discretion. On _____ , 199____ , I mailed a second copy to the occupant at the property.

    I declare under penalty of perjury under the laws of the State of California that the foregoing is true and correct.

Dated: _____ , 199____   _____

Here's another example of language in a three-day notice—a situation when the tenant failed to make agreed payments toward a security deposit which was to be paid off over a period of time.

YOU ARE HEREBY NOTIFIED that you are in violation of the lease or rental agreement under which you occupy these premises because you have violated the covenant to:

pay agreed installments of the security deposit, in the amount of $50
per month on the first day of each month (in addition to rent) until paid

in the following manner:

_failing to pay the $50 on the first day of the month of December, 19___

---

2. The Three-Day Notice To Quit

Only when a tenant's conduct is extreme, or when the lease violation can't be corrected in three days, can a three-day notice to quit just tell the tenant to leave in three days without giving the tenant the option of correcting the problem.[7]

The unconditional Three-Day Notice To Quit can be used only in one of the following situations:

Noncorrectable violation. If there is no way the violation could possibly be corrected in three days, you can use an unconditional three-day notice. The most common example is when a tenant has sublet all or part of the premises to someone else, contrary to the rental agreement or lease.

Nuisance. The tenant is causing a nuisance on the premises, repeatedly annoying neighbors.

Extreme damage. The tenant is causing a great deal of damage to the property (called "waste"). This means extreme problems such as holes punched in

---

[7]CCP § 1161(4).

the wall or numerous windows broken. This doesn't include run-of-the-mill damage caused by carelessness, in which case the tenant must at least be given a chance to correct the problem.

Illegal use. The tenant is using the property for an illegal purpose—like running a house of prostitution, dealing drugs (a special case, discussed in Section B.3, below) or even operating a legitimate business in violation of local zoning laws.

3. A Reason for Which You Must Evict— Drug Dealing

In cases of drug dealing, it's not a question of whether it's permissible to evict a tenant—it's imperative to do so. In fact, a landlord who fails to evict a tenant who deals illegal drugs on the property can face lawsuits from other tenants, neighbors and local authorities. Many landlords have recently been held liable for tens of thousands of dollars in damages for failing to evict a drug-dealing tenant; a landlord can also lose the property. (Chapter 12.C discusses penalties facing landlords who fail to evict drug-dealing tenants.) When it's a month-to-month tenancy, the tenancy should be terminated with a 30-day notice (Section A, above) as soon as you suspect illegal drug activity .

If the tenant has a fixed-term lease rather than a month-to-month rental agreement, you will have to use a Three-Day Notice To Quit. Evictions for drug dealing may be a little more difficult if the tenant has a lease rather than a month-to-month rental agreement or lives in a rent-controlled city with just-cause eviction provisions in its rent-control ordinances. (See Section C, below.)

Terminating a tenancy when drug dealing is suspected is difficult. Except for termination of non-government subsidized month-to-month tenancies in cities that don't require just cause for eviction, the termination notice must state, often in detail, the reason the tenancy is being terminated. The tenant, faced with a written accusation of a serious crime, may refuse to move, thinking that to do so would be tantamount to admitting wrongdoing.

If the tenant fights the eviction in court, a landlord who must show just cause for eviction due to a rent control ordinance or government-subsidized tenancy will have to prove that the tenant is dealing drugs, most likely by indirect (circumstantial) evidence. For example, there may be suspiciously heavy traffic in and out of the unit. Other tenants and neighbors, who are in the best position to know about goings on in the suspected dealer's apartment, may be too intimidated to testify.

A landlord faced with a potentially difficult eviction of a suspected drug-dealing tenant should take these steps, especially where he must show just cause for terminating the tenancy:

Gather evidence. Remind other tenants or neighbors that you have a strict no-drug-dealing policy (Clause 15 of our lease and rental agreements, Chapter 2) and are determined to put a stop to any drug-related activity, but that you need proof to evict the tenant. Ask them to keep records of what they see, including dates and times when the same people go into the tenant's apartment for brief periods. Ask them if they would be willing to testify in court if necessary. Keep notes of your conversations with tenants and neighbors.

Contact the tenant. Don't accuse a tenant of dealing drugs. Do say that you've received complaints about heavy traffic in and out of the unit and about disturbances that have been brought to your attention. Do not disclose the names or locations of the people who have complained. Tell the tenant that if it continues, you'll have no choice but to terminate the tenancy. Follow through with a letter, and keep a copy for your records. (We include a sample warning letter in Section C.2, below.)

Tell the police. If other tenants have been intimidated by the dealers, make an appointment to see someone at the police station. Follow through with a letter to the chief of the local police agency, and keep a copy for your records. Send a copy to the local district attorney's office. If other tenants want a building watch program, ask the police to help establish one.

Don't make an accusation of drug dealing on the termination notice unless that's the only way you can evict, and you can prove it. For example, if the tenant is behind in the rent or has repeatedly disturbed neighbors (people go in and out all night), evict on one of those grounds.

<table>
<tr><td>

Overview of Legal Eviction Process

Here's an overview of the eviction process, which often takes more than a month or two depending on whether the tenant contests the eviction. See Landlord's Law Book, Volume 2: Evictions, for complete details.

1. The landlord terminates the tenancy by serving a termination notice on the tenant, which may be a Three-Day Notice To Pay Rent or Quit, a Three Day Notice To Perform Covenant or Quit, an Unconditional Three-Day Notice To Quit or a 30-Day Notice.

The notice must be prepared and served in accordance with state and local law. If the tenant pays rent, corrects the violation or moves (depending on the particular notice), that's the end of the matter, but the tenant may still owe rent.

2. After the three or 30 days are up, and if the tenant hasn't paid the rent, corrected the violation or left, the landlord can begin an eviction lawsuit by filing an "unlawful detainer complaint," in municipal court (justice court in some rural areas). The tenant must file a written response in court usually within five days (plus applicable extensions).

3. If the tenant hasn't filed a written response in court by the deadline, the landlord wins. The court clerk issues a "Default Judgment for Possession of Premises" and "Writ of Possession," which the landlord takes to the sheriff or marshal.

If the tenant files a response, the court will set the case for trial. After trial (or if the case is decided summarily by a judge), if the landlord wins the landlord gets a judgment for possession of the property and for rent and court costs. The landlord gets a "Writ of Execution" from the clerk and gives it, and eviction instructions, to the sheriff or marshal.

4. After several days, the sheriff or marshal gives the tenant written notice he'll be forcibly evicted within five days if he doesn't move out first.

5. After five more days, the sheriff or marshal forcibly evicts any tenants who have not left, and turns the property over to the landlord.

6. After eviction, if the landlord got a Default Judgment for Possession, the landlord can go back to court and get a judgment for rent and court costs.

</td></tr>
</table>

4. Preparing the Three-Day Notice To Quit

The unconditional Three-Day Notice To Quit must contain the following:

1. The tenant's name.

2. A description of the premises—street address, apartment number (if any), city and county.

3. A demand that the tenant leave the premises within three days.

4. A specific statement as to how and approximately when the tenant illegally sublet, caused a nuisance, damaged the premises or illegally used the premises. This is the most important part of the notice, and must be drafted very carefully to clearly tell the tenant what she is doing wrong. Also, remember that you may have to prove in court that the tenant violated the lease or rental agreement, if the tenant refuses to move. This is especially important when evicting tenants for illegal uses of the premises, such as drug dealing.

5. An unequivocal statement that the lease is forfeited and that you will take legal action to remove the tenant if she fails to vacate within the three days.

6. Your signature, or that of your manager's, and the date.

7. Fill in the Proof of Service stating how the three-day notice was served on the tenant. (You fill in the proof of service on the copy after having given the original to the tenant.) See Chapter 16.C for directions on completing the Proof of Service.

A blank tear-out Three-Day Notice To Quit form is included in the Appendix. A sample form is shown below, followed by language for different situations.

SAMPLE THREE-DAY NOTICE TO QUIT

Three-Day Notice To Quit
(Improper Subletting, Nuisance, Waste or Illegal Use)

To: _____ Eric Kahn _____ ,
                          (name)

Tenant(s) in possession of the premises at:

_____ 1234 Francisco Street, Apartment 5 _____ ,
                              (street address)

City of ____ San Francisco ____ , County of ____ San Francisco ____ , California.

YOU ARE HEREBY NOTIFIED that you are required within THREE (3) DAYS from the date of service on you of this notice to vacate and surrender possession of the premises because you have committed the following nuisance, waste, unlawful use or unlawful subletting:

You have unlawfully sublet a portion of the premises to another person who now lives on the premises with you contrary to the provisions of your lease (Clause 10)

As a result of your having committed the foregoing act(s), the lease or rental agreement under which you occupy these premises is terminated. If you fail to vacate and surrender possession of the premises within three days, legal proceedings will be instituted against you to recover possession of the premises, damages and court costs.

Date: ____ May 1, 19 ____   *Lisa Kramer* _____
                                            Owner/Manager

. . . .

Proof of Service

I, the undersigned, served this notice, of which this is a true copy, on _____ , one of the occupants listed above as follows:

☐ On _____ , 199____ , I delivered the notice to the occupant personally.

☐ On _____ , 199____ , I delivered the notice to a person of suitable age and discretion at the occupant's residence/business after having attempted personal service at the occupant's residence, and business if known. On _____ , 199____ , I mailed a second copy to the occupant at his or her residence.

☐ On _____ , 199____ , I posted the notice in a conspicuous place on the property, after having attempted personal service at the occupant's residence, and business, if known, and after having been unable to find there a person of suitable age and discretion. On _____ , 199____ , I mailed a second copy to the occupant at the property.

I declare under penalty of perjury under the laws of the State of California that the foregoing is true and correct.

Dated: _____ , 199____   _____

Other language to use in Three-Day Notice To Quit:

Nuisance. "You have committed a nuisance on the premises by having or allowing loud boisterous parties at which music was played at an extremely loud volume, and at which intoxicated guests milled about outside the front door to the premises and shouted obscenities at passersby every night from February 26th through 28th, 19__."

Waste. "You committed or allowed to be committed waste on the premises in that you or your guests have punched holes in the doors and walls of the premises and broken the front living room window."

Illegal use. "You have used the premises for an unlawful use by selling illegal controlled substances to visitors to the premises, between April 1, 19_ and the present."

5. Advantage of 30-Day Notice Over Three-Day Notice

As described in Section B.2, some reasons for eviction—such as making too much noise or damaging the property—may justify evicting with an unconditional Three-Day Notice To Quit. A landlord in a non-rent control area who wants to evict a month-to-month tenant (whose rent is paid) will often be better off using a 30-day notice.

If you can evict a tenant by using a three-day notice, why give the tenant with a month-to-month tenancy a break by using a 30-day notice? Because it's good business, for several reasons:

- A tenant is far more likely to defend against an eviction lawsuit that only gives her three days to get out, rather than 30 days.

- If a tenant does force you to go to court, if your tenancy termination is based on a 30-day notice, you don't even have to list the reason in the lawsuit papers (unless the tenant has a lease or government-subsidized tenancy, or the property is in a rent control area requiring just cause for eviction). With

a three-day notice, you must clearly tell the tenant what he or she is doing wrong; the slightest omission of necessary information could render the three-day notice invalid.

- Judges are more reluctant to allow a tenant to be evicted using a three-day notice for breaching the rental agreement or causing a nuisance or damage, than they are if you use a 30-day notice.

6. Serving the Three-Day Notice

As with other types of notices, there are specific procedures for serving a three-day notice. Both kinds of three-day notices (conditional and unconditional) are served the same way.

a. When the Three-Day Notice Should Be Served

A Three-Day Notice To Perform Covenant or Quit or a Three-Day Notice To Quit can be served on a tenant on any day of the month. The only requirement is that the tenant's violations of the lease or rental agreement already have occurred. For example, if the tenant's third loud and boisterous party in a month occurred on April 15, and you're using the three disturbances as a basis for eviction, you can serve your Three-Day Notice To Quit on April 16.

If the tenant's violation of the lease or rental agreement involves a failure to do something else on a certain date, the notice should be served the day after that. For example, if a tenant must pay a security deposit installment which the lease or rental agreement says is due on the first day of the month, the tenant isn't late until the first business day after that date. If the day for the tenant to pay the money or otherwise perform the act falls on a Saturday, Sunday or holiday, he doesn't legally have to do it until the following business day.

It doesn't matter that you've earlier accepted the rent for a particular month when it comes to giving a tenant a three-day notice for a reason unrelated to rent. Just don't accept rent after you've become aware of the violation for which you'll be evicting

EXAMPLE

Your tenant Rochelle paid you the $500 rent for her apartment on October 1, then had four loud and wild parties (which lasted to 2 A.M. despite protests from other tenants) on October 5, 6, 13 and 14. Your Three-Day Notice To Quit could be given on the 15th, asking Rochelle to leave by the 18th, even though you've accepted her rent through October 31.[8] This is because Rochelle, in creating a nuisance after having paid her rent, has legally forfeited her right not only to continue under the lease or rental agreement, but also to live there for the rest of the period for which she paid rent in advance. After that, your service of the three-day notice on her, plus waiting the three days, allows you to file an eviction lawsuit. However, if you accept rent in November—well after the loud parties occurred—you can't evict on that basis with a three-day notice.

b. Who Should Serve the Notice?

The three-day notice may be served by anyone over 18, you included.

c. Whom To Serve

You should try to serve a copy of the Three-Day Notice To Perform Covenant or Quit or Three-Day Notice To Quit on each tenant to whom you rented the property. You are not legally obligated to serve all co-tenants on the same written lease or rental agreement. (See Chapter 16.D.3.) But you are required to serve all persons considered to be sub-tenants if the tenant has sublet (even illegally) and left. (See Chapter 16.D.4.) Serving all adult occupants means you won't have to worry about a co-tenant you didn't serve claiming she was a sub-tenant entitled to notice. We discuss who is and who is not a tenant in Chapter 10.

---

[8]This would be a situation in which you would probably want to give a conditional three-day notice—that is, tell the tenant to cease the offending conduct or leave.

d. How the Notice Is Served

A Three-Day Notice To Quit may be served as follows:

- Personal service
- Substituted service on another person, plus mailing, or
- Posting and mailing.

    See Chapter 16.D.4 for details on serving three-day notices. The rules for service are identical for all types of three-day notices.

e. Accepting Rent After the Notice Is Served

With conditional three-day notices, don't accept any rent unless the tenant has corrected the violation within three days—in which case, you can't evict and the tenant can stay. If the tenant doesn't correct the violation within three days, don't accept any rent unless you want to forget about evicting for the reason stated in the notice.

    Don't accept rent after you've served an unconditional three-day notice unless you want to forget about the eviction. Acceptance of the rent will be considered a legal admission that you decided to forgive the violation and continue collecting rent rather than complain about the problem.

C. Termination When Just Cause for Eviction Is Required

Quite a few cities with rent control (Berkeley, Beverly Hills, Cotati, East Palo Alto, Hayward, Los Angeles, San Francisco, Santa Monica, Thousand Oaks and West Hollywood) require a landlord to have just cause for terminating a month-to-month (or other periodic) tenancy.

    In these cities, the notice (whether 30-day or three-day) must always specify in detail the reason for termination, but there are often other requirements as well. For example, San Francisco's ordinance requires that the notice state that tenant assistance is available from the rent control board (the address and phone number of the rent board must be included). Berkeley's ordinance requires that copies of all such notices be filed with the local rent board. Some cities restrict a landlord's ability to evict fired managers (see Chapter 6). Failure to comply with technical requirements of a rent control ordinance may result in your losing a subsequent eviction lawsuit and being held liable for the tenant's court costs and attorney fees.

Some of these cities require that the landlord's reason for terminating the tenancy be specified in either a 30-day or three-day termination notice.

If your property is subject to a rent-control ordinance, obtain a copy of the ordinance and look for:

- allowable reasons for termination
- special requirements for what must be included in the termination notice
- requirements that you warn the tenants, in writing, before sending a termination notice.

1. Which Notice To Use

In rent-controlled cities requiring just cause for eviction, and where the tenancy is government-subsidized, you must have good cause to evict (even if the tenancy is from month-to-month), whether you use a three-day or 30-day notice. In "Section 8" government-subsidized tenancies, you must use a 30-day notice to evict for reasons other than nonpayment of rent.[9] But where the just-cause requirement is imposed only by a rent control law, there is only a slight advantage to using the 30-day notice when you have a choice. (See Section C.3, below, for situations where you may only use a 30-day notice.) A tenant receiving a 30-day notice might more readily move, having more time within which to do so, than if only three days' notice is

given. On the other hand, low-cost legal help to tenants is readily available from tenants' groups and other sources, and even tenants who receive the full 30-day notice may stay and fight it out anyway.

2. Reasons Allowed for Termination With a Three-Day Notice

All rent-control cities allow evictions for, among other things:

- nonpayment of rent
- violation of a lease or rental agreement provision
- causing serious damage to the premises
- causing a nuisance
- illegal use of the premises.

a. Nonpayment of Rent

In rent-controlled cities, a Three-Day Notice To Pay Rent or Quit is not much different than in areas without rent control. You can use the Three-Day Notice To Pay Rent or Quit in the Appendix, following the directions in Chapter 16. Be sure to check your local ordinance for any special requirements.

b. Violation of a Lease or Rental Agreement Provision

A Three-Day Notice To Perform Covenant or Quit, spelling out the lease or rental agreement violation and giving the tenant a chance to correct it, satisfies ordinance requirements that the tenant's misconduct be specified and that she be given a chance to correct it. (This assumes the violation is correctable.) So, with the possible exception of a requirement that the notice include the local rent control board's name, address and phone number, or that a copy be given to the board, a three-day notice based on a tenant's lease violation is no different in a rent-controlled city than in areas without rent control. Follow the

---

[9]*Gallman v. Pierce*, 639 F. Supp. 472 (N.D. Cal.1986).

directions in Section B.1, above, for serving a Three-Day Notice To Perform Covenant or Quit.

Evicting for violation of access clause of a lease or rental agreement. Many leases and rental agreements, including the forms in the back of the book, contain a clause requiring the tenant to provide the landlord access to the property as required by law—for example, to repair or maintain the premises. (See Clause 14 in Chapters 2 and13.) Some rent control ordinances allow eviction both for rental agreement or lease violations and specifically for the tenant's refusal to allow the landlord property access—provided such refusal is a violation of the lease or rental agreement. The Three-Day Notice To Perform Covenant or Quit would include language like, "…you are in violation of the lease …because you have violated the covenant to: allow Landlord access to the property as required by Civil Code Section 1954, following the giving of reasonable notice by the Landlord that he would conduct repairs to the premises on December 1, 19 , in the following manner: you refused to allow such access on December 3, 19 ."

If the tenant still refuses you access over the next three days, you may want to begin an eviction lawsuit.

Check your ordinance to make sure you comply with its requirement for such a notice.

c. Damage and Nuisance

Rent control ordinances typically allow eviction of tenants for excessively damaging the property or causing a nuisance. But most ordinances require that the tenant must first be notified of the problem in a written notice—often called a cease-and-desist notice— and be given a chance to correct the problem, no matter what it is. For example, Berkeley's ordinance allows eviction of a tenant for damaging the property (in excess of ordinary wear and tear) only if she "has refused, after written

notice, to pay the reasonable costs of repairing such damage and ceasing damaging premises."[10]

To reconcile the ordinance with state law, you can use a Three-Day Notice To Perform Covenant or Quit. This gives the tenant an option to correct. However, we prefer another method, in which two notices are used. First, send a letter that demands that the tenant correct the problem, pay to repair the damage, stop having loud parties or whatever. Second, should the tenant fail to correct the problem, serve an unconditional Three-Day Notice To Quit.

EXAMPLE

After paying the rent on December 1, Bruce held some wild holiday parties in his Santa Monica apartment on the 7th, 8th, 14th and 15th. Other tenants repeatedly complained (eventually to the police) about Bruce's parties. At these parties, a drunken guest threw a beer bottle through the front window of the apartment. Santa Monica's rent control ordinance requires that (1) before terminating a tenancy for causing excessive damage, the landlord must give the tenant a chance to pay the cost of repairs, and (2) to terminate for disturbing neighbors, the disturbances must continue following a written notice to cease.

Here's a letter addressing both issues. This should be followed by serving Bruce with an unconditional Three-Day Notice To Quit if he doesn't pay for the damage and stop his raucous parties. It should be given to the tenant in the same way as a three-day notice is served. (See Section B.2, above.) This type of warning letter can also be used in non-rent control situations where you have grounds for eviction, but feel the tenant's behavior will change given a warning notice.

---

[10]This raises some interesting legal issues regarding how far a city may go in essentially altering state procedural laws governing three-day notices. In *Birkenfeld v. City of Berkeley*, 17 Cal. 3d 129, 148-151 (1976), the California Supreme Court stated, essentially, that a more extensive digression from state law (requiring that an eviction certificate be issued by the rent board) was improper, while a less serious digression (requiring a 30-day notice to specify the reason for termination) was okay.

SAMPLE WARNING LETTER FOR TENANT DAMAGE OR NUISANCE

December 16, 19_

Bruce Wilson
950 Oceanview St.
Monica Apartments, Apt. 10
Santa Monica, CA

Dear Mr. Wilson:

This letter is to advise you that the management of Monica Apartments intends to proceed to terminate your tenancy of the above premises if you continue to conduct yourself in a manner which seriously disturbs other tenants and results in the destruction of our property.

On December 7, 8, 14 and 15, you held loud and boisterous parties, which lasted until 3 A.M. and at which very loud music was played and guests spilled out into the street. The police were called on at least three of the four occasions. This conduct has destroyed the peace and quiet of other tenants. If this conduct does not cease, your tenancy shall be terminated in accordance with local and state law.

On December 14 and/or 15, several of the party guests damaged our property, shattering the front window to your apartment and punching two holes in your bathroom wall. After a properly noticed inspection of the premises yesterday by myself and my maintenance person, I have concluded that the reasonable cost of repairing this damage is $350. If you fail to pay this sum to me within three days, your tenancy will be terminated in accordance with both local and state law.

Sincerely,

Jason Knepps
Manager

We have included a sample fill-in-the-blank Warning Notice which you can use the same way as a warning letter. A tear-out copy is included in the Appendix.

SAMPLE WARNING NOTICE
(COMPLAINTS FROM NEIGHBORS/RESIDENTS)

Warning Notice (Complaints from Neighbors/Residents)

Date: _____ December 16, 1991 _____

Memorandum from Owner /Manager to

___ Bruce Wilson _____ ,

Resident(s) of

Property at: ___ 950 Oceanview St., Apt. 10 _____

___ Santa Monica, California _____

Re: Complaints from neighbors/other residents

Several of your neighbors have complained to the management regarding to the following disturbance or condition:

___ loud noises from parties in your apartment, until 3:00 a.m. _____

_____

Approximate date of occurrence: ___ December 7, 8, 14 and 15, 199 _____

It is very important to the management that our residents be able to enjoy the peace and quiet of their homes. Disturbing or affecting neighbors is a violation of the terms of your lease/rental agreement. You are requested to take the following corrective action:

___ Keep noise within reasonable limits. No noise after midnight on ___
weekends and 10:00 p.m. on weekdays. _____

If you have any questions, please contact _____ Jason Knepps _____ ,

at ___ Manager's Office—Apartment 1. _____ .

Sincerely,

Jason Knepps _____
Owner/Manager

If Bruce fails to pay the money for repairs or has another wild party, you would prepare and serve the following unconditional Three-Day Notice To Quit.

SAMPLE THREE-DAY NOTICE TO QUIT (JUST CAUSE FOR EVICTION)

Three-Day Notice To Quit
(Improper Subletting, Nuisance, Waste or Illegal Use)

To: _____ Bruce Wilson _____,
              (name)

Tenant(s) in possession of the premises at:

_____ 950 Oceanview Street, Apartment 10 _____,
                        (street address)

City of ____ Santa Monica ____, County of ____ Los Angeles ____, California.

YOU ARE HEREBY NOTIFIED that you are required within THREE (3) DAYS from the date of service on you of this notice to vacate and surrender possession of the premises because you have committed the following nuisance, waste, unlawful use or unlawful subletting:

(1) You have continued, following a written request to cease, dated December 16, 19_, to be so disorderly as to destroy the peace and quiet of other tenants, by having a loud party December 21, 19_, which lasted until 3 a.m. and at which very loud music was played until that time. Prior to this, you conducted four similar parties, on December 7th, 8th, 14th, and 15th .(2) You have failed, following a written request, to pay the reasonable cost of repairing a shattered window and holes in walls, caused by you or your guests at one or more of such parties.

As a result of your having committed the foregoing acts, the lease or rental agreement under which you occupy the premises is terminated. If you fail to vacate and surrender possession of the premises within three days, legal proceedings will be instituted against you to recover possession of the premises, damages and court costs.

Date: ____ December 22, 19 ____   _Jason Knepps_ _____
                                          Owner/Manager

···

Proof of Service

I, the undersigned, served this notice, of which this is a true copy, on _____, one of the occupants listed above as follows:

☐ On _____, 199____, I delivered the notice to the occupant personally.

☐ On _____, 199____, I delivered the notice to a person of suitable age and discretion at the occupant's residence/business after having attempted personal service at the occupant's residence, and business if known. On _____, 199____, I mailed a second copy to the occupant at his or her residence.

☐ On _____, 199____, I posted the notice in a conspicuous place on the property, after having attempted personal service at the occupant's residence, and business, if known, and after having been unable to find there a person of suitable age and discretion. On _____, 199____, I mailed a second copy to the occupant at the property.

I declare under penalty of perjury under the laws of the State of California that the foregoing is true and correct.

Dated: _____, 199____   _____

d. Illegal Use of the Premises

Some rent control ordinances neglect to mention this as a ground for eviction. Does this mean that you can't evict a tenant who, for example, runs a house of prostitution out of her apartment? The answer, of course, is no. Virtually all written leases and rental agreements (including our form lease and rental agreement) either specify that the property be used only as a residence or that illegal use of the property is forbidden. An illegal activity, such as drug dealing, therefore constitutes a violation of the rental agreement. A Three-Day Notice To Quit could be used, and you need not give the tenant the alternative of stopping his misbehavior.

3. Reasons Allowed for Termination With a 30-Day Notice

All the reasons listed in Section C.2, above, for which a tenant's tenancy can be terminated with a three-day notice under local ordinance, apply whether the tenancy is from month-to-month (or some other period) or for a fixed term.

The just-cause eviction sections of most rent control ordinances also allow termination of the tenancy for other reasons. These reasons permit termination of a month-to-month tenancy (but not a tenancy under a fixed-term lease) by an unconditional 30-day notice, and include:

- The tenant refuses to allow the landlord access to the premises, but no lease or rental agreement clause requires the tenant to allow access.

- The landlord, after having obtained all necessary permits, intends to extensively remodel the premises, convert the dwelling to a condominium unit or demolish the structure.

- The landlord is intending to move herself or a close relative into the dwelling.

a. Tenant Refusal to Allow Access

A three-day notice can be used to terminate tenancy where the tenant refuses to allow the landlord legal access to the property—provided such refusal is a violation of the lease or rental agreement. (See Chapter 13.) If the rental agreement doesn't have an access clause, however, a 30-day notice must be used. This sort of notice should be preceded with a warning letter of the type mentioned in Section C.2, above. Also, the reason for termination should be stated in the 30-day notice. A sample notice is shown below.

b. Remodeling, Conversion or Demolition

Most rent control ordinances allow a month-to-month tenancy to be terminated by a 30-day notice if the landlord wishes to extensively remodel the premises, convert the property into a condominium unit or demolish it. The landlord must first obtain all permits necessary, and comply with other ordinances providing for notice to affected persons, the tenants included. The 30-day notice should specify in detail the reason for termination, giving the date the permits were granted by the city or county.

Some landlords have abused ordinances which allow eviction for remodeling, either by claiming nonexistent needs for extensive remodeling or failing to do the remodeling once the tenant left. In response, several cities have added safeguards to protect tenants. For example, Berkeley's ordinance requires a landlord seeking to evict a tenant for remodeling to give the tenant the right of first refusal to re-rent the property when the remodeling is done, and even to house the tenant in the interim (at the same rent) if the landlord has any other vacant rental property in the city. Again, be sure to check your local ordinance for specific requirements.

SAMPLE 30-DAY NOTICE OF TERMINATION OF TENANCY (JUST CAUSE FOR EVICTION)

30-Day Notice of Termination of Tenancy

To: _____ Hope Swensen _____,
(name)

Tenant(s) in possession of the premises at:

_____ 1234 Grove Street, Apartment 5 _____,
(street address)

City of ____ Berkeley ____, County of ____ Alameda ____, California.

     YOU ARE HEREBY NOTIFIED that effective 30 DAYS from the date of service on you of this notice, the periodic tenancy by which you hold possession of the premises is terminated, at which time you are required to vacate and surrender possession of the premises. If you fail to do so, legal proceedings will be instituted against you to recover possession of the premises, damages and costs of suit.

You have continued, following a written request to cease, dated December 10, 19 , to refuse me access to the premises as required by Civil Code Section 1954, on 12/11/9 , 12/12/9 , and 12/13/9 , despite the fact that I gave you notice 24 hours in advance, in each case, of an intent to repair a defective heater. (Rent Stabilization Ordinance, Section 13(a)(6).)

[OR]

I wish to have my son Orville Bergman, reside in the premises, there being no other vacant comparable unit in the property. (Rent Stabilization Ordinance, Section 13(a)(9).)

Date: ____ December 22, 19 ____   *Olaf Bergman* _____
                                               Owner/Manager

....

Proof of Service

    I, the undersigned, served this notice, of which this is a true copy, on _____, one of the occupants listed above as follows:

☐ On _____, 199____, I delivered the notice to the occupant personally.

☐ On _____, 199____, I delivered the notice to a person of suitable age and discretion at the occupant's residence/business after having attempted personal service at the occupant's residence, and business if known. On _____, 199____, I mailed a second copy to the occupant at his or her residence.

☐ On _____, 199____, I posted the notice in a conspicuous place on the property, after having attempted personal service at the occupant's residence, and business, if known, and after having been unable to find there a person of suitable age and discretion. On _____, 199____, I mailed a second copy to the occupant at the property.

☐ On _____, 199____, I mailed the notice by certified mail addressed to the occupant at his or her place of residence.

    I declare under penalty of perjury under the laws of the State of California that the foregoing is true and correct.

Dated: _____, 199____   _____

c. Landlord or Close Relative To Move In

Most rent control ordinances allow a month-to-month tenancy to be terminated by 30-day notice when the landlord wants to live in the property himself or move in a close relative. This basis for termination has had its share of abuse, with some landlords falsely claiming to have relatives interested in moving into the property, which would then be occupied by the relative for a very short time, if at all. Cities have tightened their ordinances to prevent abuse. For example, Berkeley's ordinance limits permissible relatives to parents and children, and requires the termination notice to give the name and relationship of the person who will move in.

Also, just cause for eviction ordinances now provide for heavy penalties against landlords who use a phony-relative ploy, as does state law. (Chapter 4.H.2 describes penalties for attempted evasion of this type of rent control ordinance provision.)

D. Termination When No Notice Is Required

Most just cause provisions of rent control ordinances also allow a landlord to evict a tenant who refuses to sign a new fixed-term lease after the old one expires. However, the new lease the landlord presents to the tenant must contain essentially the same terms as the old one, with no substantial change, and must not contain any clauses forbidden by state law (see Chapter 2.E) or local ordinance. This basis for eviction applies only where:

1. A fixed-term lease expires on a certain date;

2. The landlord has not accepted any rent after that date, and so has not converted the tenancy into a non-expiring month-to-month tenancy; and

3. The tenant has refused to sign a new lease essentially identical to the earlier one.

In this situation, the landlord does not have to give the tenant a written notice of any kind before filing an eviction lawsuit. This is because the tenancy ended of its own accord when the lease expired, and the tenant is refusing to extend it.

When a Tenant Leaves: Month-to-Month Tenancies, Fixed-Term Leases, Abandonment, and Death of Tenant

You might think, after reading Chapter 18, that many tenancies end with the landlord giving the tenant some sort of written termination notice. In fact, most tenancies end with the tenant leaving voluntarily. The tenant may give notice or leave at the end of a lease term, break the lease or just walk out before the term ends, or die. Here, we discuss these ways a tenancy legally comes to an end.

A. Termination of Month-to-Month Tenancies

Most tenancies end when the tenant decides to move and gives you 30 days' notice. If the rental agreement specifically allows for a shorter notice period, the tenant isn't required to give you a full 30 days' notice. (This is true regardless of rent control ordinances, which restrict only the landlord's ability to terminate the tenancy.)

This section discusses the tenant's liabilities and responsibilities when ending a month-to-month tenancy.

To make sure your tenant will give you the required 30 days' notice, highlight termination notice requirements in a move-in letter to new tenants. (See Chapter 7.)

1. Insisting on a Written Notice

The tenant's notice should be in writing, and should be personally served on you or your manager or mailed by certified mail.[1] In practice, many tenants mail the notice by ordinary first-class mail, which is still legally effective so long as you receive it 30 or more days before the termination date.

If the tenant simply tells you that he will be leaving in 30 days or more, it's good business to insist that the notice be in writing. If the tenant doesn't do

this, you should prepare and serve your own written 30 days' notice on the tenant. Why bother, if the tenant plans to leave anyway? Because if you don't, you may be caught between the proverbial rock and a hard place if you sign a rental agreement for a new tenant to move in and the current tenant does not move as promised. An oral promise to leave isn't legally binding, so you can't sue to force the current tenant to leave, except perhaps by three-day notice followed by an unlawful detainer suit if the rent has not been paid. But if you signed a lease or rental agreement, or even orally promised your new tenant that she could move in, you will be liable to the new tenant for the full cost of temporary housing until the existing tenant leaves, unless the agreement has a clause limiting your liabiity if you can't deliver possession on the promised date. (Clause 12 of our forms have such a provision.).

EXAMPLE
Your current tenants, the Beckers, call and tell you they plan to move in 30 days. On the basis of their promise, you sign a rental agreement with new tenants, the Owens, beginning the day after you expect the Beckers to depart. Unfortunately, that agreement has no clause limiting your liability for inability to deliver possession as promised. The Beckers later inform you (or you discover) that they won't leave as planned. Because the Beckers did not give you a written 30-day notice, you cannot sue to evict them. The best you can do is serve the Beckers with a 30-day notice. If the Owens must stay in a motel until the Beckers leave in 30 days, you are responsible for the cost, which is certain to be more than the rent you will get from the Beckers. If, on the other hand, the Beckers gave you a written 30-day notice but failed to abide by it, you could sue to evict them as soon as the 30 days are up.

2. Applying the Security Deposit to the Last Month's Rent

A month-to-month tenant may ask you to apply the security deposit toward the last month's rent, which the tenant tells you he won't be paying. Although

---

[1]CC § 1946.

this is legal if you called all or part of the tenant's initial payment "last month's rent," you are not legally obliged to apply a security or other deposit in this way.

Why should you care if a tenant doesn't pay last month's rent if the deposit, no matter what it's called, covers the rent? The problem is that you can't know in advance in what condition the property will be left. If the tenant leaves the property a mess and has already applied the security deposit to last month's rent, obviously you will have nothing left to use to repair or clean the property.

You have two choices if you are faced with a tenant who tries to use a security deposit for last month's rent. Your first is simply to do nothing. In some circumstances, if you have good reason to believe that the particular tenant will in fact leave the property clean and undamaged, this may be the best thing to do.

Your second choice is to treat the tenant's nonpayment (or partial payment) of the last month's rent as an ordinary case of rent nonpayment. You can serve a Three-Day Notice to Pay Rent or Quit on the tenant as set out in Chapter 16, and file an eviction lawsuit if the tenant doesn't pay. But because it takes a minimum of three weeks to evict even in uncontested cases, this probably won't get the tenant out much sooner than he would leave anyway. However, you can get a court judgment for the unpaid last month's rent. This means you may apply the security deposit to pay for any necessary cleaning and repair costs, with any remainder applied to the judgment for nonpayment of rent. (We show how in Chapter 20.)

EXAMPLE

On December 31, Lee and Sara give you 30 days' notice and ask you to take their last month's rent out of their deposit. Immediately, you serve them with a three-day notice to pay the remaining $450 rent or quit. Four days later, on January 8, you may bring suit (see *Volume II*). If your suit is uncontested, you can get a default judgment on January 14 and perhaps get the sheriff or marshal to evict as soon as January 20. The money part of the judgment, assuming you can collect it, will compensate you for the rent, and you'll be free to use the deposit for its proper purpose—payment of repair and cleaning costs.

3. Accepting Further Rent After a 30-Day Notice Is Given

If you accept rent for any period beyond the termination date, you cancel the termination notice and create a new tenancy. This is true whether you or your tenant sent the 30-day notice.

EXAMPLE

On April 15, George sends you a 30-day termination notice. A few weeks later, however, he changes his mind and decides to stay. He simply pays the usual $500 monthly rent on May 1. If he were intent on leaving on May 15 as promised, he should be paying only 15 days pro-rated rent. Unwittingly, you cash the $500 check for the rent for all of May, even though you've already re-rented to a new tenant who hopes to move in on the 16th. Not only will you be powerless to evict George, but if you weren't careful about limiting your liability for inability to deliver possession as promised, you'll also be liable to the new tenant for failing to put her in possession of the property as promised.

If you've already accepted "last month's rent," do not accept rent for the last month of the tenancy. If you don't want to continue the tenancy as before, but are agreeable to giving the tenant a few days or weeks more, prepare a written agreement to that effect and have the tenant sign it.

4. What To Do When the Tenant Gives Less Than 30 Days' Notice

A tenant may mail the notice two weeks before vacating, or she may just say goodbye as she hands you the keys. But a tenant's written termination notice isn't ineffective just because it gives you less than the full 30 days' notice. It is still a valid notice of termination, but you are entitled to rent for the entire 30 days from the date of the notice. (There is one restriction on your right to the rent: If the tenant moves out less than 30 days after the notice is served, you must try to re-rent the property, before you can charge the tenant for giving you too little notice. This rule is discussed below.)

EXAMPLE

On August 25, Cara gives you a note saying she'll be moving out in ten days, on September 4. You're entitled to rent for 30 days from the date of the notice, through September 24. So on September 1, when Cara tries to get by with paying pro-rated rent for her four remaining days in September, remind her that you're entitled to 24 days' pro-rated rent. Of course, if Cara pays it, she'll have the right to stay through the 24th if she wishes. If Cara doesn't pay, which is likely (a threat of an eviction suit for rent non-payment isn't likely to faze a tenant about to leave anyway), you can deduct the unpaid rent from her deposit. If the deposit won't cover this plus cleaning and damage costs, you'll have to take Cara to small claims court for the balance. (We discuss how to do this in Chapter 20.)

If a tenant leaves without giving you the 30 days' notice you're entitled to and doesn't pay rent for some or all of those days, you're entitled to the rent you've lost. But you can't collect double by charging the former tenant rent beyond the date she left, while at the same time collecting rent from a new tenant. In other words, if you immediately find a new tenant to replace the outgoing one who didn't give you the full 30 days' notice, and therefore suffer no financial loss as a result of the inadequate notice, you can't charge the outgoing tenant that extra rent. However, if there was a gap of a few days, during which time you had no paying tenant, you are entitled to the pro-rated rent for those days, plus any costs of advertising the property. You may deduct these amounts from the outgoing tenant's deposit, as discussed in detail in Chapter 20.

If you can't collect double rent, both from the outgoing tenant who didn't give sufficient notice, and from the new tenant, why should you bother getting a new tenant so quickly? Because the law requires you to take reasonable steps to minimize your losses. This is called "mitigation of damages." If you don't, and instead sit back and let the property lie vacant between the day the tenant vacates and the 30th day from the date of the notice, hoping to charge the rent for that period to the outgoing tenant's deposit, you may be in for an unpleasant surprise. You can't charge the former tenant if you didn't take reasonable steps to find a new tenant.[2]

---

[2]CC § 1951.2.

EXAMPLE

On June 25, Rick, who rents from you on a month-to-month basis, says he'll be leaving on June 30. He's liable for the rent for another 25 days, through July 25. Rick's security deposit was $500. You charge him 25 days of pro-rated rent, or $375 (his monthly rent is $450), and because the property was clean and undamaged, return the remaining $125 of the deposit. You make no effort to re-rent the place until July 26, almost four weeks after Rick left. Rick takes you to small claims court, suing for the $375. The judge may find that you should have made a reasonable effort to locate a new tenant. Based on the local housing market, which is extremely tight, the judge concludes that you probably could have found a new tenant within ten days if you listed the vacancy in the papers and with rental location agencies. The judge therefore allows you to keep only ten days' pro-rated rent, or $150, giving Rick a judgment for the $225 difference.

To summarize, if a month-to-month tenant gives you less than 30 days' written notice, you're entitled to:

1. Thirty days' rent pro-rated from the date of the written notice, less

2. Any rent you reasonably could have collected from a new tenant for the period between the day the outgoing tenant left and the end of the 30-day period, plus

3. Any reasonable advertising expenses incurred in finding that new tenant.

B. Termination of Fixed-Term Leases

As we discussed in Chapter 2, a lease lasts for a fixed term, typically six months or a year. During the term of the lease, neither you nor the tenant may terminate the tenancy unless the other party violates the lease by failing to fulfill his obligations. You would generally use a three-day notice to terminate a tenancy for violation of a lease provision. (See Chapters 16 and 18 for details.)

If, however, everything goes well, the lease simply terminates of its own accord at the end of the lease term. Unfortunately, however, this description of how a lease works is often more theoretical than real. This section of the chapter focuses on your rights and responsibilities as well as those of a tenant who leaves at the end of a lease term. This section also discusses problems which occur when a tenant breaks a lease simply by leaving before the end of the term.

When a lease converts to a month-to-month tenancy. If you accept rent for a period beyond the date when a fixed-term lease ends, you've extended the tenancy on a month-to-month basis. To terminate the tenancy at this point, follow the rules for terminating a month-to-month tenancy. (See Chapter 18.A.)

1. The Tenant Leaves at the End of the Lease Term

A fixed-term lease simply expires at the end of the term. The tenant may pick up and leave at the end of the lease term, without any further obligation. Any notice, written or oral, indicating the tenant's intent to leave before the natural expiration of the lease term is of no legal effect other than to tell you that the tenant is planning to break the lease.

Under state law, the landlord may, without giving any advance notice to the tenant, insist he move out just as the lease expires.[3] However, this is not generally a good idea. First, in cities with just-cause eviction provisions in their rent control ordinances, the ordinances do not allow eviction except for specified reasons, including when the tenant has refused to sign a new lease containing essentially the same terms. (See Chapter 18.C.)

In any case, even when no formal notice of "termination" is required, you should, as a practical matter, routinely give tenants a 30-day notice if you

---

[3]*Black v. Black*, 77 Cal. App. 82 (1926).

don't wish to continue the tenancy when the lease expires. Otherwise, as mentioned above, the lease will convert to a month-to-month tenancy. Although the tenant is theoretically required to leave at the end of the lease term, it has become so customary for a tenant to stay on a month-to-month basis, in the absence of anything said to the contrary, that it's an essential business practice to advise your tenant at least a month in advance if you won't be renewing or even extending the lease.

As with a month-to-month tenancy, a tenant with a fixed-term lease may not legally refuse to pay the rent for the last month of occupancy and insist that you take it out of the security deposit, unless you have accepted a deposit specifically called "last month's rent." (See Section A.2 , above.)

2. The Tenant Leaves Before the End of the Term

A tenant who leaves (whether or not she notifies you that she's leaving) before the expiration of a fixed-term lease and refuses to pay the remainder of the rent due under the lease is said to have "broken the lease."

A tenant renting under a lease agrees at the outset to pay a fixed total rent: the monthly rent multiplied by the number of months the lease is to last. Payment is normally to be made in monthly installments over the term of the lease. This means the tenant is liable for the entire rent for the entire lease term (except where the landlord breaches an important lease provision first). According to this rule, a landlord faced with a tenant leaving early could sue the tenant for the remaining rent she would have collected had the tenant not left early.

Make sure your tenant understands his long-term liability for rent in both the lease (see Clause 3, Chapter 2) and move-in letter (Chapter 7).

But a tenant's liability for leaving too soon is limited by the landlord's duty to mitigate damages by finding a new rent-paying tenant as soon as reasonably possible.[4] This is true whether the tenancy is under a fixed-term lease or a month-to-month arrangement (as discussed in Section A.4, above), but applies most powerfully in the lease situation.

EXAMPLE 1

Juan rented an apartment to Jorge in January for a term of one year, the monthly rent being $1,000. Everything went well until late September, when Jorge skipped out on the lease. Jorge is theoretically liable to Juan for $3,000—the rent for October, November and December. However, if Juan mitigated these damages by taking out an ad and re-renting on October 15, Jorge would owe much less. If the new tenant paid $500 for the last half of October, and $1,000 in November and December, Juan must credit the total $2,500 he got from the new tenant against Jorge's $3,000 liability. This leaves Jorge liable for only $500 for the unrented days, plus Juan's advertising costs of $20, for a total of $520.

EXAMPLE 2

Same example as above, but assume that after Jorge skips out in late September, Juan does nothing to re-rent the property, but sues Jorge in December for the three months' rent of $3,000. If Jorge can convince the court that Juan could have re-rented the property after half a month at the same rent, the court will award Juan only the $500 he would have lost had he acted more diligently.

Of course, the landlord's duty to mitigate damages only gets the tenant off the hook if it's possible to get a satisfactory new tenant to pay the same amount of rent or more. Most of the time it is, but occasionally a landlord might have problems, as could be the situation with student housing during the summer or vacation rentals off season.

Often a tenant wishing to break the lease by leaving before it expires will approach the landlord and offer to find a suitable new tenant so that the

---

[4]CC § 1951.2.

flow of rent will remain uninterrupted. It is a good idea to cooperate with a tenant who suggests this. A landlord who refuses to cooperate by accepting an excellent new tenant is almost by definition refusing to mitigate damages, and may wind up with no recovery if he sues the outgoing tenant who broke the lease.

In this context, the mitigation-of-damages rule is, in effect, a hidden lease clause requiring the landlord to be reasonable about consenting to accept a new tenant to fill out the first tenant's lease term, even where the lease flatly prohibits a sublease. In fact, about the only criterion a landlord may legitimately use to reject a replacement tenant suggested by the outgoing one—that is, with an eye to still being able to collect damages from the departing tenant—is a bad credit or renting history. Of course, if the rental market is really tight in your area, and you can lease the unit easily at a higher rent, you may not care if a tenant breaks a lease, but will want to rent the property yourself and not bother with the tenant's help.

If you and the outgoing lease-breaking tenant do agree on a replacement tenant, you can legally proceed in one of two ways. You can: (1) either agree to let the outgoing tenant sublet to the incoming one (in which case the outgoing tenant still remains liable for the remainder of the rent under the lease if the new tenant doesn't pay), or (2) you may have the new tenant enter into a new lease with you (in which case you might even want to raise the rent a little, if local rent control ordinances permit). As we discuss in some detail in Chapter 10, we believe the second alternative is the more desirable because it makes the new tenant legally responsible to you.

To summarize, where your fixed-term tenant leaves before the end of the lease, you're entitled to:

1. The remaining rent due under the lease, less

2. Any rent you could have collected from a new tenant between the time the outgoing tenant left and the end of the lease term, plus

3. Any reasonable advertising expenses incurred in finding a new tenant.

You can deduct the total of these three items, plus repair and cleaning charges, from the tenant's security deposit. (See Chapter 20.)

C. Termination by Tenant Abandoning Premises

This section describes legal means of regaining possession of your rental property, without having to go to court, when you have reason to believe the tenant simply left without intending to come back, but didn't bother to tell you about it.

Often it's hard to tell whether a tenant has left for good. People do, after all, sometimes disappear for weeks at a time, going on vacations or elsewhere. And even when a tenant doesn't intend to come back, she may leave behind enough discarded clothing or furniture to make it appear that she may plan to return. We discuss what to do with abandoned property in Chapter 21.

Often the first hint you'll have that a tenant has abandoned the premises will be when you don't receive the rent. Or you may get a call from a neighbor asking about a vacancy, or simply walk by a window and notice the lack of furniture. Unfortunately, the mere appearance that your rental property is no longer occupied doesn't give you the legal right to retake possession. It does, however, constitute legal justification to inspect the place for signs of abandonment. (See Chapter 13, on tenants' privacy.) And remember, you don't have to give 24 hours' advance notice of entering if it's "impracticable" to do so, which is certainly the case if no one's been around for days.

Inspecting Abandoned Property

Here are some tips for inspecting property you suspect has been abandoned:

- *Look in the refrigerator. Is it empty, or is most of the food spoiled?*
- *Check whether electricity has been cut off, and the mail discontinued.*
- *Look in closets to see if a substantial amount of clothing remains behind.*

If these conditions apply, the property might be abandoned.

---

1. Re-Rent the Property

Once you've determined that your tenant has probably skipped out with no intention of returning, you have several choices. First and most obvious, you can assume that the tenant won't return, and proceed to clean up, dispose of any possessions left behind (see Chapter 21) and re-rent the property. This is perfectly okay if the tenant doesn't come back, and may be your best bet if the tenant who has cleared out has not paid rent, and has left nothing behind. However, it does involve some legal risk—the tenant might return to find the place re-rented and her possessions gone. If you are too impatient, you could face heavy liability in a lawsuit. This is especially true if you retake possession during a time for which the departing tenant has paid rent.

2. Track Down the Tenant

Your second choice is to hunt down the tenant and ask whether she intends to stay away or come back. Look at the tenant's rental application and phone each personal and business reference. If that doesn't work, try asking neighbors and, finally, the police.

Why should you go to so much trouble? Because this approach beats the third alternative, which, although it protects you from liability, requires you to go without rent for a little over a month. From a business standpoint, it's far better to track down the tenant and get her to admit she isn't coming back, allowing you to retake possession immediately, than to have to follow the legally correct procedure requiring you to leave the place vacant for a month.

3. Formally Notify the Tenant of Plans To Terminate the Tenancy

The third procedure is the formal legal one. It requires that you try to notify the tenant in writing that you intend to terminate the tenancy as the result of the tenant's suspected abandonment of the premises. Unfortunately, you must wait until 14 days have passed without the tenant's having paid rent before you can initiate this procedure.[5] It involves mailing a notice to the tenant's address at the property (or any other known mailing address) on or after the 15th day of rent nonpayment. This notice should look like the sample below (a blank form is included in the Appendix of this book):

---

[5]CC § 1951.3. During this 14-day waiting period, you might as well prepare a Three-Day Notice To Pay Rent or Quit and serve it by posting and mailing. (See Chapter 16.) This way, if the tenant does show up later and indicates an intent not to leave after all, you can begin the unlawful detainer suit to get the tenant out if she won't pay the rent. However, in situations where the tenant doesn't show up, use of an unlawful detainer suit will be just as time-consuming as, and more costly than, the abandonment notice procedure discussed here.

SAMPLE NOTICE OF BELIEF OF ABANDONMENT

Notice of Belief of Abandonment
Civil Code Section 1951.3

To: _____ Alice Green _____,
                         (name)

Tenant(s) in possession of the premises at:

_____ 123 Sendaro Street _____,
                  (street address)

City of _____ Fresno _____, County of _____ Fresno _____, California.

This notice is given pursuant to Section 1951.3 of the Civil Code concerning the real property leased by you at the above address. The rent on this property had been due and unpaid for 14 consecutive days and the owner or his agent believes that you have abandoned the property.

The real property will be deemed abandoned within the meaning of Section 1951.2 of the Civil Code and your lease will terminate on _____ May 5, 19 _____, a date not less than 18 days after the mailing of this notice, unless before such date the undersigned receives at the address indicated below a written notice from you stating both of the following:

(1) Your intent not to abandon the real property;

(2) An address at which you may be served by certified mail in any action for unlawful detainer of the real property.

You are required to pay the rent due and unpaid on this real property as required by the lease, and your failure to do so can lead to a court proceeding against you.

Date: _____ April 15, 19 _____

*Ruth Clark*_____
Owner (signature)

_Ruth Clark_____
Owner (print)

_456 State Street, Fresno, California_____
(address)

Mail the notice to the tenant by first class mail at the property with extra copies mailed to any other address you have for the tenant.

To preserve her right to the property, the tenant must provide you with a written statement that indicates an intent not to abandon and provide you with a mailing address at which she may be served by certified mail with an unlawful detainer suit. If you don't receive such a response by the 18th day after mailing the notice (not counting the day of mailing), you may retake possession of the premises.[6] Just walk in and begin your usual preparation for re-renting. You don't have to go to the courthouse first. You should return or dispose of any of the tenant's abandoned possessions in the manner described in Chapter 21.

D. What To Do When Some Tenants Leave and Others Stay

When one of your tenants leaves and the other (whether a spouse, lover or roommate) remains behind, good business practice, as well as sound legal reasons, require that you take the change into account rather than ignore it. However, your best course of action, from a legal point of view at least, depends on the extent to which the person leaving is still responsible for the rent if the remaining tenant doesn't pay. We discuss the legal liability of co-tenants and sub-tenants in detail in Chapter 10. Here we review this material briefly.

1. Co-Tenant Liability

When two or more people rent property together, and all sign the same rental agreement or lease, (or enter into the same oral agreement when they move in at the same time), they are co-tenants with equal rights to occupy the premises and equal liability for the rent. This is why it's best to have all adult occupants sign the lease or rental agreement. A co-tenant who moves out and leaves a fellow co-tenant behind is still legally liable for the rent due under the lease or rental agreement until the lease period expires (unless you agree to an earlier termination) or until the month-to-month tenancy is terminated by 30-day notice.

For example, if you sign a one-year lease with Jack and Elaine, and Elaine moves out, Elaine is still jointly liable with Jack for the rent for the time left on the lease. If Jack doesn't pay the rent, you can sue Elaine in small claims court for unpaid rent. It's important to remember, though, that this suit should be separate from any eviction suit—in which only occupants can be named as defendants. (See *Volume 2, Evictions.*)

If Jack and Elaine had a month-to-month rental agreement, Elaine would be liable for the monthly rent after leaving, unless she properly terminated the tenancy, as to herself, by giving you a 30-day notice.[7] (Because the tenancy is one from month-to-month, Elaine can move out and terminate her obligation by giving you a 30-day notice.) Still, as a practical matter, if Jack stopped paying rent after Elaine left without giving a proper notice, you would sue only Jack in an unlawful detainer proceeding, since, as noted above, you can sue only occupants of the premises in that kind of suit. If you could find Elaine, you could of course file a separate small claims suit against her for all unpaid rent.

---

[6] If you served the notice personally, you need wait only 15, rather than 18, days before retaking possession. But if you had actually been able too serve the notice personally, you obviously would have long since asked the tenant if she intends to stay, and the whole notice procedure should be moot.

---

[7] This situation may differ, however, if Jack and Elaine were married, and did not intend to separate permanently. Elaine might still be liable for the rent, even after giving such a 30-day notice, if she moved out but Jack stayed, because Elaine is legally responsible for her husband's necessities of life. CC § 5121.

2. Sub-Tenant Liability

A sub-tenant is a person who rents all or part of the property from a tenant and does not sign a rental agreement or lease with the landlord. A sub-tenant is someone who either took over the property after the original tenant temporarily left, or one who simply lives with the tenant who has signed your lease or rental agreement.

If your lease or rental agreement prohibits sub-leasing, you can evict the tenant who brings in a sub-tenant for violating this lease term. If you don't evict, however, you normally have few legal rights vis-a-vis the sub-tenant who does not have a tenant-landlord relationship with you. As a result, you can't sue the sub-tenant for rent—either in small claims court or in an eviction suit.[8] However, should you rent to a married couple and neglect to get both to sign the lease, the non-signing spouse, although a sub-tenant, is liable for the rent, because each spouse is legally responsible for the necessities of life of the other.[9]

3. When a Tenant Leaves and a New Person Moves In

When a co-tenant leaves and someone else moves in, you must act decisively. While, if no new agreement is signed, the departing tenant will still be liable for the rent, this will probably not be worth too much if your tenant leaves for parts unknown. You are almost always better off to sign a lease or rental agreement with any new tenant if they are acceptable. As an added advantage, it will be clear that the outgoing tenant is no longer entitled to possession of the property. This last point may be especially important where a couple (married or not) separates. If one of them leaves and then wants to come back—against

the will of the other—you are powerless to keep that person out, if:

    a. The person who has left didn't terminate the month-to-month tenancy as to herself with a 30-day notice; or

    b. In the case of a lease, no new lease was entered into by the remaining tenant (on his own or with someone else as a co-tenant), or

    c. The couple is still married, even if a new agreement *has* been signed.[10]

If someone is moving in to replace the departing tenant, it's usually best to have the remaining tenant and the new tenant sign a new lease or rental agreement.[11] The new roommate thus becomes jointly liable for the rent.

But what happens if the new tenant isn't acceptable to you? If she hasn't moved in, simply use your authority to deny permission to sublet. If she has moved in without your permission, promptly move to evict the tenant on the basis of his violation of the lease term prohibiting sublets. (You should also name the person moving in on the eviction action—see *Volume 2, Evictions.*) If you rent under a month-to-month tenancy, a simple 30-day notice is probably your best bet.

E. Death of a Tenant

Occasionally, a landlord will be faced with the death of a tenant who lives alone. Because lawyers and public agencies are bound to be involved, you should be

---

[8]You can bring an eviction lawsuit against the sub-tenant based on nonpayment of rent, but you can get a judgment against the sub-tenant only for possession of the property and court costs, not for the rent itself.

[9]CC § 5121.

[10]Under CC § 5102, a spouse may not be excluded from the home of the other in the absence of a court order, even if a divorce is pending.

[11]If you live in a city with rent control that recognizes the concept of vacancy decontrol, such as Los Angeles, this may also be your chance to raise the rent if the remaining tenant was not part of the original group you rented to. Remember, in most cities that recognize the vacancy decontrol concept, you can only raise the rent in a shared housing when all the original tenants move out. (For more on vacancy decontrol, see Chapter 4.)

sure to comply with the law, even though your first urge may be to clear out the property and rent it as quickly as possible.

When you first suspect or learn of a death of a tenant, call the police or fire department. After the body is removed, you are required to take reasonable precautions to preserve the deceased tenant's property. Obviously, you don't want to be sued by the executor of the estate for giving away valuable property to relatives or to friends, to the detriment of the true heirs. If you can, contact the next of kin, but allow them only to remove personal effects (such as the deceased's clothing) needed for the funeral. Keep everyone else out of the premises. If more than a negligible amount of property is in the dwelling, put a padlock on the door. Open it for the public administrator for the county, or to a court-appointed executor or administrator who can show you Letters Testamentary or Letters of Administration (legal mumbo-jumbo for papers signed by a judge appointing a legal representative for the deceased's estate).

If the deceased tenant's total estate was small ($60,000 or less) or she efficiently used probate avoidance techniques, there may well be no official probate procedure and hence no court-approved executor or administrator. In this situation, if a family member of the deceased's appears and wants to take the property, you can safely release it if you receive a copy of the decedent's will, establishing that the person in question is entitled to the property, along with a declaration under penalty of perjury signed by the person to whom the property has been left.[12] If there is no will, however, and only a small amount of property remains on the premises, formal probate proceedings are unlikely and it's probably okay to release the property to close relatives—provided they sign a receipt for what they take. If you are in doubt, talk to a lawyer.

After all the deceased tenant's property is removed, consider making a claim to the deceased tenant's estate for any unpaid rent through the date the property remained on the premises. If a probate proceeding is initiated, you should submit a filled-out creditor's claim form (available from the court clerk) to the probate clerk of the superior court. You have four months in which to file your claim, beginning when the court officially appoints the estate's executor. If the estate doesn't go through probate (many small estates do not), the best you can do is bill the next of kin.

Living together note. If you rent to an unmarried couple, straight or gay, and one member of the couple dies without a will, you might be caught in a nasty crossfire between the blood relatives of the deceased and his domestic partner. In a living together situation, the blood relatives inherit unless the survivor and the deceased had a contract to share ownership of all property. This is pretty tricky stuff, and if a lot of property is involved, your best bet is to check with your lawyer.

---

[12]Probate Code § 13100.

Returning Security Deposits

As any small claims court judge will tell you, disputes over whether or not a landlord properly withheld all or part of a tenant's security deposit account for a large percentage of the landlord-tenant disputes that wind up in court. Even though landlords commonly win the suits they initiate, they sometimes don't gain very much given the time that goes into bringing the suit and the often difficult and time-consuming job of collecting the judgment. Your best protection against spending hours haggling in court over back rent, cleaning costs and damage to your property is to follow the law scrupulously when you return security deposits. And make sure your tenant knows the law and your procedures on security deposits.

This chapter shows you how to itemize deductions and refund security deposits as the law requires. It also covers the occasional necessity of taking a tenant to small claims court for unpaid rent, damage or cleaning bills not covered by the deposit.

Related Topics

- How to avoid deposit disputes by using clear lease and rental agreement provisions: Chapter 2

- Highlighting security deposit rules in a move-in letter to new tenants; taking photographs and using a Landlord-Tenant Checklist to keep track of the condition of the premises before and after the tenant moves in: Chapter 7

- How much you can charge for deposits, local requirements to pay interest on deposits and the effect of sale of the property on an owner's liability for security deposits: Chapter 5

- How to increase security deposits: Chapter 14

A. Basic Rules for Returning Deposits

The law allows you to make certain deductions from a tenant's security deposit, provided you do it cor-

rectly. The basic rule is this: Within two weeks after a tenant who has paid a deposit leaves—whether voluntarily or by eviction—you must mail the following to the tenant's last known address, or forwarding address if you have one:

1. The tenant's entire deposit, or

2. A written, itemized accounting of deductions for back rent and costs for necessary cleaning and damage repair, together with a check for any deposit balance.[1]

If you act in bad faith and keep a security deposit, or any portion of it, you may be liable for up to $200 in punitive damages should the tenant sue you in small claims court, plus 2% monthly interest on the unreturned balance of the deposit, from the date you were required to pay the deposit (two weeks after the tenant vacated). Also, judges are often skeptical about the legitimacy of a landlord's charges for cleaning and damages if the landlord never bothered to itemize these charges until the tenant raised the issue of getting the deposit back.[2]

1. Security Deposits Defined

California law defines a security deposit as any money you collect from a tenant other than first month's rent. It specifically includes "last month's rent." In other words, whether you call your tenant's up-front money a fee, deposit or charge for "rent," "cleaning," "damage" or even "keys," you must account for it under the law applicable to refundable security deposits. Anything in a lease or rental agreement to the contrary is of no legal effect.[3] (Chapter 5 discusses these rules in more detail.)

---

[1]See CC § 1950.5(e) and (1).

[2]Effective 1/1/92, CC § 1950.5(f) states, "Failure of the landlord to furnish [the] itemized statement to the tenant within two weeks ...shall not preclude the landlord from subsequently claiming and deducting from the security deposit amounts permitted....' You may want to point out this new law to a skeptical judge, but it's still better to act within the two-week period.

[3]CC § 1953(a)(1).

2. When You Rent to More Than One Tenant

When you rent to two or more co-tenants under the same agreement (where their names are all listed on the written lease or rental agreement), you don't have to return or account for any of the deposit until all the tenants leave. In other words, you're entitled to the benefit of the entire deposit until the entire tenancy ends. Any question as to whether a departing co-tenant is entitled to any share of the deposit he originally paid should be worked out between the co-tenants. Obviously, you can voluntarily work out an appropriate agreement with a departing tenant in this situation. But if you do, make sure you're adequately protected by the remainder of the deposit or require that the remaining tenants (or the new roommate, if there is one) bring the deposit up to an acceptable amount.

3. When a Tenant Is Evicted

You must follow the legal procedures for returning and accounting for security deposits whether the tenant leaves voluntarily or involuntarily, with or without the threat or use of eviction proceedings. Quite a few landlords are under the mistaken belief that they don't have to account for the deposit to a tenant who's been evicted by court order, apparently thinking the tenant's misconduct allows a landlord to pocket the entire deposit without further formality.

This is not true. Even if you win a judgment in court against a tenant for several months' unpaid rent—more than the amount of the deposit—you still must notify the tenant in writing within 14 days after the tenant departs as to how the deposit is applied toward cleaning or damage charges and the court judgment for rent. (See Section C, below.)

4. Inspecting the Premises

Although it's not legally required, we recommend that you or your manager arrange to check over the property with a tenant who's moving out. Done in a conciliatory, non-threatening way, this should alleviate any of the tenant's uncertainty concerning exactly what deductions (if any) will be made from the deposit. After all, a tenant unpleasantly surprised by the amount withheld from the deposit is more likely to take the matter to court. A Move-Out Letter that explains your inspection procedures to the tenant is shown below. You can modify this letter to your own needs using the tear-out copy provided in the Appendix.

Whether or not the final inspection is made in the tenant's presence, we suggest you check each item—for example, refrigerator or bathroom walls—on the Landlord/Tenant Checklist signed when the tenant moved in. (An excerpt is shown here. See Chapter 7 for a complete Checklist.)

EXCERPT FROM LANDLORD-TENANT CHECKLIST—General Condition of Rooms

	Condition on Arrival	Condition on Departure	Est. Cost of Repair/Replacement
Kitchen			
Floors & Floor Coverings	cigarette burn hole (1)	no charge	
Walls & Ceilings	OK	dirty wall	
Light Fixtures	OK	OK	
Cabinets	OK	no charge	
Counters	discolored		
Stove/Oven	OK		
Refrigerator	OK	N/A	
Dishwasher	N/A	N/A	
Garbage Disposal	N/A	OK	
Sink & Plumbing	OK	OK	
Smoke Detector	OK		
Other			
Other			

Note any item that needs cleaning, repair or replacement in the middle column (Condition on Departure). Where appropriate, note the Estimated Cost of Repair or Replacement in the third column; you can subtract those costs from the security deposit.

In Chapter 7, we recommend that you photograph or videotape the premises before the tenant moves in. You should do the same when the tenant leaves, to make before and after comparisons.

Finally, if you have any reason to expect a tenant to take you to court over deductions you plan to make from a security deposit, have the unit examined by another, more neutral person, such as another tenant in the same building. This person should be available to testify in court if necessary.

SAMPLE MOVE-OUT LETTER

July 5, 199

Dear Resident:

We hope you have enjoyed living here.

Before vacating, be sure to thoroughly vacuum the floors (shampoo carpets, if necessary) and clean the walls, kitchen cabinets, stove and oven, refrigerator (which should be emptied of food, turned off, with the door left open), kitchen and bathroom sink, bathtubs, showers, toilets, plumbing fixtures and

_____ deck _____.

Once you have cleaned your unit and removed _all_ your belongings, contact me at __555-1234__ to arrange for a walk-through inspection and to return the key.

Also, please provide a forwarding address where we may mail your security deposit, less any lawful deductions for the cost of necessary cleaning and repairs of damage in excess of ordinary wear and tear, and any past-due rent. We will return your deposit balance, and an itemization of any charges, within two weeks after you move out.

If you have any questions, please contact me at __555-1234__.

Sincerely,

Denise Parsons
Owner/Manager

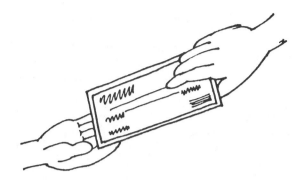

B. Deductions for Cleaning and Damages

You may deduct the following amounts from the tenant's deposit:

1. Costs of Cleaning

The reasonable costs of cleaning include taking care of such things as flea infestations left behind by the tenant's dog, cleaning the oven, removing decals from walls, getting rid of mildew in the bathroom and defrosting the freezer.

As you can imagine, many landlord-tenant disputes over deductions from security deposits deal with whether or not it was reasonable for the landlord to clean the premises after the tenant moves. Unfortunately, legal standards in this area are vague. You may legally charge for any cleaning necessary to satisfy the "average" or "reasonable" incoming tenant. That isn't much help, is it? In practical terms, this means that you can't charge a tenant for cleaning carpets, drapes or walls or repainting as a standard policy. (If repainting badly smudged walls is cheaper and more effective than cleaning, however, you can charge for repainting. See Section 2.a, below.)

You may charge only for cleaning that is actually necessary. Items for which cleaning is often

necessary—and costly—include stained carpets, drapes (particularly smoke-contaminated ones), furniture (for furnished premises) and dirty stoves, refrigerators and kitchen and bathroom fixtures. That's why we highlight these trouble spots in our move-out letter.

You can deduct a reasonable hourly charge if you or your employees do any necessary cleaning. Several large management companies we know cost out cleaning time at $20 per hour, and this is accepted by small claims courts.[4] If you have cleaning done by an outside service, be sure to keep your cancelled checks, and have the service itemize the work. By and large, small claims courts accept cleaning charges unless they are clearly unreasonable. However, if you pay teenagers the minimum wage to do the work, you can expect trouble in court if you have charged the tenant a $20 hourly rate. Also, it's wise to try to patronize only those cleaning services whose employees are willing to testify for you, or at least send a letter describing what they did in detail if the tenant sues you in small claims court, contesting your deposit deductions.

2. Repairing Damage to Property

You may deduct the cost of fixing damage, but not of fixing ordinary wear and tear. Almost as common as disputes over cleaning are those over whether or not damages were due to ordinary wear and tear. Some typical areas of disagreement concern repainting, carpets and fixtures.

Damages over and above ordinary wear and tear include obvious sorts of things, such as cigarette burns, holes in walls and broken tiles, but also more subtle breakage, such as broken refrigerator parts, missing broiler pans, water damage from hanging

---

[4]This is justified as follows. Maintenance people get $8 - $10 per hour. With benefits, this adds up to nearly $15 per hour. Supervisors who must schedule maintenance and inspect the unit (this could be you) are paid a higher hourly rate but work on any one unit for a shorter period of time.

plants and urine stains from animals. See "Costs of Cleaning," above, for advice on determining the costs of repairing damage.

Note on estimated costs. If you can't get necessary repairs made within two weeks, you may deduct an estimate of the cost from the security deposit. If the tenant subsequently sues you, be sure you make the repairs before the trial date, so that you have receipts and an itemization of the repair cost.

a. Repainting

A common argument is whether normal deterioration or the tenant's carelessness makes repainting necessary. Basically, this depends on the condition of the premises and how long the tenant has occupied them. One landlord we know uses, with excellent success, the following approach when a tenant moves out and repainting is necessary. If the tenant has occupied the premises for six months or less, the full cost of repainting (labor and materials) is subtracted from the deposit. If the tenant lived in the unit between six months and a year, and the walls are dirty, two-thirds of the painting cost is subtracted from the deposit. Tenants who occupy a unit for between one and two years and leave dirty walls are charged one-third of the repainting cost. No one who stays for two years or more is ever charged a painting fee. No matter how dirty the walls become, the landlord would always repaint as a matter of course if more than two years had passed since the previous painting. Obviously, a general rule of this type is only that, and must be modified occasionally to fit particular circumstances

What about actual damage to walls? Generally, minor marks or nicks are ordinary wear and tear, but large marks or paint gouges are the responsibility of the tenant. A large number of picture, hook or tack holes in the wall or ceiling that require filling with plaster, or otherwise patching and repainting, are usually damage that goes beyond ordinary wear and tear.

b. Cleaning Carpets or Drapes

Moderate dirt or spotting on a carpet or drapes, even if you can't get the stains out, is probably just ordinary wear and tear if the tenant has occupied the unit for a number of years. On the other hand, you would be justified in deducting from the security deposit for large rips or indelible stains in a carpet. The basic approach to take is to determine whether the tenant has damaged or substantially shortened the life of something that does wear out. If the answer is yes, you may charge the tenant the pro-rated cost of the item, taking into account how old it was, how long it might have lasted otherwise and the cost of replacement. For example, if your tenant has ruined an eight-year-old rug that had a life expectancy of 10 years, and for which a replacement would cost $1,000 at today's prices, you would charge the tenant $200 for the two years of life that would have remained in the rug had the tenant not ruined it.

c. Removing Fixtures

Many lease and rental agreements (including ours—see Clause 16, Chapter 2) forbid tenants from repairing or altering the premises—for example, by installing fixtures. If the tenant leaves behind a row of bookshelves, contrary to the provisions of the rental agreement, you can remove them, restoring property to the same condition as before they were installed, and subtract the cost from the tenant's security deposit. You do not have to return the bookcases to the tenant because, after all, you've only removed something that has become part of the premises and hence your property.

C. Deductions for Unpaid Rent

After deducting legitimate cleaning and damage charges from a tenant's security deposit, you can also deduct any unpaid rent.

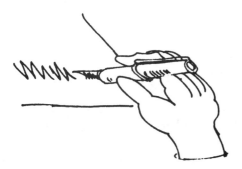

1. Month-to-Month Tenancies

If a tenant leaves owing rent, figure the exact amount by pro-rating the monthly rent for the number of days the tenant failed to pay.

EXAMPLE

Your tenant pays you the rent of $600 for March—supposedly his last month—but stays until April 5 without paying anything more. You are entitled to deduct five-thirtieths (or one-sixth) of the total month's rent, or $100, from the security deposit.

If the tenant gave less than the required 30 days' notice before leaving, you are entitled to rent for the entire 30 days, unless you re-rent, or reasonably could have re-rented, within the 30 days.

EXAMPLE

After having paid her $600 monthly rent on October 1, your tenant Sheila informs you on the 15th that she's leaving on the 25th, thus giving you only 10 days' notice when you're entitled to 30. You're entitled to rent through the 30th day, counting from October 15, or November 14, unless you found—or reasonably could have found—a new tenant in the meantime.[5] Since the rent is paid through October 31, Sheila owes you the pro-rated rent for 14 days in November. At $600 per month or $20 a day, this works out to $280, which can be deducted from Sheila's security deposit.

---

[5] We discuss your responsibility to try to find a replacement tenant in these circumstances in Chapter 19. Unless the departing tenant produces a satisfactory new tenant who will begin paying rent immediately, it is generally (but not always) assumed that it is reasonable to take up to 30 days to find a new tenant and get them moved in.

2. Leases

If a tenant leaves before a fixed-term lease expires, you are entitled to the balance of the rent due under the lease, less any rent you receive from new tenants before the end of the lease term, or could receive if you make a diligent effort to re-rent the property. If your tenant leaves more than one month early, your duty to cut your losses by finding a new tenant is usually taken seriously by courts. In other words, if you withhold more than one month's rent from the tenant's deposit and you are challenged in court, a judge is likely to want to know why you couldn't re-rent the property. (See Chapter 19.A, for a discussion of a landlord's duty to find a new rent-paying tenant as soon as possible.)

EXAMPLE

On January 1, Will leased his house to Anthony and his family for $1,200 a month. On June 30, Anthony moves out, even though six months remains on his one-year lease, making him responsible for a total rent of $7,200. Will re-rents the property on July 10, this time for $1,250 a month (prorated at $833 for the last 20 days in July), so that he'll receive a total rent of $7,083 through December 31. Because this sum is $117 less than the $7,200 he would have received from Anthony had he lived up to the lease, Will may deduct $117 from Anthony's deposit. If Will spent a reasonable amount of money to find a new tenant (for newspaper ads, rental agency commissions, etc.), he could also deduct this sum from the deposit.

3. Court Judgments for Unpaid Rent

If you sue to evict and obtain a judgment for rent through the date of the judgment, you can subtract:

- the amount of judgment, and
- pro-rated rent for the period between the date of the judgment and the date the tenant actually leaves.

EXAMPLE

You sue a tenant who fails to pay May's rent of $450, and get a judgment on June 10 for rent pro-rated through that date. The tenant doesn't leave until the 17th, when the sheriff comes and puts him out. You can deduct the following items from the deposit:

- costs of any necessary cleaning and damage
- judgment for rent through June 10
- the extra week's rent (seven days at $15/day, or $105) for the week between judgment and eviction.

Before you subtract the amount of a court judgment for unpaid rent, deduct for cleaning and damage costs and any rent not included in the judgment. The reason is simple. A judgment can be collected in all sorts of ways—for example, you can garnish the former tenant's wages or bank account—if the security deposit is not large enough to cover it. However, you are much more limited when it comes to collecting money the tenant owes you for damage and cleaning if you don't have a judgment for the amount. If you don't subtract them from the deposit, you'll have to file suit in small claims court.

But if you subtract the amount for cleaning, damage and any unpaid rent not covered in the judgment first, you will still have the judgment if the deposit isn't large enough to cover everything.

EXAMPLE 1

Amelia collected a security deposit of $1,200 from Timothy, whom she ultimately had to sue to evict for failure to pay rent. Amelia got a judgment for $160 court costs plus $1,000 unpaid rent through the date of the judgment. Timothy didn't leave until the sheriff came, about five days later, thus running up an additional pro-rated rent of $100 not reflected in the $1,160 judgment. Timothy also left dirt and damage that cost $1,000 to clean and repair.

Amelia (not having read this book) first applied the $1,200 security deposit to the $1,160 judgment, leaving only $40 to apply toward the rent of $100 which was not reflected in the judgment, as well as the cleaning and repair charges, all of which totalled $1,100. Therefore, Amelia must now sue Timothy for the $1,060 he still owes her.

EXAMPLE 2

Now, let's assume that Monique was Timothy's landlord in the same situation. But Monique applied Timothy's $1,200 deposit first to the cleaning and damage charges of $1,000 and then to the $100 rent not reflected in the judgment. This left $100 to apply to the $1,160 judgment, the balance of which she can collect by having the sheriff garnish Timothy's wages or bank account.

D. Preparing an Itemized Statement of Deductions

You must send the tenant a written itemized explanation of any deductions within two weeks after a tenant who has paid a deposit leaves. We have included three forms, which vary according to the types of deductions you are making. Blank tear-out copies are in the Appendix.

Remember, if your property is located in a city such as San Francisco, Los Angeles, Berkeley or Santa Monica, which requires you to pay interest on a tenant's entire deposit, you must also refund this amount. See the chart in Chapter 5 which summarizes the features of cities requiring interest on security deposits.

1. Returning the Tenant's Entire Deposit

If you are returning a tenant's entire security deposit, (including interest, if required), simply send a brief letter like the one below.

SAMPLE LETTER FOR RETURNING ENTIRE SECURITY DEPOSIT

Letter for Returning Entire Security Deposit

November 5, 199_____

Gerry Fraser_____
976 Park Place_____
Sacramento, CA_____

Dear Gerry_____:

Here is the itemization, as required by Civil Code Section 1950.5, of your $_____1,500_____ security deposit on the property at
_____976 Park Place_____,
which you rented from me on a _____month-to-month basis_____
on _____March 1, 19_____ and vacated on _____September 30, 19_____.

As you left the rental property in satisfactory condition, I am returning the entire amount of your entire security deposit of $_1,500___. *[Note any interest payments, if required.]*

Sincerely,

*Tom Stein*_____
Owner/Manager

---

2. Itemizing Deductions for Repairs and Cleaning

If you are making deductions from the tenant's security deposit only for cleaning and repair, use the form Security Deposit Itemization (Deductions for Repairs and Cleaning). A sample is shown below.

For each deduction, list the item and the dollar amount and attach receipts to the Itemization. If your receipts are not very detailed, add more information—for example, "carpet cleaning, $160, required by several large grease stains and candle wax imbedded in living room rug," or "plaster repair, $400, of several fist-sized holes in bedroom wall"—especially if you feel your tenant will dispute your deductions. (Sections B.1 and B.2 above will help you determine proper amounts to deduct for repairs and cleaning.)

3. Itemizing Deductions for Repairs, Cleaning and Unpaid Rent

Use the form Security Deposit Itemization (Deductions for Repairs, Cleaning and Unpaid Rent) if you have to deduct for unpaid rent as well as cleaning and repairs. A sample is shown below. You still must itemize the deduction even if you have a judgment against the tenant larger than the deposit. For instructions on itemizing deductions for repairs and cleaning, see Section 2, above.

This form also includes spaces for you to include unpaid rent not covered by a court judgment (line 6) and the amount of a court judgment you won in an eviction lawsuit (line 7). (Section C, above, shows you how to figure these amounts.)

It's better to deduct cleaning and damage costs from the security deposit before deducting any court judgment charges. (See Section C.3, above.)

If there's a court judgment involved, explain how you applied the deposit in the Comments section at the bottom of the itemization form. This makes it clear that you are demanding the balance owed and that you can still collect any part of the judgment not covered by the security deposit.

4. Mailing the Security Deposit Itemization

Your security deposit itemization should be mailed to the tenant's last known address or forwarding address, along with a check for any balance you owe, within two weeks of the tenant's departure. If the tenant hasn't left you a forwarding address, mail the itemization and any balance to the address of the rental property itself. That, after all, is the tenant's last address known to you.

If your former tenant has left a forwarding address with the post office, it will forward the mail. If you put "Address Correction and Forwarding Requested" on the envelope, as in the itemization itself, the Postal Service will notify you of the new address, for a nominal fee. This will help if the ten-

ant's deposit doesn't cover all proper deductions and you want to sue in small claims court. (See Section E, below.) It will also help you collect any judgment you have against the tenant.

If the tenant has left no forwarding address, the letter will come back to you. The postmarked envelope is your proof of your good-faith attempt to notify the tenant. It should protect you from the danger of being assessed up to $200 in punitive damages which a judge is empowered to assess you for bad-faith deposit withholding, if the tenant later takes you to small claims court.

E. Small Claims Lawsuits by the Tenant

No matter how meticulous you are about properly accounting to your tenants for their deposits, sooner or later you may be sued by a tenant who disagrees with your assessment of the cost of cleaning or repairs. Because virtually all residential security deposits are less than $5,000, almost all such suits are brought in small claims court. (Five thousand dollars is the maximum award available in small claims court.)

This section suggests several strategies for dealing with small claims suits over security deposits, including how to prepare and present a case in small claims court. For more information on small claims court procedures, see *Everybody's Guide to Small Claims Court* (California Edition), by Ralph Warner (Nolo Press).

SAMPLE SECURITY DEPOSIT ITEMIZATION (DEDUCTIONS FOR REPAIRS AND CLEANING)

Security Deposit Itemization (Deductions for Repairs and Cleaning)
Civil Code Section 1950.5

Date: ___November 8, 199___

To: Rachel Tolan   From: Lena Coleman

      123 Larchmont Lane   456 Penny Lane, #101

      Oceanside, California   San Diego, California

Property Address: ___789 Cora Court, Oceanside, California___

Rental Period: January 1, 199 to October 31

1. Security Deposit Received: $ 600

2. Interest on deposit (if required by lease or local law): $ N/A

3. Total Credit (sum of lines 1 and 2): $ 600

4. Itemized Repairs:

    Repainting of living room walls, required by
    crayon and chalk marks, $260.

                             Total Repair Cost: $ 260

5. Necessary Cleaning:

    Sum paid to resident manager for 4 hours cleaning
    at $20/hour—debris-filled garage, dirty stove and
    refrigerator.

                           Total Cleaning Cost: $ 80

6. Total Repair and Cleaning Cost (sum of lines 4 and 5): $ 340

                      Amount Tenant Owes Owner $ __

7. Net Sum Due: Total Deposit Credit (line 3)   OR
   Minus Total Repair and Cleaning Cost (line 6)

                      Amount Owner Owes Tenant $ 260

Comments:

A check for $260 is enclosed

SAMPLE SECURITY DEPOSIT ITEMIZATION (DEDUCTIONS FOR REPAIRS, CLEANING AND UNPAID RENT)

Security Deposit Itemization (Deductions for Repairs, Cleaning and Unpaid Rent)
Civil Code Section 1950.5

Date: ___December 19, 199___

To: Timothy Gottman   From: Monique Told

      8910 Pine Avenue   999 Laurel Drive

      Pacific Grove, California   Monterey, California

Property Address:____456 Pine Avenue, #7, Pacific Grove, California____

Rental Period: January 1, 199 to October 31

1. Security Deposit Received: $ 1,200

2. Interest on deposit (if required by lease or local law): $ N/A

3. Total Credit (sum of lines 1 and 2): $ 1,200

4. Itemized Repairs:

   Carpet repair $160, Drapery cleaning $140,

   Plaster repair $400, Painting of living room $100

   (receipts attached)

                                 Total Repair Cost: $ 800

5. Necessary Cleaning:

   Sum paid to resident manager for 10 hours cleaning

   at $20/hour—debris-filled garage, dirty stove and

   refrigerator.

                                 Total Cleaning Cost: $ 200

6. Defaults in rent not covered by any court judgment
   (list dates and rate):

   5 days at $20 day, November 6–November 11,

   date of court judgment to date of physical eviction $

   100

7. Amount of Court Judgment for Rent, Costs, Attorney Fees: $ 1,160

8. (✔) Total Amount Tenant Owes Owner
   (sum of lines 4, 5, 6 and 7 minus line 3): $ 1,160

   ( ) Total Amount Owner Owes Tenant $ _____

Comments:

The security deposit has been applied as follows: $1,100 for damage

and cleaning charges, $100 for defaults in rent (not covered by any court

judgment) and the remaining $100 towards payment of the $1,160 court

judgment. This leaves $1,060 still owed on the judgment. Please send

that amount to me at once or I shall take appropriate legal action to

collect the judgment.

1. When a Tenant May Sue

A tenant may file suit two weeks after leaving the premises if no deposit refund (with an itemization of what the deposit was used for) is received. If you return part of a deposit sooner than two weeks, a tenant who does not agree with your charges will most likely express that dissatisfaction by way of a letter or phone call demanding that you refund more than you did. This sort of demand is a requirement before anyone can begin a small claims suit.[6] After making a demand, the tenant can bring suit immediately. A tenant who is going to sue will probably do it fairly promptly, but has at least two years to do so.[7] Don't throw out cleaning bills, receipts for repairs, or photographs showing dirt and damages after only a few months, lest you be caught defenseless.

2. Trying To Settle a Potential Lawsuit

If you receive a demand letter from a tenant, probably your best bet is to try to work out a reasonable compromise with the tenant. Be open to the idea of returning more of the deposit to the tenant, even if you believe your original assessment of the cost of repairs and cleaning was more than fair and you feel you will surely win in court. As a businessperson, it usually doesn't make sense for you to spend a morning in court to argue over $50, $100 or even $200.

Splitting the Difference With Tenants

One landlord we know with thousands of units experiences about 250 move-outs each month. He receives about 10 complaints per month about the amount charged against deposits; charges vary widely with the circumstances, but average about $175. This landlord's general policy is to offer to settle for 50% of the disputed amount. He does this not because he thinks his original assessment was wrong, but because he finds that coming to a settlement with a tenant costs a lot less than fighting in court. However, if the settlement offer isn't accepted promptly by the tenant, he fights to win and almost always does.

If you and the tenant can't arrive at a reasonable compromise, you may wish to get help from a local landlord-tenant mediation service, described in Chapter 8.B.

If you arrive at a compromise settlement with your former tenant, you should insist that your payment be accepted as full satisfaction of your obligation to return the deposit. The best way to do this is to prepare and have the tenant sign a brief settlement agreement, such as the following. You could shorten this agreement by simply using the first two lines and the material in paragraph 6, along with the signature lines.

---

[6]CCP § 116.4(a) requires a person suing in small claims court to state under penalty of perjury that she "has demanded payment."

[7]The statute of limitations for a tenant's suit to recover a security deposit is two years if a landlord's failure to refund a deposit is viewed as a breach of an oral agreement (CCP § 339) and four years if a written lease or rental agreement is involved and failure to return a deposit can be considered a breach of it (CCP § 337).

SAMPLE SETTLEMENT AGREEMENT

Settlement Agreement

Lionel Washington, "Owner," and LaToya Jones, "Tenant," hereby agree as follows:

1. Owner rented the premises at 1234 State Avenue, Apartment 5, Los Angeles, California, to Tenant on July 1, 199_, pursuant to a written rental agreement for a tenancy from month-to-month.

2. Under the Agreement, Tenant paid Owner $1,000 as a security deposit.

3. On October 31, 199_, Tenant vacated the premises.

4. Within two weeks after Tenant vacated the premises, Owner itemized various deductions from the security deposit totalling $380 and refunded the balance of $620 to Tenant.

5. Tenant asserts that she is entitled to the additional sum of $300, only $80 of the deductions being proper. Owner asserts that all the deductions were proper and that he owes Tenant nothing.

6. To settle the parties' entire dispute, and to compromise on Tenant's claim for return of her security deposit, Owner pays to Tenant the sum of $150, receipt of which is hereby acknowledged by Tenant, as full satisfaction of her claim.

Date:___December 1, 19___   *Lionel Washington*_____
                                Lionel Washington, Owner/Manager

Date:___December 1, 19___   *LaToya Jones*_____
                                LaToya Jones, Tenant

It is no longer possible to force a settlement by writing on the check you mail to the tenant the words "paid in full" or similar wording. If the tenant crosses out such a notation on the check before cashing it, or even fails to cross it out because he didn't notice the wording, the tenant still may sue for any balance he claims is due.[8]

3. Preparing for a Small Claims Court Hearing

If no compromise is possible, and the tenant sues, the first official notification of the lawsuit you will receive will be a copy of the tenant's "Claim of Plaintiff" form. This will either be sent by certified mail or personally delivered. It will notify you of the date, time and place of the small claims court hearing.

It's still not too late at this stage to try to work out a settlement by paying part of what the tenant's suing for. However, if you compromise at this stage, insist that the tenant sign a dismissal form. This form, called a Request for Dismissal, is available from the small claims clerk.

You don't have to file any papers with the court clerk unless you want to countersue for money you feel the tenant owes you.[9] Normally, you would want to do this only if you kept the tenant's entire deposit and demanded that he pay you more. Obviously, you'll look silly if you refunded part of the deposit, admitting the tenant only owes you the amount withheld, and then change your mind and sue for more. You can, however, defend against the tenant's suit and still initiate your own later.

Before your court hearing, actively gather your evidence. The landlord always has the burden of proving the premises needed cleaning or were damaged after the tenant left.[10] Unless you prove that the place was dirty or damaged, all a former tenant needs to prove to win is that a residential tenancy existed, that she paid you a deposit and that you didn't return all of it. It is essential that you show up in court with as many of the following items of evidence as you can:

- Two copies of the Landlord/Tenant Checklist which you should have filled out with the tenant when the tenant moved in and again when she moved out. (See Chapter 7 and Section B, above.) This is particularly important if the tenant admitted, on the Checklist, to damaged or dirty conditions when she moved out.

- Photos or a video of the premises before the tenant moved in which show how clean and undamaged the place was.

- Photos or a video after the tenant left which show a mess or damage.

- An itemization of hours spent by you or your repair or cleaning people on the unit, complete with the hourly costs for the work.

- Damaged items small enough to bring into the courtroom (a curtain with a cigarette hole would be effective).

- Receipts for professional cleaning (particularly of carpets and drapes) and repair.

- One, or preferably two, witnesses who were familiar with the property, saw it just after the tenant left and who will testify that the place was a mess or that certain items were damaged. People who helped in the subsequent cleaning or repair are particularly effective witnesses. Written statements or declarations under penalty of perjury can be used, but they aren't as effective as live testimony. A sample written statement is shown below.

---

[8]CC § 1526.

[9]CCP § 426.60(b).

[10]CC § 1950.5(k).

SAMPLE DECLARATION

Declaration of Paul Stallone, Cleaner

I, Paul Stallone, declare:

1. I am employed at A & B Maintenance Company, a contract cleaning and maintenance service located at 123 Abrego Street, Monterey, California. Gina Cabarga, the owner of an apartment complex at 456 Seventh Street, Monterey, California, is one of our accounts.

2. On May 1, 199_, I was requested to go to the premises at 456 Seventh Street, Apartment 8, Monterey, California, to shampoo the carpets. When I entered the premises, I noticed a strong odor, part of what seemed like stale cigarette smoke. An odor also seemed to come from the carpet.

3. When I began using a steam carpet cleaner on the living room carpet, I noticed a strong smell of urine. I stopped the steam cleaner, moved to a dry corner of the carpet, and pulled it from the floor. I then saw a yellow color on the normally-white foam-rubber pad beneath the carpet, as well as smelled a strong urine odor, apparently caused by a pet (probably a cat) having urinated on the carpet. On further examination of the parts of the carpet, I noticed similar stains and odors throughout the carpet and pad.

4. In my opinion, the living room carpet and foam-rubber pad underneath need to be removed and replaced and the floor should be sanded and sealed.

I declare under penalty of perjury under the laws of the State of California that the foregoing is true and correct.

Dated: June 15, 199_

_____
Paul Stallone, Cleaner

---

4. The Small Claims Court Hearing

In small claims court people don't sit in a witness box. They normally stand behind a table facing the judge and explain their version of the dispute. In some courts, however, judges use other procedures, such as requesting that all parties and witnesses approach the judge's bench and proach the judge's bench and explain what went on in conversational tones.

Here is how a small claims hearing would probably begin:

Clerk: "Calling the case of *Wendy Tanaka v. Linda Lu.*"

Judge: "Well, Ms. Tanaka, since you're the plaintiff, please tell me your version of the facts first."

Wendy Tanaka: "I moved into apartment "A" at 1700 Walnut St. in Costa Mesa in the spring of 199_. I paid my landlady here my first month's rent of $900 plus a $900 security deposit. When I moved out, she withheld $540 of this, returning only $360. As I believe this constitutes a willful denial of my rights under Civil Code Section 1950.5, I am asking for not only the $540 she owes me, but $200 in punitive damages, for a total of $740. Here is a copy of the rental agreement [HANDS IT TO THE CLERK], which specifically states my deposit is to be returned to me if the apartment is left clean and undamaged. When I moved into apartment A, it was a mess. It's a nice little apartment, but the people who lived there before me were sloppy. The stove was filthy, as was the bathroom, the refrigerator, the floors and just about everything else. But I needed a place to live and this was the best available, so I moved in despite the mess. I painted the whole place—everything. My landlady gave me the paint, but I did all of the work. And I cleaned the place thoroughly too. It took me three days. I like to live in a clean house."

Judge: [LOOKING AT ONE OF THE TENANT'S WITNESSES] "Do you have any personal knowledge of what this apartment looked like?"

Witness: "Yes, I helped Wendy move in and move out. I simply don't understand what the landlady is fussing about. The place was a mess when she moved in, and it was clean when Wendy moved out."

Judge: "Ms. Lu, you may now tell your side of the story. I should remind you that you have the burden of proving that the amounts you withheld were reasonable."

Linda Lu: "Your Honor, it is true, as Ms. Tanaka testified, that the people who lived in the apartment before her were sloppy. They left things a mess, but my manager and I cleaned it up the day before Ms. Tanaka actually moved in. Here are several photographs we took after the previous tenant moved out [HANDS PHOTOS TO CLERK]. My manager, Bennie Owens, and I spent a long day cleaning the place before Ms. Tanaka moved in. We took this second set of photos to show the contrast after we cleaned it. Anyway, the point is that these photos [HANDS TO THE CLERK] also show the apartment just before Ms. Tanaka moved in. Also, when Ms. Tanaka moved in, she signed this inventory sheet [HANDS TO CLERK] indicating that all parts of the premises were clean and undamaged, right after she and Bennie Owens—who is here to testify—inspected the premises together.

It's true that Ms. Tanaka did some painting, but this was in exchange for a reduction of her first month's rent of $150 and our supplying the paint. Mr. Owens will also testify to his inspection of the premises after Ms. Tanaka left and present the pictures he took on the day she left. But before he does, I should add that Ms. Tanaka gave me only ten days' verbal notice, on October 15, before she left the apartment on October 25. Her rent was paid through the 31st, but I was unable to re-rent the property until November 10, despite the ads I put in the paper as soon as she gave me her notice. Because she didn't give me the full 30 days' notice, I charged her 10 days pro-rated rent of $150 for the rent I didn't receive within the 30-day period, as well as $120 for cleaning the apartment. I believe this was reasonable under the circumstances."

Judge: [LOOKING AT BENNIE OWENS] "What do you have to add, Mr. Owens?"

Bennie Owens: "Well, Your Honor, I did inspect the premises with Ms. Tanaka when she first moved in. She stated everything looked fine and signed the Landlord/Tenant Checklist I gave her. When she moved out on October 25, I went into the apartment and took these pictures. [HANDS THEM TO THE CLERK TO GIVE TO THE JUDGE]. Although the place wasn't a real mess, it still wasn't clean enough to re-rent right away either. The pictures I took clearly show mildew in the refrigerator, and a dirty oven. They also show a large dirt-stained area in the hall carpet, as well as a foot-square area where candle wax was imbedded in the bedroom carpet. I hired a professional cleaning service to clean the refrigerator, stove and carpet. Here's the receipt [HANDS TO CLERK]. The total was $120."

After you and your witnesses have presented your evidence as in the above example, the judge may ask a few questions and may announce a decision right there. Or the judge may take the matter "under submission," and you will be notified of the result by mail. If you lose the small claims case, you must pay the judgment within 20 days (unless you appeal), or the tenant will be able to attach your bank account or other property, or even to put a lien on the property.

A plaintiff who loses cannot appeal. As a defendant, however, you have the right to appeal an adverse small claims decision to the superior court and have a new trial, where you may be represented by an attorney (not allowed in small claims court). Before you do so, however, you should consider that the superior court judge will more than likely lean toward affirming the decision of the small claims judge. Finally, if the judge feels that you appealed the case just to harass or delay the plaintiff, and that you had no valid defense, you may have to pay the plaintiff's attorney fees, up to $1,000.[11]

Nothing that happens in small claims court affects the validity of any judgment you may already have (for example, from an earlier eviction suit) against the tenant. So, if you got a judgment against a tenant for $1,200 for unpaid rent as part of an eviction action, this judgment is still good, even though a tenant gets a judgment against you for $200 in small claims court based on your failure to return the deposit.

F. If the Deposit Doesn't Cover Damage and Unpaid Rent

If the security deposit doesn't cover the rent or cleaning or repair costs a tenant owes you, you may wish to file a lawsuit against a former tenant. In this situation, small claims court is both faster and easier to use than municipal court as long as your claim doesn't exceed $5,000, the small claims court limit.

Here we discuss only the basics of suing a tenant for back rent or damages not covered by the tenant's deposit. If you decide to go to court, we recommend *Everybody's Guide to Small Claims Court* (California Edition) by Ralph Warner. (Nolo Press).

1. The Demand Letter

If you decide that it is worthwhile to go after your tenant for money owed, your first step is to write a letter asking her to pay the amount of your claim. Although this may seem like an exercise in futility, the law requires that you make a demand for the amount sued for before filing in small claims court.[12] Your written itemization of how you applied the tenant's security deposit to the charges, which requests payment of the balance, can be considered such a demand. (See Section D, above.)

---

[11]CCP § 116.790.

[12]CCP § 116.320(b)(3).

2. Collection Agencies

If you don't want to sue in small claims court, consider hiring a licensed local collection agency to try to collect from the tenant. The agency usually keeps about one-third of what it collects for you. If it can't collect, it can hire a lawyer to sue the ex-tenant. Lawyers working for collection agencies may not sue in small claims court, however, and must sue in municipal court. Many collection agencies pay all court costs, hoping to recover them if and when they collect the resulting judgment. In exchange, however, collection agency commissions often rise to 50% or more if they've hired a lawyer to sue.

Of course, turning a matter over to a collection agency doesn't necessarily mean you wash your hands of the matter. The collection agency still takes direction from you. If the tenant defends against a lawsuit filed by a collection agency's lawyer, you must be involved in the litigation. The only way to walk away from it completely is to sell the debt (back rent or damage compensation) to the collection agency, which may pay you only a fraction of the amount owed.

3. Should You Sue?

Before you rush off to your local small claims court to file a claim against your former tenant, ask yourself three questions:

• Do I have a valid case?[13]

• Can I locate the former tenant?

• Can I collect a judgment if I win?

If the answer to any of these questions is no, think twice about initiating a suit.

Pay particular attention to the third question, about how you will collect a judgment. The best way

to collect any judgment against your ex-tenant is to garnish her wages. If she's working, there is an excellent chance of collecting if payment is not made voluntarily. You can't, however, garnish a welfare, social security, unemployment, pension or disability check or a federal paycheck. So, if the person sued gets her income from one of these sources, you may be wasting your time unless you can identify some other asset that you can efficiently get your hands on.

Bank accounts, motor vehicles and real estate are other common collection sources. But people who run out on their debts don't always have much in a bank account (or they may have moved the account to make it difficult to locate), and much of their personal property may be exempt under California debt protection laws. For example, equity in motor vehicles owned by the debtor is exempt up to $1,200, and the tools of a person's trade are exempt up to $2,500. Ordinarily and reasonably necessary household furnishings, appliances and clothing are all exempt, as is money in bank accounts which can be traced to exempt assets such as disability and unemployment benefits.[14]

4. How To Sue in Small Claims Court

If you decide a small claims court suit is worthwhile, you can file suit in the judicial district in which your premises are located or in which the tenant now resides, whichever is most convenient for you.

To start your case, go to the small claims clerk's office, pay a small filing fee (which you can recover if you win) and fill out a form called "Plaintiff's Statement to Clerk." When you have completed the form, give it to the court clerk, who will then use it to type out a Claim of Plaintiff form and assign your case a number. You will be asked to sign this form under penalty of perjury. A copy of the Claim of

---

[13]If you are a landlord with many rental units and use a local small claims court regularly, make particularly sure the cases you bring are good ones. You do not want to lose your credibility with the court in future cases by even appearing to be unfair.

---

[14]See *Collect Your Court Judgment* by Gini Graham Scott, Stephen Elias and Lisa Goldoftas (Nolo Press).

Plaintiff will go to the judge, and another must be served on the defendant.

If the person you're suing lives in the same county in which the suit is brought, your hearing date should be between 10 and 40 days from the time the papers are filed. If the defendant lives outside of the county where you bring suit, the case will be heard between 30 and 70 days from that date.[15]

When you file your papers, arrange with the clerk for a court date that is convenient for you. You need not take the first date the clerk suggests. Be sure to leave yourself enough time to get a copy of the Claim of Plaintiff form served on the defendant. The defendant is entitled to receive service of the Claim of Plaintiff form at least five days before the date of the court hearing, if he is served within the county in which the courthouse is located. If the defendant is served in a county other than the one where the trial is to take place, he must be served at least 15 days before the trial date. (If you fail to serve your papers properly on the defendant in time, there is no big hassle—just notify the clerk, get a new court date and try again.)

Small claims court sessions are usually held between 9 A.M. and 3 P.M. on working days. Larger counties are required to hold at least one evening or Saturday session per month. Ask the clerk for a schedule.

All the persons you name as defendants in a small claims case must be served with the papers. This can often be done by certified mail. The clerk of the court does the mailing for you. The fee is modest and is recoverable if you win. This method of service is both cheap and easy, but its success depends on the defendant signing for the letter. Some people never accept certified mail, knowing instinctively, or perhaps from experience, that nothing good ever comes by certified mail. The consensus among court clerks is that about 40% of certified mail services are accepted. The Claim of Plaintiff can also be served on each defendant personally, using the sheriff, marshal, private process server or any adult, except you. Or you can use substituted service, which involves giving a copy of the papers to a person at the defendant's home or workplace with a second copy mailed to her there.[16] (See Chapter 18 for a discussion of different forms of service.)

Once you've obtained your court date and had your former tenant served with the Claim of Plaintiff, you are ready to prepare for trial. See Section E.3 of this chapter on small claims suits over deposits, and *Everybody's Guide to Small Claims Court*, by Ralph Warner (Nolo Press).

At the small claims hearing, you should offer a copy of your demand letter or Security Deposit Itemization to the judge, noting that you're doing so for the purpose of showing that you made the required demand before suing. Although the judge will pay more attention to what you say in court rather than what you said in the demand letter, a coherent set of facts in writing certainly doesn't hurt.

If the tenant is suing you but has not demanded payment of the security deposit, as legally required, point this out to the judge, who may dismiss the suit on that basis.

---

[15]CCP § 1116.4.

[16]See CCP § 415.20.

Property Abandoned by a Tenant

This chapter outlines the proper steps to take to deal with property left behind by tenants who have moved out, so that you can prepare the premises for the next tenant. Obviously, you want to protect yourself from claims by the tenant who has moved out that you have destroyed or stolen her property.[1]

A. Personal Property

Whether a tenant vacates voluntarily, or with the aid of the sheriff or marshal, landlords all too often must not only clean up and repair damage, but also dispose of a pile of junk. You're much more likely to deal with a tenant's property when the tenant was evicted and wasn't allowed to take everything. The belongings of evicted tenants are not put into the street. The law enforcement officer performing an eviction will allow the tenant to carry out a few armloads of personal possessions, leaving the remainder to be locked in the premises and stored by you until the tenant can arrange to take them away.

Removing obvious trash is normally no problem, but even here you must exercise care. If you toss a moth-eaten book in the dumpster, and it turns out to have been a valuable first edition, you could have problems.

As a general rule, the more valuable the property left behind by a tenant, the more formalities you must comply with when disposing of it. In rare instances, you may have a judgment against a tenant for unpaid rent or damages to your premises, and this tenant has left behind valuable property that she never claims. If so, you can safely have the property sold and the money applied to pay your judgment, but only if you follow the legal procedures outlined in this chapter.

---

[1] In legal jargon, this is known as "unlawful conversion." Conversion occurs when you take someone else's property and convert it to your own use or benefit, either by selling it or otherwise disposing of it, or using it yourself.

You cannot touch a tenant's property until you have legally gained possession of the premises. This occurs when a tenant finally leaves voluntarily, whether or not she gives you the keys, or when the tenant is physically evicted by the sheriff, marshal or constable. If you gained possession of the property after having heard nothing from the tenant for 18 days since mailing a Notice of Belief of Abandonment (see Chapter 19), you should understand that your mailing of the abandonment notice relating to the real property—the premises—has nothing to do with any personal property abandoned inside. In other words, it only allows you to enter legally after the premises were abandoned, not dispose of property. You may dispose of property only after following the procedures described in this chapter.

1. If the Tenant Demands His Property

Ideally, a tenant who has left behind property after moving out will contact you about reclaiming it. If not, try to contact the tenant to pick up his property. If you can't reach him, look through the tenant's rental application and phone personal or business references listed there.

By all means, if a tenant is willing to pick up his propety, return everything to him, even if he owes you money. If a tenant owes you money—for example, back rent—you cannot insist that he pay you before you return his property.

There's one exception, however: You may insist the tenant pay your costs of moving and storing the property before you return his belongings. If you've kept the property on the premises the tenant vacated, you have the right to insist on being paid the pro-rated daily rental value for keeping the property on your premises and/or any out-of-pocket costs you incur after that for renting storage space. You can also subtract the value of your time for packing the tenant's property up in the first place.

However, in most situations where there is not a lot of property, we recommend that you give the tenant his belongings and forget about any charges, particularly if you didn't incur any out-of-pocket expenses. It's just not worth it to get in fights over $75 worth of used books, records and old clothes. If you insist on too high a storage charge, and the tenant refuses to pay it, you will end up having to keep or sell the tenant's property. As a result, the tenant may sue you, raising the possibility that a judge may hold you liable for the entire value of the property because your storage charge wasn't reasonable in the first place. Under state law,[2] a landlord who fails to promptly return a tenant's belongings may be liable for the value of the property plus $250 and the tenant's attorney fees.

The process by which a tenant demands his property is supposed to work this way:

- The tenant moves out, leaving personal belongings behind.

- Within 18 days, the tenant writes the landlord demanding the return of his property.

- Within five days after receiving the tenant's demand, the landlord must either return the tenant's property or notify her by letter (addressed to the tenant at the return address specified in her demand) itemizing in detail the amount of moving and/or storage charges, which the landlord demands as a condition of returning the tenant's property. (As stated above, however, we think it's less hassle to simply return the property without insisting on moving or storage charges.)

- The tenant then has three days to pay the landlord's moving and storage charges (if any) and reclaim the property.

2. If the Tenant Doesn't Demand His Property

A tenant truly interested in keeping his belongings usually won't leave anything behind. (Even tenants evicted by the sheriff or marshal usually manage to move themselves and their belongings out a day or two before the scheduled eviction date.) So, when a tenant leaves personal property, it's usually junk that has been intentionally left behind. Unfortunately, you can face serious liability for disposing of the junk, unless you use a Notice of Right to Reclaim Abandoned Property, as shown below.[3]

If, after a tenant has left, you discover property in addition to obvious trash or garbage, follow these steps:

Step 1. Take an inventory of the abandoned property and write down a list of everything you find. An objective witness (tenant or neighbor) is valuable here if you want to protect yourself from any charge that you have not done this honestly. Don't open locked trunks or suitcases or tied boxes; just list the unopened container. You may, however, open other containers to check items for value, since your method of disposing of the property depends on its total value.

Step 2. Decide whether the value of all the property—what you could get for it at a well-attended flea market or garage sale—is worth more than $300.

Step 3. You must then send the tenant a Notice of Right to Reclaim Abandoned Property. There is no time limit for doing this, but you may not legally dispose of the property until you begin the process with this notice. A sample is shown below and a blank form is included in the Appendix of this book.

On the Notice of Right to Reclaim Abandoned Property, you list:

1. The name of the tenant (and any other person you believe has an interest in the property).

---

[2]CC § 1965.

[3]See CC §§ 1980-1991.

2. The address of the premises.

3. A description of the property. If there are too many items of property to list on the form, you can list them on a separate sheet of paper labeled "Attachment A." The property must be described "in a manner reasonably adequate to permit the owner of the property to identify it."[4] Merely describing it as "household goods" is insufficient.

4. A place where the property may be claimed.

5. The value of the property, by checking the appropriate box on the form as to whether the property, in your opinion, is worth more or less than $300.

6. Your signature and date of the Notice.

Note on fixtures. If a tenant attaches something more or less permanently to the wall, such as bookshelves bolted or nailed in, it is called a "fixture." The general rule, in the absence of a lease provision otherwise, is that a fixture installed by the tenant becomes a part of the premises, which belongs to the landlord. That means a tenant who attaches bookshelves to a wall, using bolts, nails or other fasteners that can't be removed without leaving unsightly marks or more serious damage, such as large holes, is legally required to leave the shelves in place when she leaves. Fixtures are the landlord's property, and do not have to be returned to the tenant.

Mail the notice to the tenant's last known residence, which will, of course, usually be the address of your residential rental property. The postal service will forward the notice if the tenant has left a forwarding address.

You must surrender the property if the tenant contacts you within 18 days after you mailed the notice. If you haven't mailed a notice, you must surrender the property within 18 days after the tenant has left. Again, before returning the tenant's property, you have the right to charge moving and storage costs (not exceeding the pro-rated daily rental value for keeping the property on your premises), and/or any out-of-pocket costs you incur for renting storage space. However, as we mentioned, it may not be worth the hassle and risk to insist on these charges.

 Don't demand more than moving and storage charges. Even if the tenant owes you a substantial sum for back rent or damages, you may not insist on payment of that amount as a condition of returning the tenant's property, even if you've obtained a court judgment. In order to properly keep the property to have it sold and applied against such a judgment, you must have the sheriff seize the property and auction it off. The costs of doing this may exceed the value of the property, however.

a. Property Worth Less than $300

If your former tenant or other owner of the property left behind doesn't contact you within 18 days of mailing the Notice of Right to Reclaim Abandoned Property, you may keep, sell, give away, use or do anything else you wish with the property, if it is all worth less than $300.[5] In other words, it's yours. To recover from you for wrongfully disposing of the property, the tenant would have to convince a probably skeptical judge that the property was worth over $300 and that your belief that it was worth less was unreasonable.

Several landlords we know routinely put all the material left behind by the tenant, when the total value obviously does not exceed $300, in large plastic bags, which they tag and keep in their own storage room for six months or so. A few times a year, they give everything that hasn't been claimed to Goodwill Industries, the Salvation Army or some other nonprofit organization that operates second-hand stores.

---

[4]CC § 1983(b).

[5]CC § 1988.

SAMPLE NOTICE OF RIGHT TO RECLAIM ABANDONED PROPERTY

Notice of Right To Reclaim Abandoned Property
(Civil Code Section 1984)

To: _____ Scott Gold _____,
(name)

When the premises at: _____ 123 Alameda Avenue #4 _____
(street address)

City of ___ Santa Monica ___, County of ___ Los Angeles ___, California.

were vacated, the following personal property remained:

one Sony color TV, one green couch, shirts and pants, small coffee
table, standing lamp

[ ] Continued on Attachment "A" hereto.

You may claim this property at: _____ 2468 Great Street _____

City of ___ Los Angeles ___, County of ___ Los Angeles ___, California.

Unless you pay the reasonable cost of storage for all the above-described property, and take possession of the property which you claim not later than eighteen (18) days after the date of mailing of this notice indicated below, this property may be disposed of pursuant to Civil Code Section 1988.

[ ] Because this property is believed to be worth less than $300, it may be kept, sold, or destroyed without further notice if you fail to reclaim it within the time limit indicated.

[x] Because this property is believed to be worth more than $300, it will be sold at a public sale after notice has been given by publication, if you fail to reclaim it within the time limit indicated. You have the right to bid on the property at this sale. After the property is sold and the cost of storage, advertising, and sale is deducted, the remaining money will be paid over to the county. You may claim the remaining money at any time within one year after the county receives the money.

Date of Mailing: ___ October 1, 19 ___

Marilyn Winters
Owner/Manager

123 Alameda Avenue #1, Santa Monica, California
(street address)

b. Property Worth More than $300

Very seldom will a departing tenant leave behind personal effects worth more than $300. Indeed, one management company that handles several thousand units, and has done so for 30 years, tells us that they have only had this occur once. In the rare event this does occur, you must arrange for the property to be sold at a public auction and then publish a notice in the newspaper announcing the auction.[6]

The ad must be published after the 18-day period for the tenant to claim her belongings has expired, and at least five days before the date of the auction. Although your estimate of value can be based on flea market or garage sale values, actually holding a flea market or garage sale does not comply with the law, which requires a "public sale by competitive bidding." You must hire a licensed and bonded public auctioneer. (See the "Auctioneer" listings in the yellow pages of your telephone directory.)

Place your ad in the legal section of a local newspaper. The newspaper must be one of "general circulation" that has paid subscribers in the county. Most daily newspapers qualify; weekly "throwaway" newspapers delivered free of charge and which de-

pend on advertising for all their revenue do not.[7] Basically, the ad must describe the property in the same way you described it in the Notice of Right to Reclaim Abandoned Property.

Proceeds from the sale go first to pay your reasonable costs of storage, advertising and sale. You must pay the balance to the county within 30 days of the sale, unless you have a judgment for unpaid rent, in which instance you can keep the amount necessary to pay the judgment. (To do this, however, you will have to take the judgment and a "Writ of Execution," available from the court clerk, to the sheriff or marshal and give them the appropriate fee and written instructions to "levy" on the funds in the county's control. Ask the sheriff's or marshal's office for details.) In the unlikely event that money is left over, ask the county clerk for details, including a form to account for the sale proceeds. The county gets to keep the money if the tenant or other owner of the property doesn't claim it within a year.

Why should you go to all this trouble? After all, no law enforcement agency will prosecute you for failing to comply with this law. But following this procedure will protect you from any liability in the event the tenant or other owner of the property left behind shows up later and sues you for unlawful "conversion" of her property.[8] Also, if the property is worth a lot more than $300, there may be enough money left over from the proceeds of the sale, after subtracting your costs for storage, advertising and conducting the auction, to apply to any judgment you have against the tenant.

---

[6]CC § 1988.

[7]See Government Code Section 6066, and CC § 1988(b) and (c) for how to advertise and handle the proceeds of a public sale.

[8]CC § 1989(c).

EXAMPLE

After Donna went to court and obtained a judgment for eviction and $1,000 back rent against her tenant, Abbie, Abbie simply took off for parts unknown. Strangely enough, Abbie left behind a good quality color TV, a piano and a starving Persian cat. Donna sent Abbie a Notice of Right to Reclaim Abandoned Property, to which Abbie didn't respond. Donna then advertised and arranged a public auction which brought in $750. Donna applied the auction proceeds as follows: $100 storage charges, including care and feeding of the cat and pro-rated rental value for the days Abbie's property was on the premises, $100 for the cost of running the legal ad, and the auctioneer's $200 fee. This left $350 for Donna to have the sheriff apply against her $1,000 judgment.

Be careful how you use auction proceeds.
If the tenant owes you money—even for back rent—you can't use the proceeds of the sale to pay the tenant's debt unless you have a court judgment. This is because the proceeds, after subtracting costs of storage, advertising and sale, are still the tenant's property. You are not allowed to take someone else's property except to pay off a judgment.

In the above example, Donna, to enforce her judgment, should instruct the auctioneer to hold the funds in Abbie's name. Donna should then have the clerk of the court that issued the judgment issue a Writ of Execution, which Donna would, in turn, take to the local sheriff or marshal, with appropriate instructions to levy on the funds held by the auctioneer. As a practical matter, if Donna did simply take the excess auction proceeds and apply them toward the judgment (and account for it properly to the tenant if and when Abbie showed up later), it's unlikely a judge would penalize Donna, assuming her accounting was honest. And even if a judge did rule Donna's action was improper, Donna still would have the right to offset her judgment against the tenant's claims for any wrongful disposition of the property.

B. Motor Vehicles

Occasionally, a departing tenant will leave an inoperable "junker" automobile in the parking lot or garage. Unfortunately, motor vehicles are a special category of personal property to which the procedures listed in Section A above do not apply. Whether the tenant has used the street in front of your property, or the property itself, as a junk yard, you should call the local police, giving the vehicle's license number, make and model, and indicate where it's parked. If the car is parked on the street, the police will arrange to have it towed away 72 hours later, placing a notice to that effect on the windshield.[9]

If the vehicle is parked on your property, you can arrange to have it towed away within 24 hours after notifying the police, if the vehicle "lacks an engine, transmission, wheels, tires, doors, windshield, or any other major part or equipment."[10] Otherwise, the police may still arrange for the vehicle's removal after sending out an officer to see if it appears to be abandoned and tagging it.[11]

Cities have slightly different ordinances to cover this situation. In some, there is a small charge, but in many others, the city recovers towing and storage costs from the sale of the car. Several landlords have reported that the police are slow to pick up motor vehicles abandoned on private property and try to tell landlords that it's their responsibility to do a lien sale through the Department of Motor Vehicles. If a car is worth a fair amount, this is a viable alternative, as you can use the money you get from the sale to satisfy any judgment you have against the tenant. But it involves a fair amount of paperwork and is often more trouble than it's worth.

Your best approach is usually to insist that the police help you. Get a copy of the local abandoned property ordinance and refer to it if the police resist.

---

[9]Vehicle Code § 22651(k).

[10]Vehicle Code § 22658(a)(3).

[11]Vehicle Code §§ 22523(b) and 22669.

Appendix

RENTAL APPLICATION
To Be Completed Separately By Every Adult Tenant

Property Address

BACKGROUND INFORMATION AND RENTAL HISTORY

Name

Home Phone   Work Phone

Driver's License No.   Social Security No.

Current Address

Years at Address   Reason for Leaving

Owner/Manager   Phone

Previous Address

Years at Address   Reason for Leaving

Owner/Manager   Phone

Number and Type of Pets

Please List Any Water-filled Furniture You Own

Name and Relationship of Every Adult Person to Live With You

Name and Age of Every Minor Child to Live With You

EMPLOYMENT HISTORY

Current Occupation

Name and Address of Employer   Phone

Years with this Employer   Name of Supervisor   Phone

Name and Address of Previous Employer   Phone

Years with this Employer   Name of Supervisor   Phone

Monthly Employment Income (before deductions) $

Sources and Average Monthly Amounts of Other Income

        $

Monthly Income of Other Adults to Live with You $

Total Monthly Household Income (sum of the three items above) $

CREDIT HISTORY

Savings Acct. No. _____ Bank _____ Branch _____

Checking Acct. No. _____ Bank _____ Branch _____

Money Market or Similar Accounts (financial institution and account number)

_____

_____

Major Credit Card _____ Acct. No. _____

Other Credit Reference (e.g., car or student loan, department store credit card)

_____

_____

Acct. No. _____	Amount owed $ _____	Average Monthly payment $ _____
Acct. No. _____	Amount owed $ _____	Average Monthly payment $ _____
Acct. No. _____	Amount owed $ _____	Average Monthly payment $ _____
Acct. No. _____	Amount owed $ _____	Average Monthly payment $ _____

Have you ever filed for bankruptcy? _____ Have you ever been sued? _____ Have you ever been evicted? _____

Explain any "yes" to the above _____

_____

_____

MISCELLANEOUS

Vehicle Make _____ Model _____ Year _____ License Plate No. _____

Personal Reference _____

Address _____ Phone _____

Contact in Emergency _____ Relationship _____

Address _____

_____ Phone _____

I certify that all the information given above is true and correct, and I hereby authorize the Owner/Manager of the property listed above to verify any and all of the information and references provided to obtain all relevant credit information pertaining to me. I agree to pay the Owner/Manager a nonrefundable credit-checking fee of $ _____ to obtain a report on my credit from a credit reporting agency.

Date _____ Signed _____

NOTES (Owner//Manager)

RECEIPT AND HOLDING-DEPOSIT AGREEMENT

This will acknowledge receipt of the sum of $ _____ by _____ _____ , "Owner," from _____ _____ , "Applicant," as a holding deposit to hold vacant the rental property at

_____

until _____ , 19 _____ at _____ . The property will be rented to Applicant on a _____ basis at a rent of $_____ per month, if Applicant signs Owner's written _____ and pays Owner the first month's rent and a $ _____ security deposit on or before that date, in which event the holding deposit will be applied to the first month's rent.

This Agreement is contingent upon Owner receiving a satisfactory report of Applicant's references and credit history. Owner and Applicant agree that if Applicant fails to sign the Agreement and pay the remaining rent and security deposit, Owner may retain of this holding deposit a sum equal to the pro-rated daily rent of $ _____ per day plus a $ _____ charge to compensate Owner for the inconvenience.

Date: _____

_____
Applicant

Date: _____

_____
Owner

MONTH-TO-MONTH RESIDENTIAL RENTAL AGREEMENT

CLAUSE 1. IDENTIFICATION OF OWNER AND TENANT

This Agreement is made and entered into on _____ , 19 ___ ,
between _____ ,
hereinafter "Tenants," and _____ ,
hereinafter "Owner."

CLAUSE 2. IDENTIFICATION OF THE PREMISES

Subject to the terms and conditions below, Owner rents to Tenants, and Tenants rent from Owner, for residential purposes only, the premises at _____

_____ ,
California.

CLAUSE 3. DEFINING THE TERM OF THE TENANCY

The rental shall begin on _____ , 19 ____ , and shall continue on a month-to-month basis. This tenancy is terminable by Owner or Tenants and is modifiable by Owner, by the giving of 30 days' written notice to the other (subject to any local rent control ordinance that may apply).

CLAUSE 4. AMOUNT AND SCHEDULE FOR THE PAYMENT OF RENT

On signing this Agreement, Tenants shall pay to Owner the sum of $ _____ as rent, payable in advance, for the period of _____ , 19 _____ through
_____ , 19 _____ . Thereafter, Tenants shall pay to Owner a monthly rent of $ _____ , payable in advance on the first day of each month, except when the first falls on a weekend or legal holiday, in which case rent is due on the next business day. Rent shall be paid to _____ at
_____ , California.

CLAUSE 5. LATE FEES

If Tenants fail to pay the rent in full within five days after it is due, Tenants shall pay Owner a late charge of $ _____ , plus $ _____ for each additional day that the rent continues to be unpaid. The total late charge for any one month shall not exceed
$ _____ . By this provision, Owner does not waive the right to insist on payment of the rent in full on the day it is due.

CLAUSE 6. RETURNED CHECK CHARGES

In the event any check offered by Tenants to Owner in payment of rent or any other amount due under this Agreement is returned for lack of sufficient funds, Tenants shall pay to Owner a returned check charge in the amount of $_____ .

CLAUSE 7.   AMOUNT AND PAYMENT OF DEPOSITS

On signing this Agreement, Tenants shall pay to Owner the sum of $ _____ as
and for security as that term is defined by Section 1950.5 of the California Civil Code, namely
any payment, fee, deposit or charge to be used to compensate Owner for (a) Tenants' default in
the payment of rent, (b) repair of damages to the premises, exclusive of ordinary wear and tear or
(c) cleaning of the premises on termination of tenancy. Tenants, or any of them, may not,
without Owner's prior written consent, apply this security deposit to rent or to any other sum due
under this Agreement.

Within two weeks after Tenants have vacated the premises, Owner shall furnish Tenants
with an itemized written statement of the basis for, and the amount of, any of the security deposit
retained by the Owner. Owner may withhold only that portion of Tenants' security deposit
necessary (a) to remedy any default by Tenants in the payment of rent, (b) to repair damages to
the premises exclusive of ordinary wear and tear or (c) to clean the premises if necessary.

CLAUSE 8.   UTILITIES

Tenants shall be responsible for payment of all utility charges, except for the following,
which shall be paid by Owner: _____

_____ .

CLAUSE 9.   LIMITS ON USE AND OCCUPANCY

The premises are to be used only as a private residence for Tenants listed in Clause 1 of this
Agreement, a total of _____ adult occupants, and for no other purpose without Owner's prior
written consent. Guests may stay up to ten days in any six-month period if Tenants notify Owner
or Owner's representative by the third day of visiting. Occupancy by guests for more than ten
days is prohibited without Owner's written consent and shall be considered a breach of Clause 10
of this Agreement.

CLAUSE 10. PROHIBITION OF ASSIGNMENT AND SUBLETTING

Tenants shall not sublet any part of the premises or assign this Agreement without the prior
written consent of Owner.

CLAUSE 11. CONDITION OF THE PREMISES

Tenants acknowledge that they have examined the premises, including appliances, fixtures,
carpets, drapes and paint, and have found them to be in good, safe and clean condition and
repair, except as otherwise noted on the "Landlord/Tenant Checklist" which Tenants have completed and given Owner, a copy of which Tenants acknowledge receipt of, and which is hereby
deemed to be incorporated into this Agreement by this reference.

Tenants agree to (a) keep the premises in good order and repair and, upon termination of
tenancy, to return the premises to Owner in a condition identical to that which existed when
Tenants took occupancy, except for ordinary wear and tear, (b) immediately notify Owner of any
defects or dangerous conditions in and about the premises of which they become aware and (c)
reimburse Owner, on demand by Owner or his or her agent, for the cost of any repairs to the
premises damaged by Tenants or their guests or invitees.

CLAUSE 12. POSSESSION OF PREMISES

The failure of Tenants to take possession of the premises shall not relieve them of their obligation to pay rent. In the event Owner is unable to deliver possession of the premises to Tenants for any reason not within Owner's control, including but not limited to failure of prior occupants to vacate as agreed or required by law, or partial or complete destruction of the premises, Owner shall not be liable to Tenants, except for the return of all sums previously paid by Tenants to Owner, in the event Tenants choose to terminate this Agreement because of Owner's inability to deliver possession.

CLAUSE 13. PETS

No animal or other pet shall be kept on the premises without Owner's prior written consent, except properly trained dogs needed by blind, deaf or physically disabled persons and:

☐ other _____ ,

under the following conditions: _____ .

CLAUSE 14. OWNER'S ACCESS FOR INSPECTION AND EMERGENCY

Owner or Owner's agents may enter the premises in the event of an emergency, or to make repairs or improvements, supply agreed services, or exhibit the premises to prospective purchasers or tenants. Except in case of emergency, Owner shall give Tenants reasonable notice of intent to enter and shall enter only during regular business hours of Monday through Friday from 9:00 A.M. to 6:00 P.M., and Saturday from 9:00 A.M. to noon. In order to facilitate Owner's right of access, Tenants, or any of them, shall not, without Owner's prior written consent, alter or re-key any locks to the premises or install any burglar alarm system. At all times Owner or Owner's agent shall be provided with a key or keys capable of unlocking all such locks and gaining entry. Tenants further agree to provide instructions on how to disarm any burglar alarm system should Owner so request.

CLAUSE 15. PROHIBITIONS AGAINST VIOLATING LAWS AND CAUSING DISTURBANCES

Tenants shall be entitled to quiet enjoyment of the premises. Tenants shall not use the premises in such a way as to violate any law or ordinance, including laws prohibiting the use, possession or sale of illegal drugs, commit waste or nuisance, or annoy, disturb, inconvenience, or interfere with the quiet enjoyment of any other tenant or nearby resident.

CLAUSE 16. REPAIRS AND ALTERATIONS

Except as provided by law or as authorized by the prior written consent of Owner, Tenants shall not make any repairs or alterations to the premises.

CLAUSE 17. DAMAGE TO PREMISES, FINANCIAL RESPONSIBILITY AND RENTER'S INSURANCE

In the event the premises are damaged by fire or other casualty covered by insurance, Owner shall have the option either to: (a) repair such damage and restore the premises, this Agreement continuing in full force and effect, or (b) give notice to Tenants at any time within thirty (30) days after such damage terminating this Agreement as of a date to be specified in such notice. In the event of the giving of such notice, this Agreement shall expire and all rights of Tenants pursuant to this Agreement shall terminate. Owner shall not be required to make any repair or replacement of any property brought onto the premises by Tenants.

Tenants agree to accept financial responsibility for any damage to the premises from fire or casualty caused by Tenants' negligence. Tenants shall carry a standard renter's insurance policy from a recognized insurance firm or, as an alternative, warrant that they will be financially responsible for losses not covered by Owner's fire and extended coverage insurance policy. Repair of damage or plumbing stoppages caused by Tenants' negligence or misuse will be paid for by Tenants.

CLAUSE 18.   WATERBEDS

No waterbed or other item of water-filled furniture shall be kept on the premises without Owner's written consent.

CLAUSE 19.   TENANT RULES AND REGULATIONS

Tenants acknowledge receipt of, and have read a copy of, the Tenant Rules and Regulations, which are hereby incorporated into this Agreement by this reference. Owner may terminate this Agreement, as provided by law, if any of these Tenant Rules and Regulations are violated.

CLAUSE 20.   PAYMENT OF ATTORNEY FEES IN A LAWSUIT

In any action or legal proceeding to enforce any part of this Agreement, the prevailing party shall recover reasonable attorney fees and court costs.

CLAUSE 21.   MANAGER'S AUTHORITY TO SERVE AND RECEIVE LEGAL PAPERS

In addition to the Owner, any person signing this Agreement on Owner's behalf is authorized to manage the premises, and is authorized to act for and on behalf of Owner for the purposes of service of process and for the purpose of receiving all notices and demands, at the address indicated below Owner's signature below.

CLAUSE 22.   ENTIRE AGREEMENT

This document constitutes the entire Agreement between the parties, and no promises or representations, other than those contained here and those implied in law, have been made by Owner or Tenants.

CLAUSE 23.   ADDITIONAL PROVISIONS

Cross through with large X if none.

_____

_____

_____

This Agreement has been signed on the day and year first written herein.

Owner/Manager: _____

Address: _____

_____

Tenant: _____

Tenant : _____

FIXED-TERM RESIDENTIAL LEASE

CLAUSE 1.   IDENTIFICATION OF OWNER AND TENANT

This Agreement is made and entered into on _____ , 19 ___ ,
between _____ ,
hereinafter "Tenants," and _____ ,
hereinafter "Owner."

CLAUSE 2.   IDENTIFICATION OF THE PREMISES

Subject to the terms and conditions below, Owner rents to Tenants, and Tenants rent from
Owner, for residential purposes only, the premises at _____

_____ ,

California.

CLAUSE 3.   DEFINING THE TERM OF THE TENANCY

The term of the rental shall begin on _____ , 19 ____ , and
shall continue for a period of _____ months, expiring on _____ ,
19 _____ .

Note: Should Tenants vacate before expiration of the term, Tenants shall be liable for the
balance of the rent for the remainder of the term, less any rent Owner collects or could have
collected from a replacement tenant by reasonably attempting to re-rent. Tenants who vacate before expiration of the term are also responsible for Owner's costs of advertising for a replacement
tenant.

CLAUSE 4.   AMOUNT AND SCHEDULE FOR THE PAYMENT OF RENT

On signing this Agreement, Tenants shall pay to Owner the sum of $ _____ as rent,
payable in advance, for the period of _____ , 19 _____ through
_____ , 19 _____ . Thereafter, Tenants shall pay to Owner a
monthly rent of $ _____ , payable in advance on the first day of each month, except
when the first falls on a weekend or legal holiday, in which case rent is due on the next business
day. Rent shall be paid to _____ at
_____ , California.

CLAUSE 5.   LATE FEES

If Tenants fail to pay the rent in full within five days after it is due, Tenants shall pay Owner a
late charge of $_____ , plus $ _____ for each additional day that the
rent continues to be unpaid. The total late charge for any one month shall not exceed
$ _____ . By this provision, Owner does not waive the right to insist on payment
of the rent in full on the day it is due.

CLAUSE 6.   RETURNED CHECK CHARGES

In the event any check offered by Tenants to Owner in payment of rent or any other amount
due under this Agreement is returned for lack of sufficient funds, Tenants shall pay to Owner a
returned check charge in the amount of $_____ .

CLAUSE 7. AMOUNT AND PAYMENT OF DEPOSITS

On signing this Agreement, Tenants shall pay to Owner the sum of $ _____ as
and for security as that term is defined by Section 1950.5 of the California Civil Code, namely
any payment, fee, deposit or charge to be used to compensate Owner for (a) Tenant's default in
the payment of rent, (b) repair of damages to the premises, exclusive of ordinary wear and tear or
(c) cleaning of the premises on termination of tenancy. Tenants, or any of them, may not,
without Owner's prior written consent, apply this security deposit to rent or to any other sum due
under this Agreement.

Within two weeks after Tenants have vacated the premises, Owner shall furnish Tenants
with an itemized written statement of the basis for, and the amount of, any of the security deposit
retained by the Owner. Owner may withhold only that portion of Tenants' security deposit
necessary (a) to remedy any default by Tenants in the payment of rent, (b) to repair damages to
the premises exclusive of ordinary wear and tear or (c) to clean the premises if necessary.

CLAUSE 8. UTILITIES

Tenants shall be responsible for payment of all utility charges, except for the following,
which shall be paid by Owner: _____
_____ .

CLAUSE 9. LIMITS ON USE AND OCCUPANCY

The premises are to be used only as a private residence for Tenants listed in Clause 1 of this
Agreement, a total of _____ adult occupants, and for no other purpose without Owner's prior
written consent. Guests may stay up to ten days in any six-month period if Tenants notify Owner
or Owner's representative by the third day of visiting. Occupancy by guests for more than ten
days is prohibited without Owner's written consent and shall be considered a breach of Clause 10
of this Agreement.

CLAUSE 10. PROHIBITION OF ASSIGNMENT AND SUBLETTING

Tenants shall not sublet any part of the premises or assign this Agreement without the prior
written consent of Owner.

CLAUSE 11. CONDITION OF THE PREMISES

Tenants acknowledge that they have examined the premises, including appliances, fixtures,
carpets, drapes and paint, and have found them to be in good, safe and clean condition and
repair, except as otherwise noted on the "Landlord/Tenant Checklist" which Tenants have completed and given Owner, a copy of which Tenants acknowledge receipt of, and which is hereby
deemed to be incorporated into this Agreement by this reference.

Tenants agree to (a) keep the premises in good order and repair and, upon termination of
tenancy, to return the premises to Owner in a condition identical to that which existed when
Tenants took occupancy, except for ordinary wear and tear, (b) immediately notify Owner of any
defects or dangerous conditions in and about the premises of which they become aware and (c)
reimburse Owner, on demand by Owner or his or her agent, for the cost of any repairs to the
premises damaged by Tenants or their guests or invitees.

CLAUSE 12. POSSESSION OF PREMISES

The failure of Tenants to take possession of the premises shall not relieve them of their obligation to pay rent. In the event Owner is unable to deliver possession of the premises to Tenants for any reason not within Owner's control, including but not limited to failure of prior occupants to vacate as agreed or required by law, or partial or complete destruction of the premises, Owner shall not be liable to Tenants, except for the return of all sums previously paid by Tenants to Owner, in the event Tenants choose to terminate this Agreement because of Owner's inability to deliver possession.

CLAUSE 13. PETS

No animal or other pet shall be kept on the premises without Owner's prior written consent, except properly trained dogs needed by blind, deaf or physically disabled persons and:

☐ other _____ ,

under the following conditions: _____ .

CLAUSE 14. OWNER'S ACCESS FOR INSPECTION AND EMERGENCY

Owner or Owner's agents may enter the premises in the event of an emergency, or to make repairs or improvements, supply agreed services, or exhibit the premises to prospective purchasers or tenants. Except in case of emergency, Owner shall give Tenants reasonable notice of intent to enter and shall enter only during regular business hours of Monday through Friday from 9:00 A.M. to 6:00 P.M., and Saturday from 9:00 A.M. to noon. In order to facilitate Owner's right of access, Tenants, or any of them, shall not, without Owner's prior written consent, alter or re-key any locks to the premises or install any burglar alarm system. At all times Owner or Owner's agent shall be provided with a key or keys capable of unlocking all such locks and gaining entry. Tenants further agree to provide instructions on how to disarm any burglar alarm system should Owner so request.

CLAUSE 15. PROHIBITIONS AGAINST VIOLATING LAWS AND CAUSING DISTURBANCES

Tenants shall be entitled to quiet enjoyment of the premises. Tenants shall not use the premises in such a way as to violate any law or ordinance, including laws prohibiting the use, possession or sale of illegal drugs, commit waste or nuisance, or annoy, disturb, inconvenience, or interfere with the quiet enjoyment of any other tenant or nearby resident.

CLAUSE 16. REPAIRS AND ALTERATIONS

Except as provided by law or as authorized by the prior written consent of Owner, Tenants shall not make any repairs or alterations to the premises.

CLAUSE 17. DAMAGE TO PREMISES, FINANCIAL RESPONSIBILITY AND RENTER'S INSURANCE

In the event the premises are damaged by fire or other casualty covered by insurance, Owner shall have the option either to: (a) repair such damage and restore the premises, this Agreement continuing in full force and effect, or (b) give notice to Tenants at any time within thirty (30) days after such damage terminating this Agreement as of a date to be specified in such notice. In the event of the giving of such notice, this Agreement shall expire and all rights of Tenants pursuant to this Agreement shall terminate. Owner shall not be required to make any repair or replacement of any property brought onto the premises by Tenants.

Tenants agree to accept financial responsibility for any damage to the premises from fire or casualty caused by Tenants' negligence. Tenants shall carry a standard renter's insurance policy from a recognized insurance firm or, as an alternative, warrant that they will be financially responsible for losses not covered by Owner's fire and extended coverage insurance policy. Repair of damage or plumbing stoppages caused by Tenants' negligence or misuse will be paid for by Tenants.

CLAUSE 18. WATERBEDS

No waterbed or other item of water-filled furniture shall be kept on the premises without Owner's written consent.

CLAUSE 19. TENANT RULES AND REGULATIONS

Tenants acknowledge receipt of, and have read a copy of, the Tenant Rules and Regulations, which are hereby incorporated into this Agreement by this reference. Owner may terminate this Agreement, as provided by law, if any of these Tenant Rules and Regulations are violated.

CLAUSE 20. PAYMENT OF ATTORNEY FEES IN A LAWSUIT

In any action or legal proceeding to enforce any part of this Agreement, the prevailing party shall recover reasonable attorney fees and court costs.

CLAUSE 21. MANAGER'S AUTHORITY TO SERVE AND RECEIVE LEGAL PAPERS

In addition to the Owner, any person signing this Agreement on Owner's behalf is authorized to manage the premises, and is authorized to act for and on behalf of Owner for the purposes of service of process and for the purpose of receiving all notices and demands, at the address indicated below Owner's signature below.

CLAUSE 22. ENTIRE AGREEMENT

This document constitutes the entire Agreement between the parties, and no promises or representations, other than those contained here and those implied in law, have been made by Owner or Tenants.

CLAUSE 23. ADDITIONAL PROVISIONS

Cross through with large X if none.

_____

_____

_____

_____

This Agreement has been signed on the day and year first written herein.

Owner/Manager: _____

Address: _____

_____

Tenant: _____

Tenant : _____

NOTICE OF REINSTATEMENT OF TERMS OF TENANCY

To: _____ ,
          (name)

Tenant(s) in possession of the premises at

_____ ,
          (street address)

City of _____ , County of _____ , California.

    When you rented the premises described above, your rent was due and payable on the first day of each month. While the undersigned has attempted to work with you in the past, your late rental payments can no longer be tolerated.

    Therefore, please be advised that effective 30 days from the date of service on you of this notice, your monthly rent will be due and payable in advance on the first day of the month, for that month.

Date: _____   _____
                                        Owner/Manager

AGREEMENT FOR PARTIAL RENT PAYMENTS

_____ , Owner, and

_____ , Tenant, agree as follows:

1. That _____ has paid

_____

_____ on _____ , 19 ___ ,

which was due _____ , 19 _____ .

2. That _____ agrees to accept all the remainder of the rent

on or before _____ , 19 ____ and to hold off on any legal

proceeding to evict _____ until that date.

Date: _____   _____
                                        Owner

Date: _____   _____
                                        Tenant

NOTICE OF SALE OF REAL PROPERTY AND OF TRANSFER OF SECURITY DEPOSIT BALANCE
Civil Code Section 1950.5(g)(1)

To: _____ ,
(name)

Tenant(s) in possession of the premises at:

_____ ,
(street address)

City of _____ , County of _____ , California.

The real property described above was sold on _____ , 19 ___

to _____
(name of new owner)

_____ ,
(street address)

whose telephone number is _____ .
(phone number)

Your security deposit, less any deductions shown below, has been transferred to the new owner, who is now solely responsible to you for it.

Deposit Amount: $ _____

Deductions:
    Unpaid Back Rent: $ _____
    Other Deductions: $ _____
    Total Deductions: $ _____

Net Deposit Transferred
to New Owner: $ _____

Explanation of Deductions:

_____

_____ $ _____

Please contact the new owner, whose address and phone number are listed above, if you have any questions.

Date: _____   _____
                             Owner/Manager

RESIDENTIAL RENTAL PROPERTY MANAGEMENT AGREEMENT

1. This Agreement is between _____, Owner of residential real property at _____, _____, California, and _____, Manager of the property. Manager is currently renting unit number _____ of the property under a separate written rental agreement.

2. Manager shall be resident manager of the premises, beginning _____.
(date)

Manager's duties are set forth below:

RENTING UNITS
answer phone
show vacancies
accept rental applications
select tenants
accept initial rents and deposits
other (specify):

VACANT APARTMENTS
inspect apartment when tenant moves in
inspect apartment when tenant moves out
vacuum carpets
shampoo carpets
clean refrigerator
clean plumbing fixtures
wash windows
clean stove and oven
clean cabinets and closets
clean sink, showers, bathroom
wash and polish floors
clean ceramic tiles
clean light fixtures
clean tops of doorways, windows and woodwork
other (specify):

RENT COLLECTION
collect rents when due
sign rent receipts
maintain rent-collection records
collect late rents and charges
inform Owner of late rents
prepare Three-Day Notices To Pay Rent or Quit
serve Three-Day Notices To Pay Rent or Quit
serve rent-increase and tenancy-termination notices
deposit rent collections in bank
other (specify):

MAINTENANCE
vacuum and clean hallways and entry ways
replace light bulbs in common areas
drain water heaters
clean stairs, decks, facade and sidewalks
clean garage oils on pavement
mow lawns
trim shrubs
clean up garbage on grounds
other (specify):

REPAIRS
accept tenant complaints and repair requests
inform Owner of maintenance and repair needs
maintain written log of tenant complaints
handle routine maintenance and repairs, including:
plumbing stoppages
garbage disposal stoppages/repairs
faucet leaks/washer replacement
toilet-tank repairs
toilet-seat replacement
stove burner repair/replacement
stove hinges/knobs
dishwasher repair
light switch and outlet repair/replacement
heater thermostat repair
window repair/replacement
painting
replacement of keys
other (specify):

3. Manager shall be available to tenants during the following days and times (*specify*):

_____.

4. Manager shall be compensated as follows (*check box which applies*):

( ) $_____ per month, payable

___ once a week on _____

___ once a month on _____

___ twice a month on the _____ and _____ days of the month.

or

( ) $_____ per hour, plus overtime pay as required by law for time spent specifically assigned duties, payable

___ once a week on _____

___ once a month on _____

___ twice a month on the _____ and _____ days of the month.

5. If the hours required to carry out any duties may reasonably be expected to exceed _____ hours in any day or __ hours in any week, Manager shall notify Owner and obtain Owner's consent before working such extra hours, except in the event of an emergency. Extra hours worked due to emergency must be reported to Owner within 24 hours.

6. Owner will reimburse Manager for the cost of materials, not to exceed $ _____ for any repair unless authorized in advance by Owner.

7. This Agreement may be terminated by Owner or Manager at any time by written notice to the other.

8. This Agreement does not affect any provision of the rental agreement between Owner and Manager.

9. Owner and Manager additionally agree that: _____

_____.

10. All agreements relating to Manager's responsibilities are incorporated in this Agreement. Any modifications to the agreement must be in writing.

Dated:_____, 19____   _____
                                                                          Owner

Dated:_____, 19____   _____
                                                                          Manager

LANDLORD-TENANT CHECKLIST—General Condition of Rooms
(see reverse side for furnished property)

Street Address _____ Unit Number _____ City _____

	Condition on Arrival	Condition on Departure	Est. Cost of Repair/Replacement
Living Room			
Floors & Floor Coverings			
Drapes & Window Coverings			
Walls & Ceilings			
Light Fixtures			
Windows, Screens & Doors			
Front Door & Locks			
Smoke Detector			
Fireplace			
Other			
Other			
Kitchen			
Floors & Floor Coverings			
Walls & Ceilings			
Light Fixtures			
Cabinets			
Counters			
Stove/Oven			
Refrigerator			
Dishwasher			
Garbage Disposal			
Sink & Plumbing			
Smoke Detector			
Other			
Other			
Dining Room			
Floors & Floor Covering			
Walls & Ceiling			
Light Fixtures			
Windows, Screens & Doors			
Smoke Detector			
Other			
Other			

Bathroom(s)	Bath 1	Bath 2	Bath 1	Bath 2	Est. Cost of Repair/Replacement
Floors & Floor Coverings					
Walls & Ceilings					
Windows, Screens & Doors					
Light Fixtures					
Bathtub/Shower					
Sink & Counters					
Toilet					
Other					
Other					

Bedroom(s)	Bedroom 1	Bedroom 2	Bedroom 3	Bedroom 1	Bedroom 2	Bedroom 3	Est. Cost of Repair/Replacement
Floors & Floor Coverings							
Windows, Screens & Doors							
Walls & Ceilings							
Light Fixtures							
Smoke Detectors							
Other							
Other							

Other Areas	Condition on Arrival	Condition on Departure	Est. Cost of Repair/Replacement
Furnace/Heater			
Air Conditioning			
Lawn/Ground Covering			
Garden			
Patio, Terrace, Deck, etc.			
Other			
Other			

Use this space to provide any additional explanation: _____

_____

_____

_____

☐ Tenants acknowledge that all smoke detectors were tested in their presence and found to be in working order, and that the testing procedure was explained to them. Tenants agree to test all detectors at least once a month and to report any problems to Owner/Manager in writing. Tenants agree to replace all smoke detector batteries as necessary.

LANDLORD-TENANT CHECKLIST—Furnishings

	Condition on Arrival			Condition on Departure			Est. Cost of Repair/Replacement
Living Room							
Coffee Table							
End Tables							
Lamps							
Chairs							
Sofa							
Other							
Other							
Kitchen							
Broiler pan							
Ice Trays							
Other							
Other							
Dining Area							
Chairs							
Stools							
Table							
Other							
Other							
Bathroom(s)	Bath 1		Bath 2	Bath 1		Bath 2	
Dresser Tables							
Mirrors							
Shower Curtain							
Hamper							
Other							
Other							
Bedroom(s)	Bedroom 1	Bedroom 2	Bedroom 3	Bedroom 1	Bedroom 2	Bedroom 3	
Beds (single)							
Beds (double)							
Chairs							
Chests							
Dressing Tables							
Lamps							
Mirrors							
Night Tables							
Other							
Other							
Other Areas							
Bookcases							
Desks							
Pictures							
Other							
Other							

Landlord-Tenant Checklist completed on moving in on _____, 19_____, and approved by:

_____ and _____
             Owner/Manager   Tenant

_____
                              Tenant

_____
                              Tenant

Landlord-Tenant Checklist completed on moving out on _____, 19_____, and approved by:

_____ and _____
             Owner/Manager   Tenant

_____
                              Tenant

_____
                              Tenant

RESIDENT'S MAINTENANCE/REPAIR REQUEST

Date: _____

Address: _____

Resident's Name: _____

Phone (Home): _____

Phone (Work): _____

Problem: _____

_____

_____

Comments (including best time to make repairs): _____

_____

_____

_____

I authorize entry into my unit to perform the maintenance or repair requested above, in my absence, unless stated otherwise above.

_____
Resident

- -

FOR MANAGEMENT USE

Work done: _____

_____

Time spent: _____ hours

Date completed: _____ , 19 _____

Unable to complete on _____ , 19 _____ because:

_____

_____

_____

_____
Owner/Manager

TIME ESTIMATE FOR REPAIR

_____

_____

_____
_____
_____

Dear Resident:

Thank you for promptly notifying us of the following problem with your unit:

_____

_____

We expect to have the problem corrected on _____ , 19_____ , due to the following:

_____

_____

We regret any inconvenience this delay may cause. Please do not hesitate to point out any other problems that may arise.

Sincerely,

_____
Owner/Manager

SEMI-ANNUAL SAFETY AND MAINTENANCE UPDATE

Please complete the following checklist and note any safety or maintenance problems in your unit or on the premises.

Please describe the specific problems and the rooms or areas involved. Here are some examples of the types of things we want to know about: garage roof leaks, excessive mildew in rear bedroom closet, fuses blow out frequently, door lock sticks, water comes out too hot in shower, exhaust fan above stove doesn't work, smoke alarm malfunctions, peeling paint and mice in basement. Please point out any potential safety and security problems in the neighborhood and anything you consider a serious nuisance.

Please indicate the approximate date when you first noticed the problem and list any other recommendations or suggestions for improvement.

Please return this form with this month's rent check. Thank you.

The Management

Name: _____

Address: _____

_____

Please indicate (and explain below) problems with:
Floors and floor coverings
Walls and ceiling
Windows, screens and doors
Window coverings (drapes, mini-blinds, etc.)
Electrical system and light fixtures
Plumbing (sinks, bathtub, shower or toilet)
Heating or air conditioning system
Major appliances (stove, oven, dishwasher, refrigerator)
Basement or attic
Locks or security system
Smoke detector
Fireplace

Cupboards, cabinets and closets
Furnishings (table, bed, mirrors, chairs)
Laundry facilities
Elevator
Stairs and handrails
Hallway and common areas
Garage
Patio, terrace or deck
Lawn, fences and grounds
Pool and recreational facilities
Roof, exterior walls, and other structural
Driveway and sidewalks
Neighborhood
Nuisances
Other

Specifics of problems: _____
_____
_____
_____
_____
_____

Other Comments: _____
_____
_____
_____
_____

_____   _____
Date   Tenant

FOR MANAGEMENT USE

Action/Response:_____
_____
_____
_____
_____

_____   _____
Date   Owner/Manager

NOTICE OF INTENT TO ENTER DWELLING UNIT
Civil Code § 1954

To: _____ ,
(name)

Tenant(s) in possession of the premises at

_____ ,
(street address)

City of _____ , County of _____ , California.

PLEASE TAKE NOTICE that on _____ , 19____ ,

(   ) at approximately ___:___ AM/PM

(   ) during normal business hours,

the undersigned owner, or the owner's agent, will enter the said premises for the following reason:

(   ) To make or arrange for the following repairs or improvements:

_____

_____

_____

(   ) To exhibit the premises to: (   ) a prospective tenant or purchaser, (   ) workers or contractors regarding the above repair or improvement,

(   ) Other: _____

If you wish to be present, you may make the appropriate arrangements. If you have any questions or if the above-stated date or time is inconvenient, please notify the undersigned at

_____ .
(phone number)

Date: _____   _____
Owner/Manager

NOTICE OF CHANGE OF TERMS OF TENANCY

To: _____ ,
                              (name)

Tenant(s) in possession of the premises at

_____ ,
                           (street address)

City of _____ , County of _____ , California.

The terms of tenancy under which you occupy these premises are changed as follows:

(　) 　The monthly rent will be increased to $_____ , payable in advance.

(　) 　Other: _____

The change in terms of tenancy shall be effective

(　) 　_____ , 19_____ .
                        (date)

(　) 　On the 30th day following service on you of this notice. If the change of terms of
　　　tenancy is an increase in rent, the amount due on the next following due date, pro-rated
　　　at the current rental rate prior to the 30th day, and pro-rated at the increased rate
　　　thereafter, is $_____.

Date: _____   _____
                                             Landlord/Manager

THREE-DAY NOTICE TO PAY RENT OR QUIT

To: _____ ,
(name)

Tenant(s) in possession of the premises at

_____ ,
(street address)

City of _____ , County of _____ , California.

Please take notice that the rent on these premises occupied by you, in the amount of $ _____ ,
for the period from _____ to _____ ,
is now due and payable.

YOU ARE HEREBY REQUIRED to pay this amount within THREE (3) DAYS from the date of service on you of this notice or to vacate and surrender possession of the premises. In the event you fail to do so, legal proceedings will be instituted against you to recover possession of the premises, declare the forfeiture of the rental agreement or lease under which you occupy the premises, and recover rents, damages, and costs of suit.

Date: _____   _____
                                      Owner/Manager

....

Proof of Service

I, the undersigned, served this notice, of which this is a true copy, on _____ , one of the occupants listed above as follows:

☐ On _____ , 199____ , I delivered the notice to the occupant personally.

☐ On _____ , 199____ , I delivered the notice to a person of suitable age and discretion at the occupant's residence/business after having attempted personal service at the occupant's residence, and business if known. On _____ , 199____ , I mailed a second copy to the occupant at his or her residence.

☐ On _____ , 199____ , I posted the notice in a conspicuous place on the property, after having attempted personal service at the occupant's residence, and business, if known, and after having been unable to find there a person of suitable age and discretion. On _____ , 199____ , I mailed a second copy to the occupant at the property.

☐ On _____ , 199____ , I mailed the notice by certified mail addressed to the occupant at his or her place of residence.

I declare under penalty of perjury under the laws of the State of California that the foregoing is true and correct.

Dated: _____ , 199____   _____

30-DAY NOTICE OF TERMINATION OF TENANCY

To: _____ ,
(name)

Tenant(s) in possession of the premises at

_____ ,
(street address)

City of _____ , County of _____ , California.

    YOU ARE HEREBY NOTIFIED that effective 30 DAYS from the date of service on you of this notice, the periodic tenancy by which you hold possession of the premises is terminated, at which time you are required to vacate and surrender possession of the premises. If you fail to do so, legal proceedings will be instituted against you to recover possession of the premises, damages and costs of suit.

_____

_____

_____

_____

_____

_____

_____

_____

_____

_____

_____

_____

_____

_____

Date: _____   _____
                               Owner/Manager

· ·

Proof of Service

    I, the undersigned, served this notice, of which this is a true copy, on _____ , one of the occupants listed above as follows:

☐ On _____ , 199____ , I delivered the notice to the occupant personally.

☐ On _____ , 199____ , I delivered the notice to a person of suitable age and discretion at the occupant's residence/business after having attempted personal service at the occupant's residence, and business if known. On _____ , 199____ , I mailed a second copy to the occupant at his or her residence.

☐ On _____ , 199____ , I posted the notice in a conspicuous place on the property, after having attempted personal service at the occupant's residence, and business, if known, and after having been unable to find there a person of suitable age and discretion. On _____ , 199____ , I mailed a second copy to the occupant at the property.

☐ On _____ , 199____ , I mailed the notice by certified mail addressed to the occupant at his or her place of residence.

    I declare under penalty of perjury under the laws of the State of California that the foregoing is true and correct.

Dated: _____ , 199____   _____

THREE-DAY NOTICE TO PERFORM COVENANT OR QUIT

To: _____ ,
(name)

Tenant(s) in possession of the premises at

_____ ,
(street address)

City of _____ , County of _____ , California.

YOU ARE HEREBY NOTIFIED that you are in violation of the lease or rental agreement under which you occupy these premises because you have violated the covenant to:

_____
_____
_____
_____

in the following manner:

_____
_____
_____
_____

YOU ARE HEREBY REQUIRED within THREE (3) DAYS from the date of service on you of this notice to remedy the violation and perform the covenant or to vacate and surrender possession of the premises.

If you fail to do so, legal proceedings will be instituted against you to recover possession of the premises, declare the forfeiture of the rental agreement or lease under which you occupy the premises, and recover damages and court costs.

Date: _____   _____
                                      Owner/Manager

··

Proof of Service

I, the undersigned, served this notice, of which this is a true copy, on _____ , one of the occupants listed above as follows:

☐ On _____ , 199____, I delivered the notice to the occupant personally.

☐ On _____ , 199____, I delivered the notice to a person of suitable age and discretion at the occupant's residence/business after having attempted personal service at the occupant's residence, and business if known. On _____ , 199____, I mailed a second copy to the occupant at his or her residence.

☐ On _____ , 199____, I posted the notice in a conspicuous place on the property, after having attempted personal service at the occupant's residence, and business, if known, and after having been unable to find there a person of suitable age and discretion. On _____ , 199____, I mailed a second copy to the occupant at the property.

I declare under penalty of perjury under the laws of the State of California that the foregoing is true and correct.

Dated: _____ , 199____   _____

THREE-DAY NOTICE TO QUIT (JUST CAUSE FOR EVICTION)
(IMPROPER SUBLETTING, NUISANCE, WASTE OR ILLEGAL USE)

To: _____ ,
(name)

Tenant(s) in possession of the premises at

_____ ,
(street address)

City of _____ , County of _____ , California.

YOU ARE HEREBY NOTIFIED that you are required within THREE (3) DAYS from the date of service on you of this notice to vacate and surrender possession of the premises because you have committed the following nuisance, waste, unlawful use or unlawful subletting:

_____

_____

_____

_____

_____

_____

_____

_____

As a result of your having committed the foregoing act(s), the lease or rental agreement under which you occupy these premises is terminated.If you fail to vacate and surrender possession of the premises within three days, legal proceedings will be instituted against you to recover possession of the premises, damages and court costs.

Date: _____   _____
                                 Owner/Manager

....

Proof of Service

I, the undersigned, served this notice, of which this is a true copy, on _____ , one of the occupants listed above as follows:

☐ On _____ , 199____ , I delivered the notice to the occupant personally.

☐ On _____ , 199____ , I delivered the notice to a person of suitable age and discretion at the occupant's residence/business after having attempted personal service at the occupant's residence, and business if known. On _____ , 199____ , I mailed a second copy to the occupant at his or her residence.

☐ On _____ , 199____ , I posted the notice in a conspicuous place on the property, after having attempted personal service at the occupant's residence, and business, if known, and after having been unable to find there a person of suitable age and discretion. On _____ , 199____ , I mailed a second copy to the occupant at the property.

I declare under penalty of perjury under the laws of the State of California that the foregoing is true and correct.

Dated: _____ , 199____   _____

WARNING NOTICE
(COMPLAINTS FROM NEIGHBORS/RESIDENTS)

Date: _____

Memorandum from Owner/Manager to

_____ , Resident(s) of

Property at: _____

_____

Re: Complaints from neighbors/other residents

Several of your neighbors have complained to the management regarding the following disturbance or condition:

_____

_____

Approximate date of occurrence: _____

It is very important to the management that our residents be able to enjoy the peace and quiet of their homes. Disturbing or affecting neighbors is a violation of the terms of your lease/rental agreement. You are requested to take the following corrective action:

_____

_____

If you have any questions, please contact _____,

at _____.

Sincerely,

_____
Owner/Manager

NOTICE OF BELIEF OF ABANDONMENT
Civil Code Section 1951.3

To: _____ ,
(name)

Tenant(s) in possession of the premises at

_____ ,
(street address)

City of _____ , County of _____ , California.

    This notice is given pursuant to Section 1951.3 of the Civil Code concerning the real property leased by you at the above address. The rent on this property had been due and unpaid for 14 consecutive days and the owner or his agent believes that you have abandoned the property.

    The real property will be deemed abandoned within the meaning of Section 1951.2 of the Civil Code and your lease will terminate on _____ , 19 _____ a date not less than 18 days after the mailing of this notice, unless before such date the undersigned receives at the address indicated below a written notice from you stating both of the following:

    (1) Your intent not to abandon the real property;

    (2) An address at which you may be served by certified mail in any action for unlawful detainer of the real property.

    You are required to pay the rent due and unpaid on this real property as required by the lease, and your failure to do so can lead to a court proceeding against you.

Date: _____

_____
Owner (signature)

_____
Owner (print)

_____
(street address)

MOVE-OUT LETTER

_____

Dear Resident:

We hope you have enjoyed living here.

Before vacating, be sure to thoroughly vacuum the floors (shampoo carpets, if necessary) and clean the walls, kitchen cabinets, stove and
oven, refrigerator (which should be emptied of food, turned off, with the
door left open), kitchen and bathroom sink, bathtubs, showers, toilets,
plumbing fixtures and _____ .

Once you have cleaned your unit and removed all your belongings, contact
me at _____ to arrange for a walk-through inspection and to
return the key.

Also, please provide a forwarding address where we may mail your security
deposit, less any lawful deductions for the cost of necessary cleaning
and repairs of damage in excess of ordinary wear and tear, and any past-
due rent. We will return your deposit balance, and an itemization of any
charges, within two weeks after you move out.

If you have any questions, please contact me at _____ .

Sincerely,

_____

Owner/Manager

LETTER FOR RETURNING ENTIRE SECURITY DEPOSIT

_____

_____

_____

_____

Dear _____ :

Here is the itemization, as required by Civil Code Section 1950.5, of
your $_____ security deposit on the property at
_____ ,
which you rented from me on a _____
on _____ , 19_____ and vacated on
_____ , 19_____ .
As you left the rental property in satisfactory condition, I am returning
the entire amount of your entire security deposit of $ _____
_____ .

Sincerely,

_____
Owner/Manager

SECURITY DEPOSIT ITEMIZATION (DEDUCTIONS FOR REPAIRS AND CLEANING)
Civil Code Section 1950.5

Date: _____

To: _____   From: _____

_____   _____

_____   _____

Property Address: _____

Rental Period: _____

1. Security Deposit Received: $ _____

2. Interest on deposit (if required by lease or local law): $ _____

3. Total Credit (sum of lines 1 and 2): $ _____

4. Itemized Repairs: _____

   _____

   _____

   _____

   _____

   _____

                              Total Repair Cost: $ _____

5. Necessary Cleaning: _____

   _____

   _____

   _____

   _____

   _____

                              Total Cleaning Cost: $ _____

6. Total Repair and Cleaning Cost (sum of lines 4 and 5): $ _____

                              Amount Tenant Owes Owner: $ _____

7. Net Sum Due: Total Deposit Credit (line 3)   OR

   minus Total Repair and Cleaning Cost (line 6)

                              Amount Owner Owes Tenant: $ _____

Comments: _____

_____

_____

_____

_____

SECURITY DEPOSIT ITEMIZATION (DEDUCTIONS FOR REPAIRS, CLEANING AND UNPAID RENT)
Civil Code Section 1950.5

Date: _____

To: _____   From: _____

_____   _____

_____   _____

Property Address: _____

Rental Period: _____

1. Security Deposit Received: $ _____

2. Interest on deposit (if required by lease or local law): $ _____

3. Total Credit (sum of lines 1 and 2): $ _____

4. Itemized Repairs: _____

_____

_____

_____

_____

_____

                                    Total Repair Cost: $_____

5. Necessary Cleaning: _____

_____

_____

_____

_____

_____

                                    Total Cleaning Cost: $_____

6. Defaults in rent not covered by any court judgment) $_____
   (list dates and rate): _____

_____

_____ $_____

7. Amount of Court Judgment for Rent, Costs, Attorney Fees: $_____

8. ( ) Total Amount Tenant Owes Owner
       (sum of lines 4, 5, 6 and 7 minus line 3): $_____

   ( ) Total Amount Owner Owes Tenant: $_____

Comments: _____

_____

_____

_____

_____

NOTICE OF RIGHT TO RECLAIM ABANDONED PROPERTY
Civil Code Section 1984

To: _____ ,
                        (name)

When the premises at: _____
                                    (street address)

City of _____ , County of _____ , California.

were vacated, the following personal property remained:

_____

_____

( )   Continued on Attachment "A" hereto.

You may claim this property at: _____

City of _____ , County of _____ , California.

Unless you pay the reasonable cost of storage for all the above-described property, and take possession of the property which you claim not later than eighteen (18) days after the date of mailing of this notice indicated below, this property may be disposed of pursuant to Civil Code Section 1988.

( )   Because this property is believed to be worth less than $300, it may be kept, sold, or destroyed without further notice if you fail to reclaim it within the time limit indicated.

( )   Because this property is believed to be worth more than $300, it will be sold at a public sale after notice has been given by publication, if you fail to reclaim it within the time limit indicated. You have the right to bid on the property at this sale. After the property is sold and the cost of storage, advertising, and sale is deducted, the remaining money will be paid over to the county. You may claim the remaining money at any time within one year after the county receives the money.

Date of Mailing: _____

_____
Owner/Manager

_____
(street address)

RENT CONTROL CHART

The following chart provides summaries of the specifics of each city's rent control ordinance. For more detail and specifics, and any recent changes, you should obtain a copy of the appropriate ordinance from the address listed after "Administration."

BERKELEY

Ordinance Adoption Date	6/3/80; latest amendment 11/90 (ballot measure).
Exceptions	Units constructed after 6/3/80, owner-occupied single-family residences and duplexes. [Sec. 5.]
Administration	Elected 9-member Rent Stabilization Board, 2100 Milvia Street, Berkeley, CA 94704, 415-644-6128.
Registration	Required, or landlord can't raise rents.[1] Stiff penalties for noncooperation. [Secs. 8, 11.f.4, 11.g.]
Rent Formula	6/3/80 freeze at 5/31/80 levels (7/1/82 freeze at 12/31/81 levels for 3-unit and 4-unit owner-occupied properties not covered by original 1980 ordinance), plus annual adjustments by Board after investigation and hearings. [Secs. 10, 11.]
Individual Adjustments	Landlord may petition for further increase based on increased taxes or unavoidable increases in utility or maintenance costs, and on costs of capital improvements necessary to bring property up to minimum legal requirements. Increase not allowed based on increased debt service cost due to recent purchase. (If tenant agrees to join in landlord's request, a "fast track" petition method, under which a decision will be made within 30 days and without a formal hearing, may be used.) Tenant may apply for rent reduction based on poor maintenance. [Sec. 12.]
Rent-Increase Notice Requirements	None in addition to state law.
Vacancy Decontrol	No increase allowed upon vacancy. [Ordinance Sec. 6.q allows for decontrol only if rental unit vacancy rate exceeds 5% and both Board and City Council agree; this is a virtual impossibility.]
Eviction	Landlord must show just cause to evict. For other restrictions, see *Landlord's Law Book, Volume 2: Evictions.*
Penalties	Violation of ordinance is misdemeanor punishable by maximums of $500 fine and 90 days imprisonment (first offense) and $3,000 fine and one year imprisonment (second offense). [Sec. 19.] Tenant may sue in court for excess rent collected plus up to $750. [Sec.15.a]
Other Features	Landlord must place security deposits in interest-bearing savings and loan account which is insured by the Federal Savings and Loan Insurance Corporation. Landlord must credit interest against rents each December, as well as when tenant vacates. [Sec. 7, Regulation Secs. 701, 702.]

NEW BERKELEY RENT REGULATIONS

When this book went to press (September 1991), a new Rent Board majority less hostile to landlords had enacted regulations allowing owners with "historicaly low rents" (property rented below market value in 1980 when rent control was enacted) to raise rents to levels equal to 75% of what the federal government considered fair market rent in 1980, plus cumulative annual adjustments since 1980. Average rent increases are expected to be about $60, with rents of $281 for a studio, $329 for a one-bedroom apartment and $375 for a two-bedroom apartment. (However, Berkeley's City Council is demanding an Environmental Impact Report be done in order to determine the effect these new regulations will have on the city.) Check with the Rent Board for up-to-date information.

---

[1]The provision that a tenant can withhold rents if the landlord fails to register was ruled unconstitutional in *Floystrup v. Berkeley Rent Stabilization Board*, 219 Cal. App. 3d 1309 (1990).

BEVERLY HILLS

Ordinance Adoption Date	(Beverly Hills Municipal Code, Chapter 5) 4/27/79; latest amendment 8/8/89.
Exceptions	Units constructed after 10/20/78, units that rented for more than $600 on 5/31/78, single-family residences, rented condominium units. [Sec. 4-5.102.]
Administration	Appointed 7-member Rent Adjustments Board 445 N. Rexford, Beverly Hills, CA 90210, 213-285-1031.
Registration	Not required.
Rent Formula	Except for specific "surcharges" which must be justified and the rent-increase notice (see below), rents may not be increased in any 12-month period by more than 8% (10% where rents were over $600 in 1979) or a percentage based on the "Urban All Items Consumer Price Index for Los Angeles," whichever is less. (The CPI-based figure is calculated by adding the monthly CPI figures for the most recently-published 12-month period, subtracting from that a second CPI sum based on the 12-month period before that, and dividing the difference by the lesser of the two sums.) To this permitted increase, the landlord may add a "capital expenditure surcharge" so as to additionally increase the rent by up to 4% more (calculated by amortizing capital improvement costs), a "utility expense surcharge" based on owner-paid utility cost increases in excess of the allowed annual percentage increase, and a 10% surcharge for each adult tenant occupying the unit over and above any maximum number of adult occupants specified in the lease. The landlord may also pass through the amortized cost of any legally-required improvements. [Secs. 4-5.302-4-5.307.]
Individual Adjustments	Tenant who contests validity of any capital improvement surcharge or utility surcharge over and above the annual increase percentage may petition Board to request non-allowance of the surcharge. Landlord seeking increases above annual percentage increase and allowed surcharges may apply to Board for higher "hardship" increase. (Ordinance is silent on factors to be considered, but does not preclude hardship increase based on high debt service costs due to recent purchase.) [Sec. 4-5.402.]
Rent-Increase Notice Requirements	Landlord must post in the lobby, hallway, or other "public" location on the property a notice stating the name, address, and telephone number of the owner or authorized agent, and must give each tenant a copy of the notice; failure to comply with this requirement precludes increase of rents. Rent-increase notice must state the basis justifying the rent increase and advise the tenant that records and documentation verifying it will be made available for inspection by the tenant or the tenant's representative. [Sec. 4-5.309.] The justification should break down the increase into portions allowed under annual adjustment and individual surcharges.
Vacancy Decontrol	Landlord may charge any rent after a tenant vacates voluntarily, but not when landlord terminates tenancy. Once the property is re-rented, it is subject to rent control based on the higher rent. [Sec. 4-5.310.]
Eviction	Landlord must show just cause to evict. For other restrictions, see *Landlord's Law Book, Volume 2: Evictions*.
Penalties	Violation of ordinance is a misdemeanor punishable by maximums of $500 fine and six months imprisonment. [Sec. 4-5.706.] Tenant may sue in court for three times any rent in excess of legal rent collected ($500 minimum), plus attorney fees. [Sec. 4-5.705.]

CAMPBELL

Ordinance Adoption Date	1983 (Campbell Municipal Code, Chapter 6.09)
Exceptions	Single-family residences, duplexes, and triplexes. [Sec. 6.09.030(1).]
Administration	Campbell Rent Mediation program, 1245 S. Winchester Blvd. Suite 200, San Jose, CA 95128, 408-243-8565.
Registration	Not required.
Rent Formula	No fixed formula; rent increases must be "reasonable." [Sec. 6.09.150.]
Individual Adjustments	Tenants in 25% of the units (but at least three units) affected by an increase can contest it by filing a petition within 37 days, or lose the right to object to the increase. Disputes raised by tenant petition are first subject to "conciliation," then mediation. If those fail, either party may file written request for arbitration by city "Fact Finding Committee." Committee determines whether increase is "reasonable" by considering costs of capital improvements, repairs, maintenance, and debt service, and past history of rent increases. However, the Committee's determination is not binding. [Secs. 6.09.050-6.09.150.]
Rent-Increase Notice Requirements	On written request by a tenant, an apartment landlord must disclose in writing to that person the apartment numbers of all tenants receiving rent increases that same month. [Sec. 6.09.040.]
Vacancy Decontrol	No restriction on raises after vacancy.
Eviction Features	Ordinance does not require showing of just cause to evict, so 3-day and 30-day notice requirements and unlawful detainer procedures are governed solely by state law.
Note	Because this ordinance does not provide for binding arbitration of any rent-increase dispute, it is not truly a rent control ordinance. Compliance with any decision appears to be voluntary only.

COTATI

Ordinance Adoption Date
(Cotati Municipal Code, Chapter 19.19), 9/23/80 (ballot initiative); latest amendment 3/10/87.

Exceptions
Units constructed after 9/23/80 (board has authority to remove exemption), owner-occupied single-family residences, duplexes, and triplexes. [Sec. 19.12.020.D.]

Administration
Appointed 5-member Rent Appeals Board, 201 W. Sierra, Cotati, CA 94931, (707-795-5478.

Registration
Required, or landlord can't raise rents, and tenants can seek Board permission to withhold current rents (but may have to pay all or part of withheld rent to landlord after registration). [Sec. 19.12.030.O.][2]

Rent Formula
9/23/80 freeze at 6/1/79 levels, plus annual "general adjustments" by Board after investigation and hearings. [Sec. 19.12.050.] Annual general adjustment is to be adequate to cover operating cost increases and to permit net operating income to increase at 66% of the rate of increase in the CPI (Consumer Price Index [all items] for urban consumers, San Francisco-Oakland). [Regulation Secs. 3000-3002.]

Individual Adjustments
Within 30 days after Board determines annual general adjustment, landlord may petition for further increase based on increased taxes or unavoidable increases in utility or maintenance costs, and on costs of capital improvements necessary to bring property up to minimum legal requirements. Increase not allowed based on increased debt service cost due to recent purchase. Tenant may apply for rent reduction based on poor maintenance. [Secs. 19.12.060, 19.12.070, Reg. Secs. 4001-4052.]

Rent-Increase Notice Requirements
None in addition to state law.

Vacancy Decontrol
None. [Ordinance Sec. 19.12.030.P allows Board to decontrol only housing whose rental unit vacancy rate exceeds 5%; this is highly unlikely.]

Eviction
Landlord must show just cause to evict. For other restrictions, see *Landlord's Law Book, Volume 2: Evictions.*

Penalties
Tenant may sue in court for three times any excess rent collected ($500 minimum) plus attorney fees, or tenant may simply credit any excess payments against future rent payments. [Sec. 19.12.110.]

Other Features
Landlord must place security deposits in interest-bearing insured savings and loan account and credit interest to tenant when she vacates. [Sec. 19.12.150]

---

[2]Since the Board must first approve rent-withholding following a hearing, this provision may still be valid despite *Floystrup v. Berkeley Rent Stabilization Board,* 219 Cal. App. 3d 1309 (1990).

EAST PALO ALTO

Ordinance Adoption Date   11/23/83; latest amendment 4/88.

Exceptions   Units constructed after 11/23/83, units owned by landlords owning four or fewer units in city. [Sec. 5.]

Administration   Appointed 7-member Rent Stabilization Board, 2415 University Ave., East Palo Alto, CA 94303, 415-853-3100.

Registration   Required, or landlord can't raise rents, and tenants can apply to Board for permission to withhold current rents (but may have to pay all or part of withheld rent to landlord after registration). [Secs. 8, 11.E.4, 15.A.1.][3]

Rent Formula   11/23/83 freeze at 4/1/83 levels, plus annual adjustments by Board after investigation and hearings. [Secs. 10, 11.]

Individual Adjustments   Landlord may apply for further increase based on increased taxes or unavoidable increases in utility or maintenance costs, and on costs of capital improvements necessary to bring property up to minimum legal requirements. Increase not allowed based on increased debt service due to recent purchase. Tenant may apply for rent reduction based on poor maintenance. [Sec. 12.]

Rent-Increase Notice Requirements   Notices increasing rent by more than that allowed under annual across-the-board adjustment must state that it is subject to appeal by tenant petition to Board, and must list Board address and telephone number. [Sec. 12.E.]

Vacancy Decontrol   No increases allowed upon vacancy.

Eviction   Landlord must show just cause to evict. For other restrictions, see *Landlord's Law Book, Volume 2: Evictions*.

Penalties   Violation of ordinance is misdemeanor punishable by maximums of $500 fine and 90 days imprisonment (first offense) and $3,000 fine and one year imprisonment (second offense). [Sec. 19.] Tenant may sue landlord in court for excess rent unlawfully collected plus up to $500. [Sec. 15.A.4.]

Other Features   Landlord must place security deposits in interest-bearing account at an insured bank or savings and loan and credit interest against rents each December, as well as when tenant vacates. [Sec. 7.]

---

[3]Since the Board must first approve rent-withholding following a hearing, this provision may still be valid despite *Floystrup v. Berkeley Rent Stabilization Board*, 219 Cal. App. 3d 1309 (1990).

HAYWARD

Ordinance Adoption Date 9/13/83; latest amendment 1/30/90.

Exceptions Units first occupied after 7/1/79, units owned by landlord owning four or fewer rental units in the city. [Sec. 2(l).]

Administration Administered by city-manager-appointed employees of Rent Review Office, 25151 Clawiter Rd., Hayward, CA 94545-2731, 415-293-5540.

Registration Not required.

Rent Formula Annual rent increases limited in any 12-month period to 5%, plus increased utility costs if documented as specified. A landlord who has not increased the rent during a previous 12-month period may "bank" the increase by raising it 10% the next period. [Sec. 3(c),(d).]

Individual Adjustments The tenant can contest an increase of over 5% by first contacting the person specified in the notice (see notice requirements, below) for an explanation of the increase. Tenant then must file petition with the Rent Review Office before the increase takes effect (30 days) or lose the right to object to it. Disputes raised in tenant petition are heard by a mediator; if mediation fails, arbitration is mandatory and binding on both parties. Landlord may be allowed to pass on increased utility and maintenance costs and "amortize" [spread out] capital expenditures. [Sec. 5.]

**Rent-Increase
Notice Requirements** Landlord must give tenant a copy of ordinance at the beginning of the tenancy, and a document which gives the unit's rent history [Sec. 4(a)], lists improvements to the unit, and states that the previous tenant's security deposit was not used for any improper purpose [Sec. 7(d)]. Failure to comply may be grounds for denial of an otherwise-proper rent increase. Rent-increase notices must be accompanied by a blank tenant petition form, and by a second notice which either states that the increase is allowed under the 5%-increase limitation or which gives specific reasons for an increase above 5%. The notice must also include the name, address, and telephone number of the landlord or other person able to explain the increase. [Sec. 4(b).]

Vacancy Decontrol Rent controls are permanently removed from each unit after a voluntary vacancy (that is, without any legal action by or notices from the landlord, even for cause), followed by the expenditure of $200 or more on improvements by the landlord, and city certification of compliance with city Housing Code.[Sec. 8.]

Eviction Landlord must show just cause to evict, even where rent control removed by vacancy decontrol, above. For other restrictions, see *Landlord's Law Book, Volume 2: Evictions*.

Penalties Failure to provide required information to tenant is an infraction (petty offense) punishable on first, second, or third offense within 12-month period by fines of up to $100, $200 and $500, respectively. Fourth offense within 12 months is misdemeanor punishable by maximums of $1,000 fine and six months imprisonment. [Sec. 20.b.] Tenant may sue in court for excess rent collected, treble that amount or $500 (whichever is greater), and attorney fees. [Sec. 20.a.]

Other Features Ordinance requires landlords holding security deposits longer than a year to pay 6.5% annual interest, credited against the tenant's rent on his anniversary date and when deposit refunded at end of tenancy. There is, however, no requirement for separate account. Violation can subject landlord to liability for three times the amount of unpaid interest owed. [Sec. 13.]

LOS ANGELES

Ordinance Adoption Date   (Los Angeles Municipal Code, Chapter XV), 4/21/79; latest amendment 2/19/91.

Exceptions   Units constructed (or substantially renovated with at least $10,000 in improvements) after 10/1/78, "luxury" units (defined as 0,1,2,3, or 4+-bedroom units renting for at least $302, $420, $588, $756, or $823, respectively, as of 5/31/78), single-family residences, except where three or more houses are located on the same lot. [Sec. 151.02.G,M.]

Administration   Appointed 7-member Rent Adjustment Commission, 215 West 6th St., Suite 800, Los Angeles, CA 90014, 213-624-7368, or 800-654-4914 from San Pedro or San Fernando Valley.

Registration   Required.[4] [Sec. 151.11.B] Tenant may defend any unlawful detainer action on the basis of the landlord's failure to register the property [Sec. 151.09.F].

Rent Formula   Except with permission of Commission or Community Development Department, rents may not be increased by more than a 3%-to-8% percentage based on the "All Urban Consumers Consumer Price Index" for the Los Angeles/Long Beach/Anaheim/Santa Monica/Santa Ana areas. The figure is published each year by the Community Development Department on or before May 30th, and applies to rent increases to be effective the following July 1st through June 30th of the next year. The actual percentage is calculated by averaging the CPI over the previous 12-month period beginning the September 30th before that, but in any event cannot fall below 3% or exceed 8%. In addition, if the landlord pays for gas or electricity for the unit, she may raise the rent an additional 1% for each such type of utility service. [Secs. 151.06.D, 151.07.A.6.]

Individual Adjustments   Landlord may apply to the Rent Adjustment Commission for higher increase to obtain "just and reasonable return." (This does not include "negative cash flow" based on recent purchase, but does include negative "operating expense," not counting landlord's mortgage payment.) [Sec. 151.07.B] Also, landlord may apply to Community Development Department for permission to pass on to the tenant 50% of the cost of capital improvements not directly benefitting the landlord—for example, new roof costs would be considered, but not costs of renovations to manager's units or advertising signs—spread out over five or more years [Sec. 151.07.A].

Rent-Increase Notice Requirements   Landlord must post conspicuously or give tenant a copy of current registration statement showing that the property is registered with Board. [Sec. 151.05.A.] Landlord who applies to Board for a rent higher than maximum is required to provide written justification for the difference. [Sec. 151.05.C.]

Vacancy Decontrol   Landlord may charge any rent after a tenant either vacates voluntarily or is evicted for non-payment of rent, breach of a rental agreement provision, or to substantially remodel. Controls remain if landlord evicts for any other reason, fails to remodel after evicting for that purpose, or terminates or fails to renew a subsidized-housing lease with the city housing authority. Once a vacated unit is re-rented, it is subject to rent control based on the higher rent. [Sec. 151.06.C.]

Eviction   Landlord must show just cause to evict. For other restrictions, see *Landlord's Law Book, Volume 2: Evictions*.

Penalties   Violation of ordinance, including failing to include proper information in eviction notices, is a misdemeanor punishable by maximums of $500 fine and six months imprisonment. [Sec. 151.10.B.] Tenant may sue in court for three times any rent in excess of legal rent collected, plus attorney fees. [Sec. 151.10.A.]

---

[4]The ordinance's provision that tenants may withhold rents for non-registration is unconstitutional, unless ordinance allows the landlord a hearing first. See *Floystrup v. Berkeley Rent Stabilization Board*, 219 Cal. App. 3d 1309 (1990) .

Other Features

Landlord must pay 5% annual interest rate on deposits held over a year. Interest payments need only be made every five years, and when deposit refunded at end of tenancy.

Los Angeles also has a Rent Escrow Adjustment Program (REAP) ordinance that applies to all rent-controlled units. Under this ordinance, a tenant whose landlord has received a 30-day notice from local health or building inspectors to correct serious housing code violations may withhold rent and pay it to a city escrow fund, if the landlord has failed to correct the violation within the 30-day period. (See Chapter 11 for details on REAP.)

THOUSAND OAKS

Ordinance Adoption Date 7/1/80; latest amendment 3/24/87.

Exceptions Units constructed after 6/30/80, "luxury" units (defined as 0,1,2,3, or 4+-bedroom units renting for at least $400, $500, $600, $750, or $900, respectively, as of 6/30/80), single-family residences, duplexes, triplexes, and four-plexes, except where five or more units are located on the same lot. [Sec. III.L.]

Administration Appointed 5-member Rent Adjustment Commission, 2150 W. Hillcrest Drive, Thousand Oaks, CA 91320, 805-496-8604.

Registration Required. [Sec. XIV.]

Rent Formula Rents may not be increased by more than 7% in any 12-month period. Increase allowed each year is 75% of the All-Urban Consumer Price Index for the greater Los Angeles area, but not less than 3% nor more than 7%. [Secs. III.G,H, VI.]

Individual Adjustments Landlord may apply to the Rent Adjustment Commission for higher increase based on capital improvement costs, or to obtain "just and reasonable return" (does not include "negative cash flow" based on recent purchase.) [Sec. VII.]

Rent-Increase Notice Requirements Landlord must prominently post in the apartment complex a listing or map of rental units, showing which are subject to the ordinance and which are not. [Sec. VI.C.]

Vacancy Decontrol Property that becomes vacant after 5/1/81 due to tenant voluntarily leaving or being evicted for nonpayment of rent is no longer subject to any provision of the ordinance. [Sec. VI.]

Eviction Features Landlord must show just cause to evict. For other restrictions, see *Landlord's Law Book, Volume 2: Evictions*.

Penalties Tenant may sue in court for three times any rent in excess of legal rent collected, plus a penalty of up to $500 and attorney's fees. [Sec. IX.]

Other Features Landlord can exempt property from rent control by offering "freedom leases" with five-year term and yearly increase of no more than 3% where the tenant is over age 65, or three-year term with yearly increase of no more than 75% of the All-Urban Consumers CPI for the greater Los Angeles area, for non-elderly tenants.

WEST HOLLYWOOD

Ordinance Adoption Date (West Hollywood Municipal Code, Article IV, Chapter 4), 6/27/85 (ballot initiative); latest amendment 6/25/90.

Exceptions Units constructed after 7/1/79 ("just-cause" eviction requirements do apply, however). However, all exemptions (except a standard "boarding" exemption) must be applied for in registration document (see below). [Sec. 6406.]

Administration Appointed 5-member Rent Stabilization Commission, 8611 Santa Monica Blvd., West Hollywood, CA 90069, 213-854-7450.

Registration Required, or landlord can't raise rents. [Sec. 6407.]

Rent Formula 11/29/84 freeze at 4/30/84 levels, plus annual adjustments by Board of no more than 75% of the All-Urban Consumer Price Index for the greater Los Angeles area. Landlords who pay for tenants' gas and/or electricity may increase an additional 1/2 % for each such utility. [Secs. 6408, 6409.]

Individual Adjustments Landlord may apply for further increase based on unavoidable increases in utility or maintenance costs or taxes, and for capital improvements. Tenant may apply for rent reduction based on poor maintenance. [Sec. 6411.]

Rent-Increase Notice Requirements Rent-increase notice must contain statement to the effect that landlord is in compliance with ordinance, including filing and payment of required registration documents and fees. [Sec. 6409.G, Regulation Sec. 40000(f).]

Vacancy Decontrol When tenant of property other than a single-family dwelling voluntarily vacates or is evicted for cause, landlord may increase rent by additional 10%; however, no more than one such increase is permitted within any 60-month period. When tenant of single-family dwelling (where there's one unit per parcel only) voluntarily vacates or is evicted for cause (other than for occupancy by owner or relative), landlord can raise rent to any level; once the single-family dwelling is re-rented, it is subject to rent control at the new higher rent. In either case, landlord must file "vacancy increase certificate" with city and show she has repainted and cleaned carpets and drapes within previous six months, that all appliances are in working order, and that the premises are free from health or safety violations. Certificate must be filed within 30 days after re-occupancy, or landlord cannot raise rent under this provision. [Sec. 6410.]

Eviction Landlord must show just cause to evict. For other restrictions, see *Landlord's Law Book, Volume 2: Evictions*.

Penalties Violation of ordinance is misdemeanor punishable by maximums of $1,000 fine and six months imprisonment. [Sec.6414.E.] Tenant may sue landlord in court for three times any rents collected or demanded in excess of legal rents, plus attorney fees. [Sec. 6414.C.]

Other Features Landlord must credit 5-1/2% annual interest on security deposits against rents, with payments made on tenant's move-in "anniversary date" at least once every five years, as well as when tenant vacates. [Sec. 6408.B.]

WESTLAKE VILLAGE

This small city (population 10,000) has a rent control ordinance that applies to apartment complexes of five units or more (as well as to mobile-home parks, whose specialized laws are not covered in this book.) Because the city's only apartment complex of this size has undergone conversion to condominiums, there is therefore now no property (other than mobile-home parks) to which the ordinance applies, so we don't explain the ordinance here.

A